W9-APX-767

DICTIONARY OF ROMAN RELIGION

LESLEY ADKINS &
ROY A. ADKINS

Facts On File, Inc.

AN INFOBASE HOLDINGS COMPANY

Dictionary of Roman Religion

Facts On File, Inc.
11 Penn Plaza
New York, NY 10001

Library of Congress Cataloging-in-Publication Data

Adkins, Lesley.
Dictionary of Roman religion / Lesley Adkins & Roy A. Adkins.
p. cm.
Includes bibliographical references and index.
ISBN 0-8160-3005-7 (alk. paper)
1. Rome—Religion—Dictionaries. I. Adkins, Roy (Roy A.) II. Title
BL798.A35 1996
292.07'03—dc20 95-8355

Facts On File books are available at special discounts when purchased in bulk quantities for businesses, associations, institutions or sales promotions. Please call our Special Sales Department in New York at 212/967-8800 or 800/322-8755.

Jacket design by Catherine Hyman

This book is printed on acid-free paper.

Printed in the United States of America

RRD VC 10 9 8 7 6 5 4 3 2 1

CONTENTS

List of Illustrations

Illustrations 11, 17, 38, 44, 49, 57, 73, 90 and 98 are courtesy of Somerset County Museums Service

This book is dedicated to Len Shilstone
In gratitude for showing the way

ACKNOWLEDGMENTS

We would like to thank Stephen Minnitt (Somerset County Museums Service) for help in obtaining photographs, and the staff of Jessops, Taunton, Somerset for advice on photographic problems. We would also like to express our thanks to the Joint Library of the Hellenic and Roman Societies, the libraries of the University of Bristol and the University of Exeter, and the library of the Somerset Archaeology and Natural History Society for their assistance in obtaining books. We are, of course, indebted to all the authors of the published sources that we have consulted. Finally, we would like to thank our editor, Caroline Sutton, and project editor Jeffrey Golick for all their work.

INTRODUCTION

Mythology

The subject of Roman religion is quite complex. Most books and dictionaries of classical religions concentrate on Greek religion with its enormous element of mythology, with little attention paid to the diversity of Roman religion. There were very few Roman deities that had real mythologies of their own; most Roman mythology was adopted from Greek mythology, or was invented much later by writers such as poets. Because of this, Roman religion with its much lesser element of mythology has tended to be overlooked and yet is itself a fascinating subject.

Number and function of gods

There were literally thousands of gods in the Roman world, and often the only evidence for a particular god is a single occurrence of his or her name, with no clue as to what function the god performed. In many causes, the name of a god was unknown to the Romans, and they might, for example, make a dedication to the Genius loci ("spirit of the place") to get round this problem. In other cases, the real names were kept secret, and the gods were referred to by another name or not at all. For example, many gods were addressed as "Baal" (meaning "lord"), and hundreds of altars were dedicated to an anonymous god at Palmyra in Syria from the early second century, in particular with the formula "the one whose name is blessed forever." The names of the gods were kept secret by the worshippers or cult members for a variety of reasons, such as the name of the god having special powers; the names were therefore only spoken during rituals and never written down. In Gaul, more than 500 names of deities are known, three-quarters of which occur only once. Seventy to 80 percent of them are deities of water or are associated with water. In some cases, it is impossible even to guess whether a deity is a god or goddess. Even during the Roman period there were many deities whose functions had been long forgotten, although worship of them still continued. This situation led to huge problems in the Roman period, particularly for the philosophers and historians who were trying to establish some order within the rather chaotic religion of the time. Often they deduced the function of a forgotten deity from the etymology of its name, and sometimes a spurious mythology was attached to a deity on the strength of this attributed function. Unfortunately, the historians and philosophers sometimes wrongly interpreted the etymology, and even the correct etymology did not always reflect the function of the deity. The result was often more confusion rather than less.

Invention of gods

To add to this confusion, the Romans were not averse to inventing a new god to fit an occasion. An example of this practice is demonstrated by an altar found at Cologne in 1630. The altar dates to the third century and notes the restoration by Quintus Tarquilius Catulus of the *praetorium* (military commander's residence), which had been in ruins. The altar is dedicated to the "preserving gods" (*dis conservatoribus*) who had been made up to suit this particular occasion, the restoration of a building. Another example of a god apparently invented to suit an occasion is Lupercus, who was invented to account for the festival of Lupercalia. It is clear that some gods were invented because they are associated with a specific ritual or festival that is recorded much earlier (often hundreds of years earlier) than the first mention of the deity addressed by that ritual or festival. There is also evidence that some festivals were in celebration of a deity who had been forgotten, and that another deity was later invented to account for the festival.

Heroes and epithets

In Roman religion, as in Greek religion, the difference between men and gods was narrower than in later beliefs. Gods were immortal but their powers and abilities varied from deity to deity. It was not unusual to treat a living or deceased hero as a god. In this dictionary, no distinction has been made between heroes and gods. Here the term *gods* is often used to mean female goddesses as well; likewise, the term *deity* covers both gods and goddesses. These terms are used in their widest sense. The Romans had various categories of deities, such as *numen*, as well as equations and links among deities and titles and epithets for them. The result is a plethora of names, often with variant spellings, with little or no indication of exactly what each name means. It is impossible to be certain, for example, whether a Roman worshipper regarded Jupiter Conservator as different from Jupiter Fulgur or whether he or she regarded Jupiter as a single deity that had to be approached using the title, ritual and temple appropriate to the worshipper's desire. Jupiter Fulgur may therefore be an aspect of Jupiter, or else a separate distinct deity. In most cases where an epithet is applied to a god, it seems to represent an "aspect" of this deity. At other times the name of a god is linked to the name of another deity (such as Jupiter-Dolichenus). Sometimes one god is equated with (identified with) a god of another culture (such as Jupiter with Zeus).

Gods of the Greek east

In the eastern half of the Roman empire, Greek rather than Latin was the universal language, so most dedicatory inscriptions from this area are in Greek. Many such inscriptions are difficult to date, making it uncertain whether a god mentioned in such an inscription was worshipped during the Roman period or earlier. Greek deities have only been included in this dictionary if there is definite evidence that they were worshipped in a Roman manner. The major Greek gods that were identified with Roman gods are mentioned under the entries for the corresponding Roman gods; in many cases it is unclear whether dedicatory inscriptions to these gods, even when securely dated, represent a "Greek" cult or a "Roman" cult, and it is equally unclear whether such a distinction was ever meaningful in the Greek-speaking areas of the Roman empire.

Further reading

Suggestions for further reading are given at the end of many entries. Wherever possible, these are references to the more accessible books and journal articles. As such, these are not necessarily "key" references, but rather those with good summaries of the subject and bibliographies that enable the reader to pursue the subject further.

Temples

Entries for specific temples concentrate on those in the city of Rome itself; these are the temples for which there is good evidence from both archaeological and historical sources, and they often played a key role in the development of a cult. Some important temples outside the city of Rome also have individual entries, but otherwise the large number of temples throughout the Roman world are dealt with in the entries on general types of temple, such as Romano-Celtic or classical.

Incorporation of foreign gods

From earliest times, the Romans appear to have been quite willing to incorporate other peoples' gods into their religion. In many cases, particularly when a large number of deities were already worshipped by the Romans, an alien god would be identified with an existing Roman god. For example, the Greek god Zeus was identified with the Roman god Jupiter, and much of the Greek mythology of

Zeus was adopted by the Romans and applied to Jupiter. This process is known as *interpretatio Romana* (literally, "Roman translation").

Variant spellings

The study of Roman gods is fraught with difficulty, as much evidence comes from inscriptions that use variant spellings of gods' names. Moreover, many inscriptions were abbreviated, and modern scholars interpret the abbreviations differently—and do not always agree with each other. In the case of Silvanus Sinquas, for example, there are three variant spellings derived from just two inscriptions: Sinquas, Sinquatis and Sinquates. In the cases of such less well-known gods, it is never possible to be certain that their names have been recorded accurately.

Origin of deities

With some deities who were adopted by the Romans at an early stage, it is not possible to be precise about the origin of the deity. Some authorities use the term "Italian" to describe a deity adopted by the Romans from one of the non-Roman tribes living in what is now Italy. In this dictionary, if the non-Roman tribe is known, it is given as the origin of the deity, but if unknown, the deity has usually been described as "Roman" to distinguish it from the much later adoptions of deities from other peoples such as the Celts or the Germans. Readers interested in researching the possible origins of early Roman gods are advised to start with the reading references listed at the end of the entry for the deity concerned.

Gods of other peoples (such as the Celts or Germans) who the Romans adopted are usually known because of dedications to them in Latin (or sometimes Greek in the eastern empire). The dedicatory inscriptions show that the worship of these deities was to some extent Romanized. Some dedications in other languages (such as Persian) are known from the Roman world, but these deities have not been included as there is no evidence that they can in any sense be considered as Roman. The deities that are included were worshipped within the Roman world during the Roman period.

Equation of gods (syncretism)

The extent to which a given deity was adopted by the Romans and identified or equated with an existing Roman god is often unknown. There are many instances in which, for example, the name of a Celtic god is linked to or equated with that of a Roman god, but there is not necessarily any evidence that the Celtic god was ever a distinct entity. It may be that the Celtic name given to a Roman god is not the result of conflating two deities, but rather the modification of the Roman god to a Celtic function. The result in either case is likely to be a Celtic type of deity, but unless there is epigraphical evidence to show that the Celtic name represents an independent deity, we cannot be certain what has happened. In this dictionary, the Celtic element usually has its own minimal entry, with a cross-reference to a larger entry, because some modern authorities tend to refer solely to the Celtic name when they mean the entire name (for example, Gebrinius, when there is only epigraphical evidence for Mercury Gebrinius). This situation applies to gods adopted from other peoples, such as the Germans or the Phoenicians. In some instances, the people or tribe from whom a deity has been adopted is unknown or uncertain, and in this case some modern authorities identify the adopted god by the geographical region (for example, "Iberian" for Spain and Portugal or "Syrian" for the Roman province of Syria). This practice has been used in this dictionary, but the reader should be aware that continuing research may provide greater precision of origin for some of these gods in the future.

State religion

Many different religions coexisted throughout the Roman world, but there was a central collection of beliefs and rituals that Roman citizens considered to be their particular religion. This was generally known as the "state religion" because it was thought to ensure the preservation and prosperity of the city-state. This state religion grew out of the rites performed by early farming families. As the agricultural community expanded, the gods who had been asked by individuals and families to provide such favors as beneficial weather, good harvests and protection from thieves were requested to provide these benefits for the community as a whole. To make these requests and to perform rites and sacrifices for the gods, there arose a hierarchy of priests and officials, led originally by the king. The basis of this religion was the belief that gods and spirits were everywhere, responsible for all natural phenomena. Divine spirits or powers (*numina*) were thought to represent natural or abstract forces. Gods and divine spirits all had to be propitiated by suitable offerings and rituals. Since gods and spirits were omnipresent, sacrifice and religious ritual became part of daily life. The state religion is difficult to define precisely, and for many gods there is no surviving evidence of whether they were included in the state religion.

As the early Roman community evolved into an organized state, religion became closely connected with politics and society. Religion governed all political activities because it was essential for political leaders to ascertain the will of the gods before any state action. Eventually, religion came to be manipulated for partisan purposes. Initially the king was a priest, but after the expulsion of the kings (509 B.C.), the title was retained in *rex sacrorum* ("king of sacred things"). Priests were state officials, and temples and religious festivals were sometimes financed by the state.

The state religion was not static, but developed alongside Roman society, largely by absorbing gods from other cultures, particularly from Etruria and the Greek colonies in Italy. Probably the greatest change was caused by the influence of the Greek gods, who were anthropomorphic and had a developed mythology, in contrast to the more abstract early Roman *numina*. The state could intervene to introduce new state cults such as that of Magna Mater in 204 B.C. or to proscribe them (such as Bacchic rites in 186 B.C.). By the end of the republic, state religion was substantially different from that of early Rome because of the absorption of gods from other cultures.

The civil war and upheaval that took place after Julius Caesar crossed the Rubicon was attributed to neglect of the state religion. When order was restored, Augustus did much to revitalize the state religion by building temples, reviving rituals, reviving cults (such as that of Apollo) and encouraging people to attend the public religious ceremonies. The state religion remained a powerful force for another three centuries, but during that time other cults were adopted by the Romans and became increasingly popular. The expansion and subsequent administration of the empire brought huge numbers of soldiers and traders into contact with the religions of the peoples that had been incorporated into the empire. Many cults were recognized as being broadly similar to existing Roman ones, and this led to the identification of foreign gods with Roman ones. However, this process of religious absorption was not a rational or systematic one, and a foreign god could be identified with several different Roman gods, just as a Roman god was often identified with several different foreign gods from various parts of the empire. Oriental religions also made an impact on the empire, mainly because they tended to offer more to (and demand more from) their followers. Oriental religions such as Mithraism, the worship of Isis and Christianity became increasingly popular. Within the empire there was a contrast between the west, where the Roman pantheon was often adopted and merged with indigenous cults (such as those of the Celts), and the east where Greek deities, already established and linked to local gods, continued in predominance.

Introductory reading: Adkins and Adkins 1994; Brunaux 1988 (Celtic religion); Dumézil 1970 (archaic religion); Ferguson 1970, 1988a and 1988b; Henig 1984 (covers Roman Britain); Lane Fox 1986; Liebescheutz 1979; Ogilvie 1969; Webster 1986 (Celtic gods in the Roman period).

A

Abandinus A Celtic god who is known only from an inscription on a votive plaque at a Romano-British temple in Godmanchester, England. The name *Abandinus* could derive from the Celtic river name *Abona* or *Afon*, indicating a water god. The temple site at Godmanchester, where three successive temples were built, is close to the river Ouse, the early name for which was *Aban*. A water tank and a well in one of the temples also suggest worship of a water deity. However, the inscription on the votive plaque is fragmentary, and an alternative reading of the god's name is Maband, suggesting a link with MAPONUS.
Reading: Green, H. J. M. 1986; Green, M. J. 1992a, 26.

Abeona The Roman goddess who presided over a child's first steps away from its parents when it left the home.
Reading: Grimal 1986, 231 (under *Indigetes*).

Abilus A Celtic god who was worshipped at Arnay-le-Duc (in the Côte-d'Or), France. He was associated with the Celtic goddess DAMONA.
Reading: Green, M. J. 1992a, 76.

Abna An Iberian deity who is known from an inscription found near Santo Tirso, northern Portugal.
Reading: Tranoy 1981, 268.

Abnoba A Celtic goddess of hunting and the forest who was worshipped in Germany's Black Forest region. Abnoba was possibly also a goddess of fertility and a mother goddess. She was associated with the Roman goddess DIANA, with whom she was sometimes equated.
Reading: Green, M. J. 1992a, 26.

Abundantia A Roman deity who was the personification of prosperity.

Acca Larentia Also called Larentina, this obscure Roman goddess was worshipped during the Larentalia festival of December 23. The origins of this goddess are not clear, but she appears to have been connected with the founding of Rome. In one legend, the keeper of the Temple of Hercules (see HERCULES, TEMPLES OF) invited HERCULES to a game of dice, the prize being a feast and a beautiful girl called Acca Larentia. Hercules won, but he later gave her up and she married Tarutius, a wealthy Etruscan. Tarutius died shortly afterward, leaving Acca Larentia with large estates near Rome that she bequeathed to the Roman people at her death. This legend appears to have originated to justify the ownership of areas of land claimed by Rome. Another story names Acca Larentia as the wife of Faustulus, the herdsman who found Romulus and Remus with the wolf. The 12 ARVAL PRIESTS were said to have been founded in memory of her 12 children (not including Romulus and Remus, whom she adopted), who were the first arval priests.
Reading: Grimal 1986, 3; Hammond and Scullard (eds.) 1970, 2.

Acheron In Greek myth, one of the rivers of the underworld. In Latin poetry, it came to mean the underworld itself.

Acis The god of the Acis River near Mount Etna in Sicily. He was the son of the Roman god FAUNUS and of the nymph SYMAETHIS. Acis was supposed to have been a rival to the Cyclops Polyphemus for the love of the sea nymph Galatea. Polyphemus

tried to crush Acis under rocks, but Acis turned himself into a river to escape.
Reading: Grimal 1986, 8.

Acragas A local water god who was worshipped at Agrigento, Sicily.
Reading: Wilson 1990, 282.

Actian Games (Latin, *Actia*) Local games held at Actium, Greece, in honor of APOLLO. They were developed into a quinquennial festival at Actium by the emperor Augustus and were modeled on the Olympian games. They were later adopted by other Greek states.
Reading: Hammond and Scullard (eds.) 1970, 7.

Adamklissi In the Dobruja plain of Romania (formerly Roman Dacia) at Adamklissi are two Roman monuments. One is a military funerary altar, with the names of at least 3,000 Roman casualties, marking the Roman defeat in Domitian's Dacian War of Oppius Sabinus in 85. The other monument is a *tropaeum* (a trophy monument), dedicated in 109 by the emperor Trajan to MARS ULTOR to commemorate his victories over the Dacians and also called *Tropaeum Traiani* ("trophy monument of Trajan").
Reading: Hammond and Scullard (eds.) 1970, 8.

Adeona The Roman goddess who directed the steps of a child back to its home.
Reading: Grimal 1986, 231 (under *Indigetes*).

Adolenda ("Burner") A Roman deity who is known to have been invoked by the ARVAL PRIESTS in an attempt to remove an intrusive fig tree from the shrine of DEA DIA.

Adranos An indigenous god of Sicily. His cult was centered in and around the town of Adrano, on the southwest slopes of the volcano Etna. Adranos was identified with the Greek god Hephaestos (god of fire and smithing), but he also seems to have been regarded as a god of war. In some legends he was the father of the indigenous twin gods, the PALICI.
Reading: Wilson 1990, 279.

Adrasta Generally regarded as another name for the Greek goddess NEMESIS, Adrasta appears to have sometimes been regarded as a separate deity. Adrastea and Adrastia are usually taken to be variants of the name Adrasta. (See also FURIES.)

aedes (or *aedis*, pl. *aedes*) The Latin name for a house or dwelling place, also used for a dwelling place of a god—usually a temple building or shrine. It was sometimes called *aedes sacra* ("a house sacred [to a particular deity]"). The temple building *(aedes)* was usually built within a *templum*. (See also TEMPLE, *TEMPLUM*.)

aedicula (pl. *aediculae*) The Latin name for a small shrine within a TEMPLE *(aedes)*, usually set on a base, surmounted by a pediment and surrounded by columns.

aedile There were originally two plebeian magistrates known as aediles at Rome. They were named from the temple *(aedes)* of CERES, which they administered. The number of aediles increased over time, and their duties included overseeing temples and public Games (until the time of Augustus).
Reading: Hammond and Scullard (eds.) 1970, 11–12.

aedituus (the older Latin form was *aeditumnus*) A custodian or sacristan of a consecrated building (temple, *aedes sacra*) who was responsible for its upkeep and maintenance. The custodian probably always lived next to the shrine or temple. The term was also applied to the servants (usually slaves) who did the actual cleaning and maintenance work.

Aegiamunniaegus An Iberian deity who is known from an inscription on a bronze votive plaque that was dedicated to this god. The plaque, since lost, was found at Viana del Bollo, in northwest Spain.
Reading: Tranoy 1981, 296.

aegis In the Greek world, an emblem of ZEUS and ATHENA represented as a goatskin and used to create thunderstorms, disperse enemies and protect friends. It was depicted in art as a short cloak worn over the shoulders or left arm of the god or goddess (like a shield), and came to be an emblem of JUPITER and MINERVA (Fig. 69).
Reading: Hammond and Scullard (eds.) 1970, 13.

Aequitas A Roman goddess, also known as Aecetia, who presided over fair dealing as the personification of equity. During the empire, this deity was sometimes worshipped as a quality of the emperor, under the name Aequitas Augusti ("the Equity of the Emperor").

Aericura A Celto-Germanic goddess. She was sometimes depicted as a mother goddess, but appears to have been regarded mainly as a goddess of the underworld. She is probably the same deity as HERECURA. In southern Germany and the Balkans, she was worshipped in partnership with DIS PATER; together, they were probably deities of the underworld, thought to protect humans in the afterlife. The Celtic god Aericurus, known from an inscription found at Corbridge, Northumberland, England, is probably a male equivalent of Aericura.
Reading: Green, M. J. 1992a, 26.

Aernus An Iberian god who is known from inscriptions on three altars from the Braganca region of northern Portugal. The exact function of this deity is not clear, but he may have been the patron deity of the inhabitants of the region.
Reading: Tranoy 1981, 296.

Aesculapius The Latin name for the Greek god Asklepios or Asclepius, who was the son of the healing god APOLLO and Coronis, the mortal daughter of Phlegyas, a Greek king. Epidaurus in Greece was the most famous center of the cult of Asklepios, and lesser shrines were later founded in Athens (420 B.C.) and in Rome (292 B.C.). There were numerous Roman temples and shrines associated with Aesculapius, many serving as Asclepieia (healing sanctuaries). Aesculapius was sometimes identified with the Phoenician god ESHMOUN. There was a festival of Aesculapius on January 1. (See also AESCULAPIUS, TEMPLE OF; ASCLEPIEIUM.)
Reading: Jackson 1988, 138–147.

Aesculapius, temple of (Fig. 1) At Rome, a temple to Aesculapius (Aesculapium) was vowed in 292 B.C., following consultation of the Sibylline books during a severe plague there in 293 B.C.; an embassy was sent to Epidaurus in Greece to bring the worship of Aesculapius to Rome. A huge sacred snake was brought by ship to Rome, where it swam ashore to the Tiber Island (Latin, Insula Tiberina).

Fig. 1 A medallion of the emperor Antoninus Pius, dating to A.D. 143, which shows the arrival of Aesculapius in Rome. The god is depicted as the sacred snake from Epidaurus. The snake swims ashore, while to the right the god Tiberinus raises his hand in assent.

This event was treated as an omen and the temple was built there. It was dedicated on January 1, 291 B.C., and the plague stopped abruptly. The temple served as an ASCLEPIEIUM, and miraculous cures were reported. It may have been rebuilt in the mid-first century B.C. The cult at this temple included the god's daughter, HYGEIA, who was later identified with the Italian goddess Salus. The church of San Bartolomeo is believed to occupy the site today. Numerous inscriptions to Aesculapius by grateful suppliants are known.
Reading: Richardson 1992, 3–4, 210.

Aether The personification of the upper sky. Originally a Greek deity, the Romans sometimes regarded Aether as the father of JUPITER and CAELUS.
Reading: Grimal 1986, 22–23.

Africanus, Julius A third-century Christian philosopher from Aelia Capitolina. His main works were the *Chronographies*, in five books, which dealt with sacred and profane history from the Creation to A.D. 221 and formed the basis of Eusebius's *Creation*. He also wrote *Hoi Kestoi*, a miscellany of information in 24 books, mainly on magic.
Reading: Hammond and Scullard (eds.) 1970, 23.

afterlife There was no generally accepted view on an afterlife (life after death) in the Roman world. The issue was complicated by the wide range of religious beliefs. Some did not believe in an afterlife, while others believed that souls existed in a collective form in the afterlife or even that the individual souls of people survived after death. One belief was that the soul or spirit of the dead rested in the UNDERWORLD for a period of time before entering another person's body, although it became more common to believe in a world of the dead, in which the living would eventually meet up with the souls of their deceased relatives.

There was a long-lasting and widely held view that the souls or spirits of the dead lived on in their tombs or graves and could influence the fortunes of the living in an undefined way, and so offerings were regularly made in order to placate them. Gifts were brought to the tomb, libations were poured for the dead, and in some instances graves were provided with pipes and holes (see PIPE BURIALS) so that wine and food could be poured into the coffin or burial chamber itself. Holding celebrations at the tombs was also thought to appease the spirits of the dead. Belief in an afterlife sometimes gave rise to superstitious practices. Cases are known of bodies being weighted down to stop the dead from rising to haunt the living, while some corpses appear to have been decapitated for the same reason (Fig. 46). If the spirits of the dead were not propitiated, they could be spiteful, such as the *LEMURES*.

In addition to the belief that the dead lived on in their tombs, another view held that the ghosts or spirits of the dead went to the underworld and joined the MANES and *lemures;* they could only return at particular times of the year (such as at the LEMURIA); those souls that the gods of the underworld would not admit were destined to wander homeless forever. There was no concept of a separate heaven and hell, and the dead did not join the majority of the gods, only those gods of the underworld.

Around the mid-third century, there was a marked change in burial rites throughout the empire, with INHUMATION becoming more popular than the normal method of CREMATION. The reason for this is unclear: it may reflect a general increase in the hope and expectation of an afterlife as a result of the influence of the ORIENTAL RELIGIONS and NEOPLATONISM (and eventually CHRISTIANITY). The mystery religions, including Christianity, offered the promise of a resurrection with a happy afterlife (albeit defined in different ways in different religions), and helped to foster the belief that the soul (an entity defined by Plato and later philosophers) survived death. Death was seen by Christians as a release from troubles on earth, and on many tombstones the epitaphs included *RIP* (*requiescit in pace*, "rests in peace"). (See also STOICISM.)

Reading: Hammond and Scullard (eds.) 1970, 23–24; Hopkins 1983, 226–235; Jackson Knight 1970; Lattimore 1962; North 1988b; Prieur 1986; Toynbee 1971, 33–39.

Agdistis A Phrygian mother goddess whose main sanctuary was originally at Pessinus in Asia Minor. Her cult spread throughout Anatolia and then to Egypt, and by the fifth century B.C. to parts of Greece. In the Roman period she was known as Cybele or MAGNA MATER.

Reading: Hammond and Scullard (eds.) 1970, 25–26.

Aglibol A Syrian moon god who was frequently worshipped at Palmyra, Syria, in a triad with BEL and IARHIBOL. He was also frequently associated with MALAKBEL and also with BAAL SHAMIN. There was a temple to Aglibol and Malakbel in Palmyra that lasted to the end of the second century.

Reading: Drijvers 1976; Teixidor 1969, 1–11, 34–52.

Agonalia (alternatively called *dies agonales*, Agonia or Agonium) A festival held on January 9, March 17, May 21 and December 11, possibly for JANUS, although the Romans were uncertain as to which deities were involved. On each occasion the *rex sacrorum* sacrificed a ram at the Regia in Rome, but otherwise the method of celebration is unknown. A different god seems to have been honored on each occasion: Janus, Liber Pater (see LIBER), possibly VEDIOVIS and SOL INDIGES.

Reading: Palmer 1974, 144–145; Richardson 1992, 4–5; Scullard 1981, 60–61, 92, 203.

Aides An alternative spelling of HADES, who was equated with DIS.

Aius Locutius ("announcing speaker") The name given to a god whose voice was heard in 391 B.C. by a Marcus Caedicius (a plebeian) warning him

to tell the magistrates that Gauls were approaching Rome. Nobody heeded the warning and Rome was sacked by the Gauls in 390 B.C. After the Gauls were repulsed, the dictator Camillus ordered that an altar to this deity be erected, and a sacred precinct *(templum)* and shrine *(sacellum)* were dedicated to Aius Locutius near VESTA's shrine on the Nova Via at Rome where the voice was heard.
Reading: Grimal 1986, 27; Hammond and Scullard (eds.) 1970, 33; Richardson 1992, 5.

Alaisiagae (Figs. 2, 63) Germanic goddesses who were linked with MARS and MARS THINCSUS in dedications at Housesteads on Hadrian's Wall, England. One inscription names them as the "two Alaisiagae Beda and Fimmilena," while another inscription names them as "Baudihillia and Friagabis." From their association with Mars and from the dedications by Germanic troops serving on Hadrian's Wall, it is assumed that the Alaisiagae were war goddesses. They were possibly Valkyries, who chose who should die in battle. The Valkyries also led the spirits of the slain to the AFTERLIFE.
Reading: Burn 1969, 113–114.

Alator A Celtic god who was linked with the Roman god MARS as MARS ALATOR.

Alauina A Celtic mother goddess who is known from an inscription found at Manderscheid, Germany.
Reading: Wightman 1970, 226.

Albiorix A Celtic god who was linked with MARS as MARS ALBIORIX.

Albunea A water nymph of the sulphurous spring, the Albulae Aquae at Tivoli, Italy, where it forms a waterfall and flows into the Anio River. There was a dream ORACLE near this spot, and Albunea was sometimes called a SIBYL. Some ancient authors identified her with MEFITIS, while others identified her with LEUCOTHEA.
Reading: Hammond and Scullard (eds.) 1970, 35.

Alecto (also known as Allecto) One of the Roman deities known as the FURIES.

Alemona A Roman goddess who looked after the unborn child.
Reading: Ferguson 1988a, 853.

Fig. 2 Altar dedicated to the Alaisiagae and to Mars, found at Housesteads on Hadrian's Wall, England. The inscription reads: DEO MARTI ET DVABVS ALAISIAGIS ET N AVG GER CIVES TVIHANTI CVNEI FRISIORVM VER SER ALEXANDRIANI VOTVM SOLVERVNT LIBENT[ES] M[ERITO] ("To the God Mars and the two Alaisiagae and to the Divine Spirit of the Emperor, the German tribesmen of Tuihantis of the unit of Frisians of Vercovicium, Severus Alexander's Own, willingly and deservedly pay their vow"). N AVG is numen Augusti, *and Tuihantis is probably Twenthe in Holland. On the left of the altar are a knife and an ax, and on the right (not shown) a* patera *and a jug.*

Alisanos A Celtic god who was worshipped in Gaul as the divine spirit of the rock. The same god may have been worshipped as Alisonus in Burgundy, France, possibly as the patron deity of the town of Alesia. The name Alisonus is linked philologically with Alisanos, and both are generally regarded as the same god.
Reading: Green, M. J. 1992a, 28.

Allat A Syrian goddess who during the Roman period was worshipped in and around Palmyra, where she was equated with other local deities. She may have been regarded as identical to ASTARTE. By the second century she was sometimes equated with ATHENA and was represented with a helmet, *AEGIS*, spear and shield.
Reading: Teixidor 1969, 53–62.

Allecto An alternative spelling for ALECTO, who was one of the FURIES.

Almo A Roman river god who was deity of the Almo River in Latium, Italy. Almo was the father of the nymph Lara.

altar (Fig. 3) (Latin: *ara*, pl. *arae*) A small table-like structure used for sacrifices to deities. Altars were indispensible in the cults of most gods (the exception being UNDERWORLD gods, to whom offerings were made in pits). Since nearly every religious act was accompanied by a sacrifice, altars were a focus of worship and predated the use of TEMPLE buildings. The earliest altar in Rome was thought to be the Ara Maxima. When temples were built, the altar was placed outside, opposite the main door. Private houses often had small altars, or else the hearth served as an altar. There were also small public altars that served for bloodless sacrifices and for the burning of incense. Altars were also places of refuge, and suppliants came under the protection of the particular deity to whom the altar was dedicated. It was not unusual for an altar to be erected or promised to a god in exchange for a safe journey; because travel was often arduous and dangerous, wayside shrines existed for offerings during a journey.

Altars were of various shapes and sizes. Some of the earliest were U-shaped; bases of this kind have been found, including a row of 13 at Lavinium, Italy, dating from the sixth to fourth century B.C.

Fig. 3 A marble altar found at Ostia, near Rome, in Italy, with ornate relief sculpture.

In the second century B.C., hourglass-shaped altars (Fig. 112) were dedicated, and this form continued into the early empire. From about the third century B.C., altars in the shape of a vertical rectangular block were favored, taller than they were wide, with sometimes elaborate sculpture on one or more sides and a pulvinate crown. These persisted into the late empire and are found particularly as funerary altars. Indeed, apart from funerary altars, few Roman altars survive. Also rare are round altars. Sometimes altars were set on platforms approached by steps. Bronze tripods were also used for altars.

There was often a hollow *(focus)* in the upper surface of an altar where a fire could be lit to consume small sacrifical offerings such as cakes. Altars bore both the name of the god to whom the altar was dedicated and the name of the person responsible for setting it up.
Reading: Hassall 1980; Richardson 1992, 19–20.

Altor ("nourisher" or "sustainer") A Roman god of agriculture who was associated with the Roman goddess TELLUS.

Ambarvalia An annual moveable festival (one of the *FERIAE CONCEPTIVAE*) which was celebrated at the end of May (probably around May 29). It was originally a rite of lustration (purification), a procession around the fields of Rome—the *ager Romanus*

(Roman territory). It was primarily a festival of beating the boundaries to drive evil away from the fields, with rituals to purify the crops. It therefore involved worship of gods of agriculture such as CERES and BACCHUS and also of MARS, JUPITER and JANUS. It became both a private and public festival. Sacrificial animals (pigs, sheep and oxen—*suovetaurilia*) were led in procession around field boundaries and the old boundaries of Rome, and sacrifices were offered at particular locations along these boundaries. All agricultural work ceased for the day, and celebrations were held by farmers. The area within the boundaries was then deemed to be free from harm. The circumambulation of the fields survives in the ceremonies of the Christian church at Rogationtide, and in the ceremony of the beating of the bounds in English parishes before Ascension Day. The corresponding festival (AMBURBIUM) purified the city of Rome itself.
Reading: Scullard 1981, 124–125.

Ambieicer An Iberian deity who is known from an inscription found at Braga, northern Portugal.
Reading: Tranoy 1981, 269.

Ambiorebis An Iberian deity who is known from an inscription found at Braga, northern Portugal.
Reading: Tranoy 1981, 269.

Ambrose, Saint Aurelius Ambrosius, c. 339/340–397. An early Christian bishop and theologian, author of numerous works. In 374 Ambrose was chosen bishop of Milan by popular acclaim, although he had not been baptized or ordained. He was very influential in eradicating heresy (such as Arianism), paganism and Judaism, and AUGUSTINE was his most famous convert. He had increasing influence over the emperors Gratian, Valentinian II and Theodosius I, and persuaded Valentinian II to resist the plea of Symmachus and other aristocracy in 384 to restore the Altar of Victory (and therefore paganism) in the Senate-house. He refused Theodosius I communion for the massacre of 7,000 people at Thessalonica in 390 (undertaken to avenge the killing of the general Butheric) until he had done penance. He was probably responsible for persuading Theodosius I to ban pagan worship and close temples in 391. Ambrose wrote copious treatises, sermons, letters, funerary panegyrics and hymns, including *De Officiis Ministrorum (On Clergymen's Duties)*, a practical manual for priests written in 386. A *Life of Ambrose* was written by his secretary Paulinus.
Reading: Hammond and Scullard (eds.) 1970, 51.

Amburbium A rite of lustration (purification) held to purify the city of Rome (whereas the corresponding festival of AMBARVALIA purified the fields of Rome). It seems to have involved a procession around the city, accompanied by prayers and sacrifices, but little is known of the rituals involved. The Amburbium was still celebrated as late as A.D. 271. Although it seems to have been an annual moveable festival (one of the *FERIAE CONCEPTIVAE*), it appears in no calendar. The rite may have been held in February, and possibly became the Christian festival of Candlemas.
Reading: Hammond and Scullard (eds.) 1970, 51; Scullard 1981, 82–83.

Amon One of the chief gods of the Egyptians; also known as Ammon, Amoun and Amun. He was originally the god of the city of Thebes in Egypt, but his cult gradually spread through Egypt, where he was portrayed with a plumed headdress and sometimes with the head of a ram. He was the god of fertility and was supposed to initiate and then to maintain the continuity of life. In the seventh century B.C. his cult spread into Greece where he was portrayed as ZEUS with curling rams' horns on his head. From Greece, the cult of Amon spread to the Roman world, but it appears never to have been as widespread and popular as that of some of the other Egyptian deities. Having been identified with Zeus in Greece, Amon was later sometimes identified with the Roman god JUPITER.
Reading: Hammond and Scullard (eds.) 1970, 52–53.

amulet Object worn to protect the wearer against evil and to bring good luck. The division between superstition and religion in the Romans' attitude to amulets is often unclear. Many such objects may have been available for sale at shrines and temples, and were not used as votive offerings but for personal protection. Rings and pendants were common forms of amulet, with inscriptions or magical symbols engraved on them or on the semiprecious stones set into the object. The dividing

line between images of gods used for religious or for superstitious reasons is very thin, and many gems with representations of deities may well have been amulets instead of votive objects. Representations of the club of HERCULES and the Gorgon's head were also used as amulets. Gems with representations of combined heads (several human, or human and animal heads fused together) also seem to have been used as amulets. Other amulets have a fusion of two or more protective symbols, such as a combination of a phallus and a human head, or a phallus and a hand making the *MANO FICO* gesture. Amulets were also worn in Christian times. Buildings could also be adorned with amulets (such as phallic symbols). Various Latin words for amulet include *amuletum*, *bulla*, *crepundia* and *fascinum*.
Reading: Hammond and Scullard (eds.) 1970, 56.

Ananke The Greek personification of absolute obligation, she came to be regarded as the ultimate force of destiny that even the gods had to obey. In Rome, she was identified with the goddess NECESSITAS.
Reading: Grimal 1986, 40.

anatomical ex-voto A particular type of votive offering consisting of models of parts of the human body, known today as anatomical ex-votos. Ones that survive are usually made of terracotta, but other materials, such as wood and stone were also used; wood was probably the most common material but rarely survives. Someone with an ailment would deposit a model of the afflicted part of their anatomy in a shrine or temple of a god of healing. They hoped to be healed by dedicating the afflicted part to the god (and were therefore more likely to have been sacrifices in expectation of being healed, rather than votive offerings in thanks for being healed). This was a common medical practice in the Roman world, and models of every part of the anatomy are known.

Terracotta anatomical ex-votos first became popular in republican Italy, some at sanctuaries of AESCULAPIUS, but also at others where the healing deity cannot be identified—for example, at Ponte di Nona. Many have been found in the Tiber, probably originating from the sanctuary of Aesculapius on the Tiber Island in Rome. The anatomical ex-votos were probably made in kilns near the sanctuaries and sold to visitors. At the republican healing sanctuary of Ponte di Nona, over 8,000 have been found, many relating to hands and feet. Anatomical ex-votos virtually died out in Italy by the first century B.C., but they continued to be used for several centuries in Gaul and Britain. They continued to be dedicated in the Christian period, and are found in churches of Italy, Greece and other Mediterranean countries as metal plaques and wax models of the afflicted body parts.
Reading: Jackson 1988, 157–164, 169.

Ancamna A Gaulish goddess who is known from inscriptions found in the territory of the Treveri in Germany. She is represented as part of a divine couple with MARS LENUS or MARS SMERTRIUS at different shrines. She appears to have been a goddess specifically of the Treveri. Mars Lenus was a god of healing, and so Ancamna's association with him may imply that she was a healing goddess. However, at the shrine where she was associated with Mars Smertrius, clay figurines of mother goddesses may imply that she was regarded by some as a mother goddess.
Reading: Green, M. J. 1992a, 28.

Ancasta A Celtic mother goddess who is known from an inscription found at Bitterne, Hampshire, England.
Reading: Ross 1974, 268.

ancile (pl. *ancilia*) A small archaic shield with a waisted or figure-of-eight form. The 12 sacred shields of MARS carried in processions by the *salii* were of this form. They were kept at the Regia in Rome. Legend relates that the bronzesmith Mamurius Veturius made 11 *ancilia* in imitation of one that fell from the sky in Rome.
Reading: Warde Fowler 1899, 38–39, 42; York 1986, 74.

Andarte A Celtic goddess who was worshipped by the Vocontii in Gaul. She was also known as Andarta and Augusta Andarta ("Andarta of the emperor"). This goddess is also known from inscriptions dedicated to DEA AUGUSTA ANDARTA which have been found in the valley of the Drôme in southern France and also in the Roman town known as Dea Augusta (modern Die). Other local dedications to Dea Augusta are thought to belong to the goddess Andarte. Inscriptions from this area which record

instances of the rite of *taurobolium* have led to the suggestion that Andarte eventually became identified with MAGNA MATER (Cybele). Andarte may be the same as the goddess ANDRASTE.
Reading: Green, M. J. 1992a, 28 (under *Andraste*).

Andate An alternative name for the goddess ANDRASTE.

Andinus A Celtic god who is known from an inscription on an altar found in the Roman province of Upper Moesia. He appears to have been a local deity. The frequency of personal names such as Andia and Andio, which were probably derived from the god's name, suggests that his cult was more popular in Upper Moesia than the single known inscription would imply.
Reading: Mócsy 1974, 254.

Andraste According to ancient authors, she was a Celtic goddess of victory, worshipped by the Iceni in Britain. When the author Cassius Dio was writing about the rebellion in Britain in A.D. 60 led by Boudicca, queen of the Iceni, he refers to human sacrifices performed in a grove and other places which were sacred to Andraste. This goddess was sometimes called ANDATE and may also be the same as the deity ANDARTE.
Reading: Green, M. J. 1992a, 28.

Angerona Also called DIVA ANGERONA, she was the Roman goddess of secrecy and was believed to give relief from pain and worry. She was usually depicted with a finger placed on her sealed mouth, warning silence. She was worshipped at the festival of ANGERONALIA.
Reading: Hammond and Scullard (eds.) 1970, 64.

Angeronalia (also known as DIVALIA and Divalia Angeronae) A festival in honor of the goddess ANGERONA that was held on December 21. Little is known about the festival. A sacrifice to Angerona was offered in the Curia Acculeia at Rome, and the priests performed a rite in the shrine of VOLUPIA (Latin, *sacellum Volupiae*), where there was a statue of the goddess Angerona on the altar with her mouth bound and sealed. The Curia Acculeia was probably an unroofed enclosure, likely an augural station for observation of divine signs. The shrine of Volupia may have been in or adjacent to the Curia Acculeia, at the foot of the Palatine Hill. The festival was not connected with the winter solstice, which did not fall on December 21 before the Julian calendar.
Reading: Hammond and Scullard (eds.) 1970, 64; Richardson 1992, 101–102; Scullard 1981, 209–210.

Angitia A Marsian goddess who appears to have been a goddess of healing; the Marsi were a people who inhabited central Italy around Lake Fucinus and who were given Roman citizenship during the Social War (91–87 B.C.). Angitia appears to have been very popular in this area. She was sometimes referred to in the plural as Angitiae, implying that this was a collective name for several goddesses.
Reading: Hammond and Scullard (eds.) 1970, 65.

animal, sacred There were no animals regarded as incarnate gods in the Roman period, except in Egypt which had a tradition of such practices (such as the sacred Apis bull). However, many animals (including birds) were associated with particular gods, such as the woodpecker and wolf with MARS, and the ram, cockerel and tortoise with MERCURY. Geese were sacred to JUNO MONETA, and many deities were associated with SNAKES. There is no evidence that the animals themselves were worshipped.
Reading: Green, M. J. 1992b; Hammond and Scullard (eds.) 1970, 65; Toynbee 1973.

Anna and the Children Indigenous deities of Sicily who are attested at a shrine near Buscemi, Sicily. Little is known about the cult of these deities, but the dedicatory inscriptions to them are all in Greek, despite the Roman names of some of the worshippers.
Reading: Wilson 1990, 280.

Anna Perenna A Roman goddess who is usually considered to be a personification of the year because her festival was at the first full moon (March 15) of the new year, which began on March 1 in the old calendar. On this day both public and private sacrifices were offered to her. Her name may be derived from the prayer *ut annare perennaresque commode liceat* ("for leave to live in and through the year to our liking"). She was worshipped in a sacred grove on the Via Flaminia in Rome.

OVID records two stories about Anna Perenna, although they may have been his own inventions.

In one, she was an old woman who made and sold cakes to the plebeians when they seceded to the Sacred Mountain (Mons Sacer), and thus averted a famine. In another story she was identified as Anna, the sister of Dido. After Dido's suicide, she was driven from Carthage and arrived at Latium. There she met Aeneas and was set up in his household against the wishes of Aeneas' wife Lavinia. Being warned of Lavinia's hostility, Anna fled, and was carried off by Numicus, the god of a nearby stream. She became a water NYMPH whose new name, Perenna, signified eternity. The servants of Aeneas were sent to search for her and followed her tracks to the river bank, where a shape rose from the river and revealed that Anna had become a water nymph. Rejoicing at this, the servants passed the day with celebrations, and these festivities were established as the annual festival of Anna Perenna.

MARS was said to have chosen Anna as an intermediary between himself and MINERVA. Because Anna knew Minerva would never submit to Mars, she took Minerva's place, but when Mars entered the bridal chamber he recognized her and spoke angry words. This story was supposed to explain the obscenities that were sung at Anna Perenna's festival.

Reading: Grimal 1986, 43; Hammond and Scullard (eds.) 1970, 65; York 1986, 66–67.

Anociticus A Celtic god who is known from a temple at Benwell, on Hadrian's Wall, England. (See ANTENOCITICUS.)

Antenociticus (Fig. 4a and Fig. 4b) A Celtic god who is known from a temple at Benwell, on Hadrian's Wall, England. Here the remains of a life-size cult statue were found, accompanied by two altars, one of which was dedicated to Antenociticus and one to ANOCITICUS. These may be variant spellings or alternative names of the same god. This god is probably also invoked in a dedication found at Chesters, also on Hadrian's Wall, which was addressed to ANTOCIDICUS.

Reading: Green, M. J. 1992a, 30; Ross 1974, 472–473.

Antinous (Fig. 5) A favorite of the emperor Hadrian, Antinous was drowned in the Nile River in October A.D. 130, in mysterious circumstances. It is possible that Antinous deliberately drowned himself as a sacrifice to avert some danger to the empire and the emperor. After his death, Hadrian ensured that Antinous was deified and venerated as a god. Hadrian founded the city of Antinoopolis in Egypt, and the patron god of this city was Osirisantinous (Antinous equated with OSIRIS). Here his cult included ecstatic festivals, games and an ORACLE. He was sometimes equated with PAN, HERMES, SILVANUS

Fig. 4a The preserved remains of the temple of Antenociticus outside the fort at Benwell, Hadrian's Wall, England.

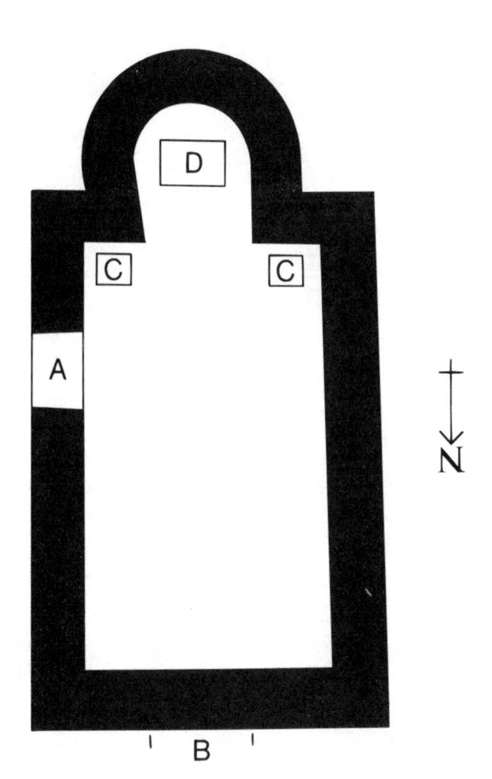

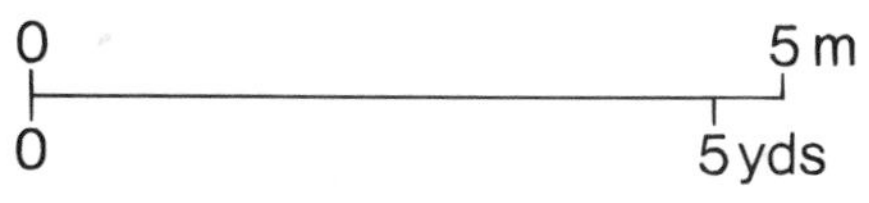

Fig. 4b Plan of the temple of Antenocitieus at Benwell, Hadrian's Wall, England. A = doorway; B = traces of doorway; C = altars; D = probable position of cult statue.

or DIONYSUS ZAGREUS, and was regarded as a savior god. The worship of Antinous was widespread in the eastern empire.

Reading: Hammond and Scullard (eds.) 1970, 71; Henig 1986, 159–160.

Antocidicus A Celtic god who is invoked in a dedicatory inscription from Chesters, Hadrian's Wall, England. He is probably the same deity as ANTENOCITICUS.

Reading: Ross 1974, 472–473.

Antonine Altar at Ephesus A huge monumental altar with very fine sculpture at Ephesus, Turkey, although discovered in a fragmentary condition. There was a monumental enclosure leading up to the sacrificial altar. Reliefs around the outside of this enclosure depicted events in the life of Lucius Verus (died A.D. 169), co-emperor with Marcus Aurelius. They included his adoption by Antoninus Pius, the gathering of the whole family and Lucius

Fig. 5 Medallion of the city of Alexandria, Egypt, portraying Antinous. His head is surmounted by a lotus flower and the Greek inscription reads "Antinous hero." He is also shown on horseback on the reverse (left), with a caduceus. *The two Greek letters indicate the 19th year of the reign of Hadrian.*

Verus's wars against the Parthians. On one side of the entrance to the sacrificial altar was a relief showing the apotheosis of Lucius Verus and on the other a scene of Artemis.
Reading: Price 1984, 158–159.

Antoninus Pius and Faustina, temple of (Latin, *templum Divi Antonini et Divae Faustinae*) Built at Rome by Antoninus Pius on the north side of the Sacra Via in the FORUM ROMANUM (Fig. 37) in honor of his deified wife Faustina (who died in 141) (Fig. 44). After his own death and deification in 161, the temple was rededicated to them both by a *senatus consultum*. It was a hexastyle temple raised on a high podium. The cella was converted into the Church of San Lorenzo in Miranda before the twelfth century.
Reading: Nash 1962a, 26–27; Richardson 1992, 11–12.

Anu A Syrian god who was originally the chief god of the Babylonians. His cult was widespread in Syria and Mesopotamia in the Roman period.

Anubis A jackal-headed Egyptian god of the dead. The Romans usually portrayed him with a dog's head, and he was sometimes depicted as a soldier in armor. His cult was introduced into Rome during the empire, along with other Egyptian deities such as Isis.
Reading: Grenier 1977; Hammond and Scullard (eds.) 1970, 78.

Apadeva A Celtic water goddess who is known from a dedicatory inscription on an altar found at Cologne, Germany.
Reading: Elbe 1975, 215.

apex (Figs. 6, 32) (pl. *apices*) A close-fitting conical hat or cap worn by *flamines* and some other priests out of doors. The term *apex* is often applied to the entire hat, although it properly referred to the top of the hat which consisted of a stick of olive wood known as a *virga*. The lower part of the hat was the *galerus*. There was a disk-like ornament at the base of the *apex* and sometimes a second stick lengthwise across the *apex* at its base. The *apex* added to their dignity, but it became smaller during the empire. That of the *FLAMEN DIALIS* was white in color as it

Fig. 6 Flamines *of late 1st-century B.C. date, dressed in the conical hat* (apex) *with the pointed spike and disk-like ornament at the base.*

was made from the skins of white animals sacrificed to JUPITER, and it was also known as the *albogalerus*.
Reading: Hammond and Scullard (eds.) 1970, 80.

Aphrodite The Greek goddess of love, beauty and fertility who was equated with the Roman goddess VENUS.

Apis The sacred bull who was worshipped in Memphis, Egypt, where he was regarded as the reincarnation of Ptah, the sovereign god of Memphis. Under Ptolemaic and Roman rule, the Apis cult expanded and its rites and feast days were given official recognition. A sacred bull was kept in its own temple and fed dainty food. The bulls came to be addressed as Osorapis. At a fixed hour each day the bull was let loose in a courtyard attached to the temple. The bull's movements were interpreted as foretelling the future: when Germanicus (adopted son of Tiberius) died, it was remembered that the sacred bull had refused delicacies offered to it by Germanicus. When a sacred bull died, it was mummified and entombed in the chambers below the temple; there was a period of fasting lasting 70 days, and a successor bull was chosen.

In the Roman period, the cult of Apis is more important to the cult of SERAPIS that originated in the worship of the Osirified sacred bulls entombed in the temple at Memphis; "Osirified" meant identified with OSIRIS, and thus brought to life to reign in the UNDERWORLD with Osiris after death.

Reading: Hammond and Scullard (eds.) 1970, 81; Kater-Sibbes and Vermaseren 1975a, 1975b and 1977.

Apollo (Fig. 7) This Greek god, son of ZEUS and LETO and brother of ARTEMIS, was never properly identified with a Roman god. First introduced to Rome as a healing god, he became a god of oracles and prophecies, as well as of hunting, music and poetry. The SIBYL at Cumae in Italy was a priestess of Apollo. Among the Greeks, Apollo had a great many titles or epithets, but only a few occur in Latin literature. His titles include Apollo Articenens (Apollo carrying the bow), Apollo Averruncus (Apollo who averts evils), Apollo Coelispex (Apollo who watches the heavens) and Apollo Culicarius (Apollo driving away midges). To the Romans, Apollo was the god of poetry, and "to drink the waters of Castalia" signified poetic inspiration. (Castalia was a NYMPH in Greek mythology who, being pursued by Apollo, threw herself into a spring on Mount Parnassus near Delphi.)

Fig. 7 Apollo playing the lyre. Statue of 2nd century A.D. from Miletus, Turkey. Apollo was the patron god of Miletus.

Apart from his epithets and titles, as Phoebus Apollo, he was worshipped as a sun god. Apollo was also identified at times with the Sabine god SORANUS. Apollo gradually became connected with ORPHISM and with NEOPYTHAGOREANISM, and he was sometimes regarded as the father of ORPHEUS and of Pythagoras. It is probably in connection with Orphism and Neopythagoreanism that the myths of Apollo are sometimes depicted in carvings on sarcophagi. Augustus regarded Apollo as his personal deity and built a temple of Apollo Palatinus at Rome next to his own house on the Palatine Hill. At Rome, games in honor of Apollo took place in July, and there was a festival on September 23. He was one of only three gods (with MARS and NEPTUNE) to whom a bull might be sacrificed. (See also entries below relating to Apollo.)
Reading: Hammond and Scullard (eds.) 1970, 81–82; Room 1983, 323–326 (for titles/epithets of Apollo); Simon 1990, 27–34.

Apollo, temples of The oldest temple of Apollo at Rome was vowed in 433 B.C. because of a plague in the city. It was dedicated in 431 B.C. (possibly July 13) by the consul Gaius Iulius. Because the cult of Apollo was a foreign one, the temple was located outside the *pomerium*, and was situated in the CAMPUS MARTIUS between the CIRCUS FLAMINIUS and the FORUM HOLITORIUM, next to the temple of BELLONA (Fig. 15). The temple was on occasions used by the Senate, especially for meeting foreign embassies and deliberating about triumphs. Its podium is beneath the cloisters of Santa Maria in Campitelli. In 1940 three of its columns were reerected. It was the only temple of Apollo in Rome until the one erected on the Palatine Hill in 28 B.C. It was probably this temple that was restored by Gaius Sosius, consul in 32 B.C., in which case it was known originally as that of Apollo Medicus, and later as the temple of Apollo Sosianus. Sosius furnished it with many works of art. An earlier restoration or rebuilding seems to have occurred in 353 B.C., and the new dedication date was September 23.

The temple of Apollo on the Palatine was called the temple of Apollo Palatinus, variously described

in Latin as an *aedes, templum* and *delubrum.* It was erected on a house plot where Octavian (Augustus) had intended to build a residence. When lightning struck during his campaign with Sextus Pompey in 36 B.C. he vowed a temple instead. It was completed and dedicated on October 9, 28 B.C., next door to Augustus's own house. The Sibylline books were transferred to this temple in 12 B.C. or earlier, and were rescued when the temple burned on March 18, A.D. 363. It was regarded as a sumptuous temple and had associated porticoes, numerous statues and libraries (where the Senate often met). The precise position of the temple is unknown, and it may have been a temple often called JUPITER VICTOR.
Reading: Nash 1962a, 28–31; Richardson 1992, 12–14; Scullard 1981, 164, 188.

Apollo Atepomarus The Celtic deity ATEPOMARUS was identified with the Greek god APOLLO in an inscription found at Mauvières, France. "Atepomarus" is sometimes translated as "Great Horseman" or "possessing a great horse". At healing shrines in other parts of Gaul, Apollo had small figurines of horses dedicated to him; since Apollo was a sun god, his association with horses may have derived from the connection of horses and the Celtic cult of the sun.
Reading: Green, M. J. 1992a, 30.

Apollo Belenus The Celtic god BELENUS was identified with the Greek god APOLLO. Apollo Belenus was both a sun god and a healing god, and was popular in parts of Gaul, northern Italy and Noricum. He is mentioned in numerous inscriptions.
Reading: Green, M. J. 1992a, 30–31.

Apollo Cunomaglus The Celtic deity CUNOMAGLUS was identified with the Greek god APOLLO. Apollo Cunomaglus is known from a shrine at Nettleton Shrub, Wiltshire, England; the shrine may have been a healing sanctuary, but Diana and Silvanus were also worshipped there, which may suggest that Cunomaglus (meaning "hound-lord") was a god of hunting. However, hunting and healing cults were often linked.
Reading: Green, M. J. 1992a, 31–32.

Apollo Grannus The Celtic god GRANNUS was linked with the Greek god APOLLO. Apollo Grannus was a god of healing who was known at Rome and over much of Europe. There are dedications to the divine couple of Apollo Grannus and the Celtic goddess SIRONA. He was often associated with medicinal springs and was also worshipped as a sun god. Grannus is mentioned as a god of healing by the ancient author Cassius Dio. This is probably the same deity as the Apollo Grannos who was invoked in an inscription found at Musselburgh, Scotland.
Reading: Green, M. J. 1992a, 32; Ross 1974, 473.

Apollo Grannus Mogounus An apparent conflation of the Celtic gods GRANNUS and MOGOUNUS with the Greek god APOLLO. This god is known from an inscription found at Horburg, Germany.

Apollo Medicus ("Apollo the Physician") A Roman god of healing who had a temple at Rome, probably the one next to the temple of BELLONA. (See APOLLO, TEMPLES OF.)

Apollo Moritasgus The Celtic god MORITASGUS was linked with the Greek god APOLLO. A dedication found at a healing shrine and temple at Alesia, France, indicates that he was a god of healing. The dedication also mentions his consort DAMONA. The temple complex at Alesia consisted of baths and a polygonal temple, as well as porticoes, possibly for the rite of INCUBATION. The dedication refers to a sacred pool in which the sick could bathe, and numerous votive models of parts of the body have been found at the site. Finds of surgeons' instruments suggest that the center of healing did not solely rely on the power of the god.
Reading: Green, M. J. 1992a, 32.

Apollo Toutiorix The Celtic deity TOUTIORIX was linked with the Greek god APOLLO. This god is known from an inscription found at Wiesbaden, Germany. Toutiorix is thought to be the same god as TEUTATES.

Apollo Vindonnus The Celtic god VINDONNUS was linked with the Greek god APOLLO. This deity was a sun god and a god of healing who had a temple at Essarois, near Châtillon-sur-Seine, France. VINDONNUS means "clear light." Many worshippers at the temple appear to have sought relief from eye afflictions since many of the votive offer-

ings to Apollo Vindonnus are bronze plaques depicting eyes, although other afflicted parts of the body are also represented in model form. There are also some offerings in the form of an image of a hand holding fruit or a cake.
Reading: Green, M. J. 1992a, 32.

Apollo Virotutis The Celtic god VIROTUTIS linked with the Greek god APOLLO. *Virotutis* probably means "benefactor of humanity." Apollo Virotutis was worshipped in Gaul.
Reading: Green, M. J. 1992a, 32.

Appias A Roman water NYMPH who was the deity of the Appian fountain near the temple of VENUS GENETRIX at Rome.

Arae Flaviae Possibly a cult center for the newly conquered Agri Decumates under the emperor Domitian; now known as Rottweil and located on the Neckar river in Germany. It may have had a monumental ALTAR such as existed at Lugdunum. The Latin name is in a plural form ("Flavian altars"). The place known as Arae Flaviae was possibly a provincial cult to the deified Vespasian and his son Titus, but there is no supporting epigraphical evidence.
Reading: Fishwick 1987, 298–299.

Arae Incendii Neronis Altars erected by Domitian in Rome to commemorate the fire of Nero in 64; they probably delimited the area that was devastated by the fire. Three altars have been found in different positions, one of which survives under no. 30 Via del Quirinale. Annual sacrifices took place at these altars at the Volcanalia.
Reading: Nash 1962a, 60–61; Richardson 1992, 21.

Ara Maxima ("greatest altar") Its full Latin description is Ara Maxima Herculis Invicti, "the altar of unconquered Hercules." An ALTAR in Rome near the Tiber River in the FORUM BOARIUM, between the CIRCUS MAXIMUS and Porta Primigenia, within the *pomerium.* It is likely to have stood between the temple of HERCULES VICTOR and the Circus Maximus. It may have been the large platform found under the church of Santa Maria in Cosmedin, but this is not universally accepted. The epithet *maxima* ("greatest") refers to its importance, not to its size. It was the earliest cult center of HERCULES in Rome. The site of the altar was supposed to have been dedicated by the Greek hero HERACLES or by EVANDER after Hercules killed the legendary CACUS. A temple of Hercules Invictus (or Hercules Victor) was later built close to the Ara Maxima. The cult at this altar was officially adopted by the state in 312 B.C. in reforms by Appius Claudius Caecus. It may have been then that the altar became known as Hercules Invictus. The form of the altar is unknown. It was probably destroyed in Nero's fire in A.D. 64 and subsequently restored. Hercules was especially popular with merchants, and tithes of booty and commercial profit were offered at this altar. Oaths were often taken at the altar and business deals agreed upon. Merchants were accustomed to giving a tithe of their profit on business deals to Hercules. The sacrificial animal at the altar was a heifer.
Reading: Palmer 1990; Richardson 1992, 186–187; Scullard 1981, 171–173.

Ara Pacis (Fig. 8) (Ara Pacis Augustae, "Altar of Peace of Augustus") An altar known from historical references (Augustus's *Res Gestae*) to have been situated on the edge of the CAMPUS MARTIUS, 1 mile (1.6 km) outside the *pomerium* of the city of Rome.

Fig. 8 Ara Pacis depicted on an as *(a bronze coin) of the emperor Nero (54–68), which was minted at Lyon in France.*

It was built by order of the Senate in honor of Augustus's safe and victorious return to Rome in 13 B.C. from campaigns in Gaul and Spain. The foundation ceremony was on July 4, 13 B.C. and it was dedicated on January 30, 9 B.C. The time lag between constitution and dedication was probably due to the time taken to undertake the detailed work.

The monumental ALTAR excavated in the Campus Martius has been identified as the Ara Pacis. There are some objections (not widely accepted) to this particular altar being the Ara Pacis; what was discovered may actually be a different monument. The original site was under the Palazzo Fiano in the Via in Lucina, a low-lying area which was once part of the Campus Martius. Several sculptured slabs were found in 1568 when the Palazzo Peretti (now Fiano) was being constructed, and further slabs were found in 1859. In 1903, the first excavations of the altar were abandoned because of technical difficulties (the site was 30 ft. [9.14 m] below ground level and was waterlogged). Excavation was renewed in 1937–38 with a technique of freezing the waterlogged soil. Most of the surviving sculptures and casts of the original sculptures were reconstructed in a modern glazed structure on the banks of the Tiber River, a short distance from the Palazzo Fiano, opposite Augustus's mausoleum, away from the original location of the altar. The whole monument was formally opened by Mussolini on September 23, 1938, in a ceremony marking the close of the Augustan Bimillennium. In antiquity, the altar faced east, but has been reconstructed north-south.

The excavated altar is of marble and is U-shaped. In its day it stood within an almost square walled precinct which measured 34 ft. 5 ins. x 38 ft. x 23 ft. (10.5 m x 11.6 m x 7 m) and had numerous carvings on both the interior and exterior walls. The altar and its precinct stood on a low podium with doors on the east and west sides. The main entrance into the precinct was by a flight of stairs. On the higher ground behind the altar was another entrance through the precinct wall for attendants with sacrificial beasts. One frieze on the precinct wall represents a sacrificial ceremony conducted by Augustus in the presence of members of his family, processions of priests and the Senate, possibly depicting the foundation ceremony (constitution) on July 4, 13 B.C. The frieze around the altar itself (of which less than one-third survives) records the dedication in 9 B.C., the scenes depicted being the *suovetaurilia* with sacrificial animals, VESTAL VIRGINS and *pontifex maximus.* The right-hand front panel of the precinct wall shows the sacrifice at Lanuvium of a sow and 30 piglets by Aeneas on his arrival from Sicily—intended to signify Augustus's safe return from abroad. The left-hand panel shows Romulus and Remus.

Reading: Billows 1993; Conlin 1992; Fishwick 1972, 171–176; Fishwick 1987, 203–210; Koeppel 1992; Patterson 1992; Richardson 1992, 287–289; Simon 1968 (in German); Toynbee 1961.

Ara Ubiorum Altar of the Ubii tribe, situated near modern Cologne. It was probably a sanctuary similar to that at Lugdunum, and was established by Augustus, possibly in 12–9 B.C. The altar (*ara)* gave its name to the Roman town of Colonia Claudia Ara Agrippensis (Cologne). The associated cult was possibly that of Roma and Augustus. The altar was probably intended as the religious and political center of Roman Germany, but ceased to exist after the destruction of Varus's legions in A.D. 9. No trace of the altar has been found.

Reading: Fishwick 1987, 137–139.

Arausio A Celtic deity who was the eponymous spirit of the town of Arausio (modern Orange), France.

Reading: Green, M. J. 1992a, 33.

Arduinna A Celtic boar goddess of the Ardennes Forest. She was probably a local goddess both of hunting and of protecting the animals of the chase, particularly boars. A statuette from the area shows her riding on a boar with a dagger in her right hand. She was sometimes conflated with the Roman goddess DIANA.

Reading: Green, M. J. 1992a, 33–34.

Area Capitolina The precinct of the temple of JUPITER OPTIMUS MAXIMUS at Rome (Fig. 15). (See CAPITOLINE HILL.)

Area Sacra di Largo Argentina An area in the southern part of the CAMPUS MARTIUS at Rome, now between the Corso Vittorio Emanuele and Via Florida. In 1926–29 a precinct containing a line of three rectangular temples (Temples A, C, D) and a round temple (Temple B) was found, of republican date, although more temples may have extended beyond the line. They were probably sited where most triumphal processions began, and the temples were likely to have been the offerings of successful generals. Before the excavation, one rectangular temple and the round temple were already known: Temple A had been built into the church of San Nicola a' Cesarini and is probably third century B.C.; Temple C is of a similar date. Temple B dates to the mid second century B.C., and Temple D to the first century B.C. The attribution of the temples is disputed; Temple B is probably that of Lutatius Catulus's temple of FORTUNA HUIUSCE DIEI and Temple D is possibly of JUPITER FULGUR; Temple A or C may have been that of JUNO CURITIS. The area was burned in the fire of Titus in A.D. 80 and was restored under Domitian.

Reading: Nash 1962a, 136–139; Patterson 1992, 196–197; Richardson 1992, 33–35, 214.

Area Sacra di Sant' Omobono A sacred precinct at the foot of the CAPITOLINE HILL on a ridge between the FORUM ROMANUM and FORUM BOARIUM (Fig. 15). It contained the twin temples of FORTUNA and MATER MATUTA.

Reading: Richardson 1992, 35–37.

Arecurius Thought to be a Celtic god of the UNDERWORLD and a male counterpart of AERICURA. He is known from an inscription on a statue of the god which was found at Corbridge, England.

Reading: Phillips 1977, 24.

Ares The Greek god of war who was equated with the Roman god MARS.

Arethusa A water NYMPH who was the personification of a freshwater spring at Syracuse on the coast of Sicily.

Reading: Wilson 1990, 281.

argei Bundles of rushes resembling people bound hand and foot. These effigies or dolls were used in certain rituals and may have represented human sacrifice, perhaps by drowning: even up to the nineteenth century, in some cultures, rivers have been regarded as requiring at least one drowning each year. Alternatively, the rituals may have been an act of purification from all the evils of the year which the *argei* personified as demons.

On March 16 and 17 a procession carrying the *argei* went to the 27 shrines (*sacraria*) situated at points throughout the Four Regions (*regiones quattuor*) of Rome; these were the four regions into which Servius Tullius is supposed to have divided Rome and were the oldest part of Rome. It is not known what was done at the shrines. Thirteen of the 27 shrines have been identified, distributed evenly throughout the four old regions—implying that there may have been originally 28 shrines (seven per region), with one dropped due to a calamity or evil omen. The number 27 is also likely; being 3 x 9, it had a mystical significance. The shrines were not associated with temples.

On May 14 (Ides), a procession carrying *argei* round the shrines took place, probably counterwise. The procession included the *FLAMEN DIALIS*, *flaminica*, VESTAL VIRGINS and the *praetor urbanus*. The procession culminated at the river Tiber, when 30 (possibly 27) effigies were thrown into the river by the Vestal Virgins from the Bridge of Sublicius. The Romans did not even know which deity was being honored or appeased in these rituals involving *argei*.

Reading: Richardson 1992, 37–39; Scullard 1981, 120–121.

Arianism The Arian heresy (Arianism), a heretical fourth-century Christian doctrine (Fig. 22). It was named after its originator, ARIUS. He was probably a Libyan by birth and became a leading presbyter at Alexandria in Egypt. In A.D. 319 (or possibly 323) Arius and his supporters (Arians) began to deny the divinity of Christ, claiming that Christ (the Son) was inferior to God (the Father), whereas orthodoxy proclaimed that they were one. Arius was condemned at the Council of Nicaea in 325, was rehabilitated c. 335 but died shortly after. Despite Arius's death, the heresy continued but a compromise with orthodox Christianity was achieved in 359, after which Arianism declined sharply in popularity (except among the Goths). Orthodoxy was finally reaffirmed at the Second Ecumenical Council of Constantinople in the church of Haghia Eirene in 391.

Reading: Hammond and Scullard (eds.) 1970, 119.

Aristides Publius Aelius Aristides Theodorus. A person through whom (because of his illness) much about healing centers of AESCULAPIUS is known. Aris-

tides was born at Mysia January 27, 118 (died c. 180) and was educated at Pergamum and Athens. A Greek rhetorician who spent much of his life giving demonstrations of his oratory, Aristides was struck down in Rome at 26 by a recurring illness that ended his public appearances and caused him to spend two years at the temples of Aesculapius at Smyrna and Pergamum. He then traveled widely and from time to time revisited the sanctuary of Pergamum and that at Epidaurus. He was author of *Hieroi Logoi (Sacred Teachings)*, an account in six books of the dreams and visions he experienced at the temple of Aesculapius (Asclepieum) at Pergamum while seeking a cure from illness. These books are a very important record of temple medicine and the fullest record of any pagan religious experience.
Reading: Hammond and Scullard (eds.) 1970, 110.

Arius A notable early Christian heretic (lived c. A.D. 260–336) whose views gave rise to ARIANISM.

armilustrium A festival of purification of weapons was held in honor of MARS in a square called the Armilustrium on the Aventine Hill on October 19 (the closing of the war season). The area must have contained an ALTAR. The *SALII* probably danced and sang with the sacred shields *(ancilia)*, purifying the military arms. The sacred shields and weapons were then put away until the next year's military campaigns.
Reading: Richardson 1992, 39–40; Scullard 1981, 195.

Arnemetia A Celtic goddess who is known from Aquae Arnemetiae ("the waters of Arnemetia," now Buxton, England), where she was probably a goddess of the medicinal springs. The name Arnemetia contains the Celtic word *nemeton* (meaning "sacred grove") and is usually interpreted as meaning "she who dwells over against the sacred grove".
Reading: Green, M. J. 1992a, 34.

Arnobius A Christian theologian, born c. 235 in North Africa. Arnobius taught rhetoric in Numidia and was converted to CHRISTIANITY c. 295. He was the author of a seven-book polemic *Adversus Nationes (Against the Pagans)*. This work is a useful source of information about paganism and about Christianity prior to the great persecutions.
Reading: Hammond and Scullard (eds.) 1970, 122.

Artaios A Celtic god who was linked with the Roman god MERCURY as MERCURY ARTAIOS.

Artemis (Fig. 9) A Greek goddess who was originally a mother goddess of fertility and of the wilderness who came to be regarded as a virgin huntress in Greek mythology. She was identified with the Roman goddess DIANA and also with a goddess wor-

Fig. 9 Artemis (fourth figure from right) depicted with many breasts in a relief sculpture at the theater at Hierapolis (Pammukale), Turkey. The sculpture is thought to represent rituals associated with Artemis, but has been mutilated.

shipped at Ephesus in Turkey. The Ephesian Artemis was a fusion between the Hellenistic goddess and an indigenous Anatolian mother goddess. This Ephesian goddess is portrayed with many breasts, in keeping with her original role, but these breasts have been interpreted by some as ripening fruit of the date palm, the scrota of bulls or symbolical ova of the sacred bee. Her virgin priestesses were called bees and her eunuch priests were called drones. The worship of Artemis was predominant in other towns in western Turkey, such as Magnesia and Perge, and she was also worshipped in towns in the eastern Mediterranean and other parts of the Roman empire. During the Roman period Artemis's temple at Ephesus was ranked as one of the seven wonders of the world.
Reading: Ferguson 1970, 21–22.

Artemis, temple of The great temple of ARTEMIS (the Artemisium) at Ephesus in Turkey was originally built in 6th century B.C. and was burnt down in 356 B.C. It was rebuilt over the next 120 years, and was still being built when Alexander the Great passed through Ephesus in 334 B.C. and offered to pay for the building work. The new temple was surrounded on all sides by a colonnade and was situated on a high platform 255 ft. (78.5 m) wide and 425 ft. (131 m) long. The Ionic columns were 60 ft. (20 m) high. The temple was three times larger than the Parthenon in Athens. From earliest times it was visited by pilgrims and tourists. It continued to be used through the Roman period and is shown on Roman coins, usually identified as the temple of Ephesian Diana. It was apparently listed as one of the seven wonders of the world by Callimachus of Cyrene (c. 305–c. 240 B.C.), who held a post in the library at Alexandria in Egypt, and also in a poem of Antipater of Sidon in the late second century B.C. The temple was destroyed by Ostrogoths in A.D. 262. By the seventeenth century its site was lost, but the temple was rediscovered in excavations in the 1860s.
Reading: Trell 1988.

Artio A Celtic goddess of forest animals who was particularly associated with bears (*artio* means "bear"). She was probably also a goddess of plenty, hunting and fertility, and is known from a statuette of the goddess with a bear and dedicatory inscription found at Muri near Berne, Switzerland, and from inscriptions found in a remote valley near Bollendorf, Trier, Germany.
Reading: Green, M. J. 1992a, 34–35.

arval priests Also called arval brothers or arval brethren *(fratres arvales).* They were pre-republican in origin, but the only reference to the existence of the arval priests in the republic is by Varro. The college was possibly extinct by the late republic and was restored by Augustus before 21 B.C. They formed the oldest priestly college in Rome and consisted of 12 priests coopted from the highest senatorial families; the reigning emperor was always also an arval priest. Arval priests retained the office for life, even if condemned and exiled. The president *(magister)* of the arval priests was elected annually, as was his assistant *(flamen).* They offered public sacrifices for the fertility of the fields (*arvum* being a plowed field), and were responsible for the rites of the goddess DEA DIA, as well as for her sacred grove. Their most important ceremony was a festival in honor of the goddess which took place in the grove in May. After the deification of Augustus, the arval priests were responsible for certain aspects of the imperial cult.

The sacred grove was situated 4.35 miles (7 km) south of Rome on the Via Campania beyond the Porta Portuensis (outside the fifth milestone), at La Magliana on the right bank of the Tiber River. It was also the religious center of the arval priests, and excavated remains include a bath building and a circular temple. A large number of inscriptions have also been found. The baths were probably for the use of the arval priests during festivals.

Much information about the arval priests is derived from their records *(Acta Fratrium Arvalium),* many of which have survived as inscriptions; some have been discovered in Rome, but most on the site of the sacred grove. The records *(Acta)* of A.D. 218 have preserved their sacred hymn *(carmen arvale).* The surviving records date from 21 B.C. to A.D. 241, although it is known that the priests continued in existence to at least A.D. 304.
Reading: Beard and North (eds.) 1990; DeLaine 1990; Hammond and Scullard (eds.) 1970, 447; Paladino 1988; Porte 1989, 111–115; Scheid 1975; Syme 1980.

Arvernus A Celtic god who was linked with the Roman god MERCURY as MERCURY ARVERNUS.

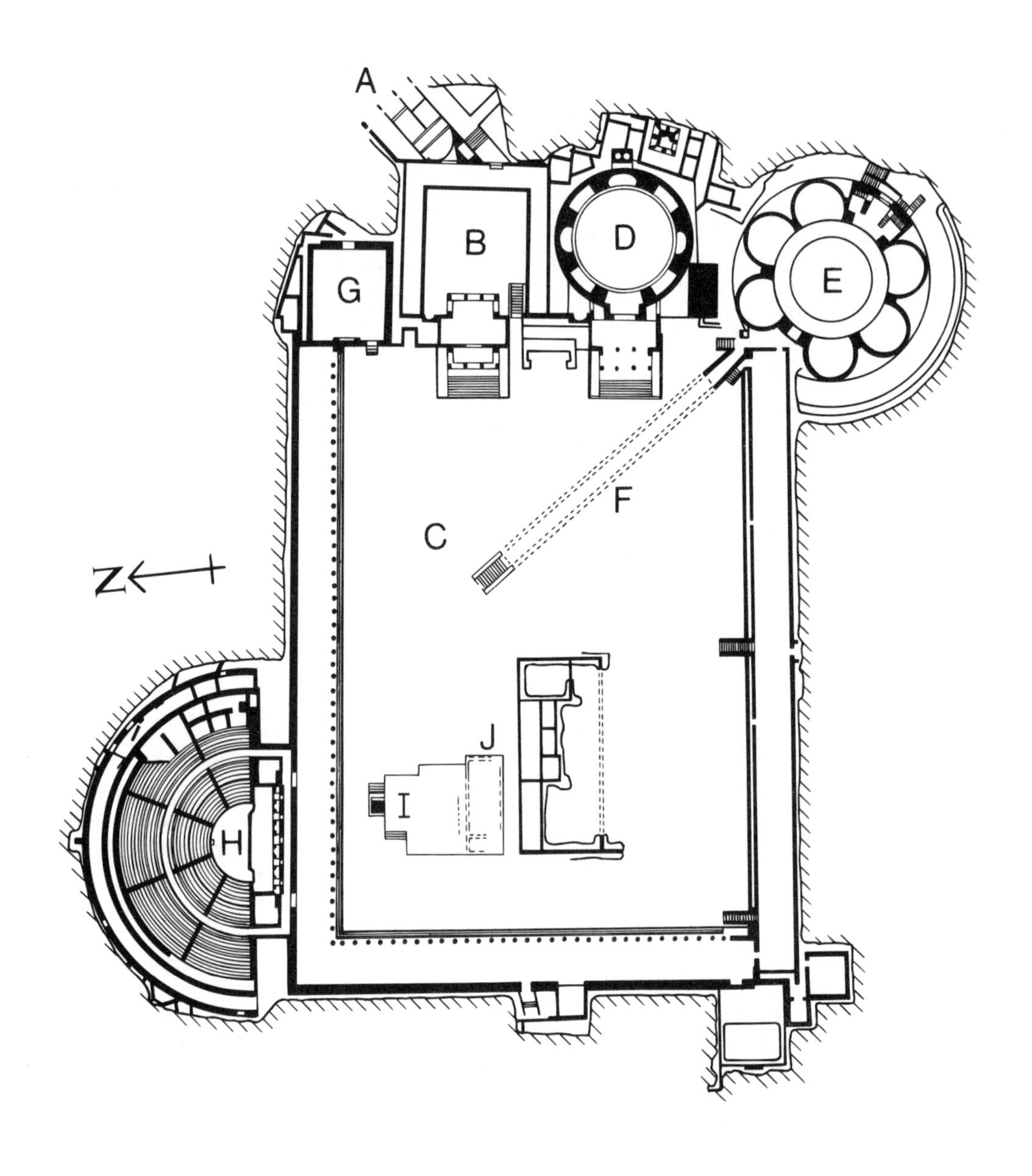

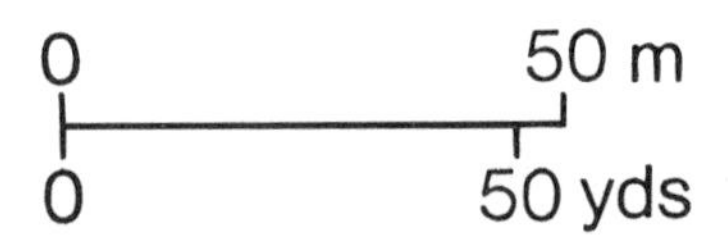

Fig. 10 Plan of the Asclepieium at Pergamum, Turkey, showing mainly Roman remains. A = Via Tecta (colonnaded way); B = forecourt or propylon (mid 2d century); C = huge courtyard; D = temple of Zeus-Asclepius (c. A.D. 150, a copy of the Pantheon; Asclepius was sometimes identified with Zeus); E = hospital; F = vaulted tunnel; G = library; H = theater; I = source of sacred spring; J = three small temples.

Asclepieium (Figs. 10, 80) (or Greek Asklepieion; pl. Asclepieia or Asklepieia) The name given to the healing sanctuaries of the god AESCULAPIUS. They were originally established in the Greek world, and consisted of temples and a range of other buildings and statues. The best known were at Epidaurus, Cos and Pergamum. Most sanctuaries stemmed from that at Epidaurus, which was restored by the Romans under Augustus. It continued in use to the time of Julian (361–363) but may have been destroyed by the Christians. At Rome there was an Asclepieium on the Tiber Island.

When each new shrine was established, a sacred snake representing the god was brought from the temple at Epidaurus. The sacred snake and temple dogs assisted in the cures. Those who were cured dedicated offerings to Aesculapius, including sacrifices of animals, cakes, money, garlands, cups and plates of precious metal, and models of the afflicted parts of the body, notably ears, eyes and limbs. They also gave an account of their medical problem and cure, inscribed on metal and stone plaques and even on votive columns which were displayed at the sanctuary. Many Christian churches were built on the sites of Asclepieia, including churches in Epidaurus, Corinth, Rome and Athens (the latter dedicated to the memory of the doctor saints). (See also AESCULAPIUS, TEMPLE OF.)

Reading: Hammond and Scullard (eds.) 1970, 129–130; Jackson 1988, 142–157, 167–169.

Asklepios (also Asclepius) The name of the Greek god of healing who was known to the Romans as AESCULAPIUS.

Astarte An alternative name for the Phoenician goddess TANIT. She may have been regarded as the same as ALLAT.

astrology Ancient astrology was the observation of heavenly bodies to ascertain their effects on human destinies. It gained a strong hold in Italy in the second century B.C. It was regarded as compatible with religion, because if the stars foretold the future, the gods must have willed it. Astrology became very fashionable in the early empire, although unlike many other forms of divination it was singled out as a target of ridicule by non-believers, including poets. Astrological signs were often incorporated into charms and amulets. From the first century, virtually everyone (including Christians and Jews) accepted the predictability of fate and the influence of the planets. Rome was particularly sensitive to the political implications, since astrology (unlike other forms of divination) claimed accurate prediction of specific events, such as the death of an emperor or the rise of a usurper. Emperors were worried that astrologers would make such predictions and thereby encourage political opponents to fulfill them, and so at times of national crisis professional astrologers were often banished from Italy and Rome (though not from other provinces). However, such bans were only temporary, and emperors had frequent recourse to astrology. It was not until AUGUSTINE's denunciation of astrology in the fourth century, and the rule of Christian emperors in the fourth and fifth centuries, that the practice of astrology was officially prohibited, although its practice nevertheless continued. Constantius II made all forms of divination (including astrology) a capital offense in 357, and this ban was repeated in 373 and 409.

Reading: Liebescheutz 1979, 119–126; Luck 1985, 309–358.

Ataecina An Iberian goddess of the UNDERWORLD who was also known as Ataegina. She was sometimes equated with the Roman goddess PROSERPINA and was worshipped in central western Spain and southern Portugal. A curse tablet found at Mérida, Spain, calls on this goddess to punish the unknown thief who has stolen six tunics, two cloaks and underwear.

Reading: Alarcão 1988, 93; Curchin 1991, 159; Keay 1988, 161.

Atargatis Also called DEA SYRIA ("Syrian Goddess"), she was originally a Syrian earth and vegetation goddess whose cult spread to Greece and to a lesser extent to the western Roman provinces. She was worshipped as a fertility goddess at her temple at Hierapolis, the greatest and holiest in Syria. Originally her consort appears to have been called Dushara or Dusares; he was regarded as subordinate to Atargatis and was thought to be a king who had died and was reborn. He was thus associated with life after death. Unlike most other deities, there was no anthropomorphic statue of Dushara, who was represented by a rectangular block of basalt. Under

Greek influence, Dushara became identified with Dionysus.

Atargatis had a second, later, consort called HADAD, a Syrian thunder god, also known as BAAL SHAMIN. Although he became identified with ZEUS, he was still subordinate to Atargatis. Her throne was flanked by lions, while his was flanked by bulls. Fish and doves were sacred to Atargatis, and at Ascalon, Israel, she was represented as half woman, half fish. She was often portrayed with symbols such as stalks of grain, vines and acanthus. Her cult spread to Egypt in the third century B.C. and to a number of Greek cities in the second century B.C., but appears to have gained little ground in the western provinces. She was sometimes identified with the Ephesian ARTEMIS. Her cult was favored for a time by the emperor Nero, and dedications to her have been found in Italy, England and the Danubian provinces.

Reading: Hammond and Scullard (eds.) 1970, 136; Ferguson 1970, 16–20; Teixidor 1969, 71–76 (evidence from Palmyra).

Atepomarus A Celtic god who was linked to the god APOLLO as APOLLO ATEPOMARUS.

atheism Literally, "a denial of the gods." Atheism in Roman times could be either a refusal to believe in any gods or to believe in the traditional pantheon of pagan gods. Atheism also meant "abandoned by the gods," and was a term of abuse applied to Christians who refused to offer incense to the emperor. Generally atheism did not incur penalties unless it was proclaimed so publicly (as in the case of Christians, who denied the pagan gods) that it aroused fear. At times of crisis people became alarmed at signs of atheism that might offend the gods with disastrous consequences. Anyone branded an atheist was liable to be made a scapegoat.

Reading: Hammond and Scullard (eds.) 1970, 138.

Athena The Greek patron goddess of Athens. She was equated with the Roman goddess MINERVA.

atrium Vestae The area associated with the VESTAL VIRGINS in Rome, east of the FORUM ROMANUM (Fig. 37). It included the open precinct, the round temple of VESTA and the residence of the Vestals. The term is today usually used more specifically for the residence of the Vestal Virgins. Access from the residence to the temple was via stairs and a corridor from the temple precinct. The atrium Vestae was a very large building, with public rooms and individual rooms for the Vestals.

Reading: Richardson 1992, 42–44; Steinby (ed.) 1993, 138–142.

Attis An Anatolian god who was also known as Atys. He was the consort of the goddess Cybele (MAGNA MATER). Phrygian myth states that Attis was the son of Nana, daughter of the river god Sangarius (a river in Asia Minor); Nana conceived him after gathering an almond or blossom from an almond tree which had risen from the severed male organs of AGDISTIS (Cybele), who was born both male and female and had been castrated by the gods. Agdistis, now purely female, loved Attis. When Attis wished to marry someone else, Agdistis was jealous and drove him mad. He castrated himself and died beneath a pine tree. Agdistis was so distressed that the other gods granted that Attis's body would not decay.

In another myth ZEUS, having tried in vain to marry Cybele, let some of his semen fall on a rock, from which the hermaphrodite Agdistis was born. Dionysus (BACCHUS) castrated Agdistis, and a pomegranate tree grew from the blood. Nana became pregnant by inserting one of the fruits of the tree in her womb and gave birth to Attis, but at Sangarius's wish she abandoned Attis, who was adopted by some passers-by. He grew to be very handsome, and King Midas of Pessinus wanted him to marry one of his daughters. Attis and his attendants became frenzied during an argument between Agdistis and Cybele. He castrated himself beneath a pine tree and died. Cybele buried Attis and the daughter of Midas, who had killed herself in despair. Violets grew around the pine tree where the blood of Attis and of Midas's daughter had fallen, and an almond tree grew over the daughter's grave. Zeus granted Agdistis that the body of Attis would not decay, and that his hair would continue to grow and his little finger move. According to legend, a festival and community of priests were founded by Agdistis at Pessinus in honor of Attis.

The poet OVID relates a different version of the legend. Attis was a boy living in the woods of Phrygia and was so handsome that he was loved by Cybele. She wanted to make him guardian of her temple, on condition that he retained his virginity, but Attis could not reject the love of the NYMPH Sagaritis. In her rage, Cybele felled a tree, to which the life of the nymph was bound, and struck Attis with madness so that he castrated himself. Afterwards, Attis was taken back into the service of Cybele.

Originally Attis was a minor part of Cybele's cult and was variously regarded as a mortal or as a god of vegetation. However, he gained official status during the reign of the emperor Claudius (41–54), and after A.D. 150 he was an equal deity with Cybele. In the later Roman empire, he appears to have been regarded as an all-powerful solar deity, and may have offered the promise of immortality to his initiates. He is usually represented as a youth dressed in a Phrygian cap and trousers. Guilds of *dendrophoroi* (tree-bearers) were associated with the worship of Attis. They also acted as burial societies, possibly because in myth Attis was buried and resurrected. The festival of Attis was known as HILARIA.

Reading: Gasparro 1985; Grimal 1986, 26–27 (under *Agdistis*), 70; Hammond and Scullard (eds.) 1970, 146–147; Vermaseren 1977.

Attis Menotyrannus The name applied to the Phrygian god MEN when linked with the god ATTIS. A number of inscriptions mentioning Attis Menotyrannus are known from Rome and Ostia in Italy.

Reading: Hammond and Scullard (eds.) 1970, 669.

Atys An alternative name for the Phrygian deity ATTIS.

Aufaniae Celtic mother goddesses also known as the MATRONAE AUFANIAE.

augur (in Latin, *augur*, pl. *augures*) A priest who was an official diviner and who alone was an authority on taking auspices (reading and interpreting signs from the gods, known as augury). Augurs were apparently created by King Numa Pompilius (715–673 B.C.). In 509 B.C. there were three augurs (one per tribe); their number gradually increased to nine by 300 B.C., to 15 under Sulla (around 81 B.C.) and to 16 under Julius Caesar. They formed a college of priests *(collegium)* and ranked second of the priestly colleges. They were originally selected from male patricians, and also from freeborn plebeians after 300 B.C. They were recruited by co-option and after 104 B.C. partly by popular election. Augurs held office for life, even if they were condemned and exiled, and mediated directly between people and gods. They ascertained divine approval (or disapproval) for military and political actions, advised the Senate and magistrates and alone could define sacred space *(templum)* on earth. The special emblem of the augur was the *lituus*.

Reading: Hammond and Scullard (eds.) 1970, 147.

Auguraculum An AUGUR's observation post in Rome where Numa Pompilius was supposedly consecrated king of Rome (715–673 B.C.). It had a primitive thatched hut (which was probably periodically rebuilt) and was situated on the Arx of the CAPITOLINE HILL. From here, the augurs took monthly auspices for the new month. The name may have been applied to the entire Arx of the Capitoline Hill.

Reading: Richardson 1992, 45, 69.

Auguratorium A building where Romulus is supposed to have taken the auspices for the new city of Rome. It was possibly located in what became Domitian's stadium, where the church of San Caesarius was situated. It was once thought to be the foundation of a building by the temple of MAGNA MATER, or the same as the Curia Saliorum. An inscription possibly refers to a restoration by the emperor Hadrian.

Reading: Richardson 1992, 45.

augury (Latin, *auspicium;* the term *augurium* probably meant the same) The reading and interpretation of signs (auspices; Latin: *auguria*) from the gods. This was an important form of divination and was originally done by reading and interpreting bird signs (flight, sound and manner of feeding). Augury was done not to foretell the future, but to find out if a proposed course of action had divine approval (whether it was *fas*, as opposed to *nefas*). The methods of taking the auspices were governed by strict rules. Magistrates had the right to take auspices, as well as augurs. Most methods of taking auspices were discredited by the first century B.C., although *extispicium* became prominent. By the first century B.C. military auspices were not taken because most commanders were by then promagistrates ("in place of a magistrate"), not magistrates, and so they had no right to take auspices. Instead, military divination became closely connected with the ritual sacrifice.

Signs from the gods could be unsolicited *(auspicia oblativa)*, such as flashes of lightning and prodigies. However, signs were usually deliberately sought *(auspicia impetrativa)* in various ways, originally by observing the flight patterns of wild birds and later the feeding habits of such captive sacred birds as chickens. *Pullarii* were licensed handlers of the sacred chickens. The auspices were taken before any event, such as a voyage, battle or meeting of the Senate. Sacred chickens were sometimes carried for this purpose by armies in the field, so that auspices could be taken before battles by observing how the chickens ate food given to them. Before the naval battle of Drepana during the siege of Lilybaeum in 249 B.C., the commander Publius Claudius Pulcher apparently disregarded the auspices. On being told that the sacred chickens would not eat, he drowned them, saying "let them drink." He was defeated, losing 93 of 123 warships, and the pious attributed the defeat to his disregard of the auspices.
Reading: North 1990; Scullard 1981, 26–27.

augustales The name given to several priesthoods or honorary offices during the empire. They were associations of freedmen who were devoted to the imperial cult and who were normally debarred from priesthoods and positions of authority. They were common in the west but rarely found in the east, except in Roman colonies. Tiberius established the *sodales Augustales* ("companions of Augustus") to preside over the worship of the deified Augustus and his family. They were modeled upon the existing *sodales Titii*. Similarly, priests were appointed to attend to the worship of other emperors after their death. In many Italian towns and some provincial ones, a board of six men *(seviri* or *seviri Augustales)* was set up to oversee the cult of "Roma and Augustus." (See also *FLAMEN AUGUSTALIS*; *SODALES*.)
Reading: Price 1984, 114.

Augusteum (pl. Augustea; Greek, Sebasteion) A temple that was dedicated to the divine Augustus.

Augustine Aurelius Augustinus (St. Augustine of Hippo), 354–430. A Christian theologian and author of numerous works. He was educated at Carthage, where he subsequently taught rhetoric, as well as in Thagaste and Rome (in 383). In 384 he became professor of rhetoric at Milan, where he met Bishop Ambrose and was converted to Christianity. In 387 he was baptized, and he returned to Africa in 388. He became bishop of Hippo in 395, where he died in 430 while Vandals besieged the town. Augustine was a prolific Christian writer, author of 93 books as well as a vast number of letters and sermons that enormously influenced western theology into the Middle Ages. Many of his works are extant, including *Confessions* (c. 397–400), a compendium of 13 books in which he gives an account of his life and analyzes his feelings and actions. *De Doctrina Christiana (On Christian Learning)* (397–426) is four books about methods of education. *De Civitate Dei (City of God)* comprises 22 books written in 413–426 following the fall of Rome to Alaric in 410; the work presents Augustine's philosophy of history, a defense of Christianity and an attack on paganism.
Reading: Hammond and Scullard (eds.) 1970, 148.

Augustus, Divus The deified emperor Augustus. He was born Gaius Octavius on September 23, 63 B.C., and was effectively emperor after his defeat of Antony in 31 B.C. He died on 19 August A.D. 14. After his death he was deified and was thence known as Divus Augustus. As the heir to Julius Caesar, he was *divi filius* ("son of a god"), a title which he seems to have used to political advantage. He was also rumored to have been conceived by APOLLO; he adopted Apollo as his protective deity, and Apollo became a key symbol during his rule. During his lifetime, Augustus accepted various honors such as the month of August being named after him, and gradually acquired a divine status. In 30 B.C. the Senate decreed that there should be offerings of wine to his *GENIUS* at all public and private banquets. The LARES AUGUSTI came to include the cult of his own *genius*, and various abstract qualities associated with the emperor were celebrated, such as Pax Augusta. In 12 B.C. Augustus became *pontifex maximus*. In c. A.D. 6 Tiberius dedicated an Ara Numinis Augusti ("altar to the *numen* of Augustus"). After his death, Augustus was consecrated *divus* on September 17, A.D. 14, and Tiberius encouraged the cult of the deified Augustus, without the association of Roma. In A.D. 15 permission was given to build a temple at Tarraco, Spain, dedicated to Divus Augustus, and in Rome Tiberius and Livia financed

a temple to Divus Augustus. A special priest *(flamen Augustalis)* to serve the cult was also established. While Tiberius's and Livia's temple was being built, a golden statue of Divus Augustus was placed in the temple of MARS ULTOR. Part of the house where Augustus was born was also converted into a shrine by the Senate. (See also AUGUSTUS, TEMPLE OF; IMPERIAL CULT.)
Reading: Fishwick 1987, 79–167.

Augustus, mausoleum of (Mausoleum Augusti) Known as the Augusteum, the mausoleum was built in 28 B.C. by Augustus as a tomb for himself and members of his family, many of whom were deified at death. The tomb was constructed on a massive scale (95.14–97.33 yds. [87–89 m] in diameter, and about 48.11 yds. [44 m] high). It was situated between the Tiber River and the Via Flaminia, probably just outside what was considered the CAMPUS MARTIUS. The exterior was once hidden by buildings constructed from the post-Roman period onwards; the tomb was used for various purposes, and the latest building was a concert hall constructed in 1907 and removed in 1934–38. The design of the tomb reflected that of late republican *tumuli*, and included public gardens. It had niches to receive urns containing the ashes of the cremations. Nerva was the last emperor to be buried there.
Reading: Nash 1962b, 38; Richardson 1992, 247–249.

Augustus, temple of (Figs. 11, 88) The temple of Divus Augustus *(templum divi Augusti)* was also referred to as Templum Augusti and Templum Novum ("new temple"). It was situated in the Forum Romanum between the Capitoline and Palatine hills and was begun by Tiberius and Livia on Augustus's death. Its exact position is unknown. It was not completed until A.D. 37, and was dedicated by the emperor Gaius (Caligula), probably on October 5. It may have been used by Caligula as a support for a wooden bridge (Pons Caligulae) connecting the Palatine and Capitoline Hills. It was destroyed by fire before 79, and was restored by Domitian and extensively restored by Antoninus Pius between 145 and 161. It was often portrayed on coins of Antoninus Pius and appeared then as an octastyle temple with Corinthian capitals and two statues. It contained many treasures, and a library established

Fig. 11 A denarius *of Antoninus Pius (coin date 140–145) showing the temple of Divus Augustus with its eight columns after its restoration. The legend reads TEMPLVM DIV AVG REST COS III ("the temple of Divus Augustus restored in his third consulship").*

by Tiberius was associated with it. The temple was last mentioned in a military diploma of 298.
Reading: Nash 1962a, 164–165; Richardson 1992, 45–46.

Aurelian Lucius Domitius Aurelianus, emperor from 270 until his death in 275. He instituted the cult of SOL INVICTUS in 274, and was apparently aiming to make it the sole state religion. At the time of his death he was planning renewed persecutions of the Christians.
Reading: Hammond and Scullard (eds.) 1970, 151–152.

Aurora The Roman goddess of the rosy dawn.

auspices (Latin, *auspicia*) Signs from the gods which were read and interpreted by AUGURY.

Avernus (1) An obscure Roman god whose name is uncertain. (See HELERNUS.)

Avernus (2) A deep lake near Puteoli, Italy, believed to lead to the UNDERWORLD.

Reading: Hammond and Scullard (eds.) 1970, 155–156.

Aveta A Celtic goddess who was worshipped at a shrine at Trier, Germany, where numerous small figurines of a mother goddess (presumably Aveta) have also been found. Some of the figurines portray a nursing goddess (*DEA NUTRIX*). Aveta appears to have been a goddess of fertility and of prosperity; she was sometimes portrayed in these figurines with a basket of fruit, and at other times with lap dogs or swaddled infants. She may also have been a goddess of healing, renewal or rebirth.
Reading: Green, M. J. 1992a, 36.

Azzanathcona A Syrian goddess who was sometimes equated with ARTEMIS.

B

Baal (pl. Baals, meaning "lord" or "master"; or spelled Bel). The name given to local sun and sky gods who were worshipped in Syria and Arabia. Baals were Phoenician deities, and originally every town in Phoenicia had its own Baal. Instead of their actual names, the name *Baal* was used for all the various local gods; this was done to prevent strangers or enemies from invoking the gods for their own purposes. The name *Baal* was even used for the great Syrian sun god whose centre of worship was at Baalbek (Heliopolis), Syria; here the great Syrian sun god (Baal) was first identified with the Greek sun god Helios and later with the Roman god JUPITER, so that he came to be invoked as Jupiter Optimus Maximus Heliopolitanus. Also at Baalbek, Baal was associated with the Syrian goddess ATARGATIS.
Reading: Drijvers 1976.

Baal Shamin An ancient god of the Canaanite and Phoenician coast dating from the second millenium B.C. His name means "Lord of the Heaven," and he was a weather god and a patron of farmers and shepherds. At Palmyra, Syria, a temple to Baal Shamin was built around A.D. 131. He was also associated with local deities including Bel, Aglibol and Malakbel. Baal Shamin was sometimes represented in Roman armor, with thunderbolts and ears of cereal crops, denoting that as well as a sky god he was also a god of protection and fertility in the Roman period.
Reading: Drijvers 1976; Teixidor 1969, 18–25.

Bacchanalia (Bacchic mysteries) The Bacchanalia was the Latin name for the secret rites or mysteries *(orgia)* performed in the worship of the god BACCHUS (the Greek god DIONYSUS). Little is known about the rites themselves, which were fundamentally Greek. They do not appear to have been associated with specific cult sites, but were performed wherever there was a group of worshippers. Surrender to Bacchic frenzy in order to achieve a sense of freedom and well-being appears to have been at the heart of these mysteries, although there were also promises of an AFTERLIFE. Livy describes wild excesses and criminal acts performed by devotees of the cult. The Bacchants were supposed to abandon their work and roam the mountains with music and dancing, and swinging torches and *thyrsi* (see *THYRSUS*). In the climax of their religious ecstacy they performed supernatural feats of strength, uprooting trees and catching and tearing apart wild animals or children, sometimes eating the flesh raw. This aspect of the mysteries symbolized the triumph of unfettered nature over man-made order. The rites of Dionysus expressed the orgiastic power of nature, and raw flesh was a sacramental meal by which the Bacchants incorporated the power of the god within themselves. Under the influence of the god, the Bacchants were said to perform miracles and display power over animals.

The wildest rites took place in Greece, but were not wholly pre-Roman. Their earliest evidence in southern Italy dates to the fifth century B.C. By the time of the adoption of the Bacchanalia by the Romans, the rites had become less wild. The Roman god Bacchus came to be worshipped in unruly processions where the spirits of the earth and fertility were represented by some of his followers wearing masks. Because of reports that the Bacchic rites had become immoral and corrupt drunken orgies, a Senate decree in 186 B.C. banned the Bacchanalia

from Rome and Italy because they introduced much disorder. Nevertheless, the cult revived despite being strictly controlled. First-century frescoes in the "Villa of the Mysteries" at Pompeii, Italy, depict Bacchic rites in a room that may have been used for the rites themselves.
Reading: Pailler 1988.

Bacchants (also Bacchantes, Bacchanals, Maenads) Followers of the cult of BACCHUS. Bacchants were mainly women and were usually depicted naked or wearing thin veils, with ivy wreaths on their heads and carrying *thyrsi* (see *THYRSUS*). Often they were depicted wearing the skins of fawns or panthers, with wreaths of ivy, oak or fir. Some were depicted carrying a *cantharus* (two-handled urn) or playing a tambourine or a double flute.

Bacchus The more common Roman name for the Greek god DIONYSUS (Dionysos), although the god was also referred to as Dionysus by the Romans. Dionysus (Bacchus) was identified with the Roman god Liber Pater (see LIBER). Dionysus was the god of the vine and also of wine, but he was also a god of mystic ecstasy, and his cult was one of the mystery religions. The cult of Dionysus appears to have originated in Asia Minor, or possibly in Thrace, and it absorbed several similar cults from that region. The cult appears to have spread rapidly throughout Greece from Thrace. The worship of Dionysus became widespread in southern Italy. By the time of its adoption (as the cult of Bacchus) by the Romans, the cult had become quite complex and had absorbed other elements, such as the role of Bacchus as the god of wine and a belief in an AFTERLIFE. Despite the god's popularity and what is known about the public worship and ritual of the cult (the BACCHANALIA), various elements of the religion were only revealed to initiates. Consequently, relatively few details are known about the secret beliefs and rites of Bacchus.

Bacchus was a popular subject of myths and legends as well as a popular subject in art, although the decoration of sarcophagi with scenes from his mythology is probably related to the deceased's belief in the cult and expectation of a happier life after death. The Bacchanalia were suppressed by the Senate in 186 B.C., and the Bacchic sanctuaries were destroyed. However, the religion continued after this date and was popular in the early centuries of the empire, with scenes from the legends continuing to appear in art. By the second century there was a group of nearly 500 worshippers at Frascati in Italy, and presumably other such groups existed. On many sarcophagi dating from the first to third centuries, there are representations of scenes from Bacchic myth, portraying Bacchus as lord of life and thus demonstrating the hope of resurrection. Bacchus was also worshipped during the festival of AMBARVALIA.
Reading: Grimal 1986, 138–140 (under *Dionysus*); Hammond and Scullard (eds.) 1970, 352–353; Hutchinson 1986a and 1986b (the cult of Bacchus in Britain); Hutchinson 1991 (review article of several books); Johns 1982, 78–82; Manfrini-Aragno 1987; Pailler 1988.

Baco A Celtic god who is known from an inscription found at Châlon-sur-Saône, France. He was probably a boar-god.
Reading: Green, M. J. 1992a, 38.

Banda An Iberian deity who was also known as Bandua. The deity is attested in a variety of inscriptions found in Portugal and northwestern Spain. The name *Banda* has been interpreted as meaning "the deity who unites or bonds together." This deity is usually interpreted as a god. However, on a silver-gilt *patera* of unknown provenance, the deity Banda Araugelensis is portrayed as a goddess carrying a *patera* and a cornucopia.

Banda has many epithets. Banda Araugelensis is thought to be the guardian deity of Araocellum, a place-name that occurs frequently in the Iberian peninsula. Banda Longobricus is recorded on an altar found at Longroiva; this village was once called Longobrica, and so Banda is assumed here to be a guardian deity of the village. It is possible that Banda Arbariaicus, Bandua Boleccus, Banda Brialeacus, Banda Isibraiegus, Banda Oilienaicus, Banda Tatibeaicus, Banda Velugus Toiraecus and Banda Vorteaeceus could be protective deities of native tribes. Altars dedicated to Banda Picius and Bandua Etobricus (or Aetobrigus) are also known. TUERAEUS may be the same deity as Banda Velugus Toiraecus, and PICIUS may be the same deity as Banda Picius, but it is also possible that these similarities result from the conflation of two different native deities. There is also a possibility that Banda Isibraiegus is the same as MERCURY ESIBRAEUS.

Reading: Alarcão 1988, 92–93, 134; Tranoy 1981, 279–280, 288.

baptistery (baptistry) A room or rooms within a church, or a detached building, used solely for Christian baptisms. By the fourth century, baptism had become a complex ritual in which the candidate was immersed or partly immersed in water, or water was sprinkled or poured over the head. The ceremony often took place in baptisteries. Ones dating from the fourth and fifth centuries have been found in western Europe; these are in a variety of styles, with square, circular, hexagonal and octagonal plans. Some contained cisterns for affusion, which was far more predominant than submersion in the western empire; submersion is likely to have taken place in natural settings such as rivers and lakes. Many baptisteries have been recognized by the evidence of tanks or fonts used for affusion, or the pouring of water over the head, and these may have been covered by insubstantial buildings or shelters. (See also LEAD TANKS.)
Reading: Thomas 1981, 202–227; Woodward 1992, 103–105.

Barciaecus An Iberian god who is known from an inscription on an altar found at Naraval, near Tineo, northern Spain. The god's name on the inscription has sometimes been interpreted as Evedutonius Barciaecus, but usually Evedutonius is read as the *gens* of the dedicator who was Lucius Servius Secundus. Barciaecus is probably a local god and patron deity of the place where the altar was found.
Reading: Tranoy 1981, 296–297.

Barrex A Celtic god who was linked with the Roman god MARS as MARS BARREX.

basilica A building with a roof supported on columns or arches and with a central nave and flanking side aisles. In the very late Roman period, beginning in the fourth century, basilicas were a model for Christian church architecture and some basilicas were actually converted into churches. For example, the Basilica Iunii Bassii in Rome was converted into the church of Sant' Andrea Catabarbara Patricia in the time of Pope Simplicius (468–483).

Baudihillia One of the ALAISIAGAE goddesses, known from an inscription from Hadrian's Wall, England.

Beda One of the ALAISIAGAE goddesses, known from an inscription from Hadrian's Wall, England.

Beissirissa A Celtic god who was identified with the Roman god JUPITER as JUPITER OPTIMUS MAXIMUS BEISSIRISSA.

Bel (meaning "Lord") A Syrian sky god who was linked with ZEUS and with the Roman god JUPITER. At Palmyra, Syria, he was often associated in a triad with the local deities IARHIBOL and AGLIBOL (from at least A.D. 32). Bel was also less frequently associated with other gods such as NERGAL, ASTARTE and BAAL SHAMIN. The triad of Bel, Iarhibol and Aglibol was also worshipped in Rome.
Reading: Teixidor 1969, 1–18.

Belatucadrus A Celtic war god, whose name means "fair shining one." He is known from approximately 28 inscriptions discovered in the vicinity of Hadrian's Wall, England. The spelling of this god's name varies a great deal, and dedications to Balatocadrus, Balatucadrus, Balaticaurus, Balatucairus, Baliticaurus, Belatucairus, Belatugagus, Belleticaurus, Blatucadrus and Blatucairus are usually accepted as variants of Belatucadrus. The god is usually referred to as Belatucadrus because this is the most frequent spelling of the name. In five inscriptions, he is equated with the Roman god MARS as MARS BELATUCADRUS. The altars dedicated to him are usually small, simple and plain, and their low quality and the variant spellings (which might reflect a low standard of literacy) have led to the suggestion that this god was mainly worshipped by people of low social status.
Reading: Coulston and Phillips 1988, 55; Fairless 1984, 225–228; Green, M. J. 1992a, 42; Ross 1974, 235–236, 466–467.

Belenus A Celtic god who was sometimes identified with the Greek god APOLLO. *Belenus* means "bright" or "brilliant." Belenus was an important Celtic sun god and healing god; he was also associated with horses. Clay figurines of horses were sometimes given to him as votive offerings. He may have been connected with the Celtic solar fire festival of Beltene on May 1. The cult of Belenus is one of the few to be recorded by ancient authors and is mentioned by Ausonius, Tertullian and Herodian. An inscription from Britain records *Belinus,*

which was probably the British form of Belenus.
Reading: Bourgeois 1991, 33; Green, M. J. 1992a, 30–31; Ross 1974, 472.

Bellona The Roman goddess of war who was also called Duellona (the old Roman form of the name) or, on rare occasions, Bellola. Bellona originally appears to have been a personification of force, but she became equated with ENYO, the Greek goddess of war. She was sometimes regarded as the wife or sister of MARS, being portrayed driving her own chariot, with a sword, spear or torch in her hand. Occasionally Bellona was identified with NERIO, the ancient cult-partner of Mars. The Cappadocian mother goddess MA was also identified with Bellona as Ma-Bellona. In Rome, Bellona had a temple near the altar of Mars (Fig. 15) and several other temples and shrines. Bellona's festival was on June 3.
Reading: Garcia Y Bellido 1967, 64–70 (*Ma-Bellona*); Grimal 1986, 75–76; Hammond and Scullard (eds.) 1970, 164.

Bellona, temple of The main temple *(aedes)* of this goddess was vowed in 296 B.C. by Appius Claudius Caecus during a battle against the Etruscans and Samnites. It was dedicated a few years later on June 3, and was situated in the CIRCUS FLAMINIUS within the CAMPUS MARTIUS at Rome (Fig. 15), near the altar of MARS. Because the temple was situated just outside the walls of Rome *(pomerium)*, it was often used by the Senate for meetings, in particular to receive foreign ambassadors and victorious generals who were requesting a triumph. In front of the temple was the *columna bellica* (column of war), a small column. In order to formally declare war on an overseas enemy, the *fetialis* would hurl a spear over the column into "enemy territory." This rite continued to at least the time of Marcus Aurelius. The temple is believed to be that discovered just east of the temple of Apollo Medicus Sosianus (Fig. 15). It was probably a hexastyle temple raised on a low podium of concrete faced with brick. The temple of the LARES PERMARINI was once identified as that of Bellona.
Reading: Nash 1962a, 202; Richardson 1992, 57–58, 94; Scullard 1981, 146.

Bellona Pulvinensis A Roman goddess known from inscriptions found in Rome that refer to a temple in a grove near the Porta Collina. Pulvinensis was equated with the Roman goddess BELLONA, and was probably an Oriental goddess, possibly the Cappadocian goddess MA.
Reading: Richardson 1992, 58.

Benedict, Saint (Benedict of Nursia) The founder of an early Christian monastery. He lived c. 480–543, born in Nursia, Italy, the son of wealthy parents. In 529 Benedict founded and ran a monastery at Monte Cassino, a mountain above the Roman town of Casinum, Italy. His views on monastic life are contained in his *Regula Monachorum*, usually known as the *Rule of Saint Benedict*, which later formed the foundations of the Benedictine order.

Bergusia A Celtic goddess who was the partner of the Celtic god Ucuetis. They are known from two inscriptions found at Alesia, France. A portrait of a divine couple from the same site may represent these deities. The female figure is represented as a goddess of prosperity, and the male figure carries a hammer. One of the inscriptions was on a large bronze vessel found in an underground room of a massive building, along with pieces of iron and bronze, suggestive of metalworking. One interpretation is that the building belonged to a craft guild; the underground room may have been a shrine dedicated to Bergusia and Ucuetis, who were probably worshipped as patrons of craftsmen and deities of prosperity.
Reading: Green, M. J. 1992a, 43, 217.

Bes (Fig. 12) An Egyptian god who was sometimes worshipped in association with the three main Egyptian deities ISIS, SERAPIS and HARPOCRATES. Bes presided over marriage and childbirth and was also a protector against evil spirits and dangerous beasts. He was portrayed as a grotesque figure, usually in the form of a dwarf with a disproportionately large head and facial features.
Reading: Hammond and Scullard (eds.) 1970, 375.

bidental (pl. *bidentales*) Any place that had been struck by lightning. The word derives from *bidens* ("with two teeth"), referring to either forked lightning or to the two-year-old animals that were traditionally sacrificed at such a site. A *bidental* was sacred ground, and had its origins in Etruscan beliefs when a place struck by lightning was walled in. Bidentals were very familiar to the Romans. A bidental was

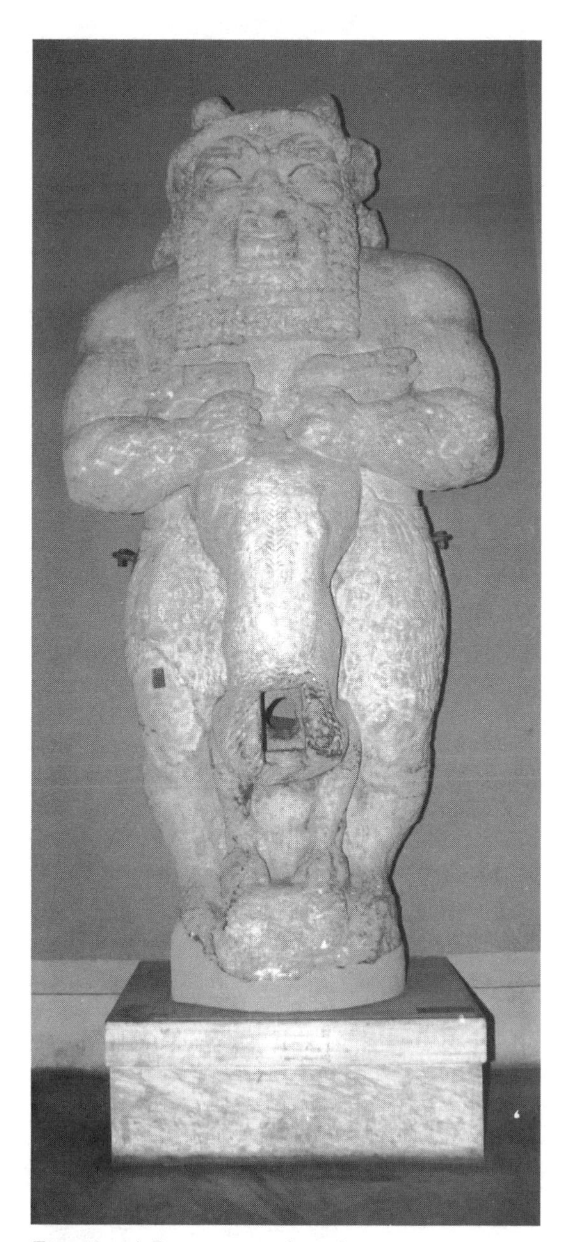

Fig. 12 A Roman copy of a 6th-century B.C. colossal statue of Bes from Amathus, Cyprus. He is holding up a headless lioness by her hind legs.

sacred to Jupiter and belonged to him alone because lightning was his prerogative. A stone inscribed *Fulgur Divom* ("Lightning of the Gods") found at Halton Chesters, England, may mark such a place. Neolithic flint and stone axes have been found on many Roman sites, including within Romano-Celtic temples, and these have been interpreted as thunderstones that were deposited in buildings to prevent lightning strikes. The adjective *bidentalis* was also applied to sacrifices at these places. A *bidental* was also the name of a priest who specialized in sacrificing two-year-old animals, particularly sheep *(bidentes)*, perhaps only at a bidental. The *decuria sacerdotum bidentalium* was the company of such priests.

Reading: Adkins and Adkins 1985 (thunderstones); Merrifield 1987, 9–16 (thunderstones); Ogilvie 1969, 58.

Bodus An Iberian god who is known from a dedicatory inscription found at Villadepalos, in the Leon region of northern Spain. It has been suggested that his name indicates a war god, but little else is known about this deity.

Reading: Tranoy 1981, 297.

Boethius Anicius Manlius Severinus Boethius, c. 480–524, a philosopher and Christian theological writer. He came from a family that had held many high offices of state in the fourth and fifth centuries. He won the favor of Theodoric the Great, becoming consul in 510 and *magister officiorum* (head of the civil service) ten years later. In 523 he was suspected of treachery, and he was executed the following year. He was buried at Pavia and was regarded as a Christian martyr, being canonized as St. Severinus. His importance derives from his being the last Latin-speaking scholar of the ancient world to be well acquainted with Greek. Some of his writings survive, including several Christian treatises. He is best known for *De Consolatione Philosophiae (Consolation of Philosophy)*, a dialogue in five books between himself and a personified Philosophy that he wrote in prison.

Reading: Hammond and Scullard (eds.) 1970, 171.

Bona Dea (Fig. 13) (also known as Bona Dia and Bona Diua) A Roman earth and fertility goddess who was worshipped exclusively by women. She was identified with the Roman goddess FAUNA, who was the wife or daughter of FAUNUS. In Roman mythology, Faunus fell in love with his daughter, Bona Dea, but she rejected him, even after he had made her drunk with wine, and he beat her with myrtle sticks. He finally had intercourse with her in the

Fig. 13 An altar dedicated to the ears (AVRIBVS) of Bona Dea (possibily the goddess who listens), found at Glanum, southern France. A small bronze dome apparently stood on top of the altar. A wreath of oak or laurel leaves surrounds two ears divided by ribbons. The altar dates from the 1st or 2nd century. Although the inscription does not mention Bona Dea, evidence from Glanum and from nearby sites indicates that this altar was part of her cult in this area.

form of a snake. In another legend, Bona Dea was the chaste wife of Faunus and excelled in the domestic arts. She became drunk on a jug of wine, and Faunus beat her to death with sticks of myrtle. In remorse, Faunus granted Bona Dea divine honors. Both legends appear to have been devised to explain why myrtle was excluded from Bona Dea's rituals and was not allowed inside her temple. It was said that because HERCULES had been excluded from the rites of Bona Dea, he founded ceremonies at his Great Altar (Ara Maxima), from which all women were excluded. (See also CARMENTIS for an alternative explanation of the exclusion of women from this ceremony.)

In Rome, there was a temple of BONA DEA SUBSAXANA on the Aventine Hill. Bona Dea had at least two temples at Ostia, and numerous inscriptions show that she was popular throughout Italy and in the provinces. The accepted sacrifice to Bona Dea was a sow. Her festival was on December 3, but it was not celebrated in her temple. Instead, it was held in a room at the house of the chief magistrate, led by his wife accompanied by the VESTAL VIRGINS, with only women present. The room was decorated with vine branches and various plants and flowers (excluding myrtle). Wine was used in the ceremony, but was referred to as milk, and the covered jar containing it was called a honey pot for the purposes of the ritual.

Reading: Brouwer 1989; Grimal 1986, 76; Hammond and Scullard (eds.) 1970, 172.

Bona Dea Subsaxana, temple of The main temple of BONA DEA in Rome was in Regio XII, below the Saxum, or Remoria, where Remus was supposed to have taken initial AUSPICES before the foundation of Rome. Her title *Subsaxana* means "below the rock." The temple was in the northeastern part of the Aventine Hill. The foundation of the temple is uncertain, possibly after the capture of Tarentum in Italy in 272 B.C. but possibly much earlier, as the temple was linked with legends of HERCULES at Rome. The temple was associated with healing, and no man was allowed inside. It was restored by Livia and by Hadrian. It was still standing in the fourth century, but no trace has been found.

Reading: Richardson 1992, 59–60.

Bona Dia An alternative name for the goddess BONA DEA.

Bona Diua An alternative name for the goddess BONA DEA.

Bonus Eventus (Fig. 14) A Roman god who personified the "successful outcome." Probably

Fig. 14 Bonus Eventus portrayed in a relief sculpture. He holds a patera *in his right hand and ears of wheat in his left.*

originally an agricultural god of good harvests, Bonus Eventus became a god of successful enterprises in general. He was very popular and had a temple in the CAMPUS MARTIUS and a statue on the Capitol at Rome. He was depicted with a cup in his right hand and ears of cereal crops in his left hand.
Reading: Hammond and Scullard (eds.) 1970, 172; Richardson 1992, 60.

Bormana A Celtic goddess of healing springs. Sometimes worshipped on her own, she was more usually associated with the Celtic god BORMO.
Reading: Green, M. J. 1992a, 48.

Bormanicus An Iberian god who is known from inscriptions on two altars found at Caldas de Vizela, south of Braga, northern Portugal. Here he was associated with healing springs. He is probably the same deity as the Celtic god BORMO.
Reading: Tranoy 1981, 269.

Bormanus A Celtic god associated with healing springs who is thought to be the same deity as BORMO.

Bormo A Celtic god associated with healing springs who was worshipped in Spain and Gaul. He is thought to be the same deity worshipped under the names Bormanus, Bormanicus and Borvo. His name is connected with "bubbling water," probably indicating hot and gaseous springs. He was sometimes associated with APOLLO, and at Aix-les-Bains, France, he may have been equated with HERCULES. He was frequently associated with a female counterpart called Bormana, and at Bourbonne-les-Bains, France, he was associated with DAMONA. An image of the god depicts him holding a goblet and with a purse and a plate of fruit. Thus, as well as being a healer, he was probably a god of fertility and plenty.
Reading: Bourgeois 1991, 29–32 (under *Borvo*); Green, M. J. 1992a, 47–48.

Borvo A Celtic god associated with healing springs who is thought to be the same deity as BORMO.
Reading: Bourgeois 1991, 29–32.

Boudina A Celtic mother goddess who is known from an inscription found at Manderscheid, Germany.
Reading: Wightman 1970, 226.

Bregans A Celtic god who was the partner of the Celtic goddess BRIGANTIA. This god is known from a single inscription found at Slack, West Yorkshire, England.
Reading: Jones and Mattingly 1990, 277, 280.

Bricta A Celtic goddess who was the partner of the Celtic god LUXOVIUS. She is known from inscriptions found at Luxeuil, France. The divine couple of Bricta and Luxovius were deities of the thermal spring at Luxeuil, where other deities were also worshipped. Little else is known about Bricta, although it has been suggested that she is linked to the Irish goddess Brigit, who became St. Brigit when Ireland was Christianized.
Reading: Green, M. J. 1992a, 50.

Brigantia A Celtic goddess who is known from inscriptions found in Britain. She is assumed to be the patron deity of the Brigantes tribe. She was sometimes equated with VICTORIA and is portrayed in a sculptured relief from Birrens, a fort north of Hadrian's Wall, England. In this relief, she is shown

wearing a mural crown and has wings (which are usually associated with Victoria). She also carries a spear, shield and a gorgon *AEGIS*, symbols usually associated with MINERVA. A single dedication to her consort, BREGANS, is known from Slack, West Yorkshire, England.
Reading: Henig 1986, 161; Jones and Mattingly 1990, 277, 280.

Brixianus A Celtic god who was linked with the Roman god JUPITER as JUPITER BRIXIANUS.

Bubastis A cat-headed Egyptian goddess. Bubastis was originally the local goddess of the city of Bubastis in Egypt, and became identified with ISIS. The Greeks identified her with ARTEMIS. She was originally a lioness-goddess, symbolizing to the Egyptians the fertilizing power of the sun. Her sacred animal later became the cat, and she was portrayed as a cat-headed woman. She was a goddess of pleasure and of protection against evil spirits and disease. There is evidence of the worship of Bubastis, along with other Egyptian deities, at Rome, Ostia and Nemi in Italy.
Reading: Hammond and Scullard (eds.) 1970, 184.

burial of the dead The Romans buried their dead by INHUMATION or CREMATION and sometimes by embalming. Cremation was the dominant rite until the first and second centuries in Italy and Rome (and by the mid-third century in the rest of the empire), when inhumation became most common. At all times, however, both cremation and inhumation were practiced. The burial of the dead was accompanied by the ritual of a funeral. Inhumations and cremations were buried in various ways, such as in graves or pits, or by being covered with a mound of earth or being placed in a tomb. The reason for burial either underground or in a tomb was to shield the dead from the view of the heavenly gods, with whom the deceased had no more to do. This avoided religious pollution and offense to the gods and their altars. It also facilitated the passage of the dead to the UNDERWORLD.

To avoid religious pollution, burials had to be outside the *pomerium* of the town (according to a law going back to the Twelve Tables), although rural burials were often close to settlement sites. One exception was the burial of newborn infants, which could take place within settlements. Until the late empire, most burials were outside towns, generally in cemeteries along the roads beyond the city gates. In a city the size of Rome, there would have been considerable difficulty in disposing of the bodies, and many urban poor had their corpses thrown into collective pits called *puticuli* (from *putescere*, to rot) outside the city; several such pits have been found. This probably occurred more frequently in times of epidemics when fuel for cremation was too costly. The control of burial regulations was the duty of the pontiffs. A place containing human remains had a right to be a *locus religiosus*, a place subject to divine law. (See also *COLUMBARIUM*; TOMB.)
Reading: Crook 1967, 133–138 (tomb law); Hopkins 1983, 201–217; Lattimore 1962 (view of death reflected in epitaphs); Reece (ed.) 1977; Toynbee 1971; Woodward 1992, 81–97.

bustum A funeral pyre, or more specifically the simple walled enclosure where the pyre was erected and the ashes were subsequently buried. The funeral pyre could be very elaborate, with a highly decorated bier. After the CREMATION, the ashes were collected in an urn which was buried within the enclosure, sometimes with a pipe for libations. The *bustum* was used over and over again by the same family. This method of burial was particularly used in the republic when cremation was popular, but it gradually died out in the empire.
Reading: Richardson 1992, 351.

C

Cabiri (also known as Cabeiri) Greek deities of fertility and of protection of sailors. Their cult was centered on the island of Samothrace in Greece. They were probably originally Phrygian deities, and different traditions record different numbers of Cabiri. One tradition recorded four Cabiri and named them as Axierus, Axiocersa, Axiocersus, and Cadmilus. The Cabiri were part of a mystery cult. Probably because of this, they were not usually individually named and were generally referred to as the "great gods." In the Hellenistic period, the cult spread rapidly throughout the Greek world and was then adopted by the Romans, particularly in Samothrace itself. In the Hellenistic period and later, the Cabiri were often confused with the DIOSCURI, who also had the function of protection of sailors. This confusion was helped by the fact that the Cabiri came to be portrayed in art as a pair of gods—an old, reclining, bearded one and a younger standing one—or later, as a pair of youths almost indistinguishable from portrayals of the Dioscuri.
Reading: Ferguson 1970, 122–123; Hammond and Scullard (eds.) 1970, 186.

Caca A Roman goddess who was regarded as the sister of CACUS and was possibly a fire goddess. In Roman myth, Caca was said to have betrayed Cacus to HERCULES by showing him where Cacus had hidden stolen oxen; in return, she was given a shrine with a perpetual flame in her honor at which the VESTAL VIRGINS worshipped.
Reading: Grimal 1986, 81; Hammond and Scullard (eds.) 1970, 186; Richardson 1992, 61.

Cacus A Roman god, possibly a fire god, who was regarded as the brother of CACA. According to Virgil, Cacus was a savage fire-breathing monster who lived on the Palatine Hill at Rome. He was the son of Vulcan, and he terrorized the countryside surrounding the Palatine Hill until he stole some cattle from Hercules. His sister, Caca, betrayed him to Hercules who killed Cacus. It is thought that Cacus and Caca were originally deities of fire, but some authorities believe that Virgil invented much of this myth and that Cacus originated in Etruscan myth, where he was known as a seer who had lived on the Palatine Hill.
Reading: Grimal 1986, 81–82; Hammond and Scullard (eds.) 1970, 186; Howatson (ed.) 1989, 105; Small 1982.

caduceus A herald's staff with two entwined snakes or serpents forming the terminals. *Caducei* of other forms are known, including a simple "tuning fork" shape. The *caduceus* became an imperial symbol of peace and prosperity. MERCURY was often depicted bearing a *caduceus* (Fig. 67).

Caelus This god was a personification of the sky. The normal Latin word for "sky" was *caelum.* He was equated with the Greek god Uranus, who was much more important in Greek religion and mythology than Caelus was in Roman religion.
Reading: Grimal 1986, 83–84.

Caesareum (pl. *Caesarea;* Greek, *Kaisareion*) An imperial site or sanctuary originally dedicated to the cult of Julius Caesar. They were more common in the east than in the west.
Reading: Price 1984, 134.

Caiva A Celtic goddess who is known from an inscription found at Pelm, Germany. The inscription, dated to October 5, A.D. 124, records the

dedication of a temple to the goddess by Marcus Victorius Pollentius and an endowment of 100,000 sesterces for maintenance of the building. Caiva is thought to be a mother goddess.
Reading: Cüppers (ed.) 1990, 520; Elbe 1975, 416.

Calaedicus A Celtic god who was linked with the Roman god SILVANUS as SILVANUS CALAEDICUS.

Calaicia An Iberian deity who is known from inscriptions on two altars found at Sobreira, near Porto, northern Portugal. It is probable that Calaicia was a patron deity of the native Callaeci tribe.
Reading: Alarcão 1988, 94; Tranoy 1981, 271.

calendar The official calendar of Rome was drawn up by the pontiffs. It contained in tabular form the dates of religious festivals and games. Calendars also held other practical information, such as foundation dates *(dies natales)* and locations of important temples, the gods to whom they were dedicated, notes on the significance of certain festivals, and lists of priests, magistrates and triumphs. Fragments of numerous calendars have survived, as have references to them in literary sources. Commentaries on calendars are known, including Ovid's *Fasti*, Varro's *Antiquitates* and Suetonius's *De Anno Romanorum (On the Year of the Romans)*. Differences do occur in the information given by the various surviving calendars.

Days on the calendar were marked with various letters, including *F* (*fastus*, when the day was not a festival) or *N* (*nefastus*, a festival day, also indicated by *NP*). Other abbreviations are *C* (for *comitialis*, when public assemblies could be held), *EN* (for *endotercisus* or *intercisus:* a day that was *nefastus* in the morning and evening but *fastus* in between), *Q ST D F* (for *quando stercus delatum fas:* when the shrine of Vesta was cleansed on June 15), *Q R C F* (for *quando rex comitiavit fas*, when the *rex sacrorum* had formal duties on March 24 and May 24).
Reading: Gordon 1990a; Porte 1989, 132–138; Scullard 1981, 41–49, 258–266; Warde Fowler 1899; York 1986.

Callirius A Celtic god who was linked with the Roman god SILVANUS and invoked as SILVANUS CALLIRIUS.

Camenae Roman goddesses who were probably originally water nymphs presiding over the springs in Rome. They were identified with the Greek MUSES and had a small shrine, spring and grove outside the Porta Capena in Rome where the VESTAL VIRGINS drew water for their rites and sprinkled the temple of VESTA daily with its water. The shrine was made of bronze. After it was struck by lightning it was moved, ultimately to the temple of HERCULES OF THE MUSES. The shrine was probably replaced by a temple. Egeria was also worshipped at this shrine. Libations were made to the Camenae with milk and water. Their festival was on August 13.
Reading: Hammond and Scullard (eds.) 1970, 198; Richardson 1992, 63–64.

camillus A boy attendant of a priest who served at sacrifices or other ceremonies.

Campestres Roman goddesses who were guardian deities of military camps and parade grounds. They are known from inscriptions on altars found in Britain and Germany. Most of the dedications to these goddesses were made by cavalrymen or by soldiers connected with the cavalry, perhaps reflecting a need for guardian deities during dangerous cavalry training.
Reading: Elbe 1975, 383, 385; Espérandieu 1931, no. 533; Phillips 1977, 86.

Campus Martius "Field of Mars," often referred to as simply Campus. An area of Rome sacred to MARS and in which altars of Mars and of DIS AND PROSERPINA were situated, as well as numerous temples. The Campus Martius was part of the flood plain of the Tiber River, being 9.84–26.24 ft. (3–8 m) above the Tiber, and was frequently flooded. It took its name from an altar of MARS (Ara Martis) and was regarded as sacred to Mars. It was therefore used as the training ground of Roman soldiers and for meetings of the *comitia centuriata*, as well as for the gathering point of triumphs. It was originally pasture, outside the *pomerium*, and was regarded by the Romans as "between the city and the Tiber." Tarquinius Superbus took over the area and planted crops, but on his expulsion it was returned to the people and rededicated to Mars. An alternative belief is that the land had belonged to Tarquinius Superbus, but on his expulsion it was dedicated to Mars.

Apart from the altar of Mars, the Campus Martius also contained a famous republican altar to Dis and Proserpina (the center of the Secular Games) and the Ara Pacis. Probably just outside the Campus Martius, but dominating it, was Augustus's mausoleum.

In time, the amount of open ground diminished as the area became built up. Numerous temples were built, many of which were victory monuments paid for by the spoils of war. They were on or close to the route of the triumphal processions, and many were constructed as a result of aristocratic rivalry. According to tradition, temples were built in the Campus Martius from the time of Romulus. They included the temples of VULCAN (attributed to Romulus); the four republican temples of the Area Sacra di Largo Argentina; the republican temples of APOLLO MEDICUS, FERONIA, BELLONA, NEPTUNE, FELICITAS, the NYMPHS, JUTURNA, LARES PERMARINI, JUNO REGINA, and FORTUNA EQUESTRIS. There was also a temple dedicated to Mars, probably situated in the north of the Campus Martius.

Julius Caesar planned to build a huge temple of Mars, but part of the site was subsequently used for the PANTHEON. Also situated in the Campus Martius were the Iseum et Serapeum (vowed by the triumvirs and built or rebuilt by Caligula), a complex that was destroyed in the great fire of 80, as was the Pantheon. Domitian built a temple of the *divi* Vespasian and Titus. Hadrian built temples of Matidia and Marciana, and Antoninus Pius built a temple of Hadrian (the Hadrianeum).

Reading: Patterson 1992, 194–200; Richardson 1992, 65–67; Steinby 1993, 220–224.

Camulos A Celtic war god who was worshipped in Britain and Gaul. In inscriptions, he was usually linked to the Roman god MARS as MARS CAMULOS, but his name survives in place names in Britain, such as Camulodunum ("Fort of Camulos," the Roman name for Colchester). It is thought that the cult of Camulos may have been important in Britain both in the Roman period and in the preceding Iron Age.

Reading: Green, M. J. 1992a, 141; Ross 1974, 234.

Candeberonius Caeduradius An Iberian god who is known from an inscription found in the area of Braga, northern Portugal.

Reading: Tranoy 1981, 271.

Candelifera ("taper-bearer") A Roman goddess who helped women in childbirth and for whom a symbolical taper or candle was lit.

Candida ("Glittering White One") This Celtic goddess is known only from an inscription found near Frankfurt, Germany, that addresses her in the dative as *Deae Candidae Reginae* ("To the Goddess Candida the Queen"—the nominative form being *Dea Candida Regina*). She was portrayed in a way similar to the usual portrayal of the Roman goddess FORTUNA, and so she may have fulfilled a similar function.

Reading: Elbe 1975, 129.

Candiedo An Iberian god who was associated with the Roman god JUPITER. He is known from an inscription on an altar found in northwestern Spain.

Reading: Tranoy 1981, 305.

Canens A Roman deity who was regarded as the daughter of JANUS and originally a NYMPH of Latium. According to legend, she was married to Picus, an early king of Latium who ruled over Laurentum, a community just below the mouth of the Tiber River. Circe (a Greek goddess powerful in magic) fell in love with Picus while he was hunting and changed him into a boar to separate him from the rest of the hunt and capture him. Picus grieved for having been separated from Canens. When Circe declared her love for him, he repulsed her, and she changed him into a woodpecker. Canens, unable to find Picus, wandered in search of him for six days and nights. Finally she collapsed in despair on the banks of the Tiber, sang for the last time and then vanished.

Reading: Grimal 1986, 87–88.

cannophorus (pl. *cannophoroi*) A reed-bearer associated with the cult of Cybele. *Cannophoroi* sometimes acted as a burial society and admitted women as members. A procession of reed-bearers took place one week before festivals of Cybele.

Reading: Vermaseren 1977, 114–115.

capite velato The head of the priest covered by his toga when the priest officiated at rituals such as a sacrifice (Fig. 88). This shielded the priest against sights and sounds of ill omen, so avoiding the need to start the ritual again. The earlier Greek rite had been conducted with the head uncovered.

Capitoline Games (Ludi Capitolini) Games *(ludi)* in honor of JUPITER that took place on October 15. They were not recorded in the calendars because they were not public games, but were given by a College of Capitolini (who were priests of JUPITER CAPITOLINUS in Rome). Their origin is uncertain, but the games were possibly held to celebrate the conquest of Veii in Italy or the saving of the Capitol from the Gauls. They may have had a pre-republican origin in honor of JUPITER FERETRIUS. Little is known of the games.

Reading: Scullard 1981, 194–195.

Capitoline Hill (Fig. 15) The smallest of the seven hills of Rome. The whole hill was known by various names, including Capitolium, mons Capitolinus, collis Capitolinus and mons Tarpeius. It was split into two peaks, known as the Capitol (or Capitolium) and the Arx. The name *Arx* implies a fortified area, but the entire area would actually have been fortified, and the area now known as the

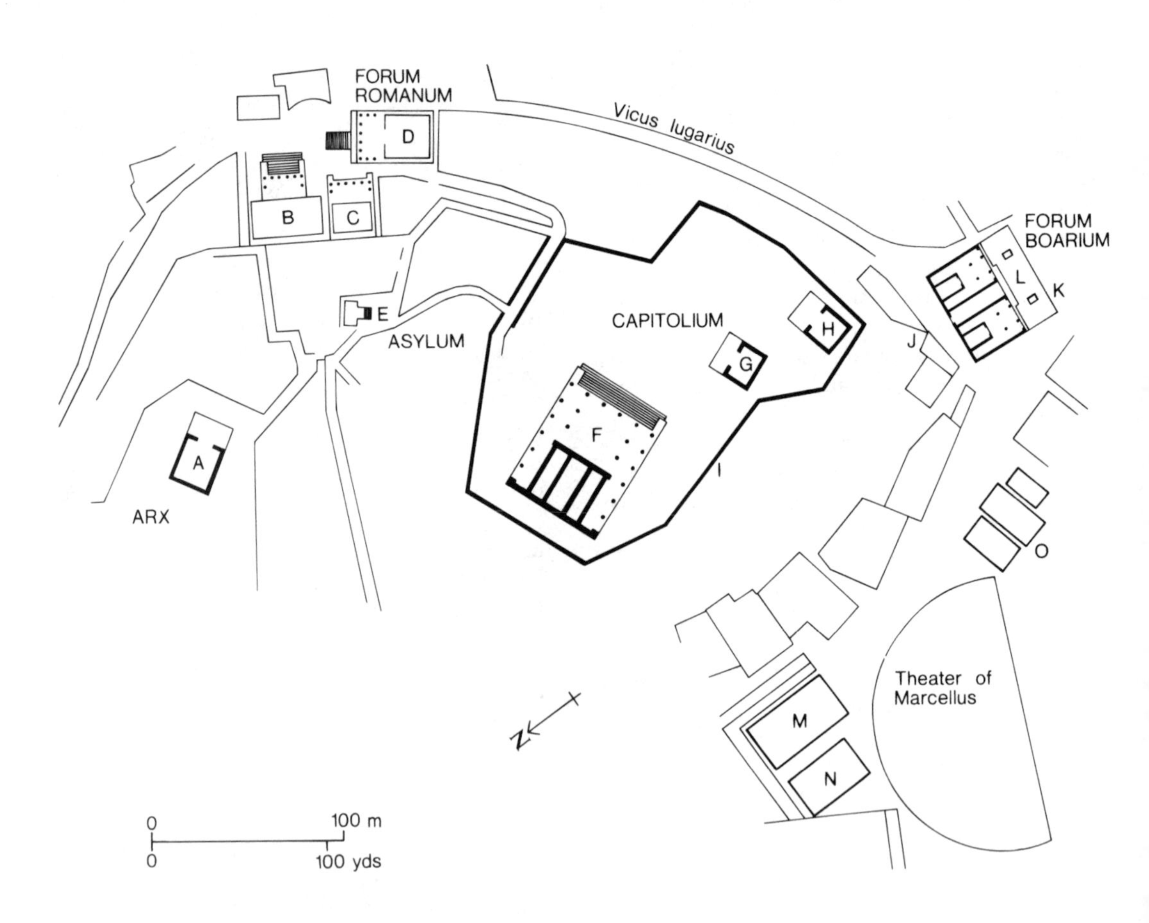

Fig. 15 Multi-period plan of the Capitoline Hill and surrounding area in Rome, showing the major religious sites. A = site of temple of Juno Moneta; B = temple of Concordia; C = temple of Vespasian; D = temple of Saturn; E = temple of Vediovis; F = temple of the Capitoline Triad; G = site of temple of Ops; H = site of temple of Fides; I = Area Capitolina; J = shrine of Carmentis; K = Area Sacra di Sant' Ombono; L = twin temples of Fortuna and Mater Matuta; M = temple of Bellona; N = temple of Apollo Medicus; O = Forum Holitorium temples (of Spes, Juno Sospita and Pietas).

Arx may have been called the AUGURACULUM. On the north summit (Arx or Arx Capitolium) was the temple of JUNO MONETA, the Auguraculum (augur's observation post; the name possibly used for the entire Arx) and a temple of CONCORDIA. On the southern summit (Capitol, originally called Saturnius mons and sometimes Tarpeius mons) was the temple dedicated to the CAPITOLINE TRIAD (CAPITOLIUM). The Capitol became the heart of the state religion. The Area Capitolina was the irregularly shaped precinct (sacred area) of Jupiter Optimus Maximus and seems to have surrounded the temple of the Capitoline Triad. Its main entrance was at the end of the street known as the *Clivus Capitolinus*, on the southeast side. The precinct was surrounded by a wall and was guarded at night by dogs under the charge of a temple attendant. Also kept in this area were geese sacred to JUNO.

There were numerous other buildings on the Capitoline Hill, including the temples of FIDES, JUPITER FERETRIUS, JUPITER CUSTOS, JUPITER TONANS, OPS, MENS and VENUS ERYCINA, as well as possibly those of MARS ULTOR and FORTUNA PRIMGENIA. There were also many altars, including a great altar to JUPITER, and numerous statues of deities in the precinct and in the temples. The temples on the Capitoline Hill were destroyed in the great fire of A.D. 80. Between the two peaks was the temple of VEDIOVIS.

Reading: Hammond and Scullard (eds.) 1970, 202–203; Richardson 1992, 31–32, 40, 68–70, 378.

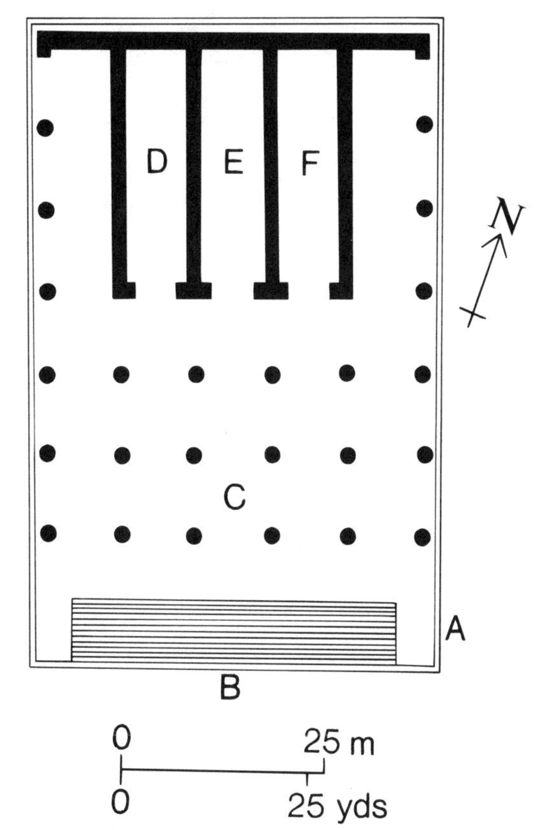

Fig. 16 The Capitoline Triad of Jupiter, Juno and Minerva shared the same temple, known as the Capitolium, but each deity had a separate cella. The plan shows the Capitolium at Rome, normally called the temple of Jupiter Optimus Maximus Capitolinus. A = podium; B = steps; C = pronaos (porch); D = cella of Juno Regina; E = cella of Jupiter Optimus Maximus; F = cella of Minerva.

Capitoline Triad As Roman religion developed, a triad of gods was formed who shared a temple on the CAPITOLINE HILL at Rome and so became known as the Capitoline Triad. They were originally JUPITER, MARS and QUIRINUS. Under Etruscan influence, the triad later consisted of Jupiter, JUNO REGINA and MINERVA, and it is the latter three who are usually referred to as the Capitoline Triad.

Reading: Dumézil 1970, 283–310.

Capitolium (Figs. 16, 56) (pl. Capitolia) The name given to any temple dedicated to the CAPITOLINE TRIAD, and in particular, to the temple on the Capitoline Hill at Rome (Fig. 15; known as the Capitolium, or *aedes Iovis Optimi Maximi Capitolini*—the temple of JUPITER OPTIMUS MAXIMUS Capitolinus). Capitolia were built on hills and prominent positions in many cities of Italy and in the provinces, particularly in the Augustan and Julio-Claudian periods. Most have a triple cella. The earliest known example outside Italy was at Emporion in Spain.

Reading: Blagg 1990, 426–427; Fishwick 1987, 253–254.

Capitolium Vetus A shrine *(sacellum)* on the Quirinal Hill in Rome dedicated to JUPITER, JUNO REGINA and MINERVA. It was thought to be older

than the temple of JUPITER OPTIMUS MAXIMUS and was still a landmark in Martial's time (later first century).
Reading: Richardson 1992, 70.

Caraedudius An Iberian deity who is known from an inscription found at Astorga, northern Spain. The function of this deity is unknown.
Reading: Tranoy 1981, 297.

Cardea A Roman goddess, also known as Carda, who presided over door hinges and thus, symbolically, over family life.
Reading: Grimal 1986, 231 (under *Indigetes*); York 1986, 80.

Caristia A family festival (also called Cara Cognatio, "Dear Relation"). Caristia was a day to renew family ties and patch up quarrels. There was a family meal and offerings to the family *lares* (see LAR) It was held on February 22, after the Parentalia (February 13–21). It continued to be celebrated in Christian times, and was converted into the feast of St. Peter and held on February 22 to at least the twelfth century.
Reading: Scullard 1981, 75–76.

carmen Any solemn saying or formula (such as spells, prayers, hymns, oaths, oracles and epitaphs), not strictly in verse but in rhythmical prose. In the first century B.C. it came to be used as the poetic word for *poetry*.
Reading: Hammond and Scullard (eds.) 1970, 205.

carmen arvale Sacred hymn of the ARVAL PRIESTS. It represents the oldest surviving example of Latin poetry. It is preserved in the inscribed records *(Acta)* of the arval priests of A.D. 218, but probably originated in the sixth or fifth century B.C.
Reading: Hammond and Scullard (eds.) 1970, 205–206.

carmen saliare Hymn of the SALII PRIESTS. It survives in fragments. An ancient hymn, it was unintelligible to the priests by republican times. A commentary was written in the late republic by Lucius Aelius Stilo Praeconus, which is the earliest known book on a religious topic.
Reading: Hammond and Scullard (eds.) 1970, 206.

Carmenta An alternative name for the goddess CARMENTIS.

Carmentalia A festival celebrated on January 11 and 15 to honor CARMENTIS. The reason for the gap between January 11 and 15 is uncertain. Festivals tended to be held on uneven days, in which case January 13 would be expected to be the second day. The festival may have been concerned with birth; many births may have occurred in January because April was the favored month for marriages.
Reading: Scullard 1981, 62–64.

Carmentis A prophetic Roman goddess of protection in childbirth, also occasionally called Carmenta. Because she was said to be a water nymph and the daughter of the Ladon River, she was possibly a water goddess. In Roman mythology, Carmentis was the mother of Evander (the first settler of Rome), but in Greek mythology, the mother of Evander was Nicostrate. Carmentis is therefore sometimes referred to as Nicostrate. She was given the name Carmentis in Rome because of her gift of prophecy (one meaning of *carmen* is "oracle" or "prophecy"), which enabled her to find the best site in Rome for her son Evander. She lived to be 110 years old and was buried at the foot of the CAPITOLINE HILL, close to the Porta Carmentalis. In another legend, she was the wife of Evander. When she refused an invitation to attend a sacrifice by HERCULES at the ARA MAXIMA, he forbade women to be present at the sacrifice thereafter (see also BONA DEA for an alternative explanation of the exclusion of women from this ceremony).

A minor *FLAMEN (flamen Carmentalis)* was assigned to her, and her festival was the CARMENTALIA. She was invoked by two names: Postverta ("feet first") and Prorsa (or Porrima, "head first"), signifying the possible positions of a child in the womb. (Or, alternatively, these names may have referred to her sisters.) The Porta Carmentalis, the gate at the foot of the Capitoline Hill, was named after her, and there was a shrine dedicated to Carmentis nearby (Fig. 15).
Reading: Grimal 1986, 89; Hammond and Scullard (eds.) 1970, 206; Richardson 1992, 72.

Carna An ancient Roman goddess of door hinges, and thus symbolically of domestic life (simi-

lar to CARDEA). Carna also came to be regarded as the protector of people's health. She was thought to dwell in a sacred wood called the Lucus Helerni (grove of Helernus) on the banks of the Tiber River. Sacrifices to Carna were offered here by the pontiffs. According to OVID, Carna was originally called Crane, and had vowed to remain a virgin. She hunted in the hills, and when a suitor approached, she made him promise to follow her into the wood. Once in the wood, she disappeared and could not be found. JANUS fell in love with her, and although she tried to hide, he found her and raped her. To make amends for what he had done, he gave her power over the hinges of doors, and she took charge of a magical branch of flowering hawthorn, which could drive away evil spells from the openings of a house. Carna also had special responsibility for protection against vampires, which were regarded as semi-human birds who tried to suck the blood of newborn babies if they were left alone in their cradles. She had a shrine on the Caelian Hill at Rome and was worshipped on June 1.
Reading: Grimal 1986, 89; Richardson 1992, 107; York 1986, 80–81.

Carpantus A Celtic god who is known from inscriptions found in the area around Fréjus and in the Haute-Garonne region, France. A dedication from the same region to a god called Carpentus is assumed to be the same deity. The similarity of names suggests that this deity had some connection with the Roman town of Carpentorate (modern Carpentras) in southern France.
Reading: Gascou and Janon 1985, 136.

Carus An Iberian god who is known from an inscription on an altar found near Arcos de Valdevez, in extreme northwestern Portugal.
Reading: Tranoy 1981, 271.

Cassiodorus Flavius Magnus Aurelius Cassiodorus, c. 490–c. 583, founder of two Christian monasteries and author of a work on monastic life. The son of a praetorian prefect of Theodoric, he was born in southern Italy. Cassiodorus held public offices and was a member of the Senate. He retired in the late 530s to devote himself to scholarship and a Christian life. In 540 he may have been taken prisoner by troops of the Byzantine Empire and was sent to Constantinople where he became influential by 550. He returned to Italy in the 550s and established two monastic foundations, including one called Vivarium in Bruttium (which survived to the seventh century). In his retirement at Vivarium, he wrote *Institutiones (Institutions)*, a guide to the religious and secular education of monks, including instruction about the copying of manuscripts. This guide became particularly influential amongst the Benedictine order.
Reading: Hammond and Scullard (eds.) 1970, 211.

Castor (Fig. 17) The brother of Pollux and one of the two Dioscuri. Castor and Pollux were originally the Greek gods Castor and Polydeuces, and were worshipped at Rome from an early date. They were known collectively as the Dioscuri but were often referred to as the Castores. Castor was always more popular, and their temple in the Forum Romanum at Rome (Fig. 37) is usually just called the temple of Castor (see CASTOR, TEMPLE OF). They were popular gods, particularly with the equites, and the common Latin oaths *mecastor* (or *ecastor*) and *edepol* were derived from their names.

The Dioscuri were sometimes identified with the DI PENATES and sometimes with the CABIRI. The latter were Oriental deities, probably of Phrygian

Fig. 17 The god Castor with his horse on a denarius *of Geta (coin date 200–202). The legend reads CASTOR.*

origin, who promoted fertility and protected sailors. Castor and Pollux came to be seen as gods of salvation. According to myth, they were notable boxers and horsemen, and so were regarded as patrons of athletes and athletic contests. They were also patrons of the Roman cavalry and, possibly because of their identification with the Cabiri, protectors of sailors, particularly against storms at sea. In Rome there was a temple of Castor in the FORUM ROMANUM and a temple of Castor and Pollux in the CIRCUS FLAMINIUS. They had festivals on January 27 and August 13.

Reading: Hammond and Scullard (eds.) 1970, 213; Scullard 1981, 65–66; Simon 1990, 35–42.

Castor, temple of A temple in the FORUM ROMANUM in Rome (Fig. 37). It was sometimes referred to as the temple of Castor and Pollux, and was officially known as *aedes Castoris* or *templum Castoris;* occasionally the terms *aedes Castorum* and *aedes Castoris et Pollucis* were used. According to tradition, it was vowed in 499 B.C. or 496 B.C. by the dictator Postumius during the battle of Lake Regillus, and again shortly afterwards when the Greek heroes Castor and Pollux were seen watering their horses at the spring of JUTURNA (LACUS IUTURNAE) in Rome. The temple was built just to the northwest of the spring and was dedicated by Postumius's son in 484 B.C. (on January 27, according to most sources, but July 15—the day of the victory—according to Livy). In 117 B.C. the temple began to be rebuilt by Lucius Caecilius Metellus, and the floor level was raised by about 9.84 ft. (3 m). In 74 B.C. Verres was in charge of restoring the temple but was accused of

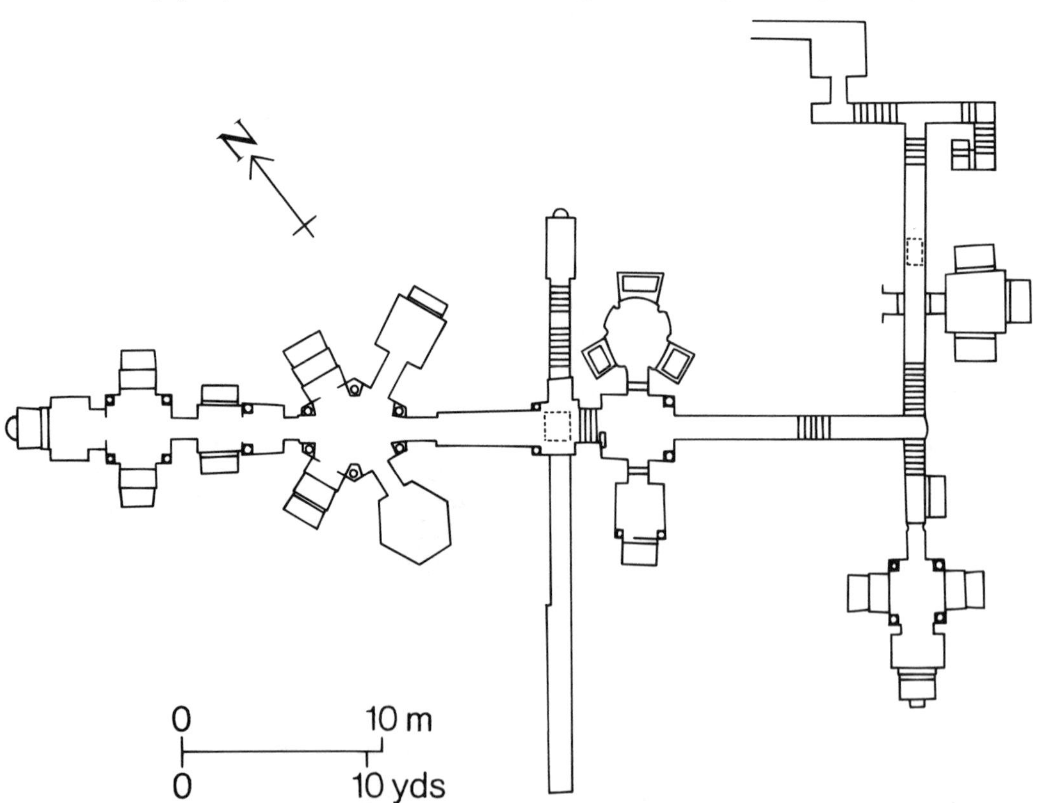

Fig. 18 Plan of the Via Latina painted Christian catacomb in Rome, discovered in 1956. It consists of corridors and galleries with loculi *in the walls. Chambers* (cubicula) *opened off the galleries, and there were also arched recesses* (arcosolia). *There were extremely elaborate paintings, mainly scenes from the Old Testament and some from the Gospels, dating to the second half of the 4th century. There were also some paintings of Hercules that seem to be for pagan believers.*

corruption by Cicero. The temple was probably destroyed in the fire of 14 or 9 B.C. Tiberius totally rebuilt it (raising it by 3.28 ft. [1 m] in height) and dedicated it in A.D. 6 in his own name and that of his brother Drusus. Caligula incorporated it into a monumental vestibule for his palace on the Palatine Hill behind it, with the two statues of the Dioscuri becoming the gatekeepers. It reverted to a temple under the emperor Claudius. The temple was restored by Domitian and renamed the temple of Castor and Minerva.

The temple was one of the finest in the Forum Romanum. At least as early as 160 B.C. it was used for various political meetings (including the Senate on frequent occasions) as well as for religious purposes. It was also used as a safe deposit for the imperial *fiscus* (treasury) and for private individuals, and in Cicero's time at least it was a repository for the standards of weights and measures. A tribunal was placed in front of the temple, and the temple became prominent in first-century B.C. political struggles, although the tribunal was little used in imperial times.

The temple as rebuilt by Tiberius was octastyle, with Corinthian capitals and a podium that stood nearly 23 ft. (7 m) high above the Sacra Via. The temple was still standing in the fourth century, but by the fifteenth century only three Corinthian columns with their entablature on the huge podium survived. It was excavated in 1871 and the main stairway was destroyed between 1871 and 1890. In the nineteenth century it was often wrongly identified, generally as the temple of JUPITER STATOR.

Reading: Scullard 1981, 65–68; Richardson 1992, 74–75; Steinby 1993, 242–245.

Castor and Pollux, temple of This temple in Rome was situated in the CIRCUS FLAMINIUS and was built around 100 B.C. Its dedication day was August 13. It was a hexastyle temple with a pronaos three columns deep approached by steps, and a transverse cella. A circular feature shown in front on the third-century marble plan of Rome *(Forma Urbis Romae)* was probably an altar.

Reading: Richardson 1992, 75–76.

catacombs (Fig. 18) Networks of underground passages carved out of soft rock in which burials of the dead were placed. There were many rock-cut tombs across the empire, including those in Petra, Jordan, with rock-cut facades, and the *hypogea* of Rome and the provinces. A *hypogeum* had niches for one or more burials and was used by pagans and Christians (Figs. 104, 105). They were family tombs for private use, but a catacomb was a public underground rock-cut cemetery, often covering a very large area on several levels. There were Jewish and Christian catacombs, and they date from the third and fourth centuries. There were catacombs in Rome and a few other Italian towns, and also in Sicily, Malta and North Africa. They had niches *(loculi)* for burial of inhumations, and many had wall paintings of a religious nature (pagan and Christian themes). Many Christian martyrs were buried in the catacombs, and a large number of the paintings date to the time of the persecutions. (See also BURIAL OF THE DEAD; CEMETERIES.)

Reading: Stevenson 1978; Toynbee 1971, 188–244.

Caturix A Celtic god who was linked with the Roman god MARS as MARS CATURIX.

Cautes (Fig. 19) One of the torchbearers commonly depicted in MITHRAISM. He was usually portrayed in Persian dress and carrying an uplifted torch representing light or day.

Fig. 19 A square relief sculpture of Cautes found on the Esquiline Hill at Rome. He is kneeling, wears a Phrygian cap and holds a torch in his left hand and a knife in his right. Height 10.63 in. (0.27 m).

Cautopates One of the torchbearers commonly depicted in MITHRAISM. He was usually portrayed in Persian dress and carrying a down-turned torch, representing night or darkness.

Cela A Roman goddess who is mentioned by some ancient authors, although little is known about her.

cemeteries (Fig. 20) Burial of the dead, either as cremations or inhumations, often took place in cemeteries, which were by law situated outside the *pomerium* of towns in order to avoid religious pollution. These were frequently along roads beyond the town gates, and many must have contained thousands of burials. Cemeteries were also located in the countryside. They were not sacred places, and were not attached to temples (although some rural cemeteries have been found close to Romano-Celtic temples). INHUMATION cemeteries often had graves laid out in rows, implying that they were all marked by wooden or stone tombstones or posts. Funerary gardens containing tombs were also frequently used for the BURIAL OF THE DEAD in the east and in Italy. Some later Christian cemeteries of Roman date had chapels, some of which developed from the shrines or mausolea of a martyr buried in the cemetery. Religious ceremonies took place at the graves of the dead at various festivals throughout the year, such as at the Parentalia and Rosalia. (See also CREMATION.)

Reading: Toynbee 1971; Woodward 1992, 81–97, 107.

Fig. 20 A table-top sarcophagus in an extensive cemetery at Hierapolis (Pammukale), Turkey, dating from Hellenistic times to the Byzantine period. The cemetery was sited outside the city walls, along the road and far up the hillside. More than 1,000 tombs are known here.

Ceres A Roman goddess of cereal crops who represented the regenerative power of nature. She was identified with the Greek goddess Demeter and was associated with the Roman earth goddess TELLUS. During a famine in 499 or 496 B.C., the Sibylline books recommended that the worship of Demeter, IACCHUS and KORE (Greek deities associated with the ELEUSINIAN MYSTERIES) should be identified with the Roman gods Ceres, LIBER and LIBERA. There was a temple on the Aventine Hill in Rome where these three deities were worshipped together, and Ceres had her own *FLAMEN*, the *flamen Cerialis*. Her festival was the CERIALIA. She was also worshipped during the SEMENTIVAE (possibly the PAGANALIA), with a sacrifice of a cake made from spelt (a type of wheat producing a fine flour) and a sacrifice of a pregnant sow on the second day of the festival. In addition, she was worshipped during the AMBARVALIA. As an earth goddess, Ceres received a sacrifice to purify the house after a funeral and was occasionally associated with the underworld. Unusually a fast in honor of Ceres *(ieiunium Cereris)* was held on October 4 (fasts were rarely practiced by the Romans).

Reading: Hammond and Scullard (eds.) 1970, 223–224; Grimal 1986, 97; Simon 1990, 43–50.

Ceres, temple of The most famous temple of Ceres in Rome was on the lower slope of the Aventine Hill, where she was worshipped with LIBER and LIBERA, the triad apparently representing the Eleusinian group of Demeter, Iacchus and Kore (see ELEUSINIAN MYSTERIES). It was usually referred to simply as the temple of Ceres. The temple was vowed by the dictator Aulus Postumius Albus after he consulted the Sibylline books because of a famine in Rome in 499 or 496 B.C. It was dedicated by the consul Spurius Cassius in 493 B.C. The temple resembled the CAPITOLIUM temple on a smaller scale and may have had three cellas for its three deities. The walls were decorated by the Greek artists Gorgasus and Damophilus; when the temple was rebuilt, their work (paintings and reliefs) was cut out and framed. The temple was very rich and had many works of art.

The temple became a center of plebeian activities and headquarters of the plebeian aediles *(aediles Cereris)* who supervised the temple. It was a repository for archives, including copies of *senatus consulta* and, later, copies of *plebiscita.* The temple also became a center of food distribution to the poor and possessed the right of asylum. It featured prominently in the CERIALIA. There were priestesses (not priests) of the temple, always brought from southern Italy, and the prayers were said in Greek. The temple was struck by lightning in 206 B.C. and again in 84 B.C. and was destroyed in the fire of 31 B.C. It was rebuilt by Augustus and dedicated in A.D. 17 by Tiberius. It was still standing in the fourth century, and its ruins probably lie beneath the present Church of Santa Maria in Cosmedin in the FORUM BOARIUM.

Reading: Scullard 1981, 102–103.

Cerialia An agricultural festival in honor of CERES. It was held April 12–19, just after the MEGALENSIA. The Cerialia was established before 202 B.C. It was originally held only on extraordinary occasions and then became an annual event in the charge of plebeian aediles. There were games in the CIRCUS MAXIMUS in Rome on the final day (Ludi Ceriales). One of the cult rituals on the last day was to let foxes loose in the Circus Maximus with burning torches tied to their tails. The FORDICIDIA was held in the middle of the Cerialia.

Reading: Richardson 1992, 80–81; Scullard 1981, 101, 102–103.

Cernenus A Celtic god who was linked with the Roman god JUPITER. This god is probably the same deity as CERNUNNOS.

Reading: Ross 1974, 181–182.

Cernunnos A Celtic god of fertility, abundance, regeneration and wild animals. He was worshipped widely in Roman times, but is also known from pre-Roman sites. He is probably the same deity as the god CERNENUS. *Cernunnos* means "peaked one" or "horned one." A sculpture bearing the name of Cernunnos was set up by sailors from the Parisi tribe in the reign of Tiberius (14–37). It depicts the god as elderly and balding with the ears of a stag as well as with human ears. The god is wearing antlers, from each of which hangs a torc (neck ring). The identification of the god rests on this one named portrait, but many other unnamed images of Cernunnos are known. He is occasionally linked with a female partner, and representations of antlered goddesses, probably female equivalents of Cernunnos, are also known.

The portraits of Cernunnos often show him with a ram-horned snake, probably a symbol of fertility, vigor and regeneration. He is sometimes accompanied by a snake without horns, probably also a symbol of fertility and regeneration. Some images have sockets on the god's head for removable antlers; it is thought that the antlers would be inserted or removed as part of a ritual reflecting the growth and shedding of antlers on a stag—a ritual of growth and regeneration. Other symbols accompanying the portraits of the god also represent abundance, and include sacks or bowls of coins or of grain, cornucopiae and fruit. The distribution of images of Cernunnos show that his cult was widespread in Gaul and was also present in Britain.

Reading: Green, M. J. 1992a, 59–61; Ross 1974, 172–220.

chi-rho (Fig. 21) (or Chi-rho) The most widely used Christian symbol. It is also known as the Constantinian symbol, monogrammed cross, monogrammatic cross, Christogram, *chrismon* and *labarum.* The earliest version was a ligature of the Greek capital letters *Chi* (like the letter *X*) and *Rho* (similar to the letter *P*). It represented the first two letters of the Greek word *Kristos* (in Latin, *Christus,* "the anointed one"). The symbol was used before 312, but achieved prominence after this date because Constantine the Great adopted it at the Battle of the Milvian Bridge. (He apparently had a dream in which the symbol was accompanied by the words *In hoc signo vince* ["In this Sign, conquer."]) The chi-rho varied in its depiction (for example, it could

Fig. 21a Chi-rho symbol with the letters alpha and omega on the side of a Roman coffin.

Fig. 21b Chi-rho symbol roughly formed by a punch on a silver pendant in the shape of a cross. One arm formed a suspension loop and the central part was a reused Roman coin. Length 1.65 in. (42 mm). It was found in a late Roman grave at Shepton Mallet, England, and dates to the 5th century. Courtesy of Somerset County Museums Service.

have single lines or double lines) and was sometimes set in a circle or wreath.

The chi-rho was often accompanied by the Greek letters *alpha* and *omega* (in upper or lower case). These were the first and last letters of the Greek alphabet, known to Christians from Revelation 1:8 and 21:6, and signified the beginning and the end. In western provinces, the chi-rho and *alpha* and *omega* would not have been understood as the Greek letters but only as Christian symbols. The chi-rho is found on numerous portable and nonportable objects such as tableware, votive plaques and lead tanks. It was replaced in popularity by the chi-rho depicted by the upright cross and letter *rho*, and later by the cross standing alone. The latter was possibly in reponse to the abolition of crucifixion as a death penalty by Constantine or to the discovery of the True Cross by Helena, mother of Constantine. The simple cross was not used as a symbol until after about 600.

Reading: Thomas 1981, 86–91, figs. 3–7; Watts 1988.

Christianity The monotheistic religion based on the life, teachings and Resurrection of JESUS CHRIST developed from the first century. Christianity initially spread rapidly to the scattered communities of Jews outside Palestine and was a completely Jewish cult. The early Christians regarded themselves as Jews, and often preached from synagogues. It might have remained a religion of a Jewish splinter group had not Paul the Apostle and subsequent missionaries deliberately spread the religion to non-Jews, ensuring increased opposition from Jews. Paul, a Jew, was originally a persecutor of Christians, but had a revelation on the road to Damascus. He believed it was his mission to spread the faith to non-Jews, and he dedicated the rest of his life to that end. From this beginning, the Christian faith continued to spread and evolve.

In its early days, the followers of Christianity believed that Jesus was alive and would soon return in glory as the Messiah. Because of this, little thought was given to organization or planning. However, as this expectation faded, attempts were made to organize and regulate the religion. Early Christian groups were controlled by a single leader or by a council of elders, but this gave way to rule by an *episcopus* (bishop). The early church and its organization were financed by offerings *(oblationes)*, but in time gifts, patronage by wealthy Christians, and tax concessions made the church rich. The posts of bishops, who controlled this wealth, were greatly sought after and sometimes fought over.

From its beginnings, Christianity was in conflict with other religions and with the civil authorities. Initially the Jews objected because some interpretations of Christianity implied that the Law of Moses was no longer valid. Despite attempts to construct a consistent and universal creed, conflicts over interpretation of the Christian faith soon grew up within the Christian community itself, leading to the formation of diverse sects and a history of internal division that has persisted to the present day.

In 64, Nero found the Christians a convenient scapegoat for the fire that destroyed much of Rome. His persecutions were not followed elsewhere in the empire, and the official attitude of tolerance towards Jews and Christians remained unchanged for a further two centuries. By the end of the second century, however, Christianity began to be regarded as a threat to the stability of the state, particularly because it demanded exclusive adherence from its followers and would not tolerate other cults.

In the second half of the second century, a coherent Christian creed was being formulated so that the religion could be more easily understood by pagans. By 200 it had become a major religion of the empire. In the third century, there is evidence that some pagans attempted to absorb the Christian god into their pantheon. Severus Alexander is supposed to have had statues of ORPHEUS, Abraham, Christ and Apollonius of Tyana in his private chapel, but the end of his reign marked the end of official tolerance of Christianity. Decius was the first emperor to try systematic extermination of the Christians, and several subsequent emperors attempted suppression. Nonetheless, at this time Christianity was becoming accepted in many communities, and by the late third century public churches were beginning to take the place of house churches.

Persecution of Christians ended in the west with the abdication of Diocletian in 305, and in the east in 311 when Galerius granted them religious freedom. In 313 Constantine and Licinius issued the Edict of Milan, which granted certain favors to Christians and officially ended persecutions. In 325 Christianity effectively became the religion of the Roman empire after the Council of Nicaea. Julian (emperor 361–363) attempted to restore paganism, but in 391 Theodosius I completed the process of making Christianity the state religion by banning all pagan worship, closing all temples and removing their state subsidies. (See also CHI-RHO, CHRISTIAN SYMBOLS, CHURCH, *MARTYRIUM,* MIRACLES, PERSECUTIONS, SAINTS.)

Reading: Brown 1972; Hammond and Scullard (eds.) 1970, 231–234; Johnson 1980; Koester and Limberis 1988; Lane Fox 1988; Potter 1988 (review article of Lane Fox 1988); Soffe 1986; Sordi 1983 (gives a history of Christianity under each emperor); Thomas 1981 (wide-ranging treatment of Christianity, not just confined to Roman Britain as its title implies).

Christian symbols The most commonly found Christian symbol is the CHI-RHO (Fig. 21), but there were other pictorial symbols including plants and animals (such as the vine, palm, fish, dolphin, pomegranate, peacock and doves), as well as the cantharus (cup or chalice). Some word squares may also have had a Christian significance. The significance of these symbols had varying origins. For example, the vine is derived from John 15:1 ("I am the true Vine . . .") and 15:5 ("I am the Vine, you are the branches . . ."). The fish was related to the concept of Christian spiritual birth in baptismal waters; in addition, the Greek word for a fish was *icthus*, linked to the acrostic *I*esous *C*hristos *Th*eo *U*ios *S*oter ("Jesus Christ, son of God, Savior"). These symbols are found scratched or engraved on portable and nonportable objects and depicted in works of art such as wall paintings.

Reading: Thomas 1981, 91–93, fig. 8.

church (Fig. 22) During the early centuries of Christianity, there seems to have been no move toward constructing special buildings (churches) for worship. Groups of Christians met for communal worship at convenient places, such as in houses, outdoors, or in hiding during times of persecution. The first churches probably used existing buildings, such as houses and villas, partly or wholly converted for use by worshippers. Even with the development of organized Christianity in the fourth century, there is little evidence for original churches, probably because of lack of funds to commission such buildings. As Christianity became more influential and the Church began to accumulate wealth,

Fig. 22 Haghia Eirene ("Divine Peace" or St. Irene) in Istanbul (Constantinople), Turkey. It was one of the first Christian sanctuaries in Byzantium, and the church was rebuilt and enlarged by Constantine the Great or by his son Constantius. It was the center of dispute between Arians and orthodox supporters of the Nicene Creed, and 3,000 people were killed in the courtyard in a religious riot in 346. The Second Ecumenical Council was held in the church in 381 and reaffirmed the Nicene Creed. The church was destroyed by fire in the Nika revolt in 532 and was rebuilt by Justinian.

churches were constructed. Inevitably their design was rooted in the traditions of Roman architecture: the basilica with aisles flanking a nave and an apse at one end greatly influenced the architecture of early churches. A number of pagan temples were converted to Christian churches, and this sometimes involved the breaking up and even hiding of pagan sculptures; alternatively, pagan temples were demolished, and their building materials were reused for a church nearby.

Many early churches still survive in some areas, including Rome and Constantinople (Istanbul), but it can be difficult in excavations to distinguish a building as a Christian church if it is no longer standing. Churches were usually oriented east-west, with the altar at east or west. There were churches inside towns (such as Bourges and Tours in France) for the communal worship of the inhabitants, and churches were also present on rural estates, either close to villas or even converted from an existing room in the villa (such as at Lullingstone villa, England). Churches were also present in major CEMETERIES outside towns (extramural or cemetery churches). Churches inside towns could not be attached to cemeteries because of burial laws. In many cases, churches in cemeteries may have evolved from the shrine or mausoleum of a martyr or saintly cleric. A cemetery church outside the town walls at Verulamium (now St. Albans), England, may have been on the site of the *MARTYRIUM* of St. Alban, and other examples include Trier and Mainz in Germany, and Arles in France.

Reading: Macdonald 1968; Thomas 1980; Thomas 1981; Woodward 1992, 98–109.

Church Wreck Off Sicily, a wreck has been found (the "Church Wreck") containing prefabricated building parts for the interior architecture of a basilica. They date to the early sixth century, the early Byzantine period when Justinian had embarked on an empire-wide program of church building. This basilica was probably destined for North Africa from Constantinople.

Cinxia The Roman deity of marriage who looked after the bride's girdle and ensured that the bride was correctly girdled.
Reading: Ferguson 1970, 68; Hammond and Scullard (eds.) 1970, 545 (under *Indigetes*).

Circus Flaminius A public square (not a circus) in Rome which was built by the censor Gaius Flaminius in 221 B.C. in the southern part of the CAMPUS MARTIUS. In it were several temples including, on the northwest, that of HERCULES CUSTOS and, on the southwest, a line of temples including that of Castor and Pollux. The Ludi Taurei were celebrated there.
Reading: Richardson 1992, 83.

Circus Maximus The oldest circus (U-shaped arena) in Rome, in which chariot and horse races took place, including horse races at the Consualia. The most important games held there were the LUDI ROMANI and the LUDI PLEBEII. Several shrines and temples were situated by and within the circus and may have originally been victory monuments erected by winning competitors. On the southwestern side of the circus was the temple of SOL and LUNA (Sun and Moon).
Reading: Richardson 1992, 84–87.

Cissonia A Celtic goddess who is known from inscriptions found in Germany. She is probably connected with the Celtic god CISSONIUS.

Cissonius A Celtic god who is usually linked with the Roman god MERCURY as MERCURY CISSONIUS. Cissonius was venerated mainly in Germany, and a dedication to Cissonius, not linked with Mercury, was found at Metz, France.
Reading: Green, M. J. 1992a, 149.

Claudius, Divus, temple of Temple of the deified emperor Claudius on the Caelian Hill in Rome. It was begun by Agrippina but was pulled down to its foundations by Nero after the fire of 64 and turned into a *NYMPHAEUM.* It was rebuilt by Vespasian. It faced the Palatine Hill and was a hexastyle temple standing on a terrace which formed one of the highest points in Rome.
Reading: Fishwick 1987, 296–297; Nash 1962a, 243; Richardson 1992, 87–88, 121.

Claudius, temple of A temple at Colchester, England, dedicated to the worship of the emperor Claudius. It was a very large temple, much bigger than many others in colonies, and was set in a large precinct. While Claudius was alive, the imperial cult probably took the form of an altar to ROMA and Augustus. The construction of the temple, and therefore its dedication, possibly took place after the death of Claudius, and it was dedicated to the *divus Claudius* (deified Claudius). There are conflicting views about the date of construction, and some believe that it was built and dedicated before his death and is therefore proof of the worship of a living emperor in the west. The remains of the temple are beneath the existing Norman cathedral.
Reading: Drury 1984; Fishwick 1972, 1987, 195–218; Fishwick 1991; Simpson 1993.

Clitumnus A Roman deity who was a personification of the Clitumnus River, near Trebiae (near modern Foligno in Umbria), Italy. The Clitumnus flowed into the Tinia River, which itself flowed into the Tiber River. It was believed that cattle who drank the water from the Clitumnus River would turn white. There were shrines dedicated to this deity at the source of the Clitumnus.
Reading: Hammond and Scullard (eds.) 1970, 253.

Clivicola The deity who presided over slopes and sloping streets.
Reading: Grimal 1986, 231 (under *Indigetes*).

Cloacina A Roman water deity who was identified with VENUS as VENUS CLOACINA.

Clodius Publius Clodius Pulcher, c. 92–52 B.C., a politician who was twice accused of religious sacrilege. Clodius appeared dressed in women's clothing at a celebration of BONA DEA held in Julius Caesar's house in December of 62 B.C. He was narrowly acquitted of the charge of religious sacrilege in May, 61 B.C., when Cicero gave evidence against him. In

55 B.C. Clodius forced his way with a band of slaves into the Megalensia games, open only to free Romans (not foreigners and slaves), creating an enormous outrage. Mob violence broke out, and Cicero attacked the sacrilege caused by Clodius, who, as aedile, was responsible for the games. In 52 B.C. Clodius was killed near a sanctuary of Bona Dea at Bovillae, Italy, and it was thought that Bona Dea had been avenged.

Reading: Brouwer 1989, 363–370; Hammond and Scullard (eds.) 1970, 254; Vermaseren 1977, 125.

Cocidius A Celtic god whose worship seems to have been confined to northern and western Cumbria and the Hadrian's Wall area of England. He appears to have been a god of woodland and hunting, and some images show him hunting in woodland. He was also a Celtic war god and is depicted with a spear and shield on two silver plaques found north of Hadrian's Wall at Bewcastle. At Ebchester there was an inscription to Cocidius Vernostonus (a Celtic god whose name means "alder tree"). Cocidius was sometimes equated with the Roman god SILVANUS and also with MARS (when he was regarded as a god of war). A *fanum Cocidi* (sanctuary of Cocidius) is mentioned in the *Ravenna Cosmography;* this was probably somewhere in the valley of the Irthing River, near Hadrian's Wall.

Reading: Fairless 1984, 228–235; Green, M. J. 1992a, 62; Ross 1974, 249–250, 467–468.

cockerel A bird that was associated with MERCURY, often appearing with him in sculpture. The exact significance of the cockerel is unknown, but it probably symbolizes a beginning, such as the start of a day or the agricultural year (in spring). The association with MERCURY may derive from Mercury's being the herald of the gods while the cockerel was herald of the day. The cockerel was also an attribute of some Celtic deities.

Reading: Green, M. J. 1992a, 62–63.

Coinquenda A Roman goddess who presided over the felling of trees.

Collatina A Roman goddess of hills who was also known as Collina.

Colossus of Nero (or *Colossus Solis Neronis*) A huge bronze statue of the emperor Nero in Rome. It originally stood in the vestibule of his Domus Aurea (Golden House). It was about 102½ to 120 Roman feet high (a Roman foot being 11.65 in, 296 mm). After Nero's death, Vespasian modified it as a statue of the god SOL, adding a radiate crown with seven rays, each 23½ Roman feet long. In about 128, Hadrian moved it to just northwest of the Colosseum amphitheater in order to build his temple of Venus and Roma. Later Commodus substituted the head with his own portrait and added attributes of his own, but after his death it was restored as Sol. It was still standing in the fourth century but was not mentioned in a late eighth- or early ninth-century account. An annual festival on June 6, in which the colossus was crowned and covered with garlands, lasted into Christian times.

Bede stated that *quamdiu stabit colossus, stabit et Roma; quando cadet, cadet et Roma; quando cadet Roma, cadet et mundus* ("as long as the colossus stands, so Rome will stand; when it falls, so Rome will fall; when Rome falls, the world will also fall"). This statement is usually taken to be about the Colosseum, but the amphitheater was not named as such until c. A.D. 1000 and his assertion actually applies to the statue.

Reading: Richardson 1992, 93–94.

columbarium (pl. *columbaria*) A large collective tomb (literally "dovecote"), usually for cremated remains and built partly or wholly underground. *Columbaria* were used particularly by *collegia* (burial clubs) or for the slaves and freedmen of large households in Rome. Many have been found in Rome, and their walls had hundreds of semicircular or rectangular niches close together to contain the ashes. Each funerary urn or chest with cremated remains was placed in its own *nidus* ("pigeonhole"). A *columbarium* for the slaves and ex-slaves of the household of the empress Livia found in 1726 in Rome contained 3,000 funerary urns.

Columbaria were initially set up by burial clubs in response to the soaring price of land in Rome, but were also adopted by rich families who had a large number of slaves and ex-slaves to bury. It was a much cheaper method of burial, and reflected the concern for the proper care of the dead, avoiding the anonymity of a mass grave. Burial clubs were often centered on a temple under the protection of a tutelary deity. The rules of one burial club (Lanuvium near Rome) survive; this particular club

was under the joint auspices of DIANA and ANTINOUS. (See also BURIAL OF THE DEAD.)
Reading: Hopkins 1983, 211–217; Toynbee 1971, 113–116.

Comedovae A triad of Celtic mother goddesses who were also referred to as *MATRES COMEDOVAE.*

commetaculum A sacred wand used by FLAMINES to clear away crowds from their path. The only known illustration of this is on the ARA PACIS.
Reading: Gordon 1990b, 221–222.

Commolenda ("smasher") A deity who is known to have been invoked by the ARVAL PRIESTS in an attempt to remove an intrusive fig tree from the shrine of DEA DIA.

Compitalia A moveable rural festival held between December 17 and January 5 (usually around January 3–5). Compitalia was celebrated in Rome on a day announced by the city praetor. It was the festival of the *lares* who were originally deities of the farmland. It was held to mark the end of the agricultural year. Shrines to the *lares* (or *LARES COMPITALES*) were erected at crossroads *(compita)* where the paths of three or four farms intersected. The shrine would be open in all four directions to allow passage for the *LAR* of each farm. A broken plowshare was hung up at the shrine (perhaps to signify work completed), as well as a wooden doll for every free person in the household and a woollen ball for every slave. The significance of the doll and woollen ball is uncertain. At the edge of each property, an altar was set up for sacrifice, which was followed by a period of feasting. Augustus transformed the worship of the *lares* at Rome, so that it became a public cult, not just a private one; worship and sacrifice were therefore conducted by a state priest on behalf of the people, rather than by private individuals. The Compitalia became an urban and a rural festival.
Reading: Alcock 1986, 115; Scullard 1981, 58–60.

Concordia (Fig. 23) A Roman goddess who was the personification of concord, perceived as agreement between members of the state or between members of groups within it, such as a guild or inhabitants of a town. Concordia was sometimes identified with Homonoia, the Greek personification of harmony. Concordia had a bronze shrine dedicated to her in Rome as early as 304 B.C., and republican temples in the FORUM ROMANUM and on the Arx. The temple in the Forum was restored by Tiberius and rededicated to Concordia Augusta, and from then on there were frequent references to Concordia Augusta, probably signifying agreement within the imperial family. There was a festival of Concordia on July 22.
Reading: Freyburger 1986, 312–317; Hammond and Scullard (eds.) 1970, 277; Scullard 1981, 167–168; Richardson 1992, 98–100.

Fig. 23 A silver denarius *of Vespasian (coin date 69–70) depicting Concordia seated facing left, with a cornucopia in her left hand and a poppy and ears of wheat in her right hand. The legend reads CONCORDIA AVG.*

Concordia, temples of The oldest and main temple of CONCORDIA stood on the northwestern side of the FORUM ROMANUM in Rome, at the foot of the CAPITOLINE HILL (Figs. 15, 37). It may have been originally vowed by the dictator Marcus Furius Camillus in 367 B.C. to celebrate the end of the struggle between the patricians and the plebeians. The temple may never have been built, and in 121 B.C. Lucius Opimius either restored this temple or built a new one in order to mark the death of Gaius Gracchus and the violent suppression of his party. It was probably dedicated on July 22. Located on a restricted site below the Capitoline Hill, the temple had an unusual plan, with a transverse cella (45.93 yds. wide × 26.24 yds.; 45 m × 24 m), wider than the hexastyle porch (37.18 yds. wide × 15.31 yds.; 34 m × 14 m). From the late second century B.C. the temple was often used by the Senate for meetings, especially when civic disorder had to be discussed. It was occasionally used for meetings by the ARVAL PRIESTS. The surviving remains represent Tiberius's lavish restoration of A.D. 7 (dedicated in A.D. 10 or 12 in the names of himself and his dead brother Drusus as the temple of Concordia Augusta). Under Tiberius, the temple seems to have become a museum in which he placed numerous works of art. It was still standing in the fourth century, but probably collapsed in the time of Pope Hadrian I (722–795).

Another temple of Concordia stood on the Arx of the Capitoline Hill and was vowed by Lucius Manlius when he was praetor in Gaul in 218 B.C. It was begun in 217 B.C. and was dedicated on February 5, 216 B.C. There was a bronze shrine near the temple which was set up in 304 B.C. by the curule aedile Gnaeus Flavius, but it was probably later destroyed. According to OVID, Livia built a temple to Concordia. A temple to Concordia Nova was also decreed by the Senate in 44 B.C. in honor of Julius Caesar but was probably never built.

Reading: Nash 1962a, 292; Richardson 1992, 98–100; Scullard 1981, 167–168.

Concordia Augusta An alternative name used during the empire for the Roman goddess CONCORDIA, when referring to "concord" or "agreement" within the imperial family.

Reading: Hammond and Scullard (eds.) 1970, 277.

Condatis A Celtic god of the confluence ("condate") of rivers in the Tyne-Tees region of England. Although a god of water and possibly of healing, he was sometimes equated with MARS.

Reading: Fairless 1984, 235–242; Green, M. J. 1992a, 66.

Conditor A Roman deity associated with storing agricultural produce, said by Fabius Pictor in the late third century B.C. to have been invoked by a priest of CERES.

Reading: Ferguson 1988a, 853; York 1986, 60.

confarreatio The oldest and most solemn form of marriage, from which divorce was virtually impossible except by an elaborate ceremony *(diffarreatio)*. Little is known of the marriage ceremony. The *FLAMEN DIALIS* and *PONTIFEX MAXIMUS* were present (possibly as witnesses or to undertake sacrifices), and the bride and groom sat with veiled heads on joined seats covered with a sheep hide. A cake made of *far* (spelt grain) had some significance, and the rite was in honor of Jupiter Farreus. Ten witnesses were required. *Confarreatio* marriage was apparently restricted to patricians and was obligatory for certain priesthoods: the three *flamines maiores* and the *REX SACRORUM*. There were no restrictions on these priests being married, but they themselves had to be born of such marriages in order to be eligible for these priesthoods.

Reading: Hammond and Scullard (eds.) 1970, 278.

consecratio Consecration of a monument such as an altar or temple. It took place after the dedication, and made the monument a *res sacra* ("sacred object") or the temple an *aedes sacra* ("sacred building"). (See also *DEDICATIO*.)

Reading: Hammond and Scullard (eds.) 1970, 278.

Consevius A Roman god of conception who was also known as Consivius.

Reading: Grimal 1986, 231 (under *Indigetes*).

constitution (from *constituere*, to found, establish or create) The inaugural foundation of a monument such as an altar or temple. The sculptured friezes on the Ara Pacis seem to depict the constitution ceremony of that altar.

Reading: Fishwick 1972.

Consualia Festivals in honor of CONSUS held on August 21 and December 15. They were possibly intended to celebrate the end of the harvest (August) and the autumn sowing (December). There was a sacrifice, offerings of first fruits, and horse races and chariot races in the CIRCUS MAXIMUS. Horses and asses were garlanded and allowed to rest. Consus had an altar in the Circus Maximus in Rome that was kept underground and was exposed on July 7 and August 21, with burnt sacrifices offered in July by the *sacerdotes publici* (state priests) and in August by the *FLAMEN QUIRINALIS* with the VESTAL VIRGINS in attendance, the latter sacrifices as part of the Consualia. The altar may also have been exposed for the Consualia on December 15.

Reading: Richardson 1992, 100; Scullard 1981, 177–178, 205.

Consus An ancient Roman god of the granary who was probably connected with the harvest and autumn sowing. Originally he may have been the god of grain stored underground. He had an underground barn and altar in the CIRCUS MAXIMUS in Rome, which was only uncovered during his festival days. He also had a temple on the Aventine Hill, and his characteristic sacrificial offering consisted of first fruits. He had two festivals, the Consualia and a festival of Consus on December 12. On July 7 a sacrifice was offered to him at the underground altar. Consus was also associated with horses, and so was sometimes identified with the Greek god of horses, Poseidon Hippios, and with Neptune.
Reading: Grimal 1986, 109–110; Hammond and Scullard (eds.) 1970, 286.

Consus, temple of A temple vowed or dedicated on the Aventine Hill in Rome by Lucius Papirius Cursor, probably in 272 B.C. when he won a victory in southern Gaul. Papirius Cursor was depicted in triumphal robes on the temple walls. It was dedicated on August 21 (or possibly on December 21, although the latter date may have marked the restoration by Augustus).
Reading: Scullard 1981, 178, 204.

Contrebis A Celtic god who is known from an inscription found at Overborough, Lancashire, England. *Contrebis* means "he who dwells among us." In another inscription found at Lancaster, England, he was identified with the Celtic god IALONUS as IALONUS CONTREBIS.
Reading: Ross 1974, 472.

Convector A Roman deity who was associated with binding the sheafs of cereal crops. He was said by Fabius Pictor in the late third century B.C. to have been invoked by a priest of CERES.
Reading: Ferguson 1988a, 853; York 1986, 60.

Copia A Roman goddess who was the personification of plenty. The *cornu Copiae* ("horn of Copia," meaning "horn of plenty") was a magic horn that provided everything its owner desired. Many other female deities were depicted holding a cornucopia.

Coronus An Iberian god who is known from a single inscription found near Guimaraes, northern Portugal. It is possible that he was regarded as the consort of the native goddess Nabia Corona.
Reading: Alarcão 1988, 93; Tranoy 1981, 273.

Corotiacus A Celtic god who was linked with the Roman god MARS as MARS COROTIACUS.

Corybantes Priests who were associated mainly with the cult of Cybele (MAGNA MATER). They were also associated with other gods who had orgiastic cults. They followed Cybele with wild dances and music, and are often confused with the Curetes, who were attendants of the goddess RHEA.

Cosunea An Iberian goddess who is known from a problematic inscription found at Citânia de Sanfins, to the south of Braga, northern Portugal. Here two sides of a granite outcrop carry inscriptions that, taken together, have been interpreted as possibly meaning "Here, with good will, were carried out the promises made to Cosunea, goddess of the Fidueneae." It is not clear who or what the "Fidueneae" are. It has been suggested, because of the similarity of name, that Cosunea may be the female counterpart of the god COSUS.
Reading: Alarcão 1988, 97; Tranoy 1981, 273.

Cosus An Iberian god who was worshipped in northwestern Spain. Five altars are known from this region, dedicated to Cosus, Cosus Calaeunius, Cosus Daviniagus, Cosus Esoaecus and Cosus Oenaecus. What the names linked with Cosus relate to is uncertain; they may be the names of local tribes, places or other deities. Other altars from this region, dedicated to Coius Deus, Cosius Viascannus, Cossua Nedoledius and Cossua Segidiaecus may be also be addressed to the same god Cosus. It is possible that the goddess COSUNEA was the female counterpart of Cosus.
Reading: Tranoy 1981, 292–293, 297.

Cotys A Thracian goddess associated with Cybele (MAGNA MATER), also known as Cotyto or Cotytto. She originally had an orgiastic cult in Athens in the fifth century B.C., which eventually spread throughout Greece and Italy. Rites in her honor were called Cotyttea.
Reading: Hammond and Scullard (eds.) 1970, 294.

Fig. 24 An altar set up by Vinomathus to Coventina. It was found at Carrawburgh, near Hadrian's Wall, England. The inscription reads: D[E]AE COVEN-[TINAE] VINOMATHVS V[OTUM] S[OLVIT] L[IBENS] M[ERITO] ("To the goddess Coventina, Vinomathus willingly and deservedly fulfilled his vow"). Height 9.44 in. (0.24 m).

Coventina (Fig. 24) The Celtic goddess of a spring at Carrawburgh near Hadrian's Wall, England. The spring fed a small pool or well that became a shrine. Although the spring had no medicinal properties, Coventina may have been regarded as a healer and also as a water goddess. She appears to have had a high status, and is referred to in some inscriptions with the titles "Augusta" and "Sancta." The excavations at the shrine produced a number of dedications to the goddess, with variations in the spelling of her name, including *Conventina, Covventina, Covontina* and *Covetna.* Among the many votive offerings and dedications in the pool of the shrine was a human skull: skulls were sometimes placed in pools and wells because of the belief that this would give the deceased an easy passage to the AFTERLIFE or renew them in the afterlife. (The head rather than the heart was regarded as the home of a person's soul or spirit.)

Coventina is usually portrayed as a water nymph. In one sculptured stone relief, she is portrayed semi-naked, reclining on lapping waves and resting on an overturned pitcher. She also holds a water-lily leaf. Another portrait shows her in triplicate pouring water from a beaker. Although generally regarded as a Romano-British goddess, she is also known from evidence at Narbonne, France, as well as in northwestern Spain, where dedications to Cohvetena and possibly Cuhvetena are also known.
Reading: Allason-Jones and McKay 1985; Green, M. J. 1986b, 154, 155, 157; Green, M. J. 1992a, 67–68; Tranoy 1981, 289 (for Spanish evidence).

Crarus An Iberian deity who is known from an inscription on an altar found at San Miguel de Laciana, near Villablino, northwestern Spain. The function of this deity is unknown.
Reading: Tranoy 1981, 297.

cremation A method of disposing of the dead by burning the corpses. The Romans burnt the dead on pyres. Imperial pyres were shaped like Roman lighthouses and usually had four tiers. They are represented on the reverses of consecration coins (showing the apotheosis of the emperor or empress), nearly always accompanied by the legend CONSECRATIO (Fig. 38). Cremations could take place in part of the cemetery set aside for that purpose (an *ustrinum*). They could also take place where the ashes were to be buried, normally over a ready-dug grave called a *BUSTUM.* Gifts and personal belongings of the dead were sometimes burnt as well. The resulting ashes and calcined bones were placed in a container, of which various types were used, including cloth bags, pottery, glass or metal vessels, gold caskets and marble chests. The vessel could be buried with grave goods (Fig. 41) or placed in a *COLUMBARIUM.*

In the first and second centuries in Rome and Italy, INHUMATION became far more popular (particularly for the wealthier classes), and by the mid-third century this was the predominant burial rite throughout the empire. This may have been due to changing beliefs in the AFTERLIFE, with cremation perceived as not allowing the soul to live on. However, the emperors continued the rite of cremation.

Jews and Christians objected to cremation, and the practice died out by the fifth century. (See also BURIAL.)
Reading: Toynbee 1971.

Creto An alternative reading of the name of the Celtic god GRETO in an inscription.

Crimisus A Roman river god, also known as Krimisos, Crinisus, Crimessus or Crimissus. The Crimisus River in Sicily is known now as the Caltabellotta River.
Reading: Wilson 1990, 282.

criobolium A rite similar to *TAUROBOLIUM* in the rites of Cybele and ATTIS, but a ram was sacrificed instead of a bull.
Reading: Vermaseren 1977, 101–107.

Cronus Also known as Cronos or Kronos. A Titan (an ancient Greek god who preceded the Olympian gods), identified with the Roman god SATURN.

Cuba A Roman goddess who protected a child while it was in bed.

Cuda A Celtic goddess who is known from an inscribed sculpture found at Cirencester, England, that depicts her as a mother goddess accompanied by three hooded *GENII CUCULLATI*. The goddess is portrayed seated with something in her lap (possibly an egg or a loaf), and the three hooded figures are standing. The nearest one appears to be giving or taking something from Cuda. The name Cuda refers to prosperity.
Reading: Green, M. J. 1992a, 72.

cult The worship of a god, goddess or hero with correct rites and ceremonies. Religious belief for the Romans was largely a matter of observing a cult or cults by performing rites and ceremonies correctly, rather than by committed belief, moral behavior or spirituality. Usually the most important part of cult ceremonies was an offering to the god by sacrifice, libation or dedication, accompanied by prayers on the theme "as I give to you, so you give to me." With time, such rituals became static and formalized, to the point where the slightest error would invalidate a ritual, which would then have to be started from the beginning.

cult image A representation (usually a statue) of a god or goddess that formed the focus of a religious site such as a temple. In temples, the cult image occupied the cella. The images were either statues or reliefs, and were usually of stone (especially marble) or bronze, and sometimes of gold, silver or ivory. Reliefs were more commonly found in *mithraea* than in other temples. It is usually impossible to be certain that a surviving statue or fragment (unless found within a temple) was originally a cult image, particularly as many cult images were deliberately destroyed in the early Christian period because of opposition to graven images. (There are many references to the destruction of cult images.) Many of the images of gods may also have been deposited as votive offerings, especially figurines, and were not necessarily cult images. Cult statues could be in a highly romanized form even in, for example, Romano-Celtic temples.

Of the thousands of images of emperors (statues and busts) erected throughout the empire, only a small proportion were honored as cult statues. These images of emperors were fairly standardized, the three main types being cuirassed, naked and civilian; but all types are found in both religious (such as temples) and secular contexts. Religious sculpture is not found in late Roman Christian contexts, although religious plate and other artefacts are common.
Reading: Gergel 1990 (review of Vermeule 1987); Henig 1980; Price 1984, 170–206 (imperial images); Vermeule 1987.

cultus The worship or veneration of a deity, and the correct observance of religious obligations. Roman religion was one of *cultus* (cult) rather than *pietas* (piety). Pietas was an attitude of dutiful respect and behavior. For the Romans, it was more important to observe correct rituals: the gods were venerated by the strict observance of rituals to make them favorably disposed, irrespective of the ethics and morals of the worshippers. It was thought that the gods required acknowledgment and propitiation of their power because they were largely spirits of natural forces. The worship of these deities was therefore designed to keep the natural forces benevolent, and rituals and ceremonies were performed to maintain peace and harmony with the gods *(PAX DEORUM)*.

Cunina A Roman goddess who looked after the child in the cradle.
Reading: Hammond and Scullard (eds.) 1970, 545 (under *Indigetes*).

Cunomaglus A Celtic god who was linked to APOLLO as APOLLO CUNOMAGLUS.

Cupid The Roman boy-god of love and son of the Roman deities VENUS and VULCAN. Cupid is an adaptation of the Greek god Eros, and like him was portrayed with wings, a bow and a quiver of arrows. Cupids are found as symbols of life after death on coffins, and this symbolism was continued in Christianity, where cupids became winged cherubs.
Reading: Jones 1990 (on coins).

Cupra A Roman goddess of the town of Cupra (near modern Grottammare), Italy. She may have been identified with the Roman goddess BONA DEA.

Curia Calabra Probably originally an enclosure or precinct representing a *templum* within the AREA CAPITOLINA in Rome for observation of the new moon. It was possibly in front of an augural hut similar to that of the AUGURACULUM.
Reading: Richardson 1992, 102.

curses The division between vows and curses is difficult to distinguish. In a strict sense, curses involve magic powers that are summoned by a sorcerer, but the term is often used to cover requests to the gods to influence events, especially to punish enemies and wrongdoers. *DEVOTIO* was the name given to a form of magical curse or charm. Curses were normally inscribed on curse tablets *(defixiones)*. (See *DEFIXIO*.)

Cyane A Roman water nymph who presided over a stream near Syracuse, Sicily. Originally Cyane was a Greek deity. According to legend, she tried to prevent the abduction of PERSEPHONE by HADES who, in anger, turned her into a pool of deep blue water.
Reading: Grimal 1986, 111.

Cyprian, Saint Thascius Caecilius Cyprianus, c. 200–258, an early Christian churchman and theological writer. Born in Carthage of a rich pagan family and educated in rhetoric, Cyprian was converted to CHRISTIANITY c. 246. He was made bishop of Carthage in 248. Persecuted by the emperors Decius and Valerian, he was executed in 258. Cyprian was a prolific author of mainly short religious treatises and letters that are a valuable source for ecclesiastical history. His writings are also a major source of information about Decius's persecutions. His *Life*, by his deacon Pontius, is the earliest surviving Christian biography.
Reading: Hammond and Scullard (eds.) 1970, 305–306.

D

Damona A Celtic goddess who was worshipped in Burgundy, France. She seems to have been a goddess of fertility and healing and was sometimes associated with APOLLO MORITASGUS, ABILUS, BORMO and with other water gods at healing springs. At Arnay-le-Duc, she was associated specifically with Abilus. At Bourbonne-Lancy, an inscription links Damona with the practice of INCUBATION, whereby pilgrims slept at healing shrines in order to have dreams or visions of the deity, who would then cure them. The name *Damona* means "great (or divine) cow."
Reading: Green, M. J. 1992a, 75–76.

dancing Some ancient dances were used in religious ceremonies, such as those of the *SALII* and ARVAL PRIESTS, and a "rope dance" of maidens in honor of JUNO was mentioned by Livy (27:37.12–15). The Romans were more restrained than the Greeks in their use of dance in religious rites, but Oriental cults introduced noisy and ecstatic dances to Rome.
Reading: Hammond and Scullard (eds.) 1970, 312.

Danubian Rider-Gods The term "Danubian Rider-Gods" refers to a goddess accompanied by one or two riders on horseback, about whom little is known. In Pannonia, Moesia and Dacia, representations on small marble or lead plaques show the goddess with one or two riders, trampling a defeated enemy. The riders are warrior deities and the goddess has overall superiority.
Reading: Tudor 1976.

Danuvius (Fig. 25) A Roman god who was the personification of the Danube River. Dedications to this deity are found in those Roman provinces through which the Danube flows.

dea Latin noun that indicates a goddess (in the nominative form), the plural being *deae*. A male deity is *deus*.

Fig. 25 Danuvius, the god of the Danube River, depicted in relief in a scene on Trajan's Column in Rome. To the left is a harbor town on the river; to the right, legionary soldiers cross the Danube using a pontoon bridge.

Dea Augusta Andarta A Celtic goddess who was also worshipped as ANDARTE, Andarta and Augusta Andarta.

Dea Caelestis ("celestial goddess") The Roman name for the Carthaginian goddess TANIT, who was usually identified with the Roman goddess JUNO CAELESTIS. Her cult does not appear to have spread outside Africa before the time of Septimius Severus (emperor 193–211). Dea Caelestis was depicted, seated on a lion, on coins of Septimius Severus. A shrine was dedicated to her (as Virgo Caelestis) on the CAPITOLINE HILL in Rome at some time before 259, when her statue was brought to Rome by the emperor Elagabalus, and she was often worshipped with SOL INVICTUS.
Reading: Garcia Y Bellido 1967, 140–151; Halsberghe 1972, 91–94; Hammond and Scullard (eds.) 1970, 187 (under *Caelestis*); Stephens 1984.

Dea Dia A Roman goddess of grain or cereal crops who was worshipped by the ARVAL PRIESTS at her festival in May. There was a grove *(lucus Deae Diae)* dedicated to this goddess near the fifth milestone on the Via Campania, 5 miles (7 km) south of Rome. The arval priests were responsible for the grove and for rites associated with the goddess.
Reading: Broise and Scheid 1993; Scullard 1981, 30.

Deae Malvisae Celto-Germanic mother goddesses who were invoked in an inscription on an altar found in the German Rhineland.
Reading: Elbe 1975, 214.

Deae Matres Celtic goddesses who were also referred to as the MATRES.

Deae Quadriviae Celtic deities of crossroads, also referred to as the Deae Quadruviae or QUADRUVIAE.

Deana An alternative name for the Roman goddess DIANA.

Dea Nutrix (pl. *deae nutrices,* "nursing goddesses") A particular form of Celtic mother goddess, usually depicted sitting in a high-backed wicker chair suckling one or two children. Pipeclay statuettes in this form have been found in Celtic areas of the empire and were manufactured in central Gaulish, Breton and Rhineland factories in the first and second centuries. Finds of these statuettes in graves suggest that Dea Nutrix was also a goddess of renewal and rebirth. Pipeclay figurines resembling the classical VENUS (sometimes called "pseudo-Venus" figurines) are also probably connected with a Romano-Celtic domestic fertility cult rather than with the worship of Venus.
Reading: Green, M. J. 1992a, 77.

Dea Syria ("Syrian Goddess") An alternative name for the goddess ATARGATIS.

decastyle A temple with ten columns on the main facade. The only example of a decastyle temple in Rome was Hadrian's temple of VENUS FELIX AND ROMA AETERNA.

Decima A Roman goddess who presided over the ninth month of pregnancy. The name meant "tenth," but actually refers to the normal ninth month, owing to the Roman method of inclusive calculation. Decima was sometimes identified as one of the FATES (*PARCAE* or *Fata*).
Reading: Ferguson 1988a, 853.

dedicatio Dedication of altars and temples. This was performed only at the completion of building work, and was undertaken by a magistrate assisted by a priest. The dedication occurred on the day the altar or temple was made over to a particular deity. An animal sacrifice took place on the anniversary of the dedication. (See also *CONSECRATIO,* CONSTITUTION.)
Reading: Fishwick 1972, 171–178; Hammond and Scullard (eds.) 1970, 318.

Deferunda ("carter") A deity who is known to have been invoked by the arval priests in an attempt to remove an intrusive fig tree from the shrine of DEA DIA.

defixio (pl. *defixiones*) A curse tablet comprising a vow to one or more gods intended to influence the actions or welfare of people against their will and the outcome of events. Over 1,500 *defixiones* are known, two-thirds of which are written in Greek and the remainder in Latin. Of the Latin examples, over half have been found in Britain. They were usually written in cursive writing (sometimes done back-to-front) and usually in vulgar Latin. They were inscribed on small thin tablets or sheets of lead or very occasionally bronze (rarely stone). Lead was the traditional medium for curse tablets until the 20th century because this material was easy to inscribe with a stilus and easy to roll up. *Defixiones* were also known as *ex(s)ecrationes*, *devotiones* or *donationes*, and in fact may not have been known as *defixiones* by the Romans. They could be inscribed with the person's name and even the desired course of action.

Because the gods of the underworld were usually called on to take action, the lead sheets were often rolled up or folded and hidden, usually by burying them, placing them in tombs or at shrines, or throwing them down wells (cursing wells are known to have continued in Britain to the nineteenth century). Alternatively, they were fixed to a tree or post; many of the curse tablets have nail holes. Many tablets were curses against thieves and were attempts to recover lost or stolen property, affect the outcome of chariot races, or bring back departed lovers. When a tablet was used to call on a god to perform such an action, the dividing line between magic and a religious vow became almost imperceptible, particularly where a reward to the god was promised in the event that the curse was fulfilled. The phrasing on some curse tablets strongly suggests that they were written by professional scribes, and it is possible that such scribes offered their services at temples and shrines, writing curses, vows and dedications as required. Many *defixiones* have been found at temple sites. (There are approximately 200 examples from Uley, England.) Wording on other tablets, with meaningful phrases combined in a clumsy, semiliterate way, suggests that they were copied from other texts.
Reading: Hassall 1980; Tomlin 1988 (includes useful bibliography).

Deganta An Iberian goddess who is known from an inscription found at Cacabelos in northwestern Spain. The form of the inscription suggests that she was the patron deity of the Argaeli tribe.
Reading: Tranoy 1981, 298.

deification The elevation of humans to the status of gods, a practice usually reserved for emperors and occasionally their family members. The deification of emperors (raising them to the status of gods) took place after their deaths, by a decree of the Senate. A deified individual was usually described as *divus* (or *diva*, in the case of female members of the imperial family). See IMPERIAL CULT.

Deiotarus A Celtic god who was worshipped in Galatia (now an area of northern Turkey). His name probably means "divine bull."
Reading: Green, M. J. 1992b, 220; Ross 1974, 385.

Dei Penates An alternative name for the PENATES (or Di Penates).

delubrum (pl. *delubra*) Generally a rather grand *TEMENOS* or *TEMPLUM* in which an *AEDES* (temple building) stood, or else a court in which an altar was sited.
Reading: Richardson 1992, 2.

Demeter One of the deities of the ELEUSINIAN MYSTERIES. She was the Greek goddess of grain or cereal crops and was equated with the Roman goddess CERES.

dendrophorus (pl. *dendrophoroi*, literally, "branch" or "tree-bearer") *Dendrophoroi* were attached to various eastern cults, although in the Roman empire they were only associated with the cult of Cybele (MAGNA MATER) in the west. Their function was to carry a pine tree symbolizing the dead ATTIS, Cybele's consort, in procession to the temple of Magna Mater in a festival held on March 22. Attis was often depicted under a pine tree. *Dendrophoroi* were in guilds of carpenters and woodworkers. The guilds sometimes acted as burial clubs or societies, possibly because in myth Attis was buried and resurrected.
Reading: Vermaseren 1977.

Deuiana An alternative name for the Roman goddess DIANA.

deus Latin noun that indicates a god (in the nominative form). The plural nominative appears variously as *di*, *dei* and *dii*. The word is also used in other contexts, such as for deified members of the imperial family and for a statue or image of a god. A female deity is *dea*.

Deverra A Roman deity whose function was the protection of newborn babies against the evil tricks of the Roman god SILVANUS and other evil spirits. According to custom, three people kept Silvanus away at a birth by sweeping the threshold with a broom, pounding the door with a pestle and striking the door with an ax. These actions were presided over by three deities: Deverra, Pilumnus and Intercidona, whose names reflect the respective actions of the ritual. The ax, pestle and broom were considered to be the symbols of civilization, powerful enough to drive away Silvanus, the spirit of uncivilized wilderness.
Reading: Grimal 1986, 374; Hammond and Scullard (eds.) 1970, 833 (under *Pilumnus*).

devotio (pl. *devotiones*) A form of sacrifice, whereby an attempt was made to gain the favor of the gods by means of the suppliant offering his own life. It was usually undertaken by military generals facing the loss of a battle. The general used a complex ritual to vow *(devovere)* himself and the enemy's army to TELLUS and the MANES (gods of the UNDERWORLD). His death in battle would be the sacrifice, implying acceptance by the gods, who in turn were obliged to take the enemy army. The general could also substitute for himself any soldier from the legion. Should a victory occur but the substitute not be killed, the latter's image (over 7 ft. [2.13 m] tall) had to be buried as the sacrifice instead.

Devotio was also the name given to a form of magical curse or charm. The wax image of a person whose death or love was desired was treated in a way thought to bring about the desired outcome. For example, the image was melted to make the person melt with love, or pierced with nails to make the victim feel pain or even die. The word *devotio* was also sometimes used to denote curse tablets, which are more commonly known as *defixiones.* (See *DEFIXIO.*)
Reading: Hammond and Scullard (eds.) 1970, 333.

Diana A Roman goddess of wild nature and woods, who was also known as Iana, Deana, Deuiana and Diuiana. Her cult spread widely from her native Italy. She was originally identified with the Greek goddess ARTEMIS and came to be regarded primarily as a protector of women, particularly in childbirth. She was also regarded as a goddess of hunting and of the moon. In Rome there was an early temple to Diana on the Aventine Hill, as well as others on the Vicus Patricius and the Vicus Longus, and another whose location is unknown. There were also shrines in Rome dedicated to Diana. Diana was sometimes associated with Celtic gods, such as APOLLO CUNOMAGLUS at Nettleton Shrub, England, and she was sometimes conflated with Celtic hunting goddesses such as ABNOBA and ARDUINNA. There was a festival of Diana in Rome on August 13.
Reading: Green, M. J. 1992a, 80; Grimal 1986, 135–136; Hammond and Scullard (eds.) 1970, 337–338; Simon 1990, 51–58.

Diana, temple of Diana's earliest temple in Rome was on the Aventine Hill, where she was usually called Diana Aventina or Diana Aventinensis. The temple was outside the *pomerium* and was apparently preceded by an altar and precinct. According to tradition, it was founded in the sixth century B.C. by King Servius Tullius and was paid for by a league of Latin towns, perhaps in order to transfer the headquarters of the Latin League from the sanctuary of Diana Nemorensis to Rome. The dedication date was August 13 (the Ides of August), a holiday especially celebrated by slaves in Italy, and the temple became a refuge for runaway slaves. It probably lay just west of the church of Santa Prisca on the Clivus Publicius; the area was sometimes called the *Collis Dianae.* There was a large precinct and a temple building, and the complex itself was often called the *Dianium.* The temple was rebuilt under Augustus by Lucius Cornificius, and was then known as the temple of Diana Cornificiana. The rules governing the precinct and its rites were inscribed in detail on a bronze stele known as the Lex Arae Dianae. The temple was still standing in the fourth century, but no trace has been found to date.
Reading: Richardson 1992, 108–109; Scullard 1981, 174.

Diana Caelestis ("Celestial Diana") The Roman goddess DIANA was sometimes worshipped with the epithet Caelestis.

Diana Nemorensis ("Diana of the woods") The name by which the Roman goddess DIANA was worshipped at her temple at Nemi, near Aricia, Italy.

Diana Nemorensis, sanctuary of This cult center of DIANA in Italy, where she was worshipped as Diana Nemorensis, was situated by Lake Nemi. The sanctuary was 16 miles (25.75 km) south east of Rome and 2 miles (3.22 km) north of Lanuvium. The Nemus wood surrounded Lake Nemi (a volcanic crater known as *Speculum Dianae*—the "mirror of Diana"). It was situated in the Alban Hills in the territory of the nearby Latin town of Aricia and was sacred to Diana. Her temple and sanctuary stood in a grove on the shores of Lake Nemi down in the crater. The temple was believed to have been an old religious center of the Latin League, having been dedicated to Diana by Egerius Baebius of Tusculum. Its priest *(rex Nemorensis)* was a runaway slave who had killed his predecessor. According to legend, only a runaway slave was allowed to break a bough from a particular tree in the wood. If he succeeded in so doing, he was entitled to fight the priest in single combat. If he killed the priest, he became the new priest, until another slave killed him in turn.

Although there is no evidence for buildings at the sanctuary before the fourth century B.C., there is evidence of worship there before that time. In the late second or early first century B.C., the sanctuary was transformed by large-scale rebuilding and landscaping. The sanctuary was a popular focus for worship, no doubt because of the proximity of the numerous villas in the area. Many votive terracotta offerings were found during late nineteenth-century excavations at the site, including figurines of men and women with children, anatomical models (some of reproductive organs, but mainly head, feet and hands), and statuettes of animals relating to Diana and the chase. Women whose prayers had been answered visited the grove in processions from Rome on Diana's festival on August 13, wearing garlands and carrying flaming torches. The festival was so popular that the early Christians adopted it as the Assumption of the Virgin. EGERIA and VIRBIUS were also worshipped at this sanctuary. The sanctuary continued in use until at least the fourth century. The rites associated with this sanctuary were the inspiration for J. G. Frazer's *The Golden Bough* (first edition published in 1890).

Reading: Beard 1993; Blagg 1986; Blagg 1993.

Diana Tifatina The name by which the Roman goddess DIANA was worshipped at her famous shrine on Mount Tifata, near Capua, Italy.

diaspora The dispersion of the Jews throughout the Roman empire. The Jews first began to disperse from their homeland after the sack of Jerusalem in 587 B.C., when Nebuchadnezzar carried away the inhabitants of southern Judaea to beyond the Euphrates. In the first century there was widespread dispersion: many Jews moved from Palestine to Egypt, and others settled in many eastern areas such as Asia Minor and Greece. There was also some settlement in the west, including Rome. Dispersed Jews tended to live in closely knit exclusive groups, and a particular characteristic of Jewish communities was the synagogue. The Jews of the Diaspora did not intervene in the first Jewish revolt of 66–70. Thousands of Palestinian Jews were sold into slavery in 70 and in 135, which increased the number of Diaspora Jews, and large communities of Jews developed in many areas of the empire. (See also JEWISH REVOLTS; JUDAISM; SYNAGOGUE.)

Reading: Hammond and Scullard (eds.) 1970, 564–565; Smallwood 1976.

Di Consentes A group of Roman deities comprised of JUPITER, JUNO, NEPTUNE, MINERVA, MARS, VENUS, APOLLO, DIANA, VULCAN, VESTA, MERCURY and CERES. The Etruscans recognized 12 great deities, six male and six female, and the idea may have been adopted by the Romans under Etruscan influence. However the Romans did not adopt the Etruscan deities, but Romanized versions of the 12 great gods of the Greeks. These deities, six male and six female, became known as the Di Consentes. There were gilt statues of these deities in the FORUM ROMANUM in Rome.

Reading: Grimal 1986, 109; Hammond and Scullard (eds.) 1970, 278–279.

Di Conserentes Roman deities who presided over procreation.

Di Conservatores ("Savior Gods") A collective term found in some inscriptions, used to address those deities who were believed to have preserved a worshipper during a difficult time. There is an altar dedicated to Di Conservatores from South Shields, England, that appears to have been set up as a thanks-offering for the safe return to Rome from Britain of the emperors Caracalla and Geta.

Reading: Phillips 1977, 59 (for inscription from South Shields).

Diespiter ("day father") The archaic nominative Latin form of Iuppiter (JUPITER), and so an alternative name for this Roman god.

dies religiosus (pl. *dies religiosi*) Any day considered to be unlucky (such as the anniversary of the defeat at the battle of Cannae), or on which there was a religious ban on business or other activities. (See also *RELIGIOSUS*.)
Reading: York 1986.

Di Inferi A collective term for the Roman gods of the UNDERWORLD, such as DIS and PROSERPINA. In Rome, the LUDI TAUREI were held every five years in honor of the *di inferi*.

Di Manes The collective spirits of the dead. (See MANES.)

Di Nixi The Roman goddesses of childbirth, also referred to as NIXI.

Dionysus (or Dionysos) A Greek god of nature who was sometimes worshipped under this Greek name and sometimes under his Roman name, BACCHUS. Dionysus became the god of the vine and of wine. He was also a god of mystic ecstasy, and his cult was one of the MYSTERY RELIGIONS. According to legend, Dionysus was the son of ZEUS and SEMELE. Semele asked Zeus to show himself to her in all his glory, but was struck dead by the sight. Zeus took the unborn Dionysus, only in his sixth month, from Semele's womb and sewed the infant up inside his thigh. At the proper time, Dionysus emerged from the thigh, alive and perfectly formed, to become "the twice-born god." Other legends describe Dionysus being driven mad by HERA and being cured by the goddess Cybele, into whose rites he was initiated. He was said to have descended into the UNDERWORLD and restored Semele to life. Hades agreed to release the shade of Semele if Dionysus gave him something that he held very dear, so Dionysus gave up the myrtle plant. On his way to the underworld, he had asked a man named Prosymnus (or Polymnus) for directions, and the man had asked for certain sexual favors from Dionysus on his return. When he returned, however, he could not fulfill his promise because Prosymnus had died; the best he could do was to plant a phallus-shaped stick in the tomb of Prosymnus. The cult of Dionysus (and subsequently, of Bacchus) reflected elements of these myths and legends.
Reading: Grimal 1986, 138–140; Hammond and Scullard (eds.) 1970, 352–353; Johns 1982, 78–82.

Dionysus Zagreus The Greek god DIONYSUS who was linked with the Cretan god Zagreus. Dionysus Zagreus was regarded as the son of ZEUS and DEMETER. According to Greek legend, the other Greek gods were jealous of Dionysus Zagreus and arranged that he be torn to pieces. The Greek goddess Pallas Athena saved his heart and took it to Zeus, who created the god Dionysus from it. This story of death and resurrection appears to have played an important part in the cult of ORPHISM, which witnessed a revival in the Roman empire.
Reading: Hammond and Scullard (eds.) 1970, 759 (under *Orphism*).

Dioscuri The collective name given to the Roman gods CASTOR and POLLUX. They were originally the Greek gods Castor and Polydeuces, who were the sons of the Greek god ZEUS and Leda, the daughter of King Thestius of Aetolia in Greece.

Di Parentes Roman spirits of ancestors. The *di parentes* of a family were the spirits of dead parents and other deceased close relations. They were worshipped at the festival called the PARENTALIA. (See also MANES.)

Di Penates Roman gods of the household, usually known as PENATES.

Dirae An alternative name for the Roman deities known as the FURIES.

Dis (A contracted form of *dives*, "rich") A Roman god of the dead and the ruler of the UNDERWORLD, also known as DIS PATER ("father of riches") and as Dives. He was equated with ORCUS and with the Greek god HADES (who was also known as Plouton). The Latin name *Pluto* is derived from the Greek Plouton or Pluton which (like *dives*) means "rich." The various names of this underworld god may reflect the richness of agricultural land and its underlying mineral wealth; this may mean that Dis was originally a deity of the fields and of the ground.

In Greek myth, Hades was one of the three sons of CRONUS and RHEA (the others being ZEUS and

POSEIDON) and ruled the underworld and the dead with his wife PERSEPHONE (PROSERPINA). When he was in the underworld, only OATHS and CURSES could reach him, and people invoked him by striking the earth with their hands. Black sheep were sacrificed to him, and those who performed the sacrifice averted their faces. Hades and his Roman equivalent Dis had very little associated cult following, and so there are few statues of Dis. In 249 B.C. and 207 B.C. the Senate ordained special festivals to appease Dis and Proserpina. In literature, Dis was regarded only as a symbol of death.
Reading: Green, M. J. 1992a, 81–82; Grimal 1986, 141, 177 (for *Hades*).

Dis and Proserpina, altar of (in Latin, *Ara Ditis Patris et Proserpinae*, "altar of Dis Pater and Proserpina") According to legend, this marble altar was miraculously discovered by the servants of a Sabine called Valesius (ancestor of the first consul). The servants were digging to lay foundations following instructions given to Valesius's children in dreams. It was found 20 ft. (6.09 m) underground, within the Tarentum on the edge of the CAMPUS MARTIUS. Valesius reburied the altar after three days of games. From the evidence of coins, the altar was round. Sacrifices were offered at this altar during the LUDI SAECULARES. It may have been uncovered for each occasion of the games, to be reburied afterwards. It was rediscovered in 1886–87 beneath the Corso Vittorio Emanuele in Rome.
Reading: Nash 1962a, 57; Richardson 1992, 110–111, 377.

Dis Pater An alternative name for DIS, the Roman god of the UNDERWORLD. As Dis Pater, he was also sometimes identified with the Sabine god SORANUS. In southern Germany and the Balkans, Dis Pater had a Celtic goddess, AERICURA, as a consort, and in *De Bello Gallico*, Julius Caesar mentions that the Gauls thought themselves descendants of Dis Pater.
Reading: Green, M. J. 1992a, 81–82.

Disciplina ("discipline") Also known as Discipulina, a Roman goddess of orderly conduct used for propaganda purposes in the later empire to help maintain order within the legions. The earliest dedication to this goddess appears to be an inscription on an altar found at Chesters, Hadrian's Wall, England. Here the dedication was to the Discipline of the emperor Hadrian and dates to his reign (117–138). Dedications were more usually "Disciplina Augusti" or "Discipulinae Augusti" ("to the Discipline of the Emperor"). Disciplina was portrayed on coins during the latter part of Hadrian's reign, and dedications are known from various parts of the empire where troops were stationed. Eight dedications are known from Britain and seven from North Africa.
Reading: Austen and Breeze 1979.

Diuiana An alternative name for the Roman goddess DIANA.

dius Latin adjective in the nominative form meaning "divine" or "possessing a supernatural power." The female form is DIA. (See also DEA DIA.)

Dius Fidius A Roman god who was sworn by in OATHS. His name is derived from *Dius* ("divine") and *fides* ("good faith," "trust"). The Dius Fidius was sometimes identified with JUPITER or with the hero HERCULES. There was a festival of Dius Fidius on June 5. He was linked with the Roman deity SEMO SANCUS, with whom he was eventually equated. In Rome there was a temple of Semo Sancus Dius Fidius on the Quirinal Hill.
Reading: Freyburger 1986, 288–294; Scullard 1981, 147; York 1986, 77–79.

Diuturna An alternative name for the Roman goddess Iuturna (JUTURNA).

Diva Angerona A Roman goddess also known as ANGERONA.

Divae Corniscae ("sacred crows") Probably local Roman deities who were worshipped at a place on the right bank of the Tiber River in Rome (possibly in a sacred grove). These "sacred crows" were said to be under the protection of JUNO, but little else is known about them.
Reading: Richardson 1992, 101.

Divalia (or Divalia Angeronae) Alternative names for the festival of ANGERONALIA.

Diva Palatua A Roman goddess who was the guardian deity of the Palatine Hill in Rome. Her

festival took place in Rome on December 11. On this day no carts or vehicles drawn by beasts of burden were allowed in the city, and sacrifices were performed by her own *FLAMEN*, the *flamen Palatualis.* Little else is known about this deity.
Reading: Scullard 1981, 104, 204.

Diva Rumina A Roman goddess also known as RUMINA.

Dives An alternative name for the Roman god DIS.

divi The collective name of some or all deified emperors. An individual emperor was usually called *divus*, but *divi* was used as a noun for deified emperors.

divination Ascertaining the will of the gods and future events through the reading and interpretation of oracles, signs, dreams and portents. The gods were believed to reveal their will to people in the form of signs or omens. Some signs, such as thunder, might be fairly obvious, but most signs were less obvious, and all needed proper interpretation. Divination included external observations of animals, plants, objects or phenomena and the observation of entrails of sacrificed animals. The Romans' many methods of divination are known today mainly from Cicero's dialogue *De Divinatione (On Divination)*, written in 45 B.C. Examples of divination included AUGURY and *EXTISPICIUM.* Some signs were deliberately sought *(impetrativa)*, such as in *extispicium*, and others were divinely sent *(oblativa)*, such as lightning.

Divination was undertaken by private individuals and by three main groups of diviners: augurs (particularly taking auspices before any public action), interpreters of prodigies and oracles (including *haruspices* and the *quindecimviri sacris faciundis*), and readers of entrails (*haruspices*) at public sacrifices.

Natural divination included the interpretation of dreams (also the basis of INCUBATION) and prophecy from the speech of someone possessed and used as a mouthpiece by a divine power or as an ORACLE, such as that at Delphi. Divination by dice or drawing lots was common, and random consultation of works of famous poets was also practiced. Unusual weather conditions were always considered significant, and from the fourth century B.C. ASTROLOGY became increasingly popular. NECROMANCY (calling up the spirits of the dead) was practiced but was not considered respectable. Early Christians saw divination as the work of the devil, and there was much official hostility and intolerance toward the practice of divination and magic. The edict of Theodosius in 391, which banned pagan worship, formally ended divination.
Reading: Luck 1985, 229–305; North 1990.

Divorum, temple of A temple in the CAMPUS MARTIUS, built by Domitian after the fire at Rome in 80 to commemorate his deified father Vespasian and brother Titus (known collectively as *DIVI*) who died in 79 and 81. It was known as Templum Divorum, and later just as Divorum (temple of the Divi). It was a large rectangular complex surrounded by porticoes, about 210 yds. long and 82 yds. wide (192 m × 75 m). It was entered from the north through a triple monumental arch. Just inside, a pair of small temples (*Aedes Divi Titi* and *Aedes Divi Vespasiani*) faced each other.
Reading: Nash 1962a, 304; Richardson 1992, 111.

divus (or *diuus*) A Latin noun in the nominative singular meaning "a god"; it was often applied to a deified emperor (followed by the emperor's name, such as Divus Augustus). The plural form (*divi*) was used as a collective noun for some or all deified emperors. (See also *DEUS*.)

DM (S) *dis manibus (sacrum)* "(sacred) to the spirits of the dead" or "to the divine shades." A formula often seen on tombstones, where the graves were dedicated to the dead collectively (the *di manes*). (See also MANES.)

dog An animal often used for sacrificial offerings, with a pre-Roman tradition in Europe. Entire skeletons of dogs have been found in Britain and on continental Europe deposited in deep pits, latrines, wells and ritual shafts, and were perhaps offerings to the UNDERWORLD. The association of dogs with the hunt may also have led to an association with the dead and therefore with the underworld. Dogs were sacrificed at the LUPERCALIA and at the ROBIGALIA. The dog was also associated with fidelity, with protection and with healing qualities in its saliva: at times they were portrayed as companions to AESCULAPIUS and other healing deities. There were

also temple dogs who cured wounds, sores and blindness by licking. Hunting dogs were also associated with such deities as SILVANUS.
Reading: Green, M. J. 1992b, 111–113, 197–203; Merrifield 1987, 46–48.

Dolichenus A local god (a BAAL) of thunder and fertility who was worshipped at Doliche, Turkey. He became regarded as a god of sky and weather and so became equated with the Roman god JUPITER as JUPITER DOLICHENUS.

Domesticae Celtic mother goddesses also known as the MATRES DOMESTICAE.

Domus Publica The residence of the *PONTIFEX MAXIMUS*, situated in the precinct of the temple of VESTA on the Sacra Via. When Augustus became *pontifex maximus* in 13 B.C., the residence was moved to the Palatine Hill and the house was given to the VESTAL VIRGINS.
Reading: Richardson 1992, 133–134.

Donatism A schismatic movement in the Christian church in North Africa in the fourth and early fifth centuries. The schism originated as a result of Diocletian's persecution (known as the Great Persecution) of Christians in 303–305. In eastern provinces, the clergy were required to perform sacrifices, but in North Africa they were obliged to surrender the Scriptures, vessels and vestments. More moderate Christians surrendered (and were termed *traditores*, "surrenderers"), arguing that a compromise was possible. Caecilian, a moderate, was elected bishop of Carthage in 311 (on the death of Mensurius, the former bishop), but dissidents opposed Caecilian and the *traditores*. They consequently elected Majorinus as rival bishop; following his death, they elected Donatus. Moderates believed that the Christian church on earth should contain both sinners and the righteous, but Donatists were puritans and considered themselves to be the church of the martyrs. They refused to accept this principle and could not therefore accept any compromise. Donatists were condemned as schismatics by legislation dating from the time of Constantine. They gained a strong foothold in North Africa but not outside Africa, except to a minor degree in Rome itself. The split persisted until the African church was destroyed by the Arabs in the seventh and eighth centuries.
Reading: Hammond and Scullard (eds.) 1970, 361–362.

Dream of Scipio *(Somnium Scipionis)* Written by Cicero, the Dream of Scipio formed the epilogue of *On the State* (*De Republica*) and was a vision of the AFTERLIFE. *On the State* was a dialogue between Scipio, Laelius and others and discusses the best form of government. The *Dream* portrays the destiny of the immortal soul, and subsequently met with Christian approval. It was said by Scipio that in his dream he heard the words *omnibus, qui patriam conservaverint, adiuverint, auxerint, certum esse in caelo definitum locum, ubi beati aevo sempiterno fruantur* (*De Republica* 6:13): "There is a sure place prepared in heaven for all who have cared for their fatherland, preserved it, contributed to its growth, increased it: a place where they may enjoy eternal life in everlasting bliss." Although Cicero was virtually forgotten in the Middle Ages, the Dream of Scipio continued to be read.
Reading: Hammond and Scullard (eds.) 1970, 237.

dreams The interpretation of dreams is an example of natural DIVINATION, a dream being interpreted by the dreamer or a professional interpreter. This is also the basis of INCUBATION.
Reading: Ogilvie 1969, 67–68.

Druidism A Celtic religion, centered in Britain, which was led by priests known as Druids. Relatively little is known about the Druidic religion because the basic doctrines were kept secret. Much of what is known comes from ancient authors such as Julius Caesar. Druidism was confined to Britain and Gaul, where the Celtic society was controlled by an elite class which had three sections: Druids, Vates and Bards. According to Caesar, Druidic power originated in Britain, which remained the center of Druidism. The only detailed account of a Druidic ritual comes from Pliny the Elder (*Natural History* 16:95). He describes the cutting of mistletoe with a golden sickle by a Druid in a white robe who climbed the tree on which the mistletoe grew. The mistletoe was allowed to fall and was caught in a white cloak held by others. Pliny also refers to the sacrifice of two white bulls and gives details of the ritual for harvesting other herbs.

The Druidic cult appears to have been centered around a belief that after death the soul passed to another body, either human or animal. This not only led to the Celts being fearless in battle, but also sanctioned the human sacrifices that seem to have been part of some Druidic rituals. Criminals, captives in battle and innocent people were at times sacrificed for various purposes, such as propitiation of the gods after disasters, thanksgiving for victories and mainly for purposes of divination; the victim was enclosed in a huge wicker construction which was set on fire.

Druids were more than priests, since they controlled the warriors, and through them the rest of the people. However, they did not have a monopoly of religious power: the Vates and the Bards also had religious functions. The Druids appear to have dominated the ruling class, and to have been a unifying element between tribes, presiding over religious assemblies involving more than one tribe. The Druids were educated and were knowledgeable in astronomy and astrology. Divination was undoubtedly part of their duties, and they were also thought to have powers over the elements and to be able to cast spells. Both Augustus and Tiberius published edicts against them, and Claudius proscribed Druidism in Gaul in 54. In 60 there was a concerted effort to break the power of the priesthood in Britain. The reason for the persecution of the Druids was allegedly the objection of the Romans to human sacrifice. However, as a unifying force among independent tribes for Celtic resistance, the Druids were also a political threat. It is difficult to assess how much effect the suppression of the Druids and of human sacrifice had on Celtic religion. The ample evidence for worship of Celtic gods after the suppression implies that it was the priesthood rather than the religion itself that the Romans wished to eradicate. However, in the fourth century Ausonius alludes to Druids in Aquitaine, so it is doubtful whether their suppression was ever complete.
Reading: Green, M. J. 1992a, 86–87; Piggott 1968; Ross and Robins 1989.

Duellona The early Roman name for the goddess BELLONA.

Durbedicus An Iberian god who is known from a dedicatory inscription found near Guimarães, Portugal. Durbedicus appears to have been a water god.
Reading: Tranoy 1981, 274–275.

E

Edict of Milan An edict of toleration, giving the Christian church and all other religious cults freedom of worship, and bringing to an end the persecutions of the Christians. It was issued by Constantine and Licinius in Milan in February 313, after Constantine defeated Maxentius.

Edict of Toleration An edict of toleration that allowed Christians the freedom to worship and ended their persecution. It was issued in April 311 by the dying Galerius, along with Constantine and Licinius, but it was immediately suppressed by Maximinus II.

Edovius An Iberian god who is known from an inscription found at Caldas de Reyes, northwestern Spain. The inscription was found in the wall of a bathhouse, and it is likely that the deity was associated with the thermal springs there.
Reading: Tranoy 1981, 289.

Edusa A Roman goddess who presided over a child's eating.
Reading: Ferguson 1988a, 853.

Egeria A Roman water goddess or water NYMPH. In legend, she was the consort and advisor of the second king of Rome, Numa Pompilius. Egeria set out the religious rituals, incantations and prayers that Numa Pompilius followed, and when he died she despaired and wept so much that she turned into a spring. She was worshipped in association with the Roman deities DIANA and VIRBIUS in a grove at Nemi near Aricia, Italy—the sanctuary of DIANA NEMORENSIS. She was also worshipped along with the Roman goddesses known as the CAMENAE at a grove outside the Porta Capena in Rome. Pregnant women sacrificed to Egeria for an easy delivery.
Reading: Grimal 1986, 144; Hammond and Scullard (eds.) 1970, 373.

Eileithyia A Greek goddess of birth who was sometimes referred to in the plural form of her name (Eileithyiae). She was identified with the Roman goddess LUCINA.

Elagabalus Emperor 218–222. He was a Syrian, born at Emesa, and was named after the Syro-Phoenician sun god Sol Invictus El Gabal of Emesa, of whom he was a priest (see EL GABAL, SOL INVICTUS). As emperor he was almost totally preoccupied by his religious duties. He made the sun god the chief deity of Rome.
Reading: Halsberghe 1972.

Elernus An obscure Roman god, whose name is uncertain. (See HELERNUS.)

Eleusinian mysteries A Greek mystery religion, in which worshippers were initiated into the secrets before they could fully take part. The initiation ceremony took place in the Eleusinion, a temple below the Acropolis at Athens. After a procession from the Eleusinion at Athens to Eleusis, a priest showed the sacred objects to the initiated in the *telesterion* (initiation hall or hall of mysteries) at Eleusis, and the mysteries were celebrated. Because most of the ritual and the sacred objects were religious secrets, virtually nothing is known about them. In general terms, the religion was linked with the myths of PERSEPHONE and DEMETER and was concerned with death and rebirth. The Eleusinian mysteries were very popular during the Roman em-

pire, and several emperors (notably Marcus Aurelius and Commodus) were initiated into the mysteries. It is noteworthy that the emperor Nero was refused initiation. Much building work took place at Eleusis in Roman times, but the sanctuary ceased to exist after 395.
Reading: Ferguson 1970, 99–101.

El Gabal (or Elagabal or Sol Invictus El Gabal) A Syrian sun deity whose worship was actively promoted in Rome by the emperor ELAGABALUS. (See also SOL INVICTUS.)

Empanda A Roman goddess who was mentioned by ancient authors, although nothing else is known about her.

emperor worship The worship of living and deceased emperors, also known as the IMPERIAL CULT.

endotercisus A day that counted as *NEFASTUS* in the morning and evening but was *FASTUS* in between; it was indicated by EN in the calendars. (See *CALENDAR*.)

Endovellicus An Iberian god who was worshipped in Spain and southern Portugal. His name is thought to mean "very black," and he may have been a god of the UNDERWORLD, although many of the dedications to him indicate that he was a god of healing. It is possible that he performed both functions, perhaps in different localities.
Reading: Curchin 1991, 157; Keay 1988, 161.

Entarabus A Celtic god who is known from an inscription found near Bastogne, Germany. He is probably the same deity as INTARABUS.
Reading: Wightman 1970, 126.

Enyo A Greek goddess of war who was identified with the Roman goddess BELLONA.

Epicureanism The philosophy formulated by Epicurus, an Athenian active around 300 B.C., about which much is known from Lucretius's writings. Epicurus believed that the gods existed in immortal bliss but neither rewarded nor punished mortals. He believed that the soul was mortal and that good could be attained and evil endured, and that there was nothing to fear from the gods and nothing to suffer in death. The aim in his philosophy was to secure a happy life, and so the moral element of his philosophy was most important. Communities of Epicureans grew up, secluding themselves from urban affairs and living an almost austere life. The effects of the philosophy on its adherents was therefore similar to that of some religious cults. With the rise of Christianity, Epicureans were denounced as atheists; although they were willing to accept the existence of a god, they did not believe that he interfered in the affairs of people, nor did they believe in an AFTERLIFE.
Reading: Ferguson 1970, 190–193; Hammond and Scullard (eds.) 1970, 390–392 (under *Epicurus*).

Epidaurus, Asclepieium of The most famous healing center of the cult of Asclepius (in Latin, AESCULAPIUS) in Greece, from which lesser shrines were founded, such as those in Athens (in 420 B.C.) and Rome (in 292 B.C.). When each new shrine to Aesculapius was established, a sacred snake (representing the god) was brought from the temple at Epidaurus. The Asclepieium (Asklepieion) at Epidaurus was approached by pilgrims along a Sacred Way from the city of Epidaurus eight miles (13 km) distant. There were numerous cult buildings, temples, a stadium, a gymnasium, a theater and a hostel, with considerable building work done during the Roman period. In A.D. 150 Pausanias visited the sanctuary at Epidaurus and noted six votive columns inscribed with many case histories; four of the columns have been found in excavations (two of which are virtually intact) and describe various miraculous cures.
Reading: Hammond and Scullard (eds.) 1970, 392; Jackson 1988, 143–150.

epitaph *(tituli sepulchrales)* An inscription on a tombstone or tomb testifying to the deceased. Epitaphs are the most common type of inscription, and the form of words varies greatly. From the Augustan age onward, they often began with *DM*, or *DIS MANIBUS* ("to the spirits of the dead") in full. There are thousands of inscriptions that begin with this formula. This is followed by the deceased's name, or sometimes *MEMORIAE* ("to the memory of") preceding the deceased's name. The careers and ages of soldiers and prominent men are often recorded, with the addition of the name of the heir,

relative or friend who erected the stone. More than 100,000 published epitaphs survive from the western empire alone, and provide a view of the Romans' belief in an afterlife. Some epitaphs give statements about the soul and its fate after death and throw light on the Romans' perception of the UNDERWORLD, the MANES and the cult of the tomb. Many of the inscriptions include set formulae such as *STTL* (*sit tibi terra levis*, "may the earth lie lightly upon you"), but even these non-original inscriptions must reflect the views of those erecting the tombstone or monument.
Reading: Lattimore 1962.

Epona A Celtic horse goddess, whose name derives from the Celtic word for horse. Her worship was most popular in eastern Gaul and on the German frontier. She was also worshipped in Britain, Dalmatia, North Africa and Rome. She had a festival in Rome, which was unique for a Gaulish deity, and this was held on December 18. There was a shrine dedicated to her at Entrains (Nièvre) in Burgundy, France. She was always portrayed on or with horses, and sometimes with *paterae* full of corn, ears of corn, baskets of fruit, a dog and a key. In some images she is portrayed holding a *mappa* (a cloth used to signal the start of horse races). Throughout the Roman world the horse was extremely important for transport, and to a lesser extent was a power source to work machinery. This is reflected in the importance of the widespread cult of Epona. Apart from her association with horses, the symbolism suggests that the goddess was also associated with water and presided over such aspects of life as fertility, healing, death and rebirth. Epona was sometimes associated with Celtic mother goddesses, and at Hagondange, Germany, she is portrayed in triplicate in the same way as the mother goddesses are often depicted.
Reading: Deyts 1992, 51–57; Green, M. J. 1984, 145–146, 195–197; Green, M. J. 1992a, 90–92; Green, M. J. 1992b, 204–207.

epulones ("Feast-organizers") A college of male priests (patricians and plebeians) established in 196 B.C. to take over the role of religious feast organization from the pontiffs. There were originally three priests (*tresviri epulones*) but their number increased to seven, possibly under Sulla, and then under Julius Caesar to 10, although they continued to be called *septemviri epulones* (seven feast-organizers). They arranged the *epulum Iovis* (feast of JUPITER), as well as the public banquets at other festivals and games. They normally held office for life and were originally coopted, but some were selected by popular election after 104 B.C.
Reading: Beard and Nash (eds.) 1990; Porte 1989, 127–130; Scullard 1981, 186–187.

epulum Iovis The feast held for senators after the sacrifices at festivals of JUPITER OPTIMUS MAXIMUS. It was arranged by the *EPULONES*. One feast took place on September 13 at the end of the LUDI ROMANI, with another on November 13 as part of the LUDI PLEBEII. Magistrates and senators attended the feast, which began with a sacrifice, possibly of a white heifer, and *mola salsa* (a ritual cake) was offered. The *epulum Iovis* may also have been in honor of JUNO and MINERVA.
Reading: Scullard 1981, 186–187, 197.

Equirria A festival of horse racing in honor of MARS held on February 27. It was said to have been established by Romulus. It was held in the CAMPUS MARTIUS in Rome, or, if that was flooded, on the Caelian Hill at a place called the Campus Martialis. A similar festival held on March 14 may have been called the Mamuralia, even though festivals were normally held on odd days of the month (see *FERIAE*). It is uncertain if chariot racing was involved in the Equirria.
Reading: Scullard 1981, 82, 89.

Erinyes Greek spirits who avenged wrongs done within families and kindred groups, especially murder within a family or clan. They also avenged offences against the gods. They were known to the Romans as Furiae (FURIES).

Eros The Greek god of love and fertility who was identified with the Roman deity CUPID.

Eshmoun (or Eshmun) The Phoenician god of health. Originally a god of vegetation and regeneration, he came to be identified with the Greek god Asclepius (Latin, AESCULAPIUS). He was particularly venerated at Sidon (modern Sayda), Lebanon.

Esus ("lord") A Celtic god who is known from the writings of the first-century Roman poet Lucan, who wrote about events that took place in the first

century B.C. (*Pharsalia* I, lines 444–446). Esus is also known from two inscriptions from Paris, France, and Trier, Germany. Lucan describes Esus as requiring human sacrifice. The god had a particular connection with willow trees and is depicted as a woodman cutting or pruning trees. At Paris, the stone with the Esus inscription has *Tarvostrigaranus* inscribed on another face. In later commentaries (from Berne, Switzerland, probably ninth century) on Lucan's *Pharsalia*, Esus is equated with MARS and MERCURY. Relatively little is known about this god, and Lucan's implication that Esus was an important Celtic deity is not supported by archaeological evidence. (See also TARVOSTRIGARANUS.)
Reading: Green, M. J. 1992a, 93–94.

Eugenius, Flavius Usurper emperor in the west 392–394. He was a friend of Symmachus, an ardent supporter of PAGANISM. Although a Christian, Eugenius sympathized with the attempt to revive pagan worship, and he restored the Altar of Victory in the Senate house.
Reading: Hammond and Scullard (eds.) 1970, 414.

Eumenides Literally, the "kindly ones," this was the euphemistic name for the Greek spirits the ERINYES, known to the Romans as Furiae (FURIES).

Eusebius of Caesarea c. 260–340, an early Christian writer and theologian. He was born in Palestine, escaped Diocletian's persecution of the Christians, and was appointed bishop of Caesarea in c. 314. He was the author (in Greek) of 46 Christian theological works, 15 of which have survived, as well as other writings, of which some fragments and translations survive. Among his extant works is *Ecclesiastical History*, an account of the rise of the Christian church from its beginnings to the early fourth century that has earned him the title "Father of Church History." The history was in 10 books and is an important source of information about the rise of the Church in the east from earliest times to 324. His other works include *Martyrs of Palestine*, an eyewitness account of the persecution of the Christians by Diocletian.
Reading: Hammond and Scullard (eds.) 1970, 423–424.

Evander A Greek deity who was associated with the Greek god PAN; both were originally worshipped in Arcadia, Greece. In Rome, Evander was associated with the worship of the Roman god FAUNUS (who was also identified with Pan) and was regarded as the first settler in Rome. According to legend, Evander founded a settlement on the Palatine Hill, called the Pallantium (or Pallanteum). His mother was worshipped in Rome as the goddess CARMENTA, but ancient authors also give the name of his mother variously as Themis, Nicostrate or Tyburtis. The

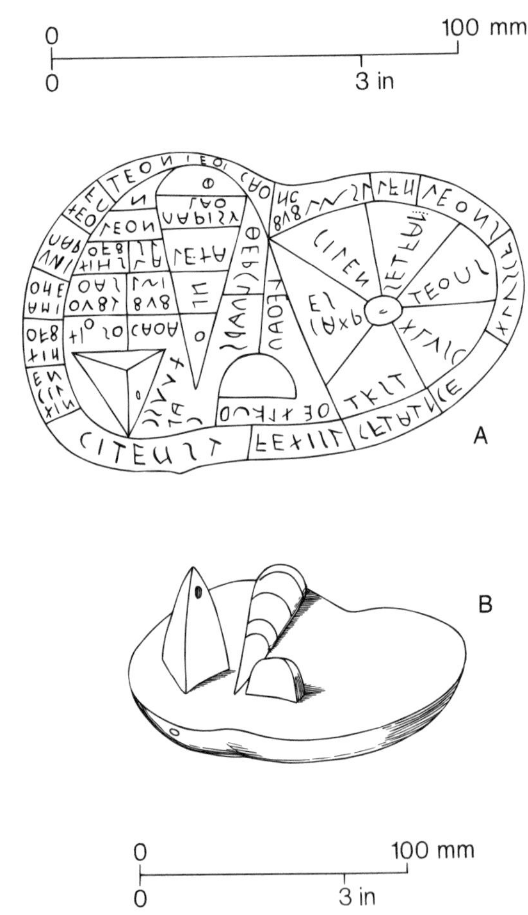

Fig. 26 A bronze model of a sheep's liver from Piacenza, Italy. A = plan view; B = oblique view drawn at a smaller scale. It is Etruscan, 3rd century B.C., *and assisted* haruspices *in* extispicium, *in interpreting good and bad omens when observing the liver of a freshly sacrificed animal. The names of Etruscan deities are engraved, and the 42 divisions probably related to regions of the sky.*

reasons given for his leaving Arcadia to settle in Rome also vary, and include him killing his father or his mother. When he settled on the Palatine Hill, Evander was welcomed by Faunus. Evander was a benevolent ruler and was thought to have introduced various skills and arts, including writing and music, as well as the cults of CERES, NEPTUNE and Pan. He was also regarded as having established the cult of HERCULES at the ARA MAXIMA. There was an altar dedicated to Evander at the foot of the Aventine Hill in Rome, near the Porta Trigemina, where sacrifices were offered annually.
Reading: Grimal 1986, 161; Hammond and Scullard (eds.) 1970, 425–426.

evocatio Transference of gods to Rome from territory under Roman control. When a town or area was conquered, its deities were regarded as conquered as well—this was done by evocation (*evocatio*), promising the deity better treatment in Rome. It was also thought that a town could be conquered if the deities (especially the one that protected the town) could be induced to leave it by EVOCATIO. Livy records the evoking of JUNO REGINA from Veii in Italy.
Reading: Hammond and Scullard (eds.) 1970, 426.

exauguration Rites conducted by augurs to ensure that a deity, known or unknown, at a particular site would not be offended by the introduction of a new deity. It could involve the deconsecration of a shrine by an AUGUR, with the deity of the shrine being promised an equal or better shrine elsewhere. It was not the same as *EVOCATIO*.

ex(s)ecratio (pl. *ex(s)ecrationes*) The invoking of a curse, and a word sometimes used for curse tablets (more commonly known as *defixiones*).

extispicium (Fig. 26) The interpretation of signs in the entrails (*exta*) of sacrificial animals (particularly the liver). It was a form of DIVINATION carried out by *haruspices* at most public sacrifices in or outside Rome. Entrails were interpreted by the color, markings and shape of the liver and gallbladder, and there is evidence that models of livers were used in the training of *haruspices*. A bronze model of a liver and gall bladder was found in 1877 at Piacenza, Italy. It was divided by engraved lines into sections which matched the parts of the sky, with the name of the ruling deity written in Etruscan in each section.
Reading: North 1990.

F

Fabulinus A Roman deity who helped children learn to talk.
Reading: Ferguson 1988a, 853.

face pot A pot with a stylized decorated face. They have been found in western provinces, particularly the Rhineland, and have been termed face pots. Head pots are similar, but the whole pot is molded in the shape of a head; they are found only in Britain. Both types may have had a ritual function, and some have been found in graves.
Reading: Braithwaite 1984.

Fagus A Celtic god who personified the beech tree (*Fagus* means "beech tree"). He was worshipped in the French Pyrenees.
Reading: Green, M. J. 1992a, 94–95.

Falacer A Roman deity who was served by a FLAMEN (the *flamen Falacer*). He appears to have been a mythical hero, but little else is known about him.

fanum (pl. *fana*) Any sacred area, including sacred groves and temples. Apart from the sanctuary of HERCULES VICTOR at Tivoli, Italy, it was a term little used in Rome itself, although it was used especially for cult centers of Oriental deities and pilgrimage shrines.
Reading: Richardson 1992, 2.

Farinus A Roman god who presided over speech.

fascinum A representation of the PHALLUS (a phallic emblem) which was worn round the neck, in particular to protect children against evil.

fasting The abstinence of food for religious purposes was rare in Roman times. It is attested by the *ieiunium Cereris* (a fast in honor of CERES in Rome, literally "a fast of Ceres"). The later mystery cults, of Oriental origin, commonly used ritual fasting. There were also some diet restrictions. For example, followers of ORPHISM were vegetarians, and the *FLAMEN DIALIS* in Rome could not eat beans.
Reading: Hammond and Scullard (eds.) 1970, 430.

fasti sacerdotales Lists of priests. Calendars that were originally compiled to list *dies fasti* and *dies nefasti* came to include lists of magistrates *(fasti consulares)*, triumphs *(fasti triumphales)* and priests *(fasti sacerdotales)*.
Reading: Hammond and Scullard (eds.) 1970, 429.

fastus *(dies fastus*, pl. *dies fasti)* A day determined by the pontiffs *(pontifices)* when it was not a religious festival and when it was therefore permitted to initiate procedures at civil law (which could presumably continue on *dies nefasti*). There were approximately 40 (possibly 42 or 43) *dies fasti* in the year, and they were marked by the letter F in the official calendars, for *fas* or *fastus* (literally, "days of speaking," when the formal words might be spoken that were required to conduct legal business). Originally, the *dies fasti* included the *dies comitiales* (about 188 to 195 days), days on which the *comitia* might meet.
Reading: Hammond and Scullard (eds.) 1970, 341; York 1986.

Fates Roman deities of destiny who were known in Latin as *Fatae*, *Fata* or PARCAE.

Fatua A Roman oracular goddess who was sometimes identified with the Roman goddess FAUNA.

Like Fauna, Fatua was a female counterpart of the Roman god FAUNUS. The name *Fatua* means "speaker."
Reading: Hammond and Scullard (eds.) 1970, 432.

Fatuclus A Roman oracular god who was often identified with the Roman god FAUNUS. The name *Fatuclus* means "speaker."

Fatuus A Roman oracular god who was often identified with the Roman god FAUNUS. The name *Fatuus* means "speaker."

Fauna A Roman goddess of fertility. The counterpart of the Roman god FAUNUS, she was sometimes regarded as his sister, wife or daughter, and was identified with BONA DEA. Fauna was worshipped as a deity of women and a fortune-teller. She was sometimes identified with the Roman goddesses MAIA and FATUA (who was also considered to be a female counterpart of Faunus). According to legend, Fauna was a young Hyperborean girl. (Hyperboreans were a legendary race of Apollo worshippers who lived in the far north.) She bore Hercules's son Latinus, the eponymous hero of the Latins (a people who lived in Latium, an area around the lower part of the Tiber River in Italy). After HERCULES left her, she married Faunus. In another story, she was the wife of the Latin King Faunus, but Hercules fell in love with her, and she bore him a son, Latinus, who was destined to be a future king of the Latins.
Reading: Grimal 1986, 162.

Faunalia A festival of FAUNUS held on December 5. It was a rural feast with sacrifices, eating, drinking and dancing. It does not occur in any of the ancient calendars, but was mentioned by Horace (*Odes* 3:18).
Reading: Johns 1986, 95.

Fauns (Fig. 27) (Latin, *Fauni*) Roman deities who were thought to be half man and half goat and who usually had horns and goats' hooves. The Roman god FAUNUS was worshipped as a pastoral deity, and the idea evolved that there were many such Fauns who were the spirits of the woods and the countryside. They were identified with Greek satyrs.

Faunus (Fig. 28) A Roman pastoral god, primarily of the forests. A hunter and promoter of agriculture, he was equated with the Greek god PAN, although he did not share Pan's goat characteristics. Faunus was originally a local god of Latium in Italy, but evidence for his cult has been found as far afield as Thetford, England. He was identified with the Roman gods FATUUS and FATUCLUS (whose names both mean "speaker"), because he was an oracular god: he was associated with the strange noises in woodland and could reveal the future in dreams and voices in sacred groves. Faunus was sometimes also identified with the Roman god INUUS. He was worshipped at the LUPERCALIA, but also had a festival in Rome on February 13 and a more popular festival in the countryside around Rome on December 5. Faunus had a temple on the Tiber Island in Rome.

The identification of Faunus with Pan (who originated in Arcadia, Greece) led Faunus to be associated with the Arcadian king EVANDER, and thus gave

Fig. 27 A copy of a bronze statuette of a Faun in the House of the Faun, Pompeii, Italy.

Fig. 28 A bronze statuette of Faunus. He carries a drinking horn and a club, and wears a crown and a panther skin.

rise to legends about the immigration of Arcadians to the area of the Palatine Hill in Rome. According to some legends, Faunus was one of the first kings of Latium, reigning before the arrival of Aeneas and his Trojans, and thus before the foundation of Rome by Romulus. He was supposed to have succeeded King Picus, and to have been succeeded by his son Latinus. According to one story, Faunus was the son of JUPITER and Circe. He was described by Virgil as the husband of Marica. (See also FAUNS.)
Reading: Grimal 1986, 162; Hammond and Scullard (eds.) 1970, 432; Johns 1982, 48–50.

Faunus, temples of Most temples of FAUNUS were in rural settings, but Livy records one temple in Rome built on the Tiber Island. It was vowed by the plebeian aediles Gnaeus Domitius Ahenobarbus and Gaius Scribonius Libo. Its dedication date was 194 B.C., on February 13 (Ides), two days before the LUPERCALIA. There was a temple of Faunus at Tivoli, Italy, where INCUBATION was practiced; a sheep was killed and the person consulting the oracle slept in its skin.
Reading: Johns 1986, 95; Richardson 1992, 148.

Fausta Felicitas A Roman goddess of good fortune who had a festival on October 9. There was a shrine (or possibly just an altar) of Fausta Felicitas on the CAPITOLINE HILL in Rome.
Reading: Richardson 1992, 148.

favissa (or *favisa*, pl. *favissae*) Vaults or subterranean chambers beneath a sacred precinct, such as the AREA CAPITOLINA in Rome, which could not be altered. They were often used for storage of damaged or excess objects dedicated to a temple. Similarly, the word *favissa* was used for pits in which such sacred items were deposited.

Febris A Roman goddess who was the personification of fever. She was greatly feared in Rome and had to be propitiated to prevent or cure fever. It is not certain whether she was a goddess of specific fevers, although some dedications to her indicate that she was regarded as a goddess of malaria, which must have been prevalent in many parts of Italy. Dedications to her are known from various parts of the empire, and she had three temples in Rome: on the Palatine Hill, on the Esquline Hill and at the head of the Quirinal Valley (the upper part of the Vicus Longus). *Remedia* (possibly meaning "charms" or "amulets") that had proved effective were deposited in these temples.
Reading: Grimal 1986, 163; Hammond and Scullard (eds.) 1970, 433; Richardson 1992, 149–150.

Februus A Roman god who appears to have been regarded as a deity of purification. The month of February was said to be sacred to this deity. February was originally the last month in the Roman year and was the month when the city of Rome was purified by sacrifices to the dead. These rites were known as the Februalia, and it is possible that the god Februus was a personification of these rituals. He was later regarded as a god of the UNDER-

Fig. 29 A coin of Faustina II (who lived c. 135–175) depicts Fecunditas with a child on each arm and two others at her side. The legend is "Fecunditas Augustae." Faustina II was the wife of the emperor Marcus Aurelius and had 12 or 13 children.

Fig. 30 A bronze coin of Antoninus Pius, with Felicitas standing and holding a capricorn and a winged caduceus.

WORLD, thought by some to be of Etruscan origin, and he was identified with DIS.
Reading: Grimal 1986, 163.

Fecunditas Augusta (Fig. 29) (or Fecunditas Augustae) A Roman goddess who was the personification of the fecundity of Roman empresses. The cult of Fecunditas Augusta flourished for about a century, particularly during the reigns of the emperors Nero (54–68), Antoninus Pius (138–161) and Marcus Aurelius (161–180). The goddess is portrayed on the reverse of coins of several empresses, either standing with children in her arms and at her feet, or seated nursing a boy and accompanied by two girls. The latter is very similar to the portrayal of a DEA NUTRIX.
Reading: Rostovtzeff 1917–18, 208–209.

Felicitas (Fig. 30) A Roman goddess or personification of good luck. She was unknown before the mid-second century B.C., when a temple was dedicated to her in the Velabrum in Rome. Another temple in Rome was erected by Marcus Aemilius Lepidus. Felicitas played an important part in the state religion during the empire, and was frequently portrayed on coins.
Reading: Champeaux 1987, 216–236; Hammond and Scullard (eds.) 1970, 434.

Felicitas, temples of The first temple of this goddess in Rome was built in the Velabrum in the CAMPUS MARTIUS by Lucius Licinius Lucullus, using booty from his campaign in Spain in 151–150 B.C. It was destroyed by fire under Claudius and was never rebuilt. Another temple was planned by Julius Caesar and was built after his death by Marcus Aemilius Lepidus on the site of the Curia Hostilia in Rome (a building that had been restored by Sulla but demolished by Julius Caesar in 44 B.C. to make way for the new temple). The temple site probably lies under the church of Saints Luca and Martina. It no longer existed by the time of Hadrian.
Reading: Richardson 1992, 150.

Feralia The public festival of the dead (*di manes*), which was held on February 21, the last day of the PARENTALIA. Offerings of food were carried to tombs by each household for use by the dead. It was equivalent to All Souls Day. It is not known if there was a public ritual: it is marked *NP* (possibly for *nefasti publici*) in imperial calendars, but *F* for *fasti* (no festival) in the Fasti Antiates, a CALENDAR of c. 70 B.C.

Reading: Scullard 1981, 74, 75.

Ferentina A Roman water NYMPH who was the deity of the Ferentina River in Latium. She had a sacred grove, and people from the whole of the Latin confederacy worshipped at her shrine.

Reading: Grimal 1986, 165.

feriae The Latin word (always used in the plural) for a holiday or festival, when people visited temples and made sacrifices to gods. These were days when the Romans renewed their relationships with particular gods, requiring additional rituals to those normally practiced. Failure to celebrate a festival or to celebrate it absolutely correctly would cause the gods to cease being benevolent. There were, therefore, important public ceremonies conducted by state officials as well as private prayers and sacrifices. The public rites took place in the temple of the god being honored by the festival. Prayers, rituals and sacrifices were conducted by the priests outside the temple. Citizens might attend the ceremonies, but only as observers and not as participants. Although a plural word, *feriae* could refer to a festival that took place on a single day. All but two of the festivals marked on the known calendars were held on odd-numbered days because even-numbered days were considered unlucky. Odd numbers were generally considered lucky, and so by implication even dates were unlucky. The two exceptions were the REGIFUGIUM and one of the EQUIRRIA festivals. There were both public festivals *(feriae publicae)* and private ones *(feriae privatae)*. The former *(feriae publicae)* comprised *feriae stativae*, *feriae conceptivae* and *feriae imperativae*. Public festivals were originally literally "feast days" when the local aristocracy paid for a meal for their poorer fellow citizens. There were many festivals during the year, but not all were public festivals recognized by the state and celebrated by state priests. However, on public holidays, work and business (legal and political) were stopped to avoid polluting the sacred day. Some work (decided by the pontiff) was permitted, and it is likely that much work went on regardless of the festival. Only the pious visited temples, while others took a holiday. Roman citizens were legally required to observe the rules about working, but they were not obliged to perform acts of worship. Although festivals always had a religious aspect, no rigid distinction was made between religious and secular activities, and festivals were often occasions of merrymaking.

The large number of festivals obviously reduced the number of working days in the year, but only the Jews (who did not observe the festivals) had a regular "rest day" by observing the Sabbath; others did not have a "weekend," and so the number of working days lost through observance of festivals was not great.

It is not clear how many festivals were celebrated outside Italy or outside Rome itself. There is little evidence for the worship of some gods, such as VEDIOVIS, outside of Rome, and none outside of Italy, so that celebration of these gods' festivals was probably geographically limited. It is likely, though, that major festivals such as the SATURNALIA were celebrated in many parts of the empire. In Rome at least, some gods and goddesses had several festival days during the year. With the rise of Christianity, many festivals were converted to the Christian calendar. For example, Caristia (February 22) was converted to the Feast of St. Peter, and LUPERCALIA (February 15) was converted to the Feast of the Purification of the Virgin Mary. Perhaps the most significant of such conversions was that of the birthday of the sun god SOL (December 25) to the birthday of Christ.

Reading: Ferguson 1988b, 913–921; Scullard 1981; Warde Fowler 1899; York 1986.

feriae conceptivae A moveable public festival or feast, rather than one with a fixed date; these festivals were therefore not recorded on the calendars. The dates for these festivals were set annually by magistrates or priests. One example was the FERIAE LATINAE.

Reading: York 1986.

feriae denicales A day sacred to the spirits of the dead. On such days, it was prohibited to irrigate fields and yoke mules.

feriae imperativae An irregular public holiday. These holidays were proclaimed by consuls, praetors or dictators for such purposes as celebrating a victory.

Reading: York 1986.

Feriae Latinae A moveable festival (*feriae conceptivae*) to honor JUPITER LATIARIS in his role as god of the Latin League. It was a joint festival of Romans and Latins at his temple on the Alban Mount, 13 miles (29.92 km) southeast of Rome. The festival was usually held at the end of April on days set by the incoming consuls at the beginning of the year. The festival dates from the time when Alba Longa, not Rome, was the chief city of Latium, but the festival survived to the end of the fourth century. JUPITER may have originally been worshipped in the festival at an altar, but from the sixth century B.C. onward he received a temple. A libation of milk was offered, and the surrounding cities brought other agricultural produce. Little puppets in the shape of humans *(oscilla)* were suspended in trees (as at the SEMENTIVAE), possibly as a substitute for earlier human sacrifice, or even simply to act as charms against evil influences. A white heifer that had never known the yoke was sacrificed and eaten in a communal meal by representatives from all the cities in the Latin League.

In the late republic this festival became increasingly important. It was still held on the Alban Mount, with the consuls being accompanied by the senior magistrates. The festival lasted one day, but it had to be repeated if there was a flaw in the proceedings. After the festival, there were two days of games (*LUDI*). This festival must have played a significant role in the people's lives, as it endured for more than 1,000 years. It was possibly suppressed by Theodosius.

Reading: Scullard 1981, 111–115; Weinstock 1971, 320–325.

feriae privatae A private festival for such events as birthdays.

feriae publicae A public festival of which there were three groups: *FERIAE STATIVAE*, *FERIAE CONCEPTIVAE* and *FERIAE IMPERATIVAE*.

Reading: York 1986, 1.

feriae stativae An annual public festival on a fixed date; these festivals were recorded in the official CALENDAR. Most occurred after the period of the waning moon (after the Ides).

Reading: York 1986, 1–3.

feriale duranum A unique papyrus from Dura-Europus, Syria, which is the most important source of information about religious practices in the Roman army. It is a CALENDAR related to one religious year of one military unit, probably dating to around 225–227. It lists various ceremonies connected with the imperial cult, those festivals of military significance and *feriae publicae*. The festivals and ceremonies probably took place in many or all military units throughout the Roman world.

Reading: Haynes 1993.

Feronia A Roman goddess of spring flowers and woods. Her cult was quite widespread in central Italy, but the main center of the cult was a town called Lucus Feroniae in Etruria. She had a grove, and later a temple, in the CAMPUS MARTIUS in Rome (built in the third century B.C.). She also had a temple at Terracina, Italy, where slaves could seek sanctuary at the altar (a Greek rather than a Roman custom), and an inscription at this temple implies that slaves were freed there. There is also evidence that her cult in Rome was linked to slaves and freedmen, and that she was sometimes identified with LIBERTAS. She was associated with FLORA and had a festival on November 13.

Reading: Hammond and Scullard (eds.) 1970, 434; Scullard 1981, 197–198.

festival (*dies festus*, pl. *dies festi*) A "festive day," a holiday in honor of a god or a feast day or other celebration. The various public games (*LUDI*) were regarded as *dies festi* (not *feriae*), and most were controlled by magistrates. *FERIAE* were a second type of festival, not only a religious festival but a holy day where no work took place; they often incorporated *ludi* in their celebrations and were under the control of priests.

festivals, Greek In the Greek provinces there were many festivals organized by the cities on regular cycles. These continued after the Roman conquest, and many became associated with the IMPERIAL CULT. There were also regular annual celebrations in cities. Examples included the ROMAIA, Sebasteia, Caesarea and Hadrianea, which were each generally held every four years.

Reading: Price 1984, 101–114, 126–132.

fetialis (pl. *fetiales*) A priest who represented Rome in diplomacy with other nations, and was involved in making treaties. The *fetiales* formed a

college *(collegium)* of 20 male priests, coopted for life from patricians and possibly later from plebeians as well. The college is believed to have been founded by one of the kings. The *fetiales* were particularly concerned with the rituals involved in declaring war and ensuring that the war was just. Livy is the main source of information about their rituals. For example, to declare war, a *fetialis* hurled a spear across the Roman boundary into enemy territory in the presence of three or more adults. To declare war on a distant nation, a *fetialis* hurled the spear into a special area in the temple of BELLONA that represented the enemy territory. A treaty was solemnized by a priest pronouncing a curse on Rome should it be the first to break the treaty, and this ritual was confirmed by the priest killing a pig with a flint instrument (*lapis silex*). The *fetiales*'s ritual implements were kept in the temple of JUPITER FERETRIUS in Rome. This college of priests may have lapsed by the end of the republic, but it was revived during Augustus's reign.
Reading: Hammond and Scullard (eds.) 1970, 435–436; Porte 1989, 93–102; Scullard 1981, 30–31.

Fides A Roman goddess who was the personification of good faith. She particularly presided over verbal contracts. Her cult was thought to be very ancient, dating to the time of King Numa. She was portrayed as an old woman with white hair and was regarded as being older than JUPITER. She had a pair of covered hands as a symbol, and anyone offering her a sacrifice had to do so with their right hand covered with a white cloth. She had a temple on the CAPITOLINE HILL in Rome (Fig. 15), and her festival was on October 1. Livy records that on this day the *flamines* rode to her temple in a hooded carriage drawn by two horses and offered sacrifices. Since no *FLAMEN* was assigned to this goddess, it may have been that priests other than *flamines* performed this ritual.
Reading: Freyburger 1986; Grimal 1986, 165; Hammond and Scullard (eds.) 1970, 436; Scullard 1981, 189–190.

Fides, temple of Also called the temple of Fides Publica and the temple of Fides Publica Populi Romani. It was built by Aulus Atilius Calatinus and was dedicated by him on October 1, 254 B.C. It stood on the CAPITOLINE HILL in Rome (Fig. 15), probably within the AREA CAPITOLINA, near the temple of JUPITER OPTIMUS MAXIMUS. It was occasionally used by the Senate for meetings, and became a repository of laws and treaties inscribed on bronze tablets, which were placed on the walls. It was restored by Marcus Aemilius Scaurus around 58 B.C.
Reading: Freyburger 1986, 259–273; Mellor 1975, 131–132; Richardson 1992, 151; Scullard 1981, 189–190.

figurine (Figs. 31, 42, 61, 67, 69) A small statuette of a deity, usually presented as a VOTIVE OFFERING. In the Roman period, figurines were made of metal (particularly bronze) and of fired clay. Many were probably made of wood, but few wooden figurines have survived. They rarely had inscriptions. Fired clay (terracotta or ceramic) figurines were very popular in Hellenistic times, and this figurine manufacturing industry continued in workshops across the Roman world. The terracotta or fired clay figurines were made in molds. Many followed Hellenistic patterns, but were often of goddesses associated with local cults. From the early second century, figurine production became important in the Allier valley of central Gaul and then in the Rhineland; figurines were made in a white clay (pipeclay) and were widely exported, particularly so-called Venus figurines and figurines of mother goddesses. Figurines were largely used for votive offerings and cult images in temples and in household shrines. The terracotta industry declined from the fourth century, possibly because of the increasing influence of CHRISTIANITY. (See also VENUS.)
Reading: Jenkins 1978.

Fimmilena One of the ALAISIAGAE Germanic goddesses who was named in an inscription found at Housesteads on Hadrian's Wall, England.

Firmicus Maternus Julius Firmicus Maternus, fourth century, from Syracuse. A writer on astrology and theology. In 334–337 he wrote a treatise on ASTROLOGY in eight books *(Mathesis)*. He was later converted to Christianity, and wrote *De Errore Profanorum Religionum (On the Error of Profane Religions)* c. 343–350, which has survived incomplete. In it, he urged Constantius and Constans to eradicate PAGANISM.
Reading: Hammond and Scullard (eds.) 1970, 439.

flamen (Figs. 6, 32) (pl. *flamines;* literally "priest" or "sacrificer") A priest appointed in charge of a

Fig. 31 A bronze figurine of Mercury found at Lamyatt Beacon, England. He wears a winged hat and shoes, and a cloak (chlamys). *He holds a money bag in his right hand; it is believed that his left hand held a* caduceus *(now missing). Height 4.25 in. (108 mm). Courtesy of Somerset County Museums Service.*

particular cult in Rome. At any time, there were 15 *flamines* in the republic, assigned to the cults of at least 13 gods: CARMENTIS, CERES, FALACER, FLORA, FURRINA, JUPITER, MARS, PALATUA, POMONA, PORTUNUS, QUIRINUS, VOLTURNUS and Volcanus (VULCAN). Many of the deities they served were obscure, suggesting that the priests had a pre-republican origin. Some *flamines* occasionally participated in the worship of other gods. The *flamines* were part of the *collegium pontificum* (college of pontiffs) under the authority of the *PONTIFEX MAXIMUS*.

Fig. 32 Drawing of a flamen *wearing the* toga praetexta *and the distinctive* apex.

The three major *flamines* (*flamines maiores*, the most ancient and most dignified) were patricians, and consisted of the *FLAMEN DIALIS*, *FLAMEN MARTIALIS* and *FLAMEN QUIRINALIS*. Lesser in status were the 12 minor *flamines* (*flamines minores*). They were plebeians who served individual deities. Only 10 are known: *flamen Carmentalis*, *Cerialis*, *Falacer*, *Floralis*, *Fur[r]inalis*, *Palatualis*, *Pomonalis*, *Portunalis*, *Volcanalis* and *Volturnalis*. Their duration of office and method of selection are unknown.

The characteristic dress of all *flamines* was the special priestly hat known as an *APEX* (Fig. 6), a thick woollen cloak (*laena*) and a laurel wreath. Municipal towns also had *flamines*. With the deification of Julius Caesar and subsequent emperors, *flamines* were also appointed in Rome and in the provinces to attend to their worship.

Reading: Beard and North (eds.) 1990; Scullard 1981, 28–29; Vanggaard 1988.

flamen Augustalis A special *FLAMEN* appointed to serve the cult of Divus Augustus (deified Augustus). This priesthood continued to the beginning of the third century. The first holder of the office (appointed for life) was Germanicus. The relationship of the priesthood to the *sodales Augustales* is not known. (See also *AUGUSTALES*.)

Reading: Fishwick 1987, 161–162, 164–167; Vanggaard 1988.

flamen Dialis A major single *FLAMEN* who served the cult of JUPITER, including participation at the Vinalia festivals and at *CONFARREATIO* ceremonies. His house was on the Palatine Hill in Rome. This priest was subject to a large number of taboos (for example, he was forbidden to see an army with its weapons) to avoid polluting his holy person, so a normal senatorial career was impossible. A patrician, he was born of parents married by *confarreatio*, and was chosen for life by the *PONTIFEX MAXIMUS*, only losing the post if a major ritual fault was committed or if his wife died. The office was revived by Augustus in 11 B.C.

Reading: Beard and North (eds.) 1990; Porte 1989, 83–85; Vanggaard 1988.

flamen Divorum A priest who served the collective cult of the *divi* (deified emperors and members of family) at the temple of DIVORUM (Templum Divorum) on the Palatine Hill in Rome. These priests (*flamines Divorum*) appear in Rome during the second century but are not attested in any record after the beginning of the third century.

Reading: Fishwick 1987, 327.

flamen Martialis A major sole *FLAMEN* who served the cult of MARS and sacrificed a horse at the October horse festival on October 15. He was a patrician born of parents married by *CONFARREATIO* and was chosen by the *PONTIFEX MAXIMUS* for life, resigning if a major ritual fault was committed.

Reading: Beard and North (eds.) 1990; Vanggaard 1988.

flamen Quirinalis A major sole *FLAMEN* who served the cult of QUIRINUS and undertook sacrifices to CONSUS and sacrifices at the ROBIGALIA and LARENTALIA. He was a patrician born of parents married by *confarreatio* and was chosen by the *pontifex maximus* for life, resigning if a major ritual fault was committed.

Reading: Beard and North (eds.) 1990; Vanggaard 1988.

flaminica Dialis Wife of the *FLAMEN DIALIS* who retained office until the death of her husband. The office was pre-republican in origin, and was subject to the same taboos as the *flamen Dialis*. She wore distinctive dress, assisted with ritual duties and regularly undertook a sacrifice of a ram to JUPITER.

Reading: Beard and North (eds.) 1990; Vanggaard 1988.

Flanona The native patron goddess of the city of Flanona (modern Plomin) in the Roman province of Dalmatia who was worshipped in the area of Istria within Dalmatia. She was identified with the Roman goddess MINERVA as MINERVA FLANATICA.

Reading: Wilkes 1969, 195.

Flora A Roman goddess of flowers and the spring. Her cult was widespread in Italy at an early date and she was worshipped by both Latin and non-Latin races. There was a month dedicated to her in the Sabine calendar, which was equivalent to April in the Roman CALENDAR. Originally Flora was the deity that made trees blossom (without which there would be no fruit), but she came to preside over everything that blooms. She had a temple in Rome on the Aventine Hill (built on advice from the SIBYLLINE BOOKS) and another temple on the

northwestern slope of the Quirinal Hill. She had her own *FLAMEN*, the *flamen Floralis*, and her festival was the FLORALIA. There was another festival of Flora on August 13. The poet OVID linked a Greek myth to Flora, identifying her with a NYMPH called Chloris.
Reading: Grimal 1986, 165; Hammond and Scullard (eds.) 1970, 442; Scullard 1981, 110–111.

Flora, temples of In a drought of 241 or 238 B.C., the Romans were advised, on consultation of the SIBYLLINE BOOKS, to build a temple to FLORA in Rome. It was built by the aediles Lucius and Marcus Publicius Malleolus. Its dedication day was April 28, and it was situated on the lower slopes of the Aventine Hill near the Circus Maximus. Restoration was begun by Augustus and finished by Tiberius in A.D. 17. It was probably restored in the 4th century by the younger Symmachus when he was consul, and the temple seems to have been a focus of gatherings of barbers. Another temple on the northwestern slope of the Quirinal Hill was possibly on the site of an altar believed to have been dedicated to her by King Tatius.
Reading: Richardson 1992, 152; Scullard 1981, 110.

Florae Referred to in the Venusine calendar for May 3. It was possibly the last day of the games of the FLORALIA, linked to Flora's temple near the CIRCUS MAXIMUS, or more likely a ceremony at Flora's other temple on the Quirinal Hill.
Reading: Scullard 1981, 118.

Floralia The agricultural festival of FLORA was originally moveable *(FERIAE CONCEPTIVAE)* but later took place on April 27 (April 28 in the Julian CALENDAR), the dedication date of her temple on the Aventine Hill. The festival was to ensure that the crops blossomed well, so that the harvest would be good. The games (Ludi Florales) within the Floralia were not held annually until 173 B.C., following a period of damage to crops. They were the responsibility of the plebeian aediles. Under the empire, games continued for six days to May 3, and began with theatrical performances and ended with circus games and a sacrifice to Flora. In the circus performances, hares and goats were let loose, and vetches, beans and lupins were scattered among the spectators, all for reasons of fertility. Part of the celebrations were nocturnal. Multicolored clothes were customary. The Floralia also came to be regarded by prostitutes as their feast. The games drew crowds of commoners and prostitutes and were more licentious than the SATURNALIA.
Reading: Scullard 1981, 110–111.

Flora Mater ("Flora the Mother") An aspect of the Roman goddess FLORA.

Flora Rustica ("Flora of the Countryside") An aspect of the Roman goddess FLORA.
Reading: Scullard 1981, 110.

Fons A Roman god of springs who was also known as Fontus. He was thought to be the son of the Roman god JANUS. Fons had a temple in Rome, possibly near a gate called Porta Fontinalis in the Servian Wall, north of the CAPITOLINE HILL. However, the Porta Fontinalis appears to have taken its name from a nearby spring rather than from the temple. There was also an altar of Fons at the foot of the Janiculum Hill. His festival was the FONTINALIA.
Reading: Grimal 1986, 165; Richardson 1992, 152–153.

Fontinalia Festival of the god FONS, which took place on October 13. In honor of this god of springs, garlands were thrown into springs and placed around the tops of wells. (See also SPRINGS, SACRED.)
Reading: Scullard 1981, 192.

Fontus An alternative name for the Roman god FONS.

footprints Representations of feet and footprints are found in a variety of contexts throughout the Mediterranean, especially North Africa and Egypt. They occur, for example, in mosaics and on stone slabs (some dedicated to one or more deities), occasionally with two pairs of feet. Some have been found in sanctuaries. These footprints may represent the epiphany of the deity or else the worshipper. They obviously have a sacred or ritual function. Representations of feet, especially footwear, occur in secular contexts, and their function in these cases is less clear. Footwear was often placed in graves next to the INHUMATION or CREMATION, possibly to assist the journey of the deceased in the UNDERWORLD.
Reading: Dunbabin 1990.

Forculus A Roman god who presided over the doors themselves, as distinct from their hinges, which were the province of the Roman goddess CARDEA. The opening and closing of a door were functions of deities, and all aspects were carefully defined.
Reading: Ogilvie 1969, 11.

Fordicidia An agricultural festival of TELLUS held in Rome on April 15. A pregnant cow (*forda* or *horda*) was sacrificed to Tellus in each of the 30 wards (*curiae*) of Rome and one on the CAPITOLINE HILL to promote fertility of cattle and the fields. The unborn calves were burnt and the ashes were used by the VESTAL VIRGINS in a purification rite in the festival of PARILIA. Apart from the FORNACALIA, it was the only festival in Rome to be organized on the basis of *curiae*.
Reading: Scullard 1981, 102.

Fornacalia A moveable festival (*FERIAE CONCEPTIVAE*) which must have started around February 5 but was celebrated no later than February 17 (QUIRINALIA). It was held in Rome on a day appointed by the leaders of the wards *(curiae)* and ended on February 17. It appears to have been celebrated to benefit the *fornaces* (ovens used for parching grain).
Reading: Hammond and Scullard (eds.) 1970, 444.

Fornax The Roman goddess who was invoked to prevent grain being burnt in grain-drying ovens (Latin, *fornaces*). She appears to have been invented to help explain the festival of FORNACALIA.
Reading: Grimal 1986, 165; Hammond and Scullard (eds.) 1970, 444.

Fors ("the Bringer") An ancient Roman goddess, possibly of providence, who was equated with the Roman goddess FORTUNA. Possibly originally a pair of deities, their names became linked as "Fors Fortuna," a phrase which eventually came to be regarded as the name of a single deity, the goddess FORS FORTUNA.
Reading: Hammond and Scullard (eds.) 1970, 445.

Fors Fortuna A conflation of the Roman goddesses FORS and FORTUNA. In Rome there were three

Fig. 33a Reconstruction of the temple of Fortuna Augusta in Pompeii, Italy. A fire burns on top of the altar in front of the temple steps. From W. Gell, Pompeiana *(1832).*

temples to Fors Fortuna across the Tiber River from the city, and a fourth was later dedicated in the Gardens of Julius Caesar, near the Tiber, in A.D. 17. There was a festival of Fors Fortuna on June 24.
Reading: Richardson 1992, 154–155; Scullard 1981, 155–156.

Fortuna Also known as FORS FORTUNA, this Roman deity was probably originally a fertility goddess. She came to be identified with the Greek goddess TYCHE, and so was regarded more generally as a goddess of fate, chance and luck. She was sometimes identified with NORTIA, an Etruscan goddess of fortune. Fortuna's main symbol is the wheel, on which she is portrayed as standing, implying instability. She was sometimes portrayed with a cornucopia and a rudder, the latter symbolizing her steering the destiny of people. She was sometimes portrayed standing, and sometimes seated, but often she was portrayed as blind. She had a festival on May 25. There was an important center of the cult of FORTUNA PRIMIGENIA at Praeneste, Italy. There was a temple of Fortuna in the FORUM BOARIUM in Rome, and possibly two others whose locations are unknown. There also appear to have been a great number of shrines dedicated to Fortuna in Rome. In his new city of Constantinople, the emperor Constantine built a temple to Fortuna. (See also FORS.)
Reading: Champeaux 1987; Hammond and Scullard (eds.) 1970, 445; Scullard 1981, 10; Simon 1990, 59–71.

Fortuna, temple of A temple situated in the Area Sacra di Sant' Omobono on a ridge between the FORUM BOARIUM and FORUM ROMANUM in Rome (Fig. 15). It formed a pair with that of MATER MATUTA, with whom it shared the same dedication day (June 11). In front of each temple was an archaic U-shaped altar. An archaic statue in the temple, apparently of gilded wood, may have been of Servius Tullius, who dedicated the temple, or it may have been of Fortuna. The temple was burned in the fire of 213 B.C. It was restored in 212 B.C.
Reading: Richardson 1992, 35–37, 155; Scullard 1981, 150–152.

Fortuna Augusta (Figs. 33a, b) An aspect of the goddess FORTUNA, referring to the fortune or

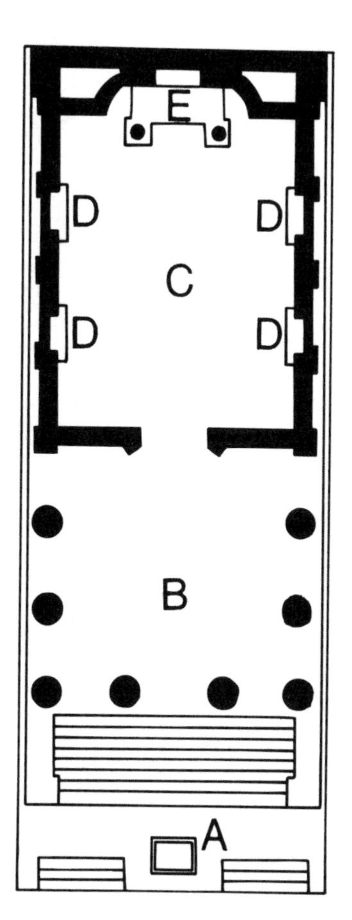

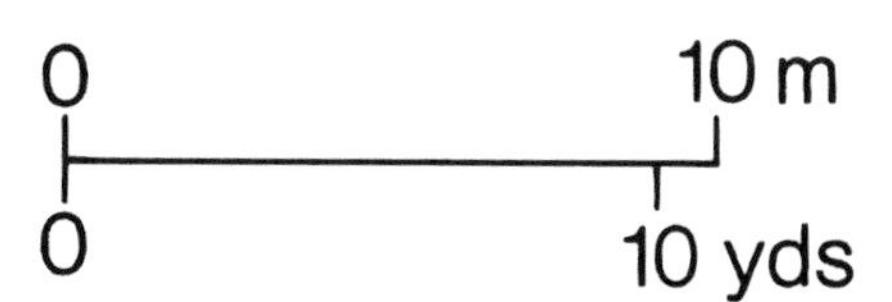

Fig. 33b Plan of the temple of Fortuna Augusta in Pompeii, Italy. It was a prostyle, tetrastyle temple with a deep pronaos. It was built by Marcus Tullius on his own land and at his own expense, and was dedicated in A.D. 3 or 4. It was situated at the intersection of the Via della Fortuna and the Via del Foro. The cult at this temple was closely associated with that of the genius *of the emperor. A = altar; B = pronaos; C = cella; D = niches for statues; E = cult statue.*

luck of the emperor. Several altars are known to have been dedicated to this deity.

Fortuna Balnearis ("Fortuna of the Baths") Dedications to this aspect of the Roman goddess Fortuna are often found in military bathhouses in frontier areas. In these bathhouses, dedications to other aspects of the goddess, such as Fortuna Salutaris ("Fortuna of health and well-being") and FORTUNA REDUX ("Fortuna the home-bringer"), are also found. This probably reflects the personal preoccupations of troops serving in a foreign land (such as health, well-being and returning home safely), and it is likely that Fortuna Balnearis also presided over these aspects of life. There are two dedications to this Roman goddess from Duratón and Gigón, Spain. These dedications probably come from specific bathhouses in the areas where they were found.
Reading: Knapp 1992, 269–270; Phillips 1977, 61 (under *Altar to Fortuna Redux*).

Fortuna Conservatrix (Fig. 34) ("Fortuna the Preserver" or "Fortuna Who Protects") There was an altar dedicated to this aspect of the Roman goddess Fortuna at the fort of Chesters on Hadrian's Wall, England.

Fig. 34 Altar dedicated to Fortuna Conservatrix. It was found at Chesters, on Hadrian's Wall, England. The inscription is: D[E]AE FORT[VNAE] CONSERVATRICI VENENVS GERM[ANVS] L[IBNTER] M[ERITO] ("Venenus, a German, willingly and deservedly set this up to the goddess Fortuna Conservatrix"). Height 2 ft 7 in. (0.78 m).

Fortuna Equestris An aspect of the Roman goddess FORTUNA whose name means "Fortune of the *equites*" (equestrian class, knights). There was a temple of Fortuna Equestris, vowed by Quintus Fulvius Flaccus in 180 B.C. during his campaign in Spain. It was situated near Pompey's theater in Rome, in the CIRCUS FLAMINIUS, and dedicated on August 13, 173 B.C. By A.D. 22 it no longer survived, possibly destroyed in the fire of 21. There was a festival of Fortuna Equestris on August 13.
Reading: Champeaux 1987, 132–154; Richardson 1992, 155–156.

Fortuna Huiusce Diei An aspect of the Roman goddess FORTUNA whose name means "Fortune of the Day" (i.e., "the present day" rather than "daytime"). Also known as Fortuna Huiusque, she was a goddess of fate, chance and luck. She had a temple in the CAMPUS MARTIUS in Rome, and there may also have been a shrine on the Palatine Hill. There was a festival of Fortuna Huiusque Diei on July 30.

Reading: Champeaux 1987, 154–170; Scullard 1981, 169.

Fortuna Huiusce Diei, temple of A temple vowed by Quintus Lutatius Catulus at the battle of Vercellae in 101 B.C. It has been identified as the round Temple B of the Area Sacra di Largo Argentina temples in the CAMPUS MARTIUS in Rome.
Reading: Champeaux 1987, 154–170; Patterson 1992, 196; Richardson 1992, 35, 156.

Fortuna Mala ("Fortune with a Beard") An altar was dedicated to this aspect of the Roman goddess FORTUNA on the Esquiline Hill in Rome.
Reading: Richardson 1992, 156.

Fortuna Muliebris ("Fortune of Women") An aspect of the Roman goddess FORTUNA who had a temple about 4 miles (6.43 km) outside Rome on the Via Latina.
Reading: Champeaux 1982, 335–373; Scullard 1981, 160–161.

Fortuna Obsequens ("Indulgent Fortune") An aspect of the Roman goddess FORTUNA who had a shrine located near the Vicus Fortunae Obsequens in Rome; it may have been on the western slope of the Caelian Hill.
Reading: Richardson 1992, 156.

Fortuna Primigenia An aspect of the Roman goddess FORTUNA whose name means "Fortune the Firstborn," probably referring to the cult of Fortuna at Praeneste and so meaning the "Original" or "First" Fortuna. There was a temple dedicated to this goddess on the Quirinal Hill in Rome, and she had a festival on November 13.
Reading: Champeaux 1982, 3–147; Richardson 1992, 156.

Fortuna Primigenia, sanctuary of (Fig. 35) A great center of the worship of FORTUNA at Praeneste (Palestrina), in Latium, Italy. It was originally a Latin sanctuary and was rebuilt on a large scale in the late republic. Praeneste was sacked during the civil wars between Sulla and the followers of Marius, but was then refounded as a veteran colony in 82/81 B.C. The complex may date to this period or may possibly date to the second half of the second century B.C. On the hillside behind the older temple were elaborate terraces on seven levels connected by ramps and staircases, and with colonnades alongside rows of vaulted rooms. At the top of the symmetrical layout was a theater, behind which was a circular temple. There was an oracular shrine here as well, which was widely consulted. This ORACLE had answers inscribed on oak tablets which were selected at random, with interpretation of the answer being left to the person consulting the oracle.
Reading: Barton 1989, 73–75; Champeaux 1982, 3–24; Scullard 1981, 100.

Fortuna Privata This aspect of the Roman goddess Fortuna was "Fortune of the Private Individual," in contrast to FORTUNA PUBLICA. She had a temple on the Palatine Hill in Rome.
Reading: Richardson 1992, 156–157.

Fortuna Publica ("Luck of the People") An aspect of the Roman goddess FORTUNA who had a festival on April 5. There were three temples of Fortuna on the Quirinal Hill in Rome, in an area that became known as "the Three Fortunes." One was dedicated to Fortuna Primigenia, and was also given the title Fortuna Publica Populi Romani ("Luck of the Roman People"); the second temple was dedicated to Fortuna Publica Citerior (*Citerior* probably meaning "nearer the center of the city"); little is known of the third temple, but it is possible that all three were dedicated to Fortuna Publica. An altar dedicated to Fortuna Populi Romani ("Fortune of the Roman people") is known from Chesterholm fort on Hadrian's Wall, England.
Reading: Coulston and Phillips 1988, 6; Richardson 1992, 158; Scullard 1981, 100.

Fortuna Redux (Fig. 36) ("Fortune the homebringer") The earliest evidence for the worship of this aspect of the Roman goddess FORTUNA is the dedication of an altar to her in Rome by the Senate in gratitude for the safe return of the emperor Augustus to Rome in 19 B.C. A temple to this goddess was built in the CAMPUS MARTIUS in Rome by the emperor Domitian to celebrate his triumphs in Germany. Altars dedicated to this goddess are known from several military bathhouses in the area of Hadrian's Wall, England.
Reading: Phillips 1977, 60–61.

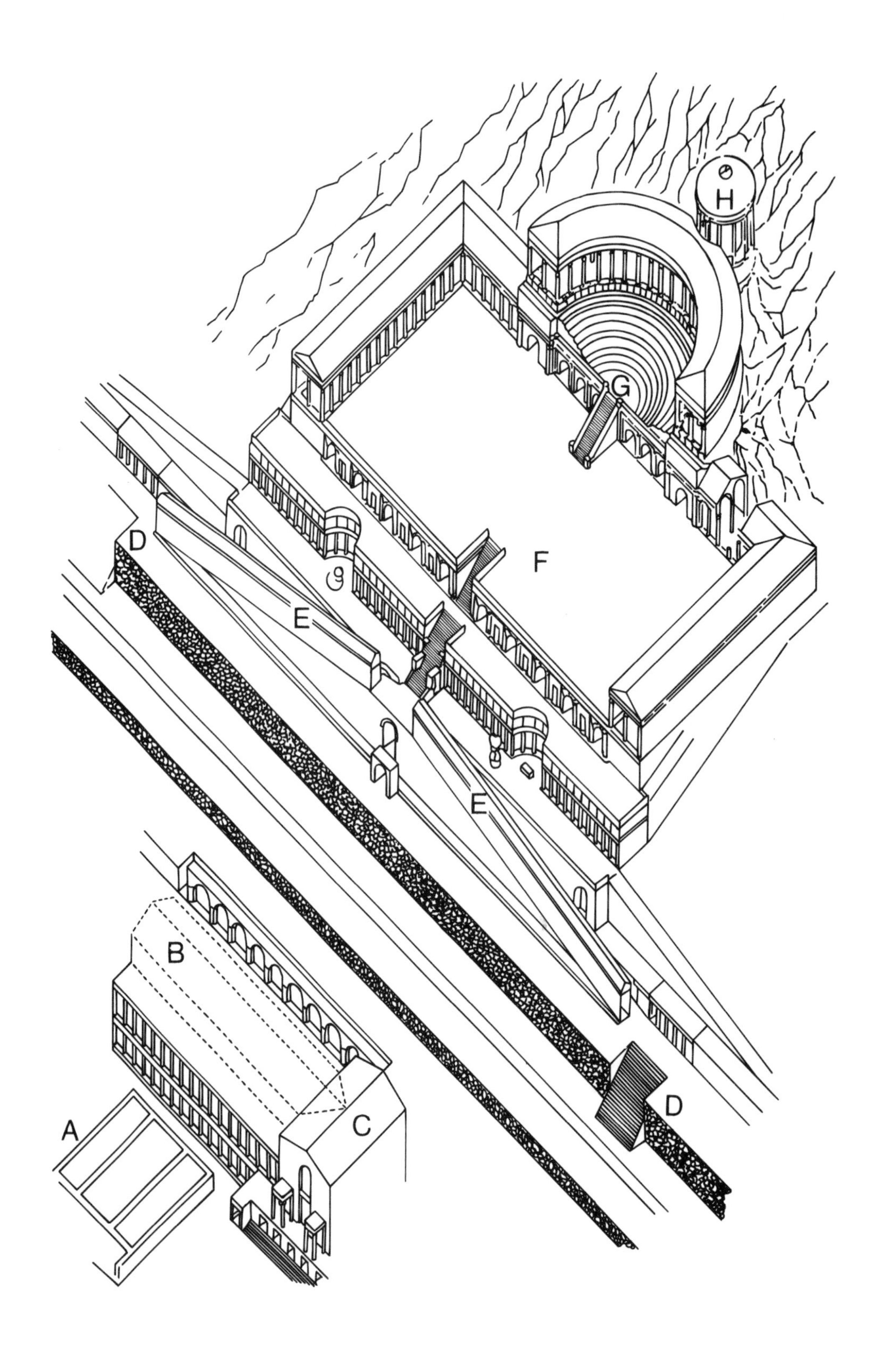

H
G
F
D
E
g
E
B
A
C
D

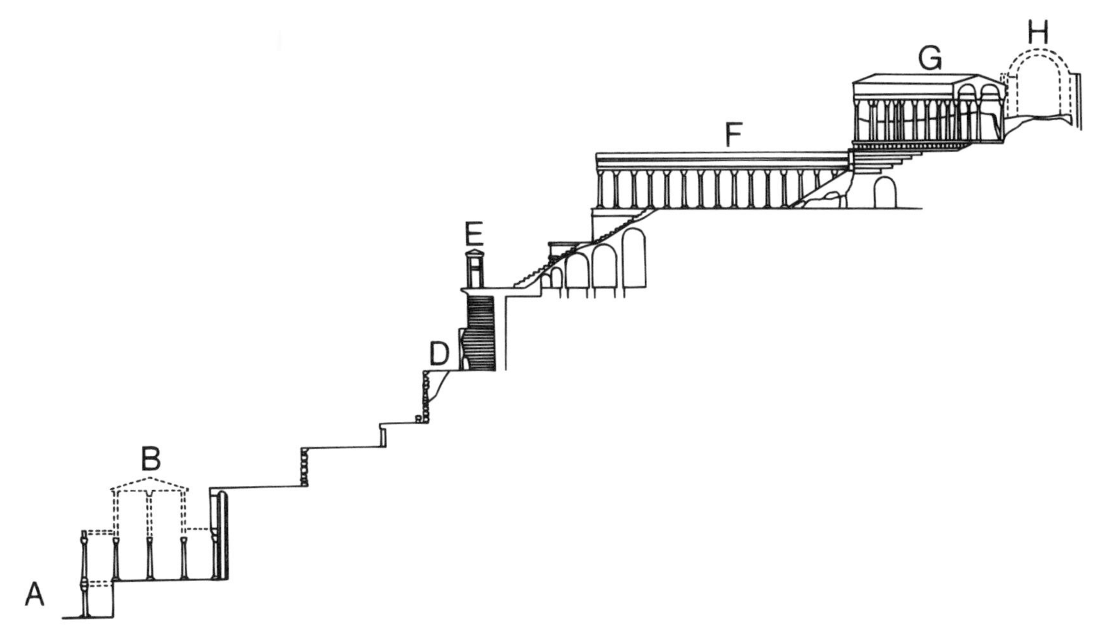

Figs. 35 a (left) and b (above) View (a) and section (b) of the sanctuary of Fortuna Primigenia at Praeneste. A = forum of town; B = basilica; C = curia; D = wall of sanctuary; E = ramps; F = courtyard; G = theater; H = temple of Fortuna.

Fig. 36 Fortuna Redux is normally shown seated on coins of Vespasian and Domitian. Here she has a cornucopia and a rudder.

Fortuna Redux, altar of (in Latin, *Ara Fortunae Reducis*) This altar to FORTUNA REDUX was constituted in Rome on October 12, 19 B.C. and dedicated on December 15, 19 B.C., probably to celebrate the return of Augustus to Rome from the east. It was probably sited in the precinct of the temple of HONOS AND VIRTUS near the Porta Capena.
Reading: Fishwick 1972, 171–176; Fishwick 1987, 203–209; Richardson 1992, 157.

Fortuna Respiciens ("Provident Fortune") An aspect of the Roman goddess FORTUNA who had a temple on the Esquiline Hill and a shrine on the Palatine Hill in Rome.
Reading: Richardson 1992, 157.

Fortuna Romana ("the Luck of Rome") An aspect of the Roman goddess FORTUNA who was a patron deity of the city of Rome. In Constantinople, the emperor Constantine built a temple to Fortuna in which he set up a statue of Fortuna Romana. Fortuna was the Roman equivalent of the Greek goddess TYCHE, and the adoption of Tyche as a patron in eastern cities is paralleled by the worship of Fortuna Romana in Rome.

Fortuna Virgo ("Fortune the Virgin") At their marriage, girls dedicated their robes to this aspect of the Roman goddess FORTUNA. She had a temple in Rome and a festival on June 11.

Fortuna Virilis An aspect of the Roman goddess FORTUNA who was worshipped during the VENERALIA. She had a shrine near an altar of VENUS and a temple, both in Rome.
Reading: Champeaux 1982, 375–409; Scullard 1981, 96–97.

Forum Boarium (or Forum Bovarium) An area of low ground in Rome between the Tiber River, CAPITOLINE HILL, Aventine Hill and Palatine Hill. It was literally a cattle market, though it may never have been used as such in Rome. It was the site of the early cult of HERCULES INVICTUS at the ARA MAXIMA, around which were erected temples and dedications to HERCULES. Also in this area were other temples, including those of FORTUNA, MATER MATUTA and PORTUNUS, and a shrine of CARMENTIS. Human sacrifice was practiced here on occasion.
Reading: Nash 1962a, 411; Richardson 1992, 162–164.

Forum Holitorium (Literally "a vegetable market") This was an area outside the Porta Carmentalis in Rome. There were four temples, devoted to JANUS, SPES, JUNO SOSPITA and PIETAS. The last three are believed to be incorporated in the fabric of the church of San Nicola in Carcere (Fig. 15).
Reading: Richardson 1992, 164–165.

Forum Romanum (Fig. 37) (or Forum Magnum) Originally the marketplace in Rome, it evolved into the business, political and ceremonial center of the city. It became increasingly built up,

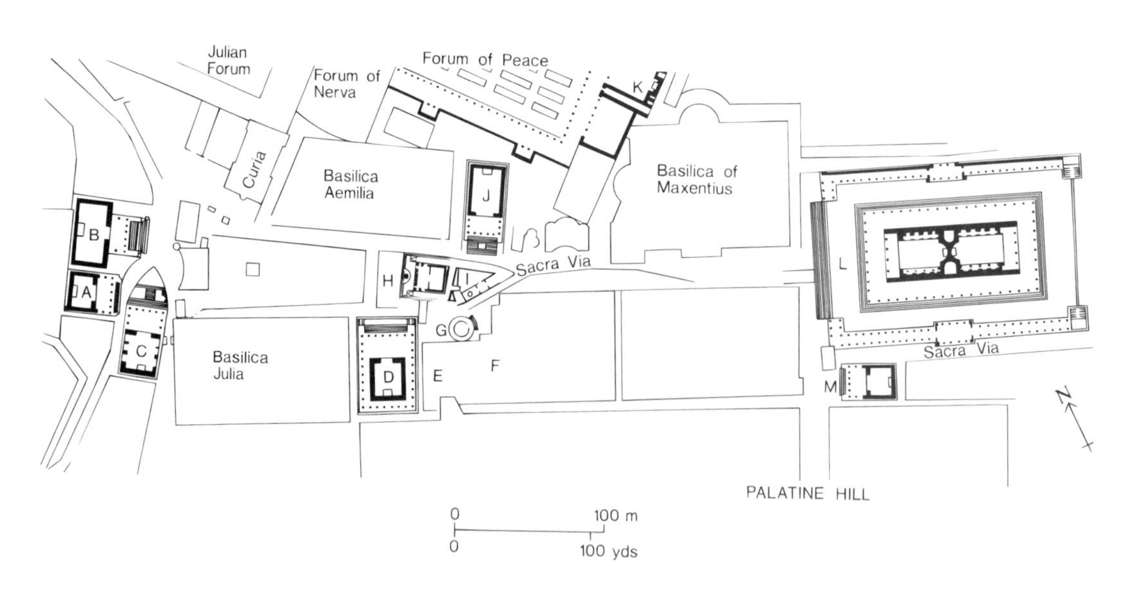

Fig. 37 Multi-period plan of the Forum Romanum and surrounding area in Rome, identifying the major religious sites. A = temple of Vespasian; B = temple of Concordia; C = temple of Saturn; D = temple of Castor; E = site of Lacus Iuturnae; F = site of atrium Vestae; G = temple of Vesta; H = temple of Divus Julius; I = Regia; J = temple of Antoninus Pius and Faustina; K = temple of Pax; L = temple of Venus Felix and Roma Aeterna; M = temple of Jupiter Stator.

including temples of SATURN, CASTOR, Divus Julius, VESTA, CONCORDIA, Divus Vespasianus, and ANTONINUS PIUS AND FAUSTINA. There was a spring of JUTURNA (LACUS IUTURNAE). The Sacra Via passed through the forum and was often the scene of ceremonies and games, including triumphal processions and funerals. The first recorded church in the forum was that of Saints Cosma and Damiano (526–530), although Santa Maria Antiqua may be older.
Reading: Grant 1970; Richardson 1992, 170–174.

Friagabis A goddess named on an inscription from Housesteads on Hadrian's Wall, England, as one of the ALAISIAGAE.

Fulgora A Roman goddess who presided over lightning.

funerals (Fig. 38) Rituals related to the BURIAL OF THE DEAD, from the point of death to the rites carried out after the burial. No ancient descriptions survive of private Roman funerary practices, but the entire procedure was intended to ensure that the body was buried or placed in a tomb with the appropriate rites, to ensure the survival of the departed soul in the AFTERLIFE. It was thought that death brought pollution, which also needed acts of purification and expiation.

Fig. 38 Funeral pyre of four tiers on the reverse of a memorial denarius *struck under Marcus Aurelius (emperor 161–180) in memory of Antoninus Pius. The obverse legend reads DIVVS M ANTONINVS PIVS, and the reverse legend reads CONSECRATIO, with the overall meaning of "sacred to the memory of the deified Antoninus Pius."*

The funeral *(funus)* was organized by professional undertakers *(libitinarii)* who provided mourning women, musicians and sometimes dancers and performers of mimes. Most funerals were fairly simple, but upper-class funerals were often elaborate, particularly if the deceased was in any way illustrious. For such a person (usually male), the body might lie in state on a bed *(lectus funebris)* in the *atrium* of his home, feet to the door. The funeral started with a procession *(pompa)* out of the city, taking a route along the main streets. The procession might pause in the forum for a ceremony of *laudatio*, during which the deceased, carried on a bier, was displayed, usually in an upright position, and a funeral oration *(laudatio funebris)* was read out.

During funerals of prominent men in the republic and early empire, part of the procession consisted of members of the deceased's family dressed as his ancestors and wearing masks of the ancestors *(imagines)*. These representatives of the ancestors rode in chariots and were a prominent part of the funeral procession. The right to publicly display ancestral images was restricted to families who had held curule magistracies.

From the forum, the procession moved outside the city to the place of burial or cremation pyre. In contrast, lower-class funerals took place soon after death, and the corpse was taken from the city by the shortest route with a less elaborate procession of mourners or none at all. The poor could belong to funeral clubs *(collegia funeraticia)*, so that the club paid the funeral expenses (see *COLUMBARIUM*). At the grave or cremation site, various rites took place, including a funeral feast *(silicernium)* for the mourners, and offerings of food and drink to the deceased. At the end of full mourning, nine days later, there was another feast *(cena novendialis)* at the grave when a libation was poured on the burial. The dead continued to be remembered throughout the year, particularly during the festivals of PARENTALIA and LEMURIA. The exact funeral and burial rites varied widely according to the beliefs of the deceased's family and local customs.

The household was considered *funesta* (polluted), and cypress or pitch-pine was hung outside the house to signify this. After the funeral, the house had to be purified, with the heir sweeping out the pollution with a special sort of broom to rid it of the ghost of the deceased.
Reading: Hopkins 1983, 217–226; Prieur 1986; Scullard 1981, 218–221.

Furies (in Latin, *Furiae* or *Dirae*) The Roman equivalent of the Greek ERINYES or EUMENIDES. These were female spirits, appointed to carry out the vengeance of the gods upon humans, punishing the guilty on earth as well as in the UNDERWORLD. According to the most ancient Roman authorities, there were three Furies, TISIPHONE, MEGARA and ALECTO, although NEMESIS was sometimes regarded as a Fury and Plutarch cites ADRASTA as one. There is some confusion here, since Adrasta was usually taken to be the same as Adrastea, another name for Nemesis. It is not clear whether Adrasta was ever regarded as a separate deity from Nemesis. The Furies were sometimes confused with FURRINA.

Furrina An obscure ancient Roman goddess, possibly of a spring or springs, who was also known as Furina. She was sometimes regarded as a NYMPH and was sometimes wrongly confused with the Furies. Furrina had a sacred grove *(lucus Furrinae)*, associated with springs, at the foot of the Janiculum Hill in Rome, near the Sublician Bridge. She also had a shrine near Arpinum, Italy. She had her own *FLAMEN* (the *flamen Furrinalis*), and her festival was the FURRINALIA. Her cult was largely forgotten by the end of the republic, and little else is known about her.
Reading: Grimal 1986, 166; Hammond and Scullard (eds.) 1970, 451; Richardson 1992, 235; York 1986, 54–55.

Furrinalia Festival of the goddess FURRINA, held on July 25, about which virtually nothing is known.
Reading: Richardson 1992, 235.

G

gallus (pl. *galli*) Eunuch priest of MAGNA MATER (Cybele). *Galli* were thought to take their name from the Gallus River in Galatia (now in Turkey) near the original temple of Cybele, or from King Gallus, or from the cockerel *(gallus)* which they took as their symbol. During ceremonies they had a wild appearance and practised self-flagellation, and on March 24 they flagellated themselves as part of the ceremonies of *dies sanguinis* (Day of the Blood). They were thought to castrate themselves in imitation of ATTIS, apparently with the most primitive of instruments such as a flint or potsherd. A carefully repaired castration clamp from the Thames River at London, decorated with busts of Cybele, may have had a ritual use by the priesthood. The fact that they willingly castrated themselves led to disbelief by many Roman writers, and Roman citizens were not allowed to serve as priests until the time of Claudius; Domitian decreed that Roman citizens were forbidden to practise emasculation (*eviratio*).

The *archigallus* was the high priest of the *galli* who was appointed for life. Not every sanctuary had its own *archigallus*, especially in the provinces. Many priestesses *(sacerdotes)* of the cult are also known, as well as assistants *(ministrae)*. The priestesses took part in the sacrifical ceremonies and processions and performed special services for women. Both the choice of *galli* and priestesses had to be sanctioned by the *QUINDECIMVIRI SACRIS FACIUNDIS*.
Reading: Vermaseren 1977, 96–101, 107–110.

Garmangabis A Germanic goddess who is known from an inscription on an altar found at Lanchester, England. The altar was dedicated to "the goddess Garmangabis" and to "the Divine Power of our Emperor Gordian" by a detachment of Germanic troops stationed in the area.

Gebrinius A Celtic god who was linked with the Roman god MERCURY as MERCURY GEBRINIUS.

genius (pl. *genii*) (Literally "begetter") A man's guardian spirit which also enabled him to beget children. In women, the corresponding guardian spirit was called Iuno (JUNO). The *genius* of the household (Genius Paterfamilias) was worshipped by the household on the birthday of the *paterfamilias* (the male head of the household), in whom it was thought to reside. Its symbol was the snake, and it was often portrayed as such in Roman art (Fig. 97). The *genius* was often worshipped with the *LAR* at the *LARARIUM*.

The idea of a *genius* was extended, so that groups of people and even places and areas had their own *genius*. This expansion resulted in a great number of *genii* presiding over groups of people, such as the Roman people, and over places such as the city of Rome and the province of Noricum.
Reading: Alcock 1986, 113–115.

Genius Augusti ("spirit of Augustus") A Roman deity who was the *genius* of the emperor. It was a decree of the Senate that at every formal dinner, both private as well as public, a libation had to be poured out to this deity.
Reading: Alcock 1986, 114.

genius cucullatus ("hooded spirit"; pl. *genii cucullati*) The name given to a series of representations, usually relief carvings in stone, of hooded deities. A *cucullus* was a hood fastened to a cloak,

and the name *genio cucullato* (dative form, "to the *genius cucullatus*") is mentioned in an inscription found at a Romano-Celtic shrine at Wabelsdorf, Austria. In Europe, the *genius cucullatus* usually appears singly, as a giant or dwarf, but in Britain three identical dwarves are usually portrayed, although a few single ones are known. *Genii cucullati* are often portrayed carrying eggs or bags of money, sometimes with scrolls, and at times they are associated with mother goddesses. They are also associated with phallic symbolism and sometimes appear as lamp fittings, with the god's phallus forming the lampholder. *Genii cucullati* appear to be Celtic deities associated with fertility and prosperity, and possibly with renewal and rebirth.
Reading: Green, M. J. 1992a, 104–105.

Genius loci (Fig. 39) ("spirit of the place") A formula used in dedications when the suppliant was uncertain of the name of the deity to whom the sacrifice was being made.

Fig. 39 A crudely cut inscription on an altar dedicated to Genius loci. The inscription reads GENIO HVVS LOCI TEXAND ET SVVE VEX COHOR II NERVIORVM ("Texandrian and [?] Suvevae soldiers in a detachment of the 2nd Nervian cohort set this up to the spirit of this place"). HVVS should be HVIVS ("this"). The altar was found at Carrawburgh, on Hadrian's Wall, England.

Genius Paterfamilias A deity who was "spirit of the head of the household." (See GENIUS.)

Genius Patriae A deity who was "spirit of the country."

Genius Publicus Populi Romani ("spirit of the community of the Roman people") Also known as the Genius Publicus or the Genius Populi Romani. In art this deity was originally portrayed as a male figure draped in an himation (a Greek garment rather like a cloak), holding a cornucopia. He was sometimes portrayed as holding a *patera* over an altar as well. In the first century B.C., however, he was portrayed as a bearded figure with a globe, scepter, crown and cornucopia, and later appeared on coinage of Vespasian as a clean-shaven young man with a cornucopia. This deity had a shrine near the temple of CONCORDIA in the FORUM ROMANUM in Rome. An annual sacrifice was made to this god on October 9.
Reading: Alcock 1986, 114; Richardson 1992, 181.

Glanis (Fig. 40) The eponymous Celtic patron deity of the town of Glanum (St. Rémy), France.

Fig. 40 An altar dedicated to Glanis, the Glanicae and Fortuna Redux, from Glanum (St. Rémy), southern France. It was found at the sanctuary of Glanis and Glanicae and was dedicated by a veteran of the Legion XXI Rapax ("grasping").

Here an altar was set up to Glanis and the Glanicae, a triad of mother goddesses associated with the town's healing springs.
Reading: Green, M. J. 1992a, 105.

Glycon A divine snake who was said to be a transformation of the god Asclepius (AESCULAPIUS). Glycon was portrayed as a snake with shaggy hair and human ears. The snake was discovered by a prophet, Alexander, in the town of Abonouteichos on the southern Black Sea coast. The prophet set up an ORACLE with the snake in Abonouteichos sometime around 150 that was active for more than 30 years, until Alexander's death. A doctor was then given charge of the shrine. At the oracle, the snake appeared to speak in answer to suppliant's questions. A mystery cult was developed at the shrine, into which those consulting the oracle were initiated. The cult of Glycon spread widely in the east and among the higher classes in Rome; Marcus Aurelius was among its followers. Much of what is known about the cult comes from the writings of the second-century poet Lucian, a contemporary of the prophet Alexander. He denounced the prophet as a fraud and the oracle as a hoax. It would appear, however, that the oracle and cult were no more fraudulent than other comparable oracles and cults.
Reading: Henig 1986, 160; Lane Fox 1988, 241–250; Tacheva-Hitova 1983, 276.

gnosticism (from *gnosis*, "knowledge") A complex religious movement based on a myth of redemption. Possibly pre-Christian in origin, it is more likely to have grown out of a fusion of ideas from pagan religion, JUDAISM and CHRISTIANITY. It came to prominence in the second century in both Christian and pagan forms, principally through the writings of Valentinus and Basilides, both of whom lived in Alexandria in Egypt. Other writers also contributed to gnostic beliefs, and eventually gnosticism spread throughout the Roman empire and beyond, as far as China. There were different sects within gnosticism; one or two gnostic cults survive today.

The basis of gnosticism was a distinction between a remote and unknowable divinity and a "Demiurge"—an inferior deity descended from this divinity. The Demiurge was the imperfect creator and ruler of the world (which was imperfect, having been made by an imperfect deity). However, some individuals were believed to possess a spark of the substance of the divinity and might hope to return to the divinity after death. A redeemer was sent by the divinity (perhaps Christ, or a redeemer still to come) who temporarily inhabited a human body and brought *gnosis* (knowledge).
Reading: Ferguson 1970, 128–131; McManners (ed.) 1990, 26–28.

Gontia A Celto-Germanic goddess who is known from an inscription from Gunzburg (Roman Guntia), Germany. It is thought, from the similarity of names, that this goddess was either the patron deity of the settlement at Gunzburg, or the deity of the river Gunz.
Reading: Elbe 1975, 142.

Gorgon's head An image, the face of which turned all who looked on it to stone, regarded as having the power to attract and hold evil powers and thus divert them from other targets. Consequently, faces or masks of the Gorgon were used as amulets, and also appeared on buildings, tombstones and coffins. Gorgo (or Medusa) was a terrible monster in Greek mythology.
Reading: Hammond and Scullard (eds.) 1970, 472.

Grannus A Celtic god who was linked to APOLLO as APOLLO GRANNUS. Grannus is mentioned as a god of healing by the ancient author Cassius Dio. *Grannos* was probably an alternative name.

Gratian Flavius Gratian, emperor 367–383. A Christian much influenced by St. AMBROSE, Gratian was the first emperor to omit the words *PONTIFEX MAXIMUS* from his title. He ordered the Altar of Victory to be removed from the Senate house in Rome, despite the protests of Symmachus.
Reading: Grant 1985, 266–268; Hammond and Scullard (eds.) 1970, 476.

grave goods (Figs. 41a, b, 46) Objects of varying kinds placed with the burials of the deceased. Many burials, both inhumations and cremations, were furnished with grave goods, presumably for use by the deceased person in an AFTERLIFE and to make their life more pleasant there, although Christian burials have few or no grave goods. The range of grave goods probably reflects the beliefs and wealth of the deceased's family. A wealthy person's burial would be likely to contain a variety of vessels full of food and drink, a flagon and *patera* for ritual libations, perhaps a gold ring as a symbol of high status, and almost anything else that the dead might be thought to require in the afterlife, including perfumes such as myrrh and frankincense. Poorer burials had only a few grave goods—often one or two vessels, food and drink and a few personal items.

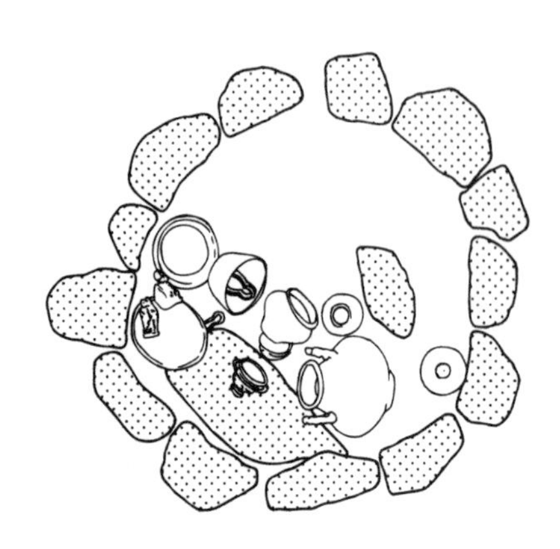

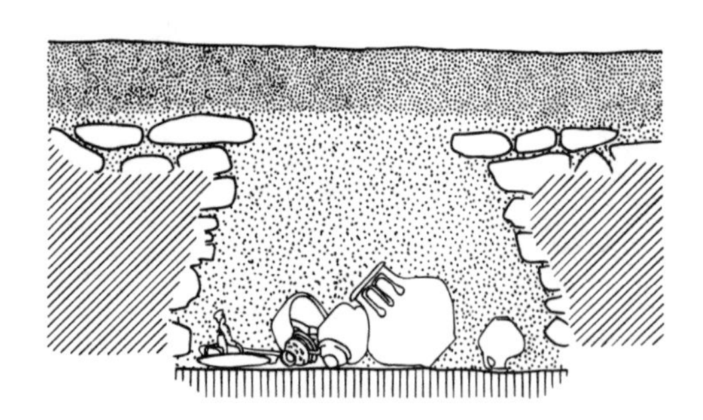

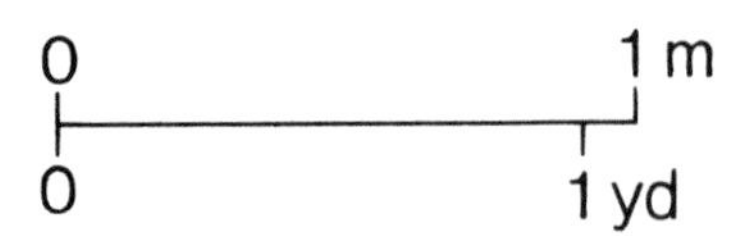

Some inhumations have a coin in the mouth as the traditional fee for Charon, the mythical ferryman who took the dead across the river Styx into the UNDERWORLD. Coins were also placed in cremations. Many inhumations and cremations had a pair of hobnailed boots or shoes (placed, not worn by the deceased, in the grave) and sometimes lamps as grave goods, all possibly for the deceased's jour-

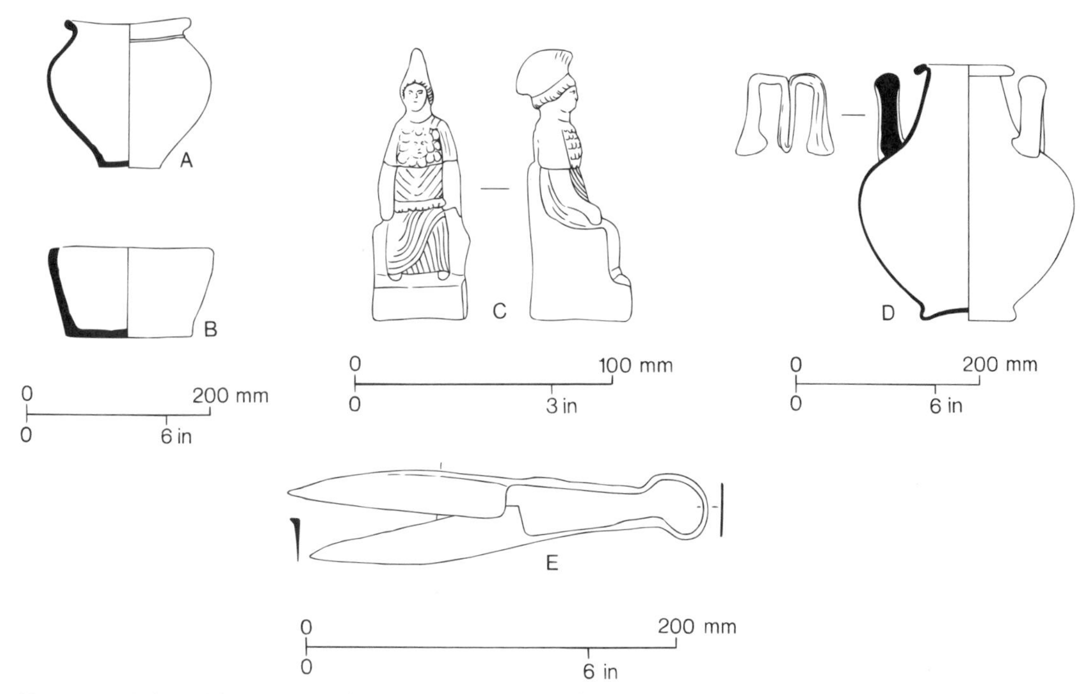

Figs. 41 a (left) and b (above) A plan (a) and section (b) of a cremation in a small stone-lined pit accompanied by many grave goods, including pottery vessels, a lamp, glass vessels, shears and figurines. Some of the grave goods are drawn separately: A = cooking pot; B = dish; C = terracotta figurine of a throned Minerva; D = glass jar; E = iron shears. Based on a cremation from the cemetery at Wederath-Belginum, Germany.

ney through the underworld. Hobnailed boots are found only in burials of the Celtic provinces, not the Mediterranean provinces. Offerings of food and drink were also made to the dead after burial, probably to keep their souls alive, and pipes and holes led directly to the burials in some cases to facilitate this. Some Romans left money in their wills so that their relatives could make regular offerings of food and drink.
Reading: Merrifield 1987, 64–76; Toynbee 1971.

Greater Quinquatrus A five-day festival and holiday that took place on March 19–23. March 19 was called *Quinquatrus* and came to be regarded as the start of this festival in honor of MARS. The Greater Quinquatrus came to be called *Quinquatria*.
Reading: Scullard 1981, 92–94.

Greto (or possibly Creto) A Celtic god who is known from an inscription at Stumpfer Turm, Germany.
Reading: Wightman 1970, 222.

Griselicae Celtic mother goddesses also known as the MATRES GRISELICAE.

grove, sacred (Latin, *lucus* or *nemus*) The oldest kind of cult place, many of which are known to have had altars and temples. In Sicily, Italy and Rome works of art are known to have been placed in these groves, possibly as votive offerings. There were numerous groves in Britain, Gaul and Germany, where they were often associated with water cults. (See also *LUCUS*.)
Reading: Beard 1993; de Cazanove 1993; Scheid 1993.

H

Hadad ("Lord of Heaven") A Syrian thunder god, also known as BAAL SHAMIN. He was thought to inhabit the mountaintops and to be associated with the sky. He became a consort of ATARGATIS (although subordinate to her) and was identified with ZEUS. Atargatis's throne was flanked by lions, but Hadad's by bulls. At Heliopolis, Lebanon, Hadad became equated with JUPITER as JUPITER HELIOPOLITANUS.
Reading: Ferguson 1970, 18.

Hades (or Aides) The Greek god who was lord of the UNDERWORLD. His name means "the unseen," and the title Pluton ("the rich one") was often applied to him. He was equated with the Roman god DIS.
Reading: Hammond and Scullard (eds.) 1970, 484.

Hadrian, mausoleum of The burial place in Rome of the deified Hadrian and of subsequent emperors and members of the imperial family. It was also called the Antoninorum Sepulcrum and the Hadrianium. (It was not called a mausoleum in the Roman period.) Now famous as the Castel Sant' Angelo, it is situated on the right bank of the Tiber River. It may have been completed by Antoninus Pius in 139, the year after Hadrian's death. It was used as the burial place of Hadrian and his family and emperors up to Caracalla. Circular in plan, it resembles a huge drum 58.5 yds. (64 m) in diameter. It was probably originally 19.2 yds. (21 m) in height, with two circular stories above a square base measuring 97.33 yds. (89 m). The structure was initially topped by a mound of earth with a small high third story.
Reading: Nash 1962b, 44; Richardson 1992, 249–251.

Hadrian, temple of A temple of Hadrian at Cyzicus, Turkey, cited in one list as one of the seven wonders of the ancient world. It is generally described as a temple of Hadrian, but ZEUS may actually have been the chief deity. The temple was built or finished by Hadrian, who was himself honored in it. The games held at Cyzicus were known as the Hadrianea Olympia, showing that Hadrian was certainly honored there, but also indicating that Zeus Olympios was involved as well. The temple had three stories, one of which was underground. It was in a ruinous condition in 1444 when it was described by Cyriacus of Ancona.
Reading: Price 1984, 153–155, 251–252.

Hadrianeum A temple of Divus Hadrianus (deified Hadrian) built by Antoninus Pius in Rome and dedicated by him in 145. It was known (like many temples of Hadrian) by the name *Hadrianeum.* The temple was converted into Rome's stock exchange and is visible in the Piazza di Pietra; it was formerly identified as the Basilica of NEPTUNE.
Reading: Nash 1962a, 457; Richardson 1992, 184–185.

Haides An alternative name for the Greek god HADES, who was lord of the UNDERWORLD and was equated with the Roman god DIS.

Hammer god An important Celtic deity who was worshipped in Gaul. He was represented either with a consort or alone; a few representations are dedicated to Sucellus. Over 200 images of the Hammer god are known, on stone monuments and as bronze figurines. Most depict the god bearded, with a short belted tunic, a heavy cloak, a long-handled hammer and a small pot or goblet. Other symbols

(such as a wine barrel and a dog) imply that the god had a range of spheres of influence. Stone votive hammers and altars decorated with hammer symbols are thought to be connected with his cult. He appears to have been associated with wine production, healing springs and the sun in different localities. It is likely that he also had many other associations. His function is complex and not fully understood, but he appears to be linked to prosperity and plenty as well as to nature.
Reading: Deyts 1992, 84–94; Green, M. J. 1984, 142–144; Green, M. J. 1992a, 110–112.

Harimella A Germanic goddess who is known from an inscription on an altar found at Birrens, Scotland. This goddess is otherwise unknown, but the dedication appears to have been made by one of the soldiers of the garrison at Birrens which was drawn from the Rhineland area of Germany. She is thought to be a goddess from the same region.
Reading: Keppie and Arnold 1984, 8.

Harpocrates The Roman and Greek name for the Egyptian deity Horus. In Egyptian mythology Horus was the son of the goddess ISIS and was a heroic figure who avenged the death of his father Osiris. He was usually worshipped with other Egyptian deities such as ISIS and SERAPIS.
Reading: Hammond and Scullard (eds.) 1970, 531.

haruspex (pl. *haruspices*, literally "gut-gazer") Someone who carried out haruspicy, a form of DIVINATION. *Haruspices* were originally Etruscan diviners or soothsayers in Rome. They were believed to be interpreters of the will of the gods. They came to rival and overlap with the role of augurs (see AUGUR), although they had no religious authority in Rome and were probably not organized into a college until the empire. This college *(ordo haruspicium)* of 60 *haruspices* was headed by a chief *haruspex* (known as a *summus*, *primarius* or *maximus haruspex*).

Haruspices interpreted three main phenomena: the entrails from sacrificed animals (*exta*, a process known as *extispicium*—Fig. 26), unnatural events (*monstra*—portents and prodigies, from *monere*, "to warn") and flashes of lightning *(fulgura)*, all of which were regarded as indications of the will of the gods (prodigies and lightning being warnings). Entrails were interpreted by the color, markings and shape of the liver and gallbladder, and there is evidence that models of livers were used in the training of *haruspices*. An interpreter of lightning was called a *fulgurator*. Lightning was interpreted by its frequency and the region of the sky in which it appeared. *Haruspices* were not official priests, but they are known from many parts of the empire, although the names of very few individual *haruspices* are known. The *haruspices* who interpreted prodigies may have been lower-class citizens than those who read *exta* at sacrifices. Haruspicy continued to the time of Theodosius II (408–450) and continued to be discussed to at least the sixth century.
Reading: Hammond and Scullard (eds.) 1970, 489; MacBain 1982 (on *haruspices* and prodigies); North 1990.

hastiferus (pl. *hastiferi*) A religious college associated with the cult of BELLONA and of MAGNA MATER (Cybele). They were once thought to be the same as the *dendrophoroi* (see *DENDROPHORUS*). They are known from several inscriptions, three of which are from the METROON at Ostia, Italy, and others from Germany (Cologne and Castel). Their name means "spearbearers," possibly in the sense of a ceremonial bodyguard carrying cult spears, although there is controversy over the meaning of the name.
Reading: Fishwick 1967.

Hebe A Greek goddess who was the personification of adolescence and youthful beauty. She was identified with the Roman goddess JUVENTAS.

Hecate Originally a Greek goddess of the UNDERWORLD who presided over magic and enchantments, often worshipped at crossroads and represented with three (occasionally four) faces or bodies. Hecate was the sister of the goddess Latona (Greek goddess LETO) and was often identified with the Roman goddess DIANA.
Reading: Hammond and Scullard (eds.) 1970, 490.

Helernus A Roman god, possibly of the UNDERWORLD. There is uncertainty about his name, which possibly was Elernus or Avernus. He was worshipped in his own sacred grove on February 1. It may have been below the Palatine Hill in Rome, near the Tiber River, but very little is known about this deity.
Reading: Scullard 1981, 72.

Helios The Greek god of the sun, identified with the Roman god SOL.

Hephaestus The Greek god of fire, particularly the fire in the smithy, who was identified with the Roman god VULCAN.

Hera The Greek goddess of marriage and the life (particularly the sexual life) of women. She was the wife of ZEUS and was identified with the Roman goddess JUNO.

Heracles A Greek hero who was sometimes worshipped as a god. He was worshipped as the god HERCULES by the Romans.

Hercules (Fig. 42) The Roman equivalent of the Greek hero HERACLES. Hercules was worshipped as a god of commercial enterprise and of victory (as HERCULES INVICTUS or Victor). In line with his reputation for gluttony, there were no restrictions on what could be sacrificed to Hercules; he could eat or drink anything. There were numerous temples to Hercules in Rome, many of them round (Fig. 43), including ones dedicated to HERCULES POMPEIANUS, HERCULES CUSTOS, Hercules Invictus, HERCULES VICTOR and HERCULES OF THE MUSES. There was an altar of Hercules Invictus (ARA MAXIMA) where oaths were often taken and business deals agreed. Hercules was sometimes identified with the Phoenician god MELQART. He was also linked to a number of Celtic names, the most popular being HERCULES MAGUSANUS. In Gallia Narbonensis he was called HERCULES ILUNNUS and Hercules Ogmios (see OGMIOS), and at Silchester, England, he was called HERCULES SAEGON. The chalk hill-figure known as the Cerne Abbas Giant, at Cerne Abbas, Dorset, England, is probably a portrait of Hercules, dating to the Roman period in Britain.
Reading: Grant 1971 (includes myths of Hercules); Green, M. J. 1992a, 118; Scullard 1981, 157; Simon 1990, 72–87.

Hercules, temples of One temple was situated outside the Porta Collina in Rome, at the farthest point of Hannibal's advance on Rome in 211 B.C. It has not been located. Another temple was found on the left bank of the Tiber River near the Pons Aelius. It was a small round temple, and may

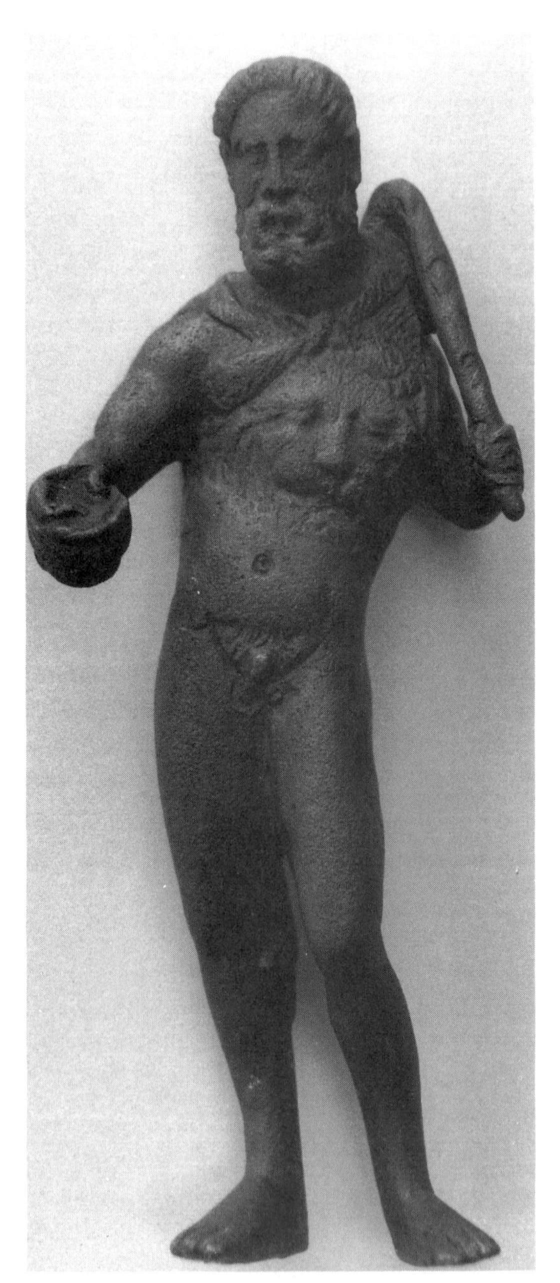

Fig. 42 Bronze figurine of Hercules found at Lamyatt Beacon, England. He is naked apart from a lion skin across the upper part of his body. He holds a wine cup in his right hand and a club in his left. Courtesy of Somerset County Museums Service.

have been dedicated to HERCULES or possibly to LIBER.
Reading: Richardson 1992, 185.

Hercules Custos ("Hercules the Custodian") A god also known as Hercules Magnus Custos ("Hercules the Great Custodian") who had a festival on June 4. In Rome he had a temple in the CIRCUS FLAMINIUS.
Reading: Richardson 1992, 186; Scullard 1981, 146.

Hercules Custos, temple of (Hercules Magnus Custos) The temple of Hercules the Custodian in the west end of the CIRCUS FLAMINIUS in Rome. It was probably the temple built on the orders of the SIBYLLINE BOOKS after Hannibal's initial victories in 218 B.C. Its dedication day was June 4. It was probably restored by, rather than built by, Sulla. Nothing is known about the cult and architecture of the temple.
Reading: Palmer 1990; Richardson 1992, 186; Scullard 1981, 146.

Hercules Ilunnus The Celtic god ILUNNUS who was linked with the Roman god HERCULES as Hercules Ilunnus. He was worshipped in the province of Gallia Narbonensis (Provence, France).
Reading: Green, M. J. 1992a, 118.

Hercules Invictus ("Unconquered Hercules") A Roman deity often mistaken or conflated with HERCULES VICTOR ("Hercules Victorious"). There were several temples in Rome dedicated to one or other of these gods, but in several cases ancient authors attribute the same temple to one or both of them. There were festivals of Hercules Invictus on August 12 and 13.
Reading: Richardson 1992, 186–189; Scullard 1981, 171.

Hercules Magnus Custos An alternative name for the Roman god HERCULES CUSTOS.

Hercules Magusanus A Celtic god who was linked with the Roman god HERCULES. He was the most popular of the Celtic gods linked with Hercules. Hercules Magusanus is known from 11 dedications found in northeast Gaul.
Reading: Green, M. J. 1992a, 118.

Hercules of the Muses, temple of A temple situated in the CIRCUS FLAMINIUS in Rome, just northwest of the Porticus Octaviae. It was built by Marcus Fulvius Nobilior after his campaigns in Ambracia in 189 B.C. and probably after his triumph of 187 B.C. Nine statues of MUSES from Ambracia and one of HERCULES playing the lyre were placed in the temple. In 187 B.C. Marcus Fulvius Nobilior also put a small bronze shrine *(aedicula)* of the CAMENAE or Muses in the temple; the shrine dated from the time of Numa and had been in the temple of HONOS AND VIRTUS after being struck by lightning. The temple is usually referred to in Latin as "Herculis Musarum Aedes," but as "Aedes Herculis et Musarum" by Servius, who also indicates that it was only dedicated to the Muses after the transfer of Numa's bronze shrine. The temple was restored by Lucius Marcus Philippus in 29 B.C. and was enclosed within the Porticus Philippi. The dedication date was June 30. Like many temples of Hercules, it was round.
Reading: Palmer 1990; Richardson 1992, 187.

Hercules Pompeianus, temple of A rectangular temple in Rome was restored or built by Pompey (Gnaeus Pompeius Magnus). Its dedication day was August 12 and it was apparently sited near the CIRCUS MAXIMUS. It had an archaic style with a wooden roof decorated with terracotta or bronze sculptures. Remains of a temple under part of the church of Santa Maria in Cosmedin may be this temple (destroyed in the time of Pope Hadrian I (772–795) when he rebuilt and enlarged the church). It may have been sited near the ARA MAXIMA and may also have been known as the temple of HERCULES INVICTUS, but this is very uncertain.
Reading: Richardson 1992, 187–188.

Hercules Saegon A Celtic god linked with the Roman god Hercules. He is known from an inscription at Silchester, England. Saegon may be a different form of the name *Segomo*, meaning "victorious."
Reading: Green, M. J. 1992a, 118.

Hercules Saxanus ("Hercules of the Rocks") The name given to HERCULES in his role as patron god of quarrymen.

Hercules Triumphalis ("Hercules Triumphant") A statue of this aspect of the Roman god

HERCULES stood in the FORUM BOARIUM in Rome, probably somewhere along the route of triumphs. Whenever a triumph was celebrated, the statue was dressed in triumphal robes. Legend ascribed the statue to EVANDER.

Reading: Richardson 1992, 188; Scullard 1981, 215.

Hercules Victor ("Hercules Victorious") An aspect of the Roman god HERCULES who appears to have been frequently confused with HERCULES INVICTUS.

Hercules Victor, temples of (Fig. 43) The number of temples dedicated to HERCULES VICTOR in Rome and their location are subject to varying opinions owing to the difficulties of interpreting the surviving Latin texts and the architectural and epigraphical evidence. There was one temple in the FORUM BOARIUM and a different one by the Porta Trigemina (which was also in the Forum Boarium). Little is known of the temple of Hercules Victor or Invictus by the Porta Trigemina. Its dedication day was August 13.

The temple to Hercules Victor situated in the Forum Boarium may have been the round temple known to have contained a painting by the poet Pacuvius, the subject of which is uncertain. It is this temple which was probably excavated and destroyed under Pope Sixtus IV (1471–1484), during which time a cult image of gilded bronze was discovered. A reconstruction drawing of the excavated temple was made later by Baldassare Peruzzi (in 1503–1513). That temple stood just to the northeast of the Church of Santa Maria Cosmedin, and was perhaps built by Titus Quinctius Flamininus in the 190s or 180s B.C. or by an Aemilius (but not by Scipio Aemilianus as has been argued). It was round, Hellenistic in style, with columns on a low stepped podium, which surrounded a round cella of marble masonry. It could have been designed by a Greek architect. Its anniversary date was June 29 or December 21. June 29 appears to relate to a rebuilding, possibly after the great fire of 31 B.C.

Fig. 43 Round temple, probably of Hercules Victor, in the Forum Boarium near the Tiber River. It was once thought to be the temple of Vesta.

Another temple to Hercules Victor was vowed in 145 B.C. by Lucius Mummius. It was possibly situated on the Caelian Hill in Rome. It was dedicated by him after his triumph over the Achaeans in 145 B.C. and before his censorship of 142/141 B.C. Two inscriptions provide the only evidence for the temple, which has never been found.

Another round temple, still extant and built in marble, overlooked the Tiber River (Fig. 43). It was just outside the city walls in the city port, near the Forum Boarium. It is now opposite the Church of Santa Maria in Cosmedin. It was formerly known as the temple of VESTA. It has sometimes been identified as the temple of Hercules Victor (or Invictus) that was also known as the temple of Hercules Olivarius. That temple is known to have existed in the area, but this identification is not widely accepted.

Reading: Palmer 1990; Richardson 1992, 188–189; Scullard 1981, 171–172.

Herecura A Celto-Germanic goddess who is known from inscriptions found at Stuttgart, Germany. This goddess is probably the same deity as AERICURA.

Reading: Espérandieu 1931, nos. 347, 564.

Hermes The Greek deity who was messenger of the gods and was identified with the Roman god MERCURY.

Hermes Devoris An Iberian god linked with the Greek god HERMES. This deity is known from an inscription on an altar found near Chaves, northern Portugal. Gaius Cexaecius Fuscus dedicated the altar; if he is the same person as a *FLAMEN* mentioned in an inscription from Tarragona, Spain, the altar near Chaves was set up in the second half of the second century.

Reading: Tranoy 1981, 302.

hero The worship of superhuman dead men and women, real or imaginary, was a phenomenon of the Greek world but was not widespread in Roman religion. Some Greek heroes (such as HERCULES) were worshipped as gods by the Romans, and were often identified with other gods in the Roman pantheon.

Reading: Hammond and Scullard (eds.) 1970, 505–506.

Hestia The Greek goddess of the hearth who was identified with the Roman goddess VESTA.

hexastyle A temple building with six columns on the main facade.

Hilaria A festival in honor of ATTIS held on March 25. There were many days in March leading up to this festival when ceremonies took place, such as March 23, which was a day of mourning, and March 24, which was the *dies sanguinis* (Day of the Blood) when priests flagellated themselves and undertook other rites, including a *TAUROBOLIUM.* March 25 was probably a day of rejoicing, a resurrection, from the word *hilaris* ("cheerful"). It is attested in Rome from the time of Antoninus Pius (138–161). The festivities in honor of Attis were mainly intended for committed worshippers, although they were admitted into the official religious calendars. Those in honor of his consort MAGNA MATER (Cybele) were fixed national holidays.

Reading: Vermaseren 1977, 113–124.

Hilary, Saint Hilarius, c. 315–367. An early Christian bishop and theologian from Poitiers. He was converted to Christianity and became bishop of Poitiers c. 353. He was opposed to ARIANISM, and spent several years in exile in Asia Minor because of his opposition. He was author of numerous theological works, including *On the Trinity* in 12 books, commentaries on Matthew and on the Psalms, and *De Synodis seu de Fide Orientalium (On Synods or on the Faith of the Peoples of the East)*, which is a valuable source of information for ecclesiastical history. He is regarded as the greatest western theologian of his age.

Reading: Hammond and Scullard (eds.) 1970, 515.

Hippolytus A Greek god who was identified with VIRBIUS (a Roman god worshipped with DIANA and EGERIA in a grove at Lake Nemi, Italy). According to legend, Hippolytus, who was devoted to the Greek goddess ARTEMIS (identified with the Roman goddess Diana), was killed by POSEIDON. At the request of Artemis, Hippolytus was brought back to life by Asclepius (AESCULAPIUS), and Artemis then took Hippolytus to her sanctuary by Lake Nemi.

Reading: Grimal 1986, 216; Hammond and Scullard (eds.) 1970, 519.

holocaust A blood sacrifice which was completely burnt.

Honos Also called Honor, this Roman deity was the personification of honor. There was a temple dedicated to Honos outside the Porta Collina in Rome. There was also a temple of Honos and Virtus near the Porta Capena, and another, probably on the slope of the Capitoline Hill. A festival of Honos was held on July 17.
Reading: Scullard 1981, 165–166.

Honos and Virtus, temple of A double temple, initially founded as a single temple to Honos by Quintus Maximus during the Ligurian War and built in Rome in 234 B.C., or possibly built by Quintus Fabius Maximus Rullianus in the early third century B.C. Marcus Claudius Marcellus restored the temple and rededicated it to Honos and Virtus in 208 B.C., but the pontiffs forbade this on the grounds that the deities could not share the same cella. He therefore added a new cella for VIRTUS, making it a double temple, which his son dedicated in 205 B.C. It stood just inside the Porta Capena and contained many works of art, representing booty from Marcellus's capture of Syracuse. A bronze shrine *(aedicula)* of the CAMENAE or MUSES dating from the time of Numa was moved to this temple for a while after it had been struck by lightning. The temple was restored by Vespasian; it may have been damaged or destroyed in the fire of Nero. It is last mentioned in the fourth century.
Reading: Richardson 1992, 190.

Hora A Roman goddess who was the wife of the Roman god QUIRINUS, but was sometimes regarded as the consort of the Roman god VULCAN. Consequently, celebrations in her honor took place during the VOLCANALIA on August 23.

Horus An Egyptian god who was known to the Romans as HARPOCRATES.

Hveteris Probably an alternative name of the Celtic deity VITIRIS.

Hvitiris Probably an alternative name of the Celtic deity VITIRIS.

Hygeia The daughter of the Greek god ASCLEPIUS. This goddess was also known as Hygia. Hygeia (meaning "health") was worshipped as part of the cult of AESCULAPIUS. She was later identified with the Roman goddess SALUS.
Reading: Hammond and Scullard (eds.) 1970, 533.

hypogeum (pl. *hypogea*) (Figs. 104, 105) Rock-cut tombs found in Rome and the provinces (particularly Roman Syria). A *hypogeum* had *loculi* or niches for holding one or more burials and were used by pagans and Christians. These *hypogea* were family tombs for private use. (See also CATACOMBS.)
Reading: Toynbee 1971, 188–244.

I

Iacchus A Greek god who was identified with the Roman god LIBER. He was variously regarded as the son of DEMETER, the son of PERSEPHONE, or the son of DIONYSUS and the nymph Aura. He was sometimes thought to be the consort of Demeter, and because of the similarity of his name to BACCHUS, was often identified with Bacchus or Dionysus.
Reading: Hammond and Scullard (eds.) 1970, 537.

Ialona A Celtic goddess who was the female equivalent of the Celtic god IALONUS. She was worshipped at Nîmes, France.
Reading: Green, M. J. 1992a, 124.

Ialonus A Celtic god who was a personification of the land, the precise nature of which is uncertain, since it relies on interpretation of his name. It can mean a deity of clearings or cultivated fields, or possibly a deity of the woodland glade. The female equivalent of Ialonus, the Celtic goddess IALONA, is known from Nîmes, France.
Reading: Green, M. J. 1992a, 124.

Ialonus Contrebis The Celtic god IALONUS who was identified with the Celtic god CONTREBIS. Ialonus Contrebis ("Ialonus who dwells among us") is invoked in an inscription found at Lancaster, England.
Reading: Green, M. J. 1992a, 124; Ross 1974, 472.

Iamblichus c. 250–330, born at Chalcis in Syria. A Neoplatonist philosopher with an interest in magic. He studied in Rome or Sicily. His extant writings (in Greek) include a defense of ritualistic magic, *De Mysteriis (On Mysteries)*, a useful work for information on fourth-century superstition.
Reading: Hammond and Scullard (eds.) 1970, 538.

Iana An alternative name for the Roman goddess DIANA.

Ianuaria A Celtic goddess who is known from a shrine at Beire-le-Châtel, France. A stone statue portrays her as a young girl with curly hair, wearing a heavy pleated coat and holding a set of pan pipes. The shrine, at a healing spring, also contained images of APOLLO (a healing god), triple-horned bulls and doves. With these associations, she may have been a goddess of music and/or healing, but nothing else is known about her.
Reading: Green, M. J. 1992a, 125.

Ianus The Latin name for the Roman god JANUS.

ianus (pl. *iani*) A passageway that could be closed at either end, originally a bridge or crossing across the *pomerium* of a town and representing a permanently inaugurated *templum*. The word came to be applied to gateways and entrances to sacred precincts; it is not known if all *iani* were regarded as sacred. There were three important *iani* in Rome: the Ianus Primus, Ianus Medicus and Ianus Geminus. The latter was the temple of JANUS GEMINUS.
Reading: Richardson 1992, 205–206; York 1986, 82.

Iarhibol (or Yarhibol) A Syrian deity who was worshipped as a triad of deities at Palmyra, Syria, with AGLIBOL and BEL. Also at Palmyra, Iarhibol was the patron god of the spring of Efca and a national god of the Palmyrenes. He was probably a sun god and acquired the character of a god of justice and of oracles.
Reading: Teixidor 1969, 1–11, 29–34.

Icovellauna A Celtic goddess who was worshipped in eastern Gaul. There are a number of dedicatory inscriptions to her from Metz, in northeast France, and from Trier, Germany. She appears to have been a goddess of healing springs.
Reading: Green, M. J. 1992a, 125.

Ides (Latin, Idus) The 15th day in long months and 13th in others. They were days of the full moon, and were *FERIAE PUBLICAE,* sacred to Jupiter. The *FLAMEN DIALIS* sacrificed a sheep to JUPITER at the temple of JUPITER OPTIMUS MAXIMUS in Rome, and other rituals must have taken place at other temples of Jupiter.
Reading: York 1986, 2.

ieiunium Cereris ("a fast of Ceres") A fast held in Rome in honor of CERES. It was prescribed by the SIBYLLINE BOOKS in 191 B.C., and was held every five years, and every year on October 4 by Augustus's time. Because the advice came from the Sibylline books, the idea of the fast is therefore Greek in origin (fasting being rare in Roman times).
Reading: Scullard 1981, 190–191.

Ilunnus A Celtic god who was linked with the Roman god HERCULES as HERCULES ILUNNUS.

imagines Masks of ancestors. There was a custom in Rome of preserving masks of ancestors *(imagines).* Until the end of the second century B.C. they were of wax, and then other materials were used, including marble busts. Memories of the individual personalities of the dead were kept alive in these busts and masks. For the Romans, the seat of life was in the head rather than in the heart, so ancestral busts had more than just decorative significance. With the better-quality statues and busts that survive, it is difficult to know if they were simply works of art or were ancestral busts with a religious significance. *Imagines* were used in funerary ceremonies, but were normally kept in the *atrium. Imagines* of deified emperors were not carried in these funerary ceremonies, as they were believed to have escaped death by being transported to heaven.
Reading: Hammond and Scullard (eds.) 1970, 542.

imperial cult (Figs. 44, 45) The worship of the living emperor, his family and ancestors and of deceased emperors; also referred to as emperor worship or ruler cult. This practice was extremely widespread throughout the empire and was especially common in Asia Minor. In the west, deified deceased emperors were closely associated with the cult of ROMA. In the eastern (Hellenistic) provinces, before the worship of emperors, there had been a ruler cult of other Roman leaders. With the expansion of the empire in the late republic, Rome came to rule eastern Hellenistic nations, whose people were accustomed to venerating their living rulers as gods, and who readily transferred their worship to Roman rulers. The earliest instance of the ruler cult applied to a Roman official was that of Gaius Marcellus, in whose honor a festival (the *Marcellia*) was established at Syracuse in Sicily after he had captured the city from the Carthaginians. This festival was later abolished by Verres, who set up his own games. The first Roman in the east to receive a permanent cult was Titus Quinctius Flamininus, who had liberated Greece. This cult lasted for three centuries in Greece, continuing to at least the second century. Various other living Roman magistrates were also honored in the late republic with priests and religious games. However, Cicero declined statues, shrines and a temple offered to him in Asia Minor. Generals such as Pompey, Julius

Fig. 44 A silver denarius *of the deified Faustina I, wife of Antoninus Pius. The legend reads DIVA FAUSTINA.*

Fig. 45 The restored temple of Hadrian at Ephesus, Turkey, with its distinctive arched facade along the main street. Originally it was probably dedicated to Artemis, the cult statue being of Artemis. Later it became part of the imperial cult and was dedicated to Hadrian.

Caesar and Mark Antony were also honored with cults.

Julius Caesar was the first leader to be awarded divine honors (deified) by the Senate, probably before his death (see JULIUS, DIVUS). It was subsequently common in Rome for an emperor to be deified after his death and be described as *divus*, or sometimes as *deus*. In the Greek world the emphasis was on the living ruler, who could be called *theos* (god) in his own lifetime. Augustus was the first emperor to be deified but his successor Tiberius was not deified.

Once permanent Roman rulers existed (initially the emperor Augustus), there was no further need for eastern provinces to establish cults of individual Roman magistrates, and instead the cult was transferred to the living emperor and his family. Augustus thought that the practice of worshipping living rulers as gods would be politically provocative if encouraged in the west; in theory, he had restored the republic and so could not be a monarch, let alone a god. Since the practice could not be eradicated in the east, he instead ruled that the cult of the living emperor could only be practiced by non-Roman provincials if it was associated with the worship of the goddess Roma. In 29 B.C. the cities of Asia requested permission to dedicate one or more temples to Augustus, but instead he allowed a temple of Roma and Divus Iulius to be erected at Ephesus and Nicaea for resident Roman citizens, and a temple of Roma and Augustus for non-citizens at Pergamum and Nicomedia.

Augustus was deified in A.D. 14, and his successor Tiberius encouraged the worship of the deified Augustus as the imperial cult, and not the cult of himself as living ruler in association with Roma. There were exceptions to his policy; for example, in A.D. 26 Tiberius allowed the erection of a temple to himself, Augustus's widow Livia and the personified Senate in Smyrna (but only because it was in an eastern province). Livia was deified in 42, and Claudius was next to be deified. This led to the cult of the *divi* (deified emperors).

Emperors tried to ensure that it was the *GENIUS* or *NUMEN* (spiritual power embodied in the emperor normally associated with deities) and not the living emperor that was worshipped, although in practice the living emperor seems to be worshipped. Evidence from inscriptions shows that various qualities attributed to the emperor were personified and worshipped, including Virtue, Health, Victory, Safety, Discipline and Fortune. For example, there are several altars dedicated to Fortuna Augusta, meaning the fortune or luck of the emperor (*Augustus* being a title originally given to the first emperor and subsequently the current reigning emperor; the Greek equivalent was *Sebastos; Augusti* or *Sebastoi* referred to the emperors collectively, including the living emperor). Vespasian in particular stressed many abstract qualities which were depicted on his coinage. In time, most deities were related to the emperor by the epithet *Augustus.*

Nero allowed himself to be depicted as a god even in Rome, in particular through many statues (which were destroyed after his death). He was frequently portrayed as the god APOLLO and the god HELIOS with a golden diadem. The building of the Domus Aurea (Golden Palace) in Rome was to be a palace of the sun, with a colossal statue of Nero-Helios (the Colossus of Nero) placed in the vestibule. Nero was never officially deified after his death, although many emperors were. (Deceased emperors whose memories were officially damned were not deified). Not only emperors, but also members of the household and associates could be deified (Fig. 44). For example, Livia was deified in the reign of Claudius, and she received sacrifices from the VESTAL VIRGINS. On his deathbed, Vespasian is recorded by Suetonius (*Divus Vespasianus* 23:4) to have said: *Vae puto deus fio* ("Alas, I believe I am becoming a god"), although it is possible that he was joking about deification.

The deified emperors became part of the formulae and liturgy of state religion. The worship of the emperor became a test of loyalty to Rome: subjects were free to worship whatever gods they chose, provided they also paid homage to the emperor. There is evidence from fragments of calendars from the Augustan period that festivals or celebrations devoted to the living emperor or his family took place about twice a month. By the time emperor worship was accepted by the Romans, the emperor was the center of the cult, and the association of Roma was superfluous. Eventually Roma disappeared from, or was absorbed into, the imperial cult, particularly in the eastern provinces. In the west, temples associated with the imperial cult generally imply the cult of one or more deified emperors.

There were numerous temples, sanctuaries, altars and statues associated with the imperial cult, and they were often located in the most prominent and prestigious positions available in a city. Emperors in the east were often honored in temples or sanctuaries dedicated to other gods (Fig. 45). Associated with the imperial cult were abstract symbols of the oak wreath civic crown (or oak swags), laurel trees and *clupeus virtutis* (shield of virtue), which are found on a range of monuments, especially altars. The imperial cult was especially popular in the first and second centuries, continuing to the mid-third century.

Reading: Etienne 1958 (imperial cult in Iberian peninsula); Fears 1988; Fishwick 1987 (concentrates on the west); Friesen 1993 (imperial cult in Asia); Mellor 1975 (cult of Roma associated with imperial cult); Neverov 1986; Price 1984 (emphasis on Asia Minor).

Imporcitor A Roman deity who was associated with the harrowing of the land or plowing with furrows. He was said by Fabius Pictor in the late third century B.C. to have been invoked by a priest of CERES.

Reading: Ferguson 1988a, 853; York 1986, 60.

Inciona A Celtic goddess who was worshipped as the partner of the Celtic god VERAUDINUS. This divine couple is known only from an inscription at Widdenberg, Luxembourg. It is likely that they are deities of that specific locality.

Reading: Green, M. J. 1992a, 125–126.

incubation A commonly practised form of natural DIVINATION. A sick person slept in a temple of a healing god (usually AESCULAPIUS) so that the god could appear in a dream vision and suggest a cure or even effect a direct cure. A patient first had to observe three days of ritual purity followed by various sacrifices, such as a gift of money and an offering

of cakes. The patient usually slept in a chamber in the temple precinct, wearing a laurel wreath, and hoped for a vision of the god. A god was also sometimes approached in this way for other purposes, such as to help locate lost property.
Reading: Bourgeois 1991, 242–246; Hammond and Scullard (eds.) 1970, 543–554; Jackson 1988, 145–147.

Indigetes (or Indigites) The *di indigetes* was a collective term used by the Romans for a group of Roman deities. Which particular deities belonged to this group is not entirely clear, and the meaning of the term is much disputed. One view is that they were minor deities of extremely limited function (usually a single small function), such as the goddess CINXIA, who looked after brides' girdles, or EDUSA, who looked after a child's eating. These single-function deities reflect the numerous anxieties that were present in daily life; for example, fear that harm would come to a child as it took its first steps away from its parents might prompt a sacrifice to the goddess ABEONA. Because these minor deities had such limited functions, they were extremely numerous and were really *numina* (see NUMEN) rather than fully conceived deities. However, some deities (for example, PROSERPINA) acquired more than one function, and under the influence of Greek mythology, they took on a more developed personality. Consequently, it is often difficult to tell whether a god or goddess was originally one of the Indigetes.

It is not entirely accepted that these deities were minor and of single function. There is some evidence that more important deities, such as APOLLO, were included in this collective term. Another explanation is that the term means indigenous or native gods, as opposed to imported or foreign gods, but, again, this view is not universally accepted.
Reading: Grimal 1986, 231; Hammond and Scullard (eds.) 1970, 544.

inhumation (Fig. 46) A method of burying the dead without cremating the corpse. The bodies were buried underground or placed in tombs. The body was usually protected in some way, probably only by a sack or shroud for poor burials. Wooden coffins were common, some lined with lead, but there were also lead coffins as well as stone coffins known as sarcophagi (Fig. 20), some of which were carved

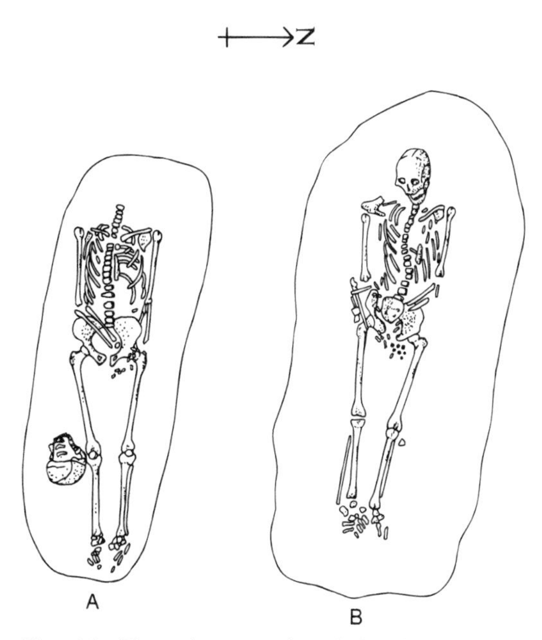

Fig. 46 Two inhumation burials based on examples found in a cemetery at Lankhills, Winchester, England. A *is a decapitated burial, possibly done to prevent the spirit from haunting the living.* B *is an extended inhumation with several coins placed near the hands as grave goods for the afterlife.*

and could be very ornate. Graves could also be lined with stones or wood, or the body protected by roof tiles or even broken amphorae. Young infants were usually buried rather than cremated, often near houses. Presumably they were not thought to cause religious pollution. In some regions, embalming was carried out, including the encasing of bodies in gypsum plaster inside coffins. Christian burials tended to lay the corpse along an east-west axis.

Inhumation became more popular than cremation in Rome and Italy in the first and second centuries, and the practice spread to the rest of the empire by the mid-third century. This was possibly because of a growing belief in an AFTERLIFE (which a cremated person might not achieve) or the result of a growing fashion that favored the more ostentatious rites and monuments associated with inhumation. Furthermore, Christians and Jews objected to cremation. Christians also objected to elaborate tombs; many Christians were buried in simple catacombs (Fig. 18). Later on wealthy Christians began

to use sarcophagi. Most inhumations were in an extended position; those in a crouched position are usually pre-Roman in date, although the position of hands, arms and legs in extended burials can vary. Some burials were face downwards and some had the head severed and placed by the feet or between the legs, possibly to prevent the haunting of the living.
Reading: Hopkins 1983, 226–235; Prieur 1986; Toynbee 1971, 33–39.

Innin An alternative name for the Syrian deity ISHTAR.

Ino According to Greek legend, a mortal who incurred the wrath of the Greek goddess HERA. When Hera drove Ino mad, Ino threw herself into the sea, but she was transformed into a sea goddess. She was also identified with the Greek goddess LEUCOTHEA and with the Roman goddess MATUTA.
Reading: Grimal 1986, 259.

Insitor A Roman deity of grafting trees, said by Fabius Pictor in the late third century B.C. to have been invoked by a priest of CERES.
Reading: Ferguson 1988a, 853; York 1986, 60.

Insula Tiberina (Tiber Island) The only island in the Tiber River at Rome. It was also known as Insula or Insula Aesculapii (Island of Aesculapius). A temple of AESCULAPIUS was first built there (dedicated in 291 B.C.), and then temples and shrines to JUPITER IURARIUS, FAUNUS, SEMO SANCUS, TIBERINUS and VEDIOVIS.
Reading: Nash 1962a, 508; Richardson 1992, 109–110.

Intarabus A Celtic woodland god known from two inscriptions found at Trier, Germany. In one of the inscriptions, Intarabus is equated with the Roman god MARS. Intarabus is probably the same deity as ENTARABUS.
Reading: Wightman 1970, 214, 215, 226.

Intercidona One of three Roman deities whose function was the protection of newborn babies against the evil tricks of the Roman god SILVANUS and other evil spirits. (See DEVERRA.)

interpretatio Romana (literally, "Roman translation") A term used by the historian Tacitus (*Germania* 43) to denote the identifying or pairing of one or more native gods with a Roman equivalent (such as SULIS with MINERVA). This process of syncretism stemmed from the Roman practice of not challenging traditional beliefs, but allowing native gods to come over to the Romans. In many cases, the native gods may have continued to be worshipped in a fairly traditional way, with only limited influence from Roman practices. Generally, the native gods were conflated with one of the major gods of the Graeco-Roman pantheon and often had a double name, such as SULIS MINERVA or APOLLO CUNOMAGLUS. This practice was a feature mainly of the western provinces. It did not mean that the native deity and the Roman one were considered to be equal in every respect. Thousands of native deities became assimilated, although their names are not often known. Some Roman gods assumed Celtic traits, and this reverse process is known as *interpretatio Celtica.*
Reading: Ferguson 1988a, 856.

Inuus An ancient Roman god, probably of fertility or sexual intercourse. His name was thought by some to be connected with the word *inire*, meaning "to copulate." He was named by Livy as the god who was originally worshipped at the LUPERCALIA. He was sometimes identified with the Roman god FAUNUS.
Reading: Hammond and Scullard (eds.) 1970, 432 (under *Faunus*).

I O M Abbreviation for Jupiter Optimus Maximus (nominative form) or Iovi Optimo Maximo (dative form) meaning "(To) Jupiter Best and Greatest."

Iovantucarus A Celtic god who was equated with the Celtic god LENUS at Trier, Germany, where he appears to have been worshipped as a protector of youth. He is also known to have been equated with the Roman god MERCURY.
Reading: Green, M. J. 1992a, 126.

Irene The Greek goddess of peace who was identified with the Roman goddess PAX.

iseum (pl. *isea*) The name given to a shrine or temple for the worship of ISIS. Apart from Isis, other gods (such as SERAPIS) were worshipped in these

temples, but Isis was always the prime deity. The best-preserved Roman *iseum* is at Pompeii, Italy. (See also ISIS, TEMPLE OF.)
Reading: Wild 1981.

Ishtar Also known as INNIN, this Syrian deity was originally a Babylonian deity (the personification of the planet Venus). The cult of this deity was widespread in Syria and Mesopotamia in the Roman period.

Isis (Figs. 47a, b) Egyptian mother goddess, whose son HORUS (called HARPOCRATES in the Roman world) was a heroic figure who avenged the death of his father OSIRIS (known to the Romans as SERAPIS or Sarapis). Osiris was restored to life by Isis. Herodotus identified Isis with DEMETER, but in the early Hellenistic period, she was identified with APHRODITE. The worship of Isis reached Rome early in the first century B.C., and was a mystery religion requiring initiation. By the early first century A.D. the cult was flourishing throughout the empire. She was usually worshipped in association with Serapis, ANUBIS and Harpocrates, and there might also be other divine attendants such as BES. The triad of Isis, Harpocrates and Serapis represented the power of creation.

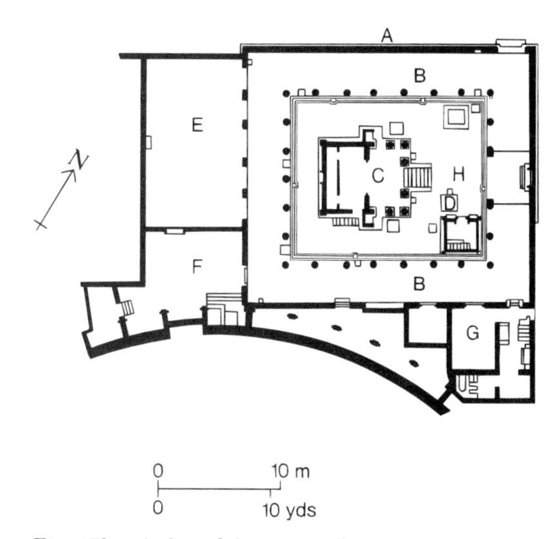

Fig. 47b A plan of the temple of Isis at Pompeii, Italy. The complex was surrounded by a high wall (A) with a single entrance so that the ceremonies could not be publicly viewed; B = portico; C = temple; D = main altar; E = meeting hall; F = initiation hall; G = priests' lodgings; H = courtyard.

Fig. 47a The columns of the portico of the temple of Isis, at Pompeii, Italy, looking south toward the temple building, which stands on a podium and is approached by steps.

A goddess of fertility and marriage, Isis was represented as loving and compassionate to individual suppliants. She was often portrayed as a loving mother, nursing her baby son Horus, an image that is often similar to portrayals of the Virgin Mary in the Christian church. She is also commonly portrayed with a ritual bucket *(situla)* for holy Nile river water (a significant part of the religion) and a rattle *(sistrum)* (Fig. 96), both objects used in her worship. The folds of her robe are sometimes shown tied in the shape of the hieroglyph *ankh* (the Egyptian symbol for "life"), and her headdress has a sun disc surrounded by a crescent moon or cow's horns. The cult of Isis involved initiation, baptism and service and promised eventual salvation. There were profes-

sional Egyptian priests. A shrine or temple to Isis was called an *ISEUM*. In Rome, the chief temple of Isis was in the CAMPUS MARTIUS, and there was at least one other temple, and several shrines, dedicated to Isis or to Isis and Serapis in various parts of the city.
Reading: Ferguson 1970, 23–26; Heyob 1975 (women in the cult); Leclant and Clerc 1972, 1974, 1985, 1991 (contains a comprehensive bibliography); Turcan 1989, 77–127; Wild 1981 (includes discussion of the use of Nile water in the cult); Witt 1971.

Isis, temple of The main temple of ISIS in Rome in the CAMPUS MARTIUS, often called Isis Campensis. It was adjacent to the temple of SERAPIS; the two collectively were known as *Iseum et Serapeum*. It was probably built in 43 B.C. and may have been destroyed by Tiberius. A new temple may have been built under Caligula and burned in the great fire of Titus in 80. It was rebuilt by Domitian and restored by Severus Alexander, who adorned it with statuary. Numerous discoveries of works of art, including Egyptian sculpture and obelisks, have been found in the vicinity. (See also *ISEUM*.)
Reading: Nash 1962a, 510; Richardson 1992, 211–212.

itineraries Routes for travelers, including Christian pilgrims. Many itineraries date from the late Roman to medieval period and gave routes to the Holy Land and to other holy sites (such as Rome) for Christian pilgrims. They include the fourth-century Jerusalem (or Bordeaux) Itinerary *(Itinerarium Burdigalense sive Hierosolymitanum)*. This is an itinerary from Bordeaux to Jerusalem which gives various routes on a Christian pilgimage to Jerusalem by way of Arles, Turin, Milan, Constantinople and Antioch, with an alternative return journey. The *Peregrinatio Aetheriae* (journey of Aetheria), dating from c. 400, is an account of a pilgrimage to the Holy Places.
Reading: Stevenson 1978, 45–47.

Iuno The Latin name for the Roman goddess JUNO. It was also the name for the guardian spirit that every woman was believed to possess, the equivalent of the *GENIUS* of a man.

Iunones A Celtic triple version of the goddess JUNO. Iunones was the name of a triad of Celtic mother goddesses worshipped in the territory of the Treveri in Gaul.
Reading: Green, M. J. 1992a, 126.

Iuppiter (or rarely, Iupiter) The Latin form of the Roman god JUPITER.

Iustitia A Roman goddess who was the personification of justice. She was equated with the Greek goddesses Dike and Astraea and was sometimes referred to in inscriptions as Iustitia Augusta ("justice of the emperor"). According to legend, she once lived happily among mortals, but their wrongdoing forced her to take flight. She took refuge in the sky, becoming the constellation of Virgo.
Reading: Hammond and Scullard (eds.) 1970, 560.

Iuturna The Latin name for the Roman goddess JUTURNA.

Iuventas (or Iuventa) The Latin name for the Roman goddess JUVENTAS.

J

Janus (in Latin, Ianus) The Roman god of beginnings and also the god of gates and doorways. He was worshipped under different names (such as JANUS BIFRONS), according to which of his aspects was most relevant to the needs of the suppliant. Janus was one of the oldest Roman gods. According to legend, he had ruled jointly with a mythical king called Camesus. Janus was supposed to have built a city on a hill, which became known as the Janiculum. He had a wife called Camise or Camasenea, and one of his children was Tiber. When Camesus died, Janus ruled Latium alone. He was supposed to have taken in SATURN, who had been driven from Greece by his son, JUPITER. While Janus reigned on the Janiculum, Saturn reigned in Saturnia, a village on the CAPITOLINE HILL. The reign of Janus was said to have been a golden age of peace and plenty, and when he died he was deified. Other legends were attached to him, including one related to the temple of JANUS GEMINUS (Fig. 49). There was another temple of Janus in the FORUM HOLITORIUM in Rome.

As god of beginnings, Janus was the first to be named in any list of gods in a prayer, and the first to receive a portion of a sacrifice. The first month of the Roman Julian CALENDAR was named after him, and January 1 was dedicated to him. This was the beginning of the new year, and it was customary to exchange small gifts: lamps to light the way through the new year were particularly popular. There was also a festival of Janus on August 17.
Reading: Grimal 1986, 241; Hammond and Scullard (eds.) 1970, 561; Simon 1990, 88–93; York 1986, 203–205.

Janus, temple of The oldest temple in the FORUM HOLITORIUM in Rome. It was built by Gaius Duilius after his naval victory over the Carthaginians at Mylae in 260 B.C. The dedication day was August 17 (the PORTUNALIA). The temple may have been near the theater of Marcellus or outside the Porta Carmentalis, but its position has not been identified. Augustus began its restoration, which was finished by Tiberius, with a dedication date of October 18, A.D. 17. A temple previously identified as this one is now thought to be that of BELLONA (just north east of the temple of APOLLO MEDICUS).
Reading: Nash 1962a, 500.

Janus Bifrons (Fig. 48) ("Janus with two faces") The Roman god JANUS depicted as having two faces

Fig. 48 A coin of Commodus (emperor 180–193) showing the emperor represented as Janus Bifrons, holding a virga *(rod). On the left the four seasons pass under an arch, and on the right a naked child (the Novus Annus—new year) advances holding a cornucopia.*

on a single head, one looking backwards and one looking forwards. This frequent depiction is sometimes regarded as symbolic of the fact that it is possible to pass in two directions through a gateway or doorway.

Janus Clusivus The Roman god JANUS who closed doors. He was invoked to ensure that the closing of a door resulted in good rather than harm.
Reading: Ogilvie 1969, 11.

Janus Geminus, temple of (Fig. 49) Referred to by contemporary writers as a shrine (*sacellum* or *sacrarium*), and the most important shrine of JANUS in Rome. It originally stood between the FORUM ROMANUM and the Julian Forum and was a permanently inaugurated bridge—*ianus*—carrying the road known as the Sacra Via over the Cloaca (a sewer or drain) to the Comitium (assembly area). It was probably a double bridge, as it was known as Ianus Geminus (twin); when the doors at each end of the bridge had to be closed for religious reasons, the other half of the bridge could still function.

Accounts of its foundation ascribe it variously to the time of Titus Tatius and more popularly to

Fig. 49 Reverse of an as *(bronze coin) of Nero, showing the temple of Janus Geminus with its doors closed, signifying peace. The legend reads PACE P R VBIQ PARTA IANVM CLVSIT SC ("Peace being provided everywhere for the Roman people, he closed the Janus").*

Numa Pompilius, as a sign of peace and war. When Rome was at war, the doors were open, when at peace, they were closed. During the war with Titus Tatius, when the Romans were hard-pressed, a huge force of very hot water gushing from the temple of Janus Geminus pushed back the enemy. This apparently explained why the doors were kept open in time of war—so that Janus could come to the aid of the Roman people if needed. They were closed throughout Numa's reign; again after the First Punic War; in 235 B.C.; in 30 B.C. (after the battle of Actium); twice under Augustus; and several times in the imperial period.

The shrine must have been moved to make way for the building of a basilica in 179 B.C. (when the Cloaca was diverted as well). It was apparently not rebuilt as a double bridge, but probably as a small rectangular structure *(ianus)* with long masonry walls and double doors at each end (as shown on coins of Nero). There may not have been a roof. Domitian subsequently moved this *ianus* to the Forum of Nerva (Forum Transitorium), where he replaced it with a *ianus* with an image of Janus with four faces, one of Rome's two Janus Quadrifrons; it must have been sited in the southwest of the Forum of Nerva, spanning the Cloaca. The old site was covered over and the Curia was built there. Later a new temple was built in front of the Curia, consisting of a small square shrine entirely of bronze. This was probably built before A.D. 193.
Reading: Richardson 1992, 207–209.

Janus Pater ("Janus the Father") Under this name, the Roman god JANUS was regarded as a god of creation.

Janus Patulcius The Roman god JANUS who opened doors. He was invoked to ensure that the opening of a door resulted in good rather than harm.
Reading: Ogilvie 1969, 11.

Jerome, Saint Eusebius Hieronymus ("Jerome" is an English version of *Hieronymus*), c. 347–420, an early Christian theologian and translator of the Bible. He was born at Stridon in Dalmatia of a prosperous Christian family. He was educated in Rome, where he was baptized c. 366, and subsequently traveled a great deal. In approximately 374 he went to Antioch, where he began theological studies and learned Greek, although he remained devoted to Latin literature. From 375 to 378 he lived in the desert of Chalcis on Syria's frontier and learned Hebrew, returning to Antioch and then to Constantinople (c. 379) and Rome (382–385), where he was secretary to Pope Damasus. He aroused the Pope's hostility, however, and left Rome, finally settling in Bethlehem as head of a monastery. He spent the rest of his life in scholarship and debate.

Jerome was an unsurpassed scholar and wrote in classical Latin. His most important work, which took 20 years to complete, was the translation of most of the Bible from the original languages into Latin in order to correct the serious errors in the earlier Old Latin versions that were then current. The Vulgate (*editio vulgata* or *lectio vulgata*—"common text") is the Latin version of the Bible most widely used in the west today, and consists mainly of the translations of the various texts by St. Jerome. The oldest extant manuscript of the Vulgate is the *Codex Amiatinus*, written at Wearmouth or Jarrow, England, between c. 690 and 700. His other main works include the *Chronicle*, a translation of Eusebius with a supplement covering the period 324–378. He also wrote *De Viris Illustribus (On Famous Men)*, an account of 135 eminent Christian writers, and at least 63 biblical commentaries. In addition there is a collection of 154 letters (some of them forgeries), written between 370 and 419, including 10 received from St. AUGUSTINE, although most were written by Jerome.

Reading: Hammond and Scullard (eds.) 1970, 562–563.

ΜΗΘΕΝΑΑΛΛΟΓΕΝΗΕΙΣΠΟ
ΡΕΥΕΣΘΑΙΕΝΤΟΣΤΟΥΠΕ
ΡΙΤΟΙΕΡΟΝΤΡΥΦΑΚΤΟΥΚΑΙ
ΠΕΡΙΒΟΛΟΥΟΣΔΑΝΛΗ
ΦΘΗΕΑΥΤΩΙΑΙΤΙΟΣΕΣ
ΤΑΙΔΙΑΤΟΕΞΑΚΟΛΟΥ
ΘΕΙΝΘΑΝΑΤΟΝ

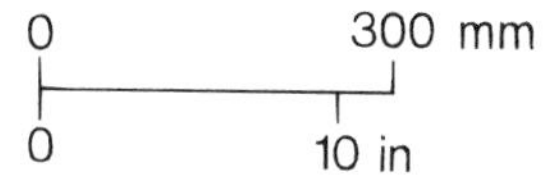

Fig. 50 This inscription forbade access for all but Jews to the precinct of the temple of Jerusalem, on pain of death. It was written in Greek for foreigners to understand. It dates to the end of the 1st century B.C. *and was found in 1871. It was engraved on a block of creamy-white limestone that measured $22\frac{1}{2}$ in. × $33\frac{1}{2}$ in. (570 mm × 850 mm). The letters were painted red, and read: "No foreigner may pass the barrier and enclosure surrounding the temple. Anyone who is caught doing so will be himself to blame for his resulting death."*

Jerusalem, temple of

(Fig. 50) The temple of the Jews in Jerusalem. The Jews built their second temple in Jerusalem when the Persian king Cyrus allowed them to return there from exile in Babylon. It was dedicated in 516 B.C., and Judaism was centered on this temple whose high priest and priests ruled Judaea and collected taxes. Jews of the DIASPORA paid a tax for this temple. In 167 B.C. under the reign of Antiochus IV it was rededicated to Olympian Zeus, but after the Maccabean Revolt it was reconsecrated to Yahweh in 164 B.C. Herod the Great replaced this small temple with a massive third temple; the building work began in 19 B.C. and was largely completed by 9 B.C. There was a great open courtyard, with colonnades along the sides, which anyone could enter. In the middle of the courtyard was a low wall or fence enclosing the temple, and notices in Greek and Latin forbade entrance to anyone but Jews. The temple consisted of a porch, central hall and shrine and was about 164 ft. (50 m) long. During the Jewish revolt (66–70) it became a fortress. By August A.D. 70, all of Jerusalem was in Roman hands except the temple. It was destroyed by Titus and was left in ruins. It was never rebuilt, and only parts of the platform and surrounding wall survive.

Reading: Smallwood 1976.

Jesus Christ

A Jew who was regarded by some as a prophet and by others as a political agitator; he was later considered to be a deity ("the son of God"), and the Christian religion was based on writings about his life and teachings. The majority of information about Jesus comes from the four gospels of the New Testament of the Bible. These were written after his death and were later collated and edited with regard to their religious, rather than historical, content. There are factual inconsistencies among the four gospels, and very little incontrovertible historical evidence has survived within them. It has been estimated that the information contained within the gospels covers no more than a total of 50 days of the life of Jesus. The exact date of birth of Jesus is unknown; it is usually calculated as around the beginning of the first century A.D. with A.D. 4 and A.D. 6 commonly put forward as likely dates.

Many periods of Jesus's life are completely unknown, but it is known that he visited towns in the Roman province of Judaea, teaching and apparently performing miracles. His teachings were based firmly on Judaism but were unfavorable to the religious establishment. He spent his last days in Jerusalem and was tried as a revolutionary before Pontius Pilate (procurator of Judaea 26–36), having been previously tried and sentenced to death by the Jewish authorities. Because he was a Jew rather than a Roman citizen, the trial Jesus received by Pontius Pilate was no more than confirmation of the original death sentence, and was for the Romans an act of political expediency. As a result, Jesus was crucified (a type of punishment normally confined to slaves) c. A.D. 30. He was buried in a rock-cut tomb and, according to his followers, was resurrected three days later. He was claimed by his followers to be the Messiah or Christ (both meaning "Lord's anointed"), who was prophesied in the Old Testament writings. Many Old Testament prophecies promised the arrival of a Messiah who would deliver the Jewish nation from all its sufferings. The spread of CHRISTIANITY by Paul and subsequent missionaries almost obliterated the historical evidence for the life and work of Jesus Christ.
Reading: Wilson 1992.

Jewish Revolts A series of revolts by Jews against the Romans. The first revolt was from A.D. 66 to 70. There had been a gradual drift to war, largely due to internal dissension between Jewish factions and a growing conflict with the Romans. The revolt spread throughout Palestine, and in 67 Vespasian was placed in charge of subduing it. By 69 the revolt was confined to Jerusalem, and it never extended to the DIASPORA Jews. Titus extinguished the revolt with his capture of Jerusalem in 70 and his destruction of the temple.

From 115 to 117 there was a huge revolt of Diaspora Jews. It began against Romans and Greeks in Cyrenaica in 115 and spread to Alexandria, most of Egypt and Cyprus. It ended in 117 with the Jewish population virtually destroyed in those areas; the Jews were excluded from Cyprus, and they never recovered their numbers or prosperity in Egypt and Cyrenaica.

In 132 another revolt of the Jews broke out in Palestine, led by Simeon Bar-Cochba ("Son of the Star"), when Hadrian established Jerusalem as a military fortress (Aelia Capitolina), so ending Jewish hopes of rebuilding the temple. This revolt was suppressed in 135 by Julius Severus (previously governor of Britain), with great devastation and loss of life suffered by the Jews. This defeat led to the final dispersion of the Jews. In 135 Hadrian forbade the Jews to enter Jerusalem, but after his death Antoninus Pius abolished persecution of the Jews.
Reading: Grant 1973; Schwartz 1988; Smallwood 1976.

Josephus Flavius Josephus, (c. 37 or 38 to after 94 or 95), born in Jerusalem, died in Rome. A Jewish historian of priestly descent, and a Pharisee. His first work, *Bellum Iudaicum (History of the Jewish War)*, in seven books, was originally written in Aramaic. His remaining works were written in Greek, including *Antiquitates Iudaicae (Jewish Antiquities)*, a history of the Jews from the Creation to 66, published in 20 books c. 93/94. His third work was the autobiographical *Vita* (Life), a reply to the allegations that he had instigated and organized one of the JEWISH REVOLTS. His last work, in two books, is widely known under the title given to it by Jerome, *Contra* (or *In*) *Apionem (Against Apion)*; in English it is commonly called *Concerning the Antiquity of the Jews.* This was a defense of Jews against anti-Semitism as personified in Apion, an Alexandrian Greek scholar.
Reading: Hammond and Scullard (eds.) 1970, 565.

Judaism An ancient monotheistic eastern religion of Judaea and Babylonia. It insisted on the worship of one god (Yahweh) alone and was based on the temple at Jerusalem. Prior to the sixth century B.C., Yahweh had been the chief god, but other deities (such as BAALS and ASTARTE) had also been worshipped. The term "Jew" actually means someone who lived in the hill-country district around Jerusalem, but it came to mean anyone who worshipped the God of Israel.

Jews regarded their god as the sole creator of all things, and the giver of all natural and moral law. They also regarded the Jewish nation as the people especially chosen by God to receive his revelation and to play the central role in human salvation. Of all the religions in the ancient world before CHRISTIANITY, Judaism was exclusive in allowing belief in and worship of only one god with only one acceptable way of worshipping that god. Worship of other gods was forbidden, and it was this aspect of Jewish religion that made it appear to the Romans at best intolerant and at worst impious and dangerous. This was not a serious problem for the Romans, since Judaea was a very small part of the empire, and Diaspora Jews elsewhere in the empire generally maintained a low profile. However, Jews were legally entitled by the Romans to follow their national religion as a *religio licita* because they were an ancient people and had been allies of Rome since the second century B.C. Tolerance of Jews (including Christians) by the pagan Romans persisted into the first century A.D., despite growing nationalism on the part of the Jews and hostility between Jews and Christians.

From c. 200 B.C. the Jews were ruled by an aristocracy of senior priests presided over by the high priest who was responsible for collection of taxes and maintenance of peace, but there were many internal divisions and conflicts. From A.D. 6 the Roman province of Judaea was governed by procurators, and opposition to direct Roman rule resulted in the foundations of a nationalist movement. After the first Jewish Revolt (66–70), the priests (who had officiated at the temple, now destroyed) were replaced as the supreme Jewish religious body by a group of rabbis (teachers); they were not priests and their head (the Nasi) replaced the high priest. The rabbis at Jamnia (Jabneh) took over the organization of the religious calendar and regulation of festivals, and Jamnia became a center of rabbinic learning. Especially after the second revolt, Rabbinic Judaism became predominant, which kept Judaism alive, although the Diaspora Jews tended to be unaffected.

Judaism was not exclusive to the Jewish nation, since non-Jews could convert to the religion, but there was no active missionary work to encourage such conversions. However, the dispersion of the Jews (the DIASPORA) throughout the empire, particularly after the destruction of the temple in Jerusalem in 70, laid the foundations for the rise of Christianity. It was from these small groups of Jews throughout the empire that Christianity initially spread, making use of the network of communications that linked these groups. Jews retained their own language and wrote in Aramaic, but the language of the Diaspora Jews was predominantly Greek, even in the western provinces. (See also JERUSALEM, TEMPLE OF.)

Reading: Gordon 1990c, 244–245; Grant 1973; Hammond and Scullard (eds.) 1970, 563–565; Schwartz 1988; Smallwood 1976.

Jugatinus A Roman god who was thought to preside over mountain ridges or possibly marriage, depending on the interpretation of the etymology of the word *Jugatinus*.

Julian (II) the Apostate Emperor 360–363; named "the Apostate" by Christian writers because he reinstated pagan cults and temples after CHRISTIANITY had become established as the Roman state religion. Julian was brought up in Cappadocia and was given a Christian education, but he acquired a passion for the classics and the old gods. He completed his education at Ephesus in Turkey (where he was influenced by the pagan philosopher Maximus) and at Athens. When he came to power, he professed his PAGANISM openly and attempted a pagan revival, proclaiming general tolerance for all religions. Julian's own religious beliefs come under the system known as Neoplatonist solar monotheism (that is, he believed in Neoplatonism and also that the sun god was the only true god, with no others existing; he saw no contradiction between this belief and Neoplatonism). He was the last pagan emperor, and after his death Christianity regained its prominence.

Reading: Bowder (ed.) 1980, 117–118; Browning 1975; Grant 1985, 251–254; Hammond and Scullard (eds.) 1970, 567–568.

Julius, Divus The deified Julius Caesar (Divus Julius) was granted divine honors by the Senate.

There appeared to have been a gradual process leading up to his deification, and it is argued that this occurred before, not after, his death. In the east, Caesar promoted his cult and built Caesarea (see CAESAREUM). In 63 B.C. he became *PONTIFEX MAXIMUS* for life, and from 47 B.C. onward he acquired several priesthoods. He also claimed divine descent from VENUS through Aeneas, and planned to build a temple to VENUS GENETRIX. Various privileges of a sacral nature were granted to him by the Senate, such as his image being carried with those of the gods in processions and a public sacrifice being carried out on his birthday. A temple was decreed by the Senate (but apparently never built) to be dedicated to Clementia Caesaris. In February 44 B.C., just before his death, Caesar was decreed a cult image *(simulacrum)* and a priest *(FLAMEN)*, with Mark Antony chosen to serve as the priest of the Divus Iulius. It therefore appears that he was deified in his lifetime, in February 44 B.C. A cult of the assassinated Caesar grew up on the site of his cremation, and it appears that his cult was encouraged in Rome, Italy and the provinces. (See also IMPERIAL CULT.)

Reading: Fishwick 1987, 56–57; Weinstock 1971.

Julius Divus, temple of The temple built on the site of Julius Caesar's cremation. After his cremation, a column and an altar were erected on the site. At the end of April 44 B.C., the consul Dolabella removed the column. In 42 B.C., the building of the temple of Divus Julius was begun; it was completed by Octavian (Fig. 37). It was dedicated on August 18, 29 B.C. The temple was hexastyle, and in the cella was a colossal statue of Julius Caesar, apparently *CAPITE VELATO* and holding a *LITUUS*, which accords with his role as an AUGUR and also as *PONTIFEX MAXIMUS*. In front of the temple was a high platform or rostra, known as the Rostra Aedis Divi Iuli. It incorporated a circular structure that could have been the original altar over the site of the cremation; alternatively, it may have been the Puteal Libonis. The rostra was decorated with the beaks of warships captured at the battle of Actium, and was used by the emperors for public addresses. The temple had the right of asylum, and the arval priests met there. The temple was repaired by Hadrian. (See also IMPERIAL CULT.)

Reading: Nash 1962a, 512; Richardson 1992, 213–214, 322.

Juno (Latin, Iuno) An ancient and important Roman goddess with many epithets. One of the CAPITOLINE TRIAD, Juno was equated with the Etruscan goddess Uni and was the wife of JUPITER, chief of the Roman gods, and mother of MARS. Juno was also identified with the Greek goddess HERA, who was the daughter of CRONUS and RHEA and the sister and wife of ZEUS. The KALENDS of every month was sacred to Juno, and she had festivals on July 1 and September 13.

Juno was worshipped under various titles or epithets, including *Interduca* ("she who leads the bride into marriage"), *Domiduca* ("she who leads the bride to her new home"), *Cinxia* ("she who looses the bride's girdle"), *Lucetia* ("bringer of light"), *Pomana* ("goddess of fruit"), *Pronuba* ("matron of honor") and *Ossipagina* ("bone setter" or "bone strengthener"). Some of these titles may have been invented as poetic descriptions and may not actually have been used in the cult of the goddess.

Reading: Hammond and Scullard (eds.) 1970, 568–569; Palmer 1974, 3–56.

Juno Caelestis ("Celestial Juno") The Roman goddess JUNO identified with the Carthaginian goddess TANIT, who was also known to the Romans as DEA CAELESTIS or Virgo Caelestis. Tanit was a mother and fertility goddess. In the Roman city of Carthage, the goddess Juno Caelestis had an ORACLE and was the chief deity of the city.

Reading: Hammond and Scullard (eds.) 1970, 187–188 (under *Caelestis*); Simon 1990, 94–106.

Juno Caprotina (very occasionally Juno Capratina) JUNO apparently was a Roman goddess of fertility. In this aspect, she was worshipped at the Feast of the Serving Women (NONAE CAPROTINAE) on July 7.

Juno Curitis The Roman goddess JUNO as "Juno protector of spearmen." She was also known as Juno Curritis and Juno Quiritis. Juno may have originally derived her name "Curitis" from the word *curiae*, because Juno was said to have been worshipped in each of the 30 military and political administrative units *(curiae)* of Rome that were set up by Romulus. It was also thought that the name was derived from *curis*, the Sabine word for "spear," and so Juno Curitis came to have a military aspect. As well as in her widespread cult in Rome, she was worshipped

in Falerii and Beneventum, Italy. A prayer to this goddess is known from the Tiburtine region in Italy: "Juno Curitis, protect my fellow natives of the curia with your chariot and shield." Juno Curitis is the only deity whose cult is known to have been universal in the *curiae* of Rome. Here she was worshipped at sacrificial suppers where first fruits and cakes made from spelt and barley were served with wine in a simple and old-fashioned way. Juno Curitis had a temple in the CAMPUS MARTIUS in Rome and a festival on October 7.
Reading: Palmer 1974, 5.

Juno Curitis, temple of A temple of JUNO CURITIS in the CAMPUS MARTIUS in Rome, possibly Temple A or C in the AREA SACRA DI LARGO ARGENTINA. Its dedication day was October 7.
Reading: Richardson 1992, 214.

Juno Lucetia The Roman goddess JUNO worshipped as "the bringer of light." Her consort, JUPITER, was sometimes addressed as Jupiter Lucetius ("Jupiter bringer of light").

Juno Lucina JUNO as a goddess of light and childbirth. This was an early aspect of the Roman goddess Juno. She probably originally derived the name *Lucina* from *lucus* (meaning "grove"). A temple in a grove on the Esquiline Hill in Rome was dedicated to her in 375 B.C., and Pliny records that the goddess took her name from this grove, in which there was an ancient tree where the VESTAL VIRGINS hung up offerings of locks of their hair. Later, the name *Lucina* was thought to indicate a goddess of light, and at least by the second century B.C., Juno Lucina came to be regarded as a goddess of childbirth, the newborn child having been "brought to light." Women who worshipped this goddess had to untie any knots on their clothing and unbind their hair to remove symbolically any hindrance to safe delivery. King Servius Tullius was said to have ordered that a coin should be placed in her temple for every birth to record the growth of the population. The Romans sometimes identified Lucina with EILEITHYIA, a Greek goddess of childbirth. Juno Lucina was worshipped at the MATRONALIA festival on March 1.
Reading: Palmer 1974, 19–21; Scullard 1981, 86–87.

Juno Martialis The Roman goddess JUNO who was portrayed on coins issued by Trebonianus Gallus (emperor 251–253). She is shown seated on a throne, sometimes in a round domed temple, with a bird and jars at her side. Sometimes she holds a scepter and sometimes an orb. The nature of this portrait suggests that the name *Martialis* does not mean "warlike," but more likely refers to the month of March: according to a late Roman CALENDAR of festivals, Juno Martialis had a festival on March 7. Trebonianus Gallus's home town was Perugia, Italy, to which he accorded special privileges, and it is possible that Juno Martialis can be identified with JUNO PERUSINA. Some modern authors, therefore, refer to her as Juno Martialis Perusina.
Reading: Palmer 1974, 32–33.

Juno Moneta (Fig. 51) The Roman goddess JUNO with the epithet *Moneta*, which possibly means "remembrancer" or "one who warns." It is likely that the original derivation of the title *Moneta* came from the word *mons* ("hill"), but according to legend, the title was given to Juno because her sacred geese had warned *(monere)* Manlius of an impending attack by the Gauls in 390 B.C., and thus saved the Capitol. Another legend explains the title by a voice that issued from Juno's temple warning the people to sacrifice a pregnant sow as expiation after an earthquake. Later (in 273 B.C.), a coin mint was set up in or near the temple, so that *moneta* possibly came to mean first "mint" and then "money"; alternatively, the mint gave Juno her title. The mint continued in use at least to the time of Augustus. Juno Moneta had a temple on the CAPITOLINE HILL

Fig. 51 A silver denarius *of the Carisia family dating to 46 B.C. On the obverse is the head of Juno Moneta, and on the reverse are represented symbols of coin minting (Vulcan's cap above the anvil, hammer and tongs of a mint worker) and the name of T. Carisius (one of the* tresviri monetales *in Rome).*

in Rome (Fig. 15). There were festivals of Juno Moneta on June 1 and October 10.
Reading: Hammond and Scullard (eds.) 1970, 698; Scullard 1981, 127.

Juno Moneta, temple of (or Juno Moneta Regina) A major temple in Rome, situated on the Arx of the CAPITOLINE HILL (Fig. 15). Its precise position is uncertain. It was vowed in a war with the Gauls by Marcus Furius Camillus in 345 B.C., and was dedicated on June 1, 344 B.C. Celebrations held at the temple on October 10 probably commemorate a later restoration. The Linen Books (Librei Lintei) were stored in the temple.
Reading: Nash 1962a, 515; Richardson 1992, 215; Scullard 1981, 127.

Juno Opigena The Roman goddess JUNO regarded as the daughter of OPS, a Roman goddess of abundance. Juno Opigena was regarded as a goddess of childbirth and presided over women in labor.

Juno Perusina JUNO as the Roman goddess of Perusia (modern Perugia), Italy. Her cult was imported to Rome by Octavian (Augustus): in 40 B.C. Octavian besieged Perugia and eventually captured it, and he was supposed to have had a dream which instructed him to take the statue of Juno from Perugia to Rome. However, there is no record of a subsequent cult of Juno Perusina in Rome, and little else is known about her. Some modern authors have identified her with JUNO MARTIALIS and sometimes refer to her as Juno Martialis Perusina.
Reading: Palmer 1974, 32–33.

Juno Populona Also known as Juno Populonia. An ancient Roman goddess known as early as the period of monarchy in Rome (eighth–sixth centuries B.C.). The word *populus* later came to mean "people," but at that time it had the meaning of "infantry"; although there was no professional army during the monarchy period, the army was made up of ordinary citizens called to arms, and so the difference between "infantry" and "people" is not as great as might appear. Juno Populona was therefore regarded as a goddess of people when they were under arms, and consequently she was a goddess of soldiers. She was also regarded as the patroness of marriage, and so indirectly of the increase in population. As a result, she came to be regarded as a goddess of the people.
Reading: Palmer 1974, 6–7.

Juno Quiritis An alternative name for the Roman goddess JUNO CURITIS.

Juno Regina ("Juno the Queen") An aspect of the Roman goddess JUNO, and part of the CAPITOLINE TRIAD (Fig. 16). There was a temple of Juno Regina on the Aventine Hill in Rome, and another in the CIRCUS FLAMINIUS. The festival of Juno Regina was on September 1. (See also JUPITER OPTIMUS MAXIMUS, TEMPLE OF.)
Reading: Scullard 1981, 183.

Juno Regina, temples of A temple was vowed in 396 B.C. by Marcus Furius Camillus during the siege of Veii in Italy to persuade the goddess to abandon Veii and come to Rome, a process of *EVOCATIO*. Following his victory over Veii, he built the temple on the Aventine Hill dedicated on September 1, 392 B.C. It contained a wooden cult statue of the goddess brought by Camillus from Veii. The temple lies close to the church of Santa Sabina. It was restored by Augustus but is not mentioned after this date. Offerings were made by women at this temple, and after the temple was struck by lightning in 207 B.C., Juno Regina received offerings that had previously been made to other gods.

Another temple to Juno Regina was vowed by Marcus Aemilius Lepidus during the Ligurian Wars. It was sited in the CIRCUS FLAMINIUS, within the CAMPUS MARTIUS. It was next to the temple of JUPITER STATOR and was dedicated by Aemilius Lepidus on December 23, 179 B.C. In 156 B.C. a portico between this temple and that of FORTUNA was struck by lightning. The temple may have been rebuilt after 146 B.C., but this temple was struck by lightning in 134 B.C. It was rebuilt by Octavia, and was burned in the fire of Titus in 80. Domitian probably rebuilt it, and it was again burned in 203. Septimius Severus and Caracalla restored it, and much remains of this latest rebuilding.
Reading: Richardson 1992, 215–217; Scullard 1981, 183.

Juno Seispita An alternative name for the Roman goddess JUNO SOSPITA.

Juno Sispes (Juno Sispes Mater Regina, literally "Juno, Savior, Mother and Queen") Originally the chief goddess of the town of Lanuvium (to the south of Rome), also worshipped by the Romans from 338 B.C. onward. In that year, after the dissolution of the Latin League (an association of towns in Latium, which attempted an unsuccessful revolt against Roman domination in a war from 340 to 338 B.C.), the Romans exchanged citizenship and religious cults with the Lanuvians. The cult came under the control of the pontiffs, and initially the Roman consuls made an annual visit to Lanuvium to sacrifice to Juno Sispes. Later, there were at least two temples to Juno Sispes in Rome. The Roman adoption of this cult was as much a political as a religious act, part of the Roman domination of Lanuvium.

Juno Sispes is portrayed on coins wearing a goatskin with the head and horns forming a helmet, shoes turned up at the toes, and with a spear, shield and chariot. Sometimes she is portrayed with a snake, and sometimes with a crow or raven. She seems to have had military associations, and was regarded by some as a protector of the state. Some of the rites performed at Lanuvium suggest that she may originally have been a fertility goddess. Juno Sispes later appears to have evolved into JUNO SOSPITA.

Reading: Palmer 1974, 30–32; Scullard 1981, 71 (under *Sospita*).

Juno Sororia JUNO as a Roman goddess of protection of girls at puberty. She had a festival on October 1.

Juno Sospita ("Juno the Savior") The Roman goddess Juno apparently as a later version of JUNO SISPES, and who was also known at an earlier period as Juno Seispiter or Juno Seispita. She was regarded as protector of the state. In Rome there was a temple of Juno Sospita in the FORUM HOLITORIUM (Fig. 15) which was vowed in 197 B.C. and dedicated in 194 B.C. Juno Sospita Mater Regina ("Juno Savior, Mother, Queen") was a goddess mainly of fertility and protection; she had a festival on February 1.

Reading: Palmer 1974, 30–32 (under *Sispes*); Richardson 1992, 217–218 (for temple); Scullard 1981, 70–71.

Jupiter The Roman sky god who was identified with the Greek god ZEUS. His Latin name was Iuppiter, or rarely, Iupiter in the nominative form. The genitive form was Iovis and the dative Iovi. In English he is also sometimes called Jove. The archaic nominative form was Diespiter, derived from Zeus and *pater* ("father"). Like Zeus, he was regarded as the chief of the gods; as such, he was sometimes identified with the Egyptian god AMON. He was also regarded as the husband of JUNO and father of MERCURY. Jupiter had many epithets and was worshipped in many aspects (such as Jupiter Custos—"Jupiter the Custodian") or associated with other gods (such as JUPITER BRIXIANUS). The Roman god VEDIOVIS was closely connected with Jupiter, but was regarded by the Romans as his opposite (that is, harmful).

Originally, Jupiter appears to have been a sky god who controlled the weather, particularly rain and lightning. A place struck by lightning *(BIDENTAL)* was considered sacred to Jupiter. Jupiter is apparently portrayed as the Celtic sky god on JUPITER COLUMNS. He is also sometimes portrayed with a spoked wheel, a symbol of the Celtic sun god. There were festivals of Jupiter on March 15, May 15 and October 15, and he was worshipped in the festival of VINALIA PRIORA on April 23. The CAPITOLINE GAMES took place on October 15, and the LUDI PLEBEII on November 4–17, both in honor of Jupiter.

Reading: Ferguson 1970, 33–36; Green, M. J. 1984, 217–264; Hammond and Scullard (eds.) 1970, 569; Simon 1990, 107–118; York 1986, 76–79.

Jupiter Beissirissa A Celtic god who was identified with the Roman god JUPITER. He is known from a dedicatory inscription to JUPITER OPTIMUS MAXIMUS BEISSIRISSA found at Cadéac, Hautes-Pyrénées, southern France.

Reading: Green, M. J. 1992a, 127.

Jupiter Brixianus A Celtic god who was identified with the Roman god JUPITER. He is known from Brescia, northern Italy. The name *Brixianus* is related to the name *Brescia* (Roman Brixia), and it is likely that the deity was a god of that locality.

Reading: Green, M. J. 1992a, 127.

Jupiter Capitolinus ("Jupiter of the Capitol") The name sometimes given to the Roman god JUPITER OPTIMUS MAXIMUS on the CAPITOLINE HILL in Rome. (See JUPITER OPTIMUS MAXIMUS, TEMPLE OF.)

Jupiter Cernenus The Celtic god CERNENUS who was linked with the Roman god JUPITER. He is known from a dedicatory inscription found in Gaul.
Reading: Ross 1974, 181–182.

Jupiter columns (Fig. 52) The god JUPITER apparently portrayed as the Celtic sky god on stone columns known as Jupiter columns (or Jupiter-Giant columns). About 150 of these columns are known, mainly in northeast Gaul and the Rhineland within the territory of the Lingones, Mediomatrici and Treveri tribes. The columns were up to 49 ft. (15 m) high. The column base was a four-sided plinth, on top of which was an octagonal plinth which supported the column itself. These plinths were decorated with images of deities, usually related to the planets, sun and moon, with dedicatory inscriptions to Jupiter and JUNO. The column was often ornamented to symbolize a tree. At the very top of the column, the capital supported a carved group of figures, commonly a horseman riding down a monster with snake limbs. The horseman sometimes wears armor, often brandishes a thunderbolt, and sometimes uses the Celtic solar symbol of the wheel as a protective shield. Although the columns have inscriptions dedicating them to Jupiter, Jupiter is not normally portrayed on horseback. The figures on top of the columns are accompanied by all the symbols of the Celtic sky god rather than symbols associated with Jupiter. It is therefore likely that the figures are of Jupiter portrayed as the Celtic sky god.
Reading: Bauchhenss and Noelke 1981; Green, M. J. 1984, 173–179; Green, M. J. 1986, 67–68.

Fig. 52 Copy of a small Jupiter column at Bitburg, Germany. Fragments of the original column are on display in the local museum.

Jupiter Conservator ("Jupiter the Savior") A shrine dedicated to this Roman god was built on the CAPITOLINE HILL in Rome. It was built by Domitian, before he became emperor, on the site of the house of an *AEDITUUS* who had sheltered him when Vitellius's supporters stormed the Capitoline Hill in 69. Domitian later built a temple of Jupiter Custos, possibly on the same site.
Reading: Richardson 1992, 218.

Jupiter Digus An Iberian god named Digus who was linked with the Roman god JUPITER. He is invoked in an inscription found in the mountains of the region of Orense, northwest Spain.
Reading: Tranoy 1981, 302 (under *I.O.M. Geius*).

Jupiter Dolichenus (Fig. 53) A local god (a Baal) of sky and weather, originally worshipped in Doliche, Turkey, and who became equated with the Roman god Jupiter. The cult was spread westward through the empire by soldiers, slaves and merchants, and Jupiter Dolichenus came to be regarded as a god of the universe (including the heavens) and

Fig. 53 Jupiter Dolichenus is flanked by Hercules and Minerva on the front side of a silvered bronze votive plaque. Jupiter Dolichenus is in military dress, standing on a bull, and holds a double-edged ax in his right hand and a lightning bolt in his left. On his left Victory offers him a crown, and on the right is a flaming altar. Above him are busts of the Sun and Moon (Sol and Luna). The votive tablet was dedicated by a centurion of the cohors I Alpinorum. *It was found at Kömlöd, Hungary (Lower Pannonia).*

of safety and success (including military success); he was identified with JUPITER OPTIMUS MAXIMUS and had JUNO REGINA as his consort. He was also sometimes identified with JUPITER HELIOPOLITANUS. He was usually portrayed wearing Roman military uniform, standing on a bull, and holding a double-headed ax and a thunderbolt. Together with MITHRAS, Jupiter Dolichenus was the most prominent of the Oriental deities to be worshipped by the army. There were shrines of Jupiter Dolichenus on the Esquiline Hill and the Aventine Hill in Rome. The main sanctuary of the cult in Doliche was sacked by the Persians in the mid-third century, and the cult subsequently lost support.
Reading: Hammond and Scullard (eds.) 1970, 359; Haynes 1993, 145–152; Hörig and Schwertheim 1987; Popa and Berciu 1978 (cult in Dacia); Speidel 1978; Tacheva-Hitova 1983, 235–249 (in Moesia Inferior and Dacia); Turcan 1989, 156–166.

Jupiter Elicius An aspect of the Roman god JUPITER who was considered by many ancient authors to regulate rainfall. *Elicius* means "drawn out" or "elicited," such as by prayer or incantation. There was an altar to Jupiter Elicius on the Aventine Hill in Rome that was believed to have been erected by King Numa to consult the god by AUGURY to determine which prodigies should be considered as omens.
Reading: Ogilvie 1969, 12; Richardson 1992, 218–219.

Jupiter Feretrius An aspect of the Roman god JUPITER whose function is not understood. The name *Feretrius* is obscure, but may mean "one who blesses weapons," "maker of agreements" or perhaps "the striker" (from *ferire*, "to strike" or "to strike dead"). There was a temple dedicated to this god on the CAPITOLINE HILL in Rome.
Reading: Richardson 1992, 219; York 1986, 217.

Jupiter Feretrius, temple of Traditionally believed to have been established by Romulus in Rome high on the CAPITOLINE HILL as a *templum* to receive the *spolia opima* (booty or trophies) that he had taken from Acron, king of Caenina. A small temple was built either at that time (eighth century B.C.) or soon afterward, and it was Rome's oldest temple. It was probably always a small temple, with the long sides measuring less than 15 ft. (4.57 m). The temple was tetrastyle with Tuscan columns. It was associated with a sacred oak tree, although some ancient authors maintained that the oak tree was cut down when the temple was built. Apart from the trophies kept in the temple, it also served as a repository for ritual implements used by the *fetiales.* There was no cult statue, only a scepter by which the *fetiales* swore, and a flint instrument *(lapis silex)* with which they sacrificed pigs. It was in a dilapidated condition when it became one of the first temples to be restored by Augustus. No trace of the temple has ever been found.
Reading: Richardson 1992, 219; Scullard 1981, 194–195.

Jupiter Fulgur The Roman god JUPITER who hurled thunderbolts or lightning in the daytime

(distinguished from SUMMANUS, who hurled them by night). A temple, which was open to the sky, was dedicated to this god in the CAMPUS MARTIUS in Rome. There was a festival of Jupiter Fulgur on October 7.
Reading: Richardson 1992, 219; Scullard 1981, 191.

Jupiter Heliopolitanus (Fig. 54) ("Jupiter of Heliopolis") The Roman god JUPITER equated with the Syrian god HADAD at Heliopolis (modern Baalbek, Lebanon). Hadad was a thunder god, the consort of ATARGATIS. Evidence of the cult of Jupiter Heliopolitanus is known from Athens and Rome, as well as from Italy, Pannonia, Gaul and Britain. He was sometimes identified with JUPITER DOLICHENUS. A temple to Jupiter Heliopolitanus was built on the Janiculum Hill in Rome and was destroyed by fire, probably around 341.
Reading: Ferguson 1970, 34; Richardson 1992, 219–220 (for temple); Turcan 1989, 145–156.

Fig. 54 A statue to Jupiter Heliopolitanus from Es Suhne, Syria, dating to the 2nd century. It was dedicated by the commander of the 2nd cohort.

Jupiter Invictus ("Unconquered Jupiter") An aspect of the Roman god JUPITER who had a festival on June 13. He may be the same as JUPITER VICTOR.
Reading: Richardson 1992, 227.

Jupiter Ladicus A local Iberian mountain god identified with the Roman god JUPITER. He was worshipped in northwest Spain as the deity of Mount Ladicus.
Reading: Green, M. J. 1992a, 127.

Jupiter Lapis The Roman god JUPITER who presided over the taking of solemn oaths. He was associated with the stones (*lapis* being Latin for "a stone") that were used in taking oaths; presumably the stones were believed to be thunderbolts.
Reading: Hammond and Scullard (eds.) 1970, 569.

Jupiter Latiaris The name by which the Roman god JUPITER was known when worshipped on the Mons Albanus (Alban Mount). This volcano was the dominant peak of the Alban Hills, 13 miles (20.92 km) southeast of Rome. Jupiter Latiaris was worshipped in the FERIAE LATINAE festival on March 27 in his role as god of the Latin League. The festival took place on the Alban Mount, originally at an altar, but from the sixth century B.C., at a temple. No trace of the temple remains, but the Via Triumphalis leading to it has been identified.
Reading: York 1986, 77.

Jupiter Leucetius An alternative spelling of JUPITER LUCETIUS.

Jupiter Liber Under this name the Roman god JUPITER was regarded as a god of creativity or creative force. He had a festival on September 1.
Reading: York 1986, 77.

Jupiter Libertas The Roman god Jupiter linked with the goddess LIBERTAS. There was a festival in Rome on April 13, and a temple on the Aventine Hill in Rome.
Reading: Richardson 1992, 221.

Jupiter Lucetius (or Jupiter Leucetius) The Roman god JUPITER worshipped as "the bringer of light." His consort, JUNO, was sometimes addressed as Juno Lucetia ("Juno bringer of light").
Reading: York 1986, 76.

Jupiter Milichius (Fig. 55) (or Zeus Meilichios, "Gracious Zeus") In about 200 B.C. a pre-Roman temple to Zeus Meilichios was built at Pompeii in Italy, and was probably rebuilt and rededicated to Jupiter Milichius by the early Roman colony in the early first century B.C. The identification of the actual temple depends on a pre-Roman Oscan inscription which was found at the site. The cult was particularly favored by the Greeks in Sicily, but was rare among the Romans. The deity was especially associated with agriculture and abundant crops, and was the patron of farmers. The temple was modest and seems to have been used as a temporary place of worship for the CAPITOLINE TRIAD (JUPITER, MINERVA and JUNO) when their nearby temple was destroyed in the earthquake of 62.
Reading: Richardson 1988, 80–82.

Jupiter Optimus Maximus ("Jupiter Best and Greatest") The supreme Roman god. Jupiter was so commonly worshipped in this form that *Iuppiter Optimus Maximus* was usually abbreviated to *I O M*. After contact with the east, he became known as "Jupiter Highest and Supremest" *(Iuppiter Summus Exsuperantissimus)*. He was worshipped above all other gods, particularly in Spain, Dacia and Pannonia. The LUDI ROMANI, games in honor of Jupiter Optimus Maximus, took place in September, with a festival on September 13. Jupiter Optimus Maximus shared temples known as *Capitolia* with JUNO REGINA and MINERVA, the three deities making up the CAPITOLINE TRIAD (Fig. 16).
Reading: Ferguson 1970, 34.

Jupiter Optimus Maximus, temple of (Figs. 16, 56) This temple on the CAPITOLINE HILL in Rome (Fig. 15) was apparently vowed by King Tarquin in his wars with the Sabines. According to legend, part

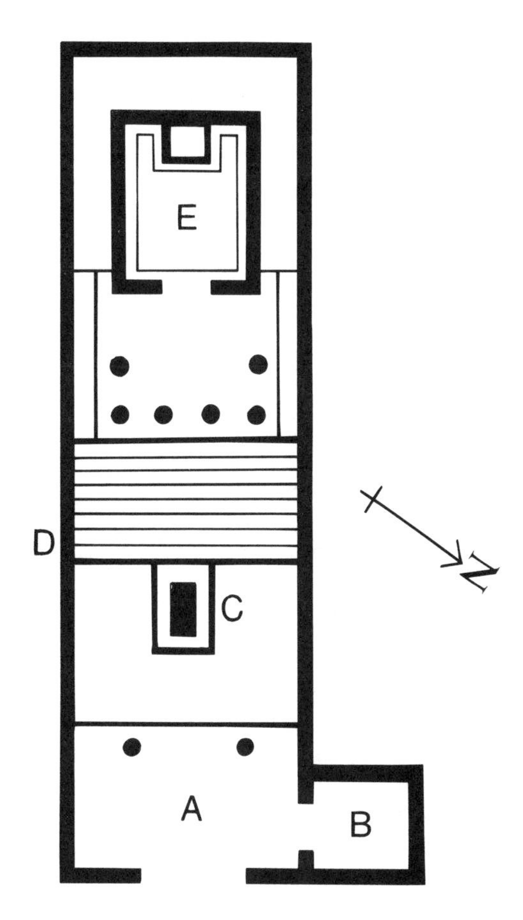

Fig. 55 Plan of the temple of Jupiter Milichius at Pompeii, Italy. A = colonnade; B = sacristy; C = large altar; D = steps; E = cella.

of the area had been occupied by other deities. They agreed to EXAUGURATION and were moved to make room for the new temple in honor of JUPITER OPTIMUS MAXIMUS. TERMINUS alone refused to move, a stand that was regarded as a good omen; JUVENTAS was added later as a deity who had also refused exauguration. The shrines of Terminus and Juventas were incorporated in the new building. Later on,

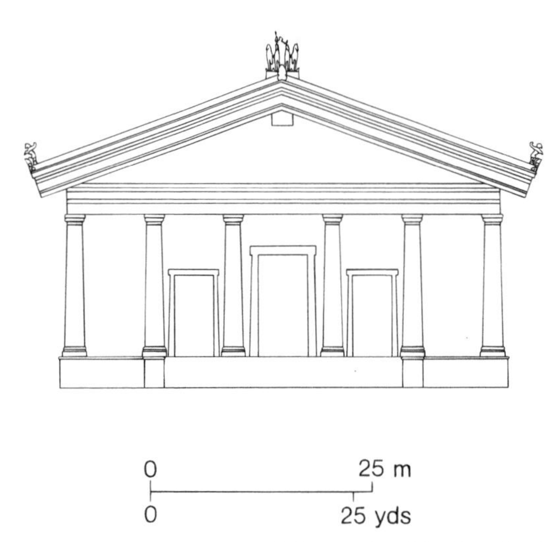

Fig. 56 Reconstruction of the temple of Jupiter Optimus Maximus Capitolinus in Rome. The facade has six Tuscan columns; the three doors lead to the three cellas.

MARS was also believed to have refused to move. The temple was dedicated on September 13, 509 B.C. by Marcus Horatius Pulvillus, the first consul of the republic.

It was the oldest republican temple in Rome, and was a triple temple dedicated to Jupiter Optimus Maximus, his consort JUNO REGINA and his daughter MINERVA (the CAPITOLINE TRIAD). It was situated on the Capitol, in the AREA CAPITOLINA. The temple was also known as the Capitolium, the temple of JUPITER CAPITOLINUS or the temple of Jupiter Optimus Maximus Capitolinus. A gold statue of VICTORIA was placed in the temple, sent by Hiero of Syracuse to encourage the Romans after their defeat at the battle of Lake Trasimene in 217 B.C. The temple was the center of state religion in Rome: victorious generals ended their processions there and offered part of their spoils to Jupiter, and consuls sacrificed there when entering office.

The first temple was probably of mud brick faced with stucco. It was burned down and rebuilt several times but seems to have retained its original Tuscan style and plan. There were three cellas side-by-side. The middle cella was dedicated to Jupiter Optimus, the right one to Minerva and the left one to Juno Regina. The cult statue of Jupiter was of terracotta and showed him brandishing a thunderbolt. There would have been cult statues for Juno and Minerva, and each deity had a separate hearth altar. The temple platform was 180 × 210 Roman feet (174.75 ft. × 204 ft.; 53.26 m × 62.14 m). The HEXASTYLE pronaos was deep, with three rather than two rows of widely spaced columns. The roof was of wood with terracotta decoration; because Terminus had to be under an open sky, the temple was not roofed over above the site of his shrine.

In 193 B.C. the temple was repaired and restuccoed, and after the Third Punic War a mosaic floor was laid in each cella. In 142 B.C. the coffered ceiling was gilded. The temple became a repository of treasures deposited by victorious generals, and many were removed in 179 B.C. because there were too many. The temple was burnt down on July 6, 83 B.C., and even the SIBYLLINE BOOKS kept in a stone chest underground were lost. The temple was rebuilt to the original plan with the funding of Sulla, a task carried out largely by Quintus Lutatius Catulus in 69 B.C. The temple was frequently struck by lightning and was renovated and repaired by Augustus in 26 B.C. and in 9 B.C. This temple was burnt down in A.D. 69 during the storming of the Capitol by supporters of Vitellius. The rebuilding by Vespasian (to the same plan, but made taller) took five years (70–75). Vespasian's temple was burnt down in the great fire of Titus in 80, and Domitian rebuilt it lavishly in 82, at a cost of 12,000 gold talents for the gilding alone. Its plunder was begun by Gaiseric in 455.

In the early republic, in an important ritual held on the Ides of September, the *praetor maximus* or another magistrate would drive a nail into the wall of the temple *(cella Iovis)*. The purpose of this ritual may have been to ward off evil. It was not carried out after the third century B.C.

Reading: Nash 1962a, 530; Richardson 1992, 221–224; Scullard 1981, 166, 186–187.

Jupiter Optimus Maximus Beissirissa The Celtic god BEISSIRISSA who was identified with the Roman god JUPITER OPTIMUS MAXIMUS. He is known from an inscription found at Cadéac, Hautes-Pyrénées, France.

Jupiter Optimus Maximus Geius An Iberian god, Geius, who was linked with the Roman god JUPITER OPTIMUS MAXIMUS. This god is known from

an inscription on an altar dedicated to "I.O.M. Geius" found at Servoy, near Verin, northwest Spain.
Reading: Tranoy 1981, 302.

Jupiter Optimus Maximus Tanarus A Celtic thunder god linked to the Roman god JUPITER OPTIMUS MAXIMUS. An inscription on an altar found at Chester, England, is addressed to Jupiter Optimus Maximus Tanarus ("Jupiter Best and Greatest Tanarus"). It was dedicated by a Roman soldier in the mid-second century. It is likely to refer to the Celtic god TARANIS, who was often identified with Jupiter.
Reading: Green, M. J. 1992a, 205–207 (under *Taranis*).

Jupiter Parthinus Also known as Jupiter Partinus, a Celtic god identified with the Roman god JUPITER. This deity is known from inscriptions found on the borders of northeast Dalmatia and Upper Moesia. The name *Parthinus* may be associated with the local tribe of the Partheni.
Reading: Green, M. J. 1992a, 127.

Jupiter Pistor ("Jupiter the Baker") JUPITER as the Roman god of bakers. According to legend, while the Capitol in Rome was besieged by Gauls and provisions were beginning to run out, Jupiter appeared to the defenders in a dream and told them to hurl their most precious possession at the enemy. Following this advice, the Romans baked all their remaining flour into loaves of bread. They threw them at the Gauls, who despaired of ever starving out the Romans, who apparently had such abundant provisions. The siege was therefore raised, and in gratitude, an altar was dedicated to Jupiter Pistor on the top of the CAPITOLINE HILL. It is more likely that the name *Pistor* is linked to thunder, and that the legend was an attempt to explain a name that was not understood.
Reading: Grimal 1986, 376; Richardson 1992, 224.

Jupiter Poeninus A Celtic god who was identified with the Roman god JUPITER and worshipped in the Alps around the Great St. Bernard Pass. A sanctuary with votive plaques dedicated to Jupiter Poeninus was established here in the Iron Age and continued in use into the Roman period. It is possible that POENINUS is the same deity as POININUS who is known from Turnovo, Bulgaria, where he is equated with the Roman god SILVANUS.
Reading: Dorcey 1992, 75; Green, M. J. 1992a, 127.

Fig. 57 A silver denarius *of Gordian III, with the reverse showing the figure of Jupiter Stator carrying a spear. The legend reads IOVIS STATOR.*

Jupiter Propugnator ("Jupiter the Defender" or "Jupiter the Champion") There was a temple dedicated to this aspect of the Roman god JUPITER on the Palatine Hill in Rome.
Reading: Richardson 1992, 224.

Jupiter Stator (Fig. 57) An aspect of the Roman god JUPITER. "Jupiter Stayer of the Rout" caused the people or troops to stop their flight, rally and stand their ground. There were festivals of Jupiter Stator on June 27 and September 5.
Reading: Richardson 1992, 225.

Jupiter Stator, temples of According to legend, one temple to JUPITER STATOR was vowed by Romulus in the battle between the Sabines and Romans. A temple building was never constructed, but in 294 B.C. the consul Marcus Atilius Regulus made a similar vow during a battle with the Samnites when the Romans rallied and stood their ground. A temple was built in Rome in the location where Romulus had laid out a *templum*, at the foot of the Palatine Hill on the Sacra Via (Fig. 37), just southwest of the Arch of Titus. Foundations of the temple were discovered when a medieval tower was being demolished in 1829. Its dedication day was June 27. It was PROSTYLE, HEXASTYLE, with a square cella and a deep porch. On November 8, 63 B.C., the Senate met here for the only recorded time, when Cicero delivered his first oration against Catiline.

Another temple was situated in the CIRCUS FLAMINIUS. It was adjacent to the later-built temple of JUNO REGINA, but its date of construction is disputed; possibly before the early second century B.C. It was rebuilt by Octavia, and burned in the fire of Titus. It was subsequently restored by Domitian and possibly later by Septimius Severus as well.

Reading: Nash 1962a, 534; Richardson 1992, 225–226.

Jupiter Taranis A Celtic god of thunder, TARANIS, who was linked to the Roman god JUPITER as Jupiter Taranis.

Jupiter Tonans ("Jupiter the Thunderer") An aspect of the Roman god JUPITER who had a temple on the CAPITOLINE HILL in Rome which was vowed by Augustus after he was nearly struck by lightning in 26 B.C. There was a festival of this god on September 1.

Reading: Richardson 1992, 226–227.

Jupiter Uxellinus A Celtic god who was identified with the Roman god JUPITER. This deity was a local high mountain god, worshipped in Austria.

Reading: Green, M. J. 1992a, 127.

Jupiter Victor ("Victorious Jupiter") An aspect of the Roman god JUPITER who had a festival on April 13 and a temple on the Palatine Hill in Rome. He may be the same as JUPITER INVICTUS.

Reading: Richardson 1992, 227.

Justinian I Emperor from 527 to 565 and suppressor of Christian heresy and PAGANISM. Justinian became sole emperor of the eastern part of the empire in 527. As part of his attempt to restore order and to regain the western provinces (which had been lost to the barbarians), he drastically reinforced the laws against pagans, Jews and heretics. He was a strongly religious person who believed that the greatness of the empire depended on God's favor. His religious reforms were therefore made in concert with administrative reforms and military attempts to regain lost provinces—all were practical moves to restore the empire's greatness.

Reading: Adkins and Adkins 1994, 37; Hammond and Scullard (eds.) 1970, 571.

Juturna A Roman water NYMPH known in Latin as Iuturna or Diuturna. She was also regarded as a goddess of healing. According to legend, Juturna was the sister of CASTOR and POLLUX. Originally this goddess was the spirit of the river Numicus, but she later became identified with the spirit of the spring in the southwest corner of the FORUM ROMANUM in Rome, near the temple of Castor. This site, with a formal pool and shrine, was known as the Lacus Iuturnae (spring of Juturna) (Fig. 37). Juturna also had a temple in the CAMPUS MARTIUS in Rome, near the Aqua Virgo. It was vowed by Gaius Lutatius Catulus, consul in 242 B.C. Its dedication day was January 11, the same as one of the two days of the CARMENTALIA festival. Juturna's festival, the JUTURNALIA, was on January 11.

Reading: Grimal 1986, 245; Scullard 1981, 62.

Juturnalia A festival of JUTURNA held on January 11. It is mentioned by OVID but appears in no calendars.

Reading: Warde Fowler 1899, 293.

Juventas The modern form of the name of the Roman goddess known in Latin as Iuventas or Iuventa. Her function was the protection of youth (men of military age). When a man first put on an adult toga, it was customary to make an offering of money to the goddess at a small shrine in the cella of MINERVA within the temple of JUPITER OPTIMUS MAXIMUS. Juventas came to be regarded as a protector of youth in a more general sense and so was sometimes identified with the Greek goddess HEBE. There was a temple of Juventas near the CIRCUS MAXIMUS in Rome, and she may have had a festival on December 19.

Reading: Hammond and Scullard (eds.) 1970, 561; Richardson 1992, 228.

K

Kalends (Latin, Kalendae) The first day of the month, sacred to JUNO, especially the first day of the month of March. A minor pontiff with the *REX SACRORUM* offered a sacrifice after the new moon appeared, and announced the date of the NONES.
Reading: Scullard 1981, 126; York 1986, 2.

Kore An alternative Greek name for the Greek goddess PERSEPHONE.

Kybebe An alternative Lydian Greek name for the Anatolian goddess Cybele (MAGNA MATER).

Kybele An alternative Greek name for the Anatolian goddess Cybele (MAGNA MATER).

L

Lactans A Roman god who promoted the growth of young corn.

Lactantius Lucius Caecilius (or Caelius) Firmianus Lactantius, c. 245–c. 325, a Christian writer and apologist. He was from North Africa. He studied rhetoric, converted to Christianity, and achieved considerable fame as an author and apologist. Only his Christian works survive, all written after the Christian persecutions began, most notably *De Opificio Dei (On God's Handiwork)* (303–304), *De Ira Dei* (*On the Wrath of God*, possibly 314) and *Divinae Institutiones (Divine Institutions)*, written in seven books between 303 and 313. Because of his style, he came to be called the "Christian Cicero" in the Renaissance.
Reading: Hammond and Scullard (eds.) 1970, 575–576.

Lacus Iuturnae A spring-fed pool in the FORUM ROMANUM in Rome, (Fig. 37) associated with a shrine (*aedicula*) of the goddess JUTURNA. The pool was between the temple of CASTOR and the atrium Vestae. Here the DIOSCURI were seen watering their horses after the battle of Lake Regillus in 496 B.C. and apparently again after the battle of Pydna in 168 B.C. The pool was excavated in 1900 and a basin 6.95 ft. (2.12 m) deep was found. About 13 ft. (4 m) to the south was the shrine. It may have become a healing cult center by the second century—statues of AESCULAPIUS and APOLLO have been found in the area. Water from the pool was used in official sacrifices in Rome.
Reading: Nash 1962b, 9; Richardson 1992, 230–231.

Ladicus An Iberian god who was linked with the Roman god JUPITER as JUPITER LADICUS.

Laesus An Iberian deity who was known from an inscription on an altar found near Vinhais, Portugal. The altar was dedicated by Elanicus Taurinus, who was probably a native of the region, but nothing else is known about the deity Laesus.
Reading: Tranoy 1981, 275.

Laha A Celtic goddess who was worshipped in the foothills of the Pyrénées, France. She appears to have been a water goddess associated with springs. She may be connected with the Iberian god LAHUS PARALIOMEGUS.
Reading: Tranoy 1981, 289 (under *Lahus Paraliomegus*).

Lahus Paraliomegus An Iberian god who is known from an inscription found at Lugo, northwest Spain. He may be connected with the Celtic goddess LAHA.
Reading: Tranoy 1981, 289.

Lamiae Tres ("Three Witches") Possible Celtic deities known from a dedication on an altar found at Benwell on Hadrian's Wall, England. Witches were not normally considered as deities, and this dedication appears to be unique. It is possible that they were similar to the Celtic mother goddesses known as the MATRES. The Latin word *lamia* (pl. *lamiae*) means "ogre" as well as "witch"; in order to frighten naughty children, the name was also given to a child-eating monster, who always had a child in her stomach. It is most unlikely that the dedication to the three Lamiae was used in the direspectful way that the translation "witch" or "ogre" might imply in a modern context.
Reading: Blagg 1982, 126; Hammond and Scullard (eds.) 1970, 577 (for *Lamia the child-stealer*).

lapis manalis A stone used as a rain charm. It was kept in the temple of MARS outside the Porta Capena in Rome; in periods of drought the pontiffs carried it through the streets to induce rain. By the late second century it was regarded as a stone that closed the entrance to the UNDERWORLD (but it was not associated with the *MUNDUS*).
Reading: Richardson 1992, 244; York 1986, 37.

lar (pl. *lares*) Household deities whose original character is unclear. Each Roman household had its own protective *lar* or deity. MANIA was allegedly the mother of the *lares*, but OVID states that LARA was their mother. It is possible that the *lares* were originally farmland gods (possibly gods of the dead), later introduced into households as *lares familiares*, or guardian spirits. By the late republic, they were guardian spirits of the house and household (Fig. 97) and were worshipped at the household hearth on the KALENDS, NONES and IDES of each month. It was the role of the *paterfamilias* to ensure the continued protection of the *lar*, and to maintain a *lararium* (shrine to the household gods), usually in a corner of the *atrium*.

In parallel with the domestic situation, the Romans came to recognize many types of *lares* such as the *LARES COMPITALES* who presided over crossroads, and the *lares publici* (or *lares praestites*) who protected the whole city. There was a temple dedicated to the *lares* at the head of the Sacra Via in Rome, and there were festivals of the *lares* on June 27 and December 22.
Reading: Hammond and Scullard (eds.) 1970, 578–579; Richardson 1992, 232 (temple); Simon 1990, 119–125.

Lara A Roman NYMPH who was the daughter of the Roman god ALMO, the deity of the Almo River in Latium. In mythology Lara was a talkative nymph whose tongue was cut out by JUPITER, and so she was worshipped in Rome with the epithet *Tacita* or *Muta* ("silent" or "mute"). Some ancient authors equated her with LARUNDA and MANIA. OVID regarded her as the mother of the *lares*, though this description was possibly his own invention.
Reading: York 1986, 53.

lararium (Figs. 58, 97) (pl. *lararia*) A late Latin and modern term for *AEDICULA*. *Lararia* were private household shrines or chapels found particularly at Pompeii in Italy. They mainly took the form of simple gabled niches in the wall, niches painted on the wall, or small freestanding shrines. One or two *lares* and a *GENIUS* of the *paterfamilias* portrayed as a male (bearded) snake and sometimes also as a man with head religiously covered by his toga are depicted on them. Sometimes there were objects in the *lararia* as well, such as statuettes and paintings of deities to which the household was attached. When PAGANISM was finally banned by Theodosius I in 392, the household cult and such shrines were also banned.
Reading: Dowden 1992, 30; Ferguson 1988b, 921–922.

Fig. 58 A lararium *discovered in the Via della Statuto, Rome, in 1883, with images of the household's ancestors in the niches.*

Laraucus An Iberian mountain god who is known from inscriptions found in northern Portugal and northwest Spain. He was worshipped in the Serra do Larouco mountains (whose name apparently derives from him). The god LAROCUS is probably the same deity. He was linked with REVA as Reva Laraucus at Ginzo de Limia, in northwest Spain.
Reading: Alarcão 1988, 94; Tranoy 1981, 281.

Larentalia (later called the Larentinalia) The festival of ACCA LARENTIA, held on December 23. It consisted of funeral rites at the supposed tomb of Acca Larentia and was celebrated by the pontiffs and the *FLAMEN QUIRINALIS*.
Reading: Scullard 1981, 211–212.

Larentina A Roman goddess worshipped at the festival of LARENTALIA and who was also known as ACCA LARENTINA.

lares Augusti The "guardian spirits of the emperor." (See *LARES COMPITALES*.)

lares compitales Roman deities *(lares)* who presided over the crossroads. Each district *(vicus)*, into which Rome was divided, had a central point where roads met (a *compitum*). At these places, the two *lares* from the two adjoining areas presided over the crossroads. Shrines were erected to these *lares compitales*, and they were worshipped at the COMPITALIA, which was an agricultural festival.

In 7 B.C. Augustus reorganized Rome into 265 *vici*, ensuring that there was a shrine at each *compitum*. He ordered that two statues of the *lares* and one of the *GENIUS* of Augustus himself should be placed in each shrine, and that sacrifices should be made during the Compitalia. This gave the *lares*, previously a private cult, a public aspect. The epithet "Augusti" became attached to the figures of the *lares* and *genius*, and the cult of the *lares Augusti* developed. (See *LAR*.)
Reading: Alcock 1986, 115; Fishwick 1987, 85.

lares permarini Roman deities *(lares)* who protected sailors. A temple in the CAMPUS MARTIUS in Rome was dedicated to them in 179 B.C.
Reading: Scullard 1981, 210.

Lares Permarini, temple of A temple to the deities who protected sailors, vowed by Lucius Aemilius Regillus in 190 B.C. during a naval battle against the fleet of Antiochus the Great. It was dedicated by Marcus Aemilius Lepidus on December 22, 179 B.C. It was situated in the CAMPUS MARTIUS in Rome and is thought to be the temple once incorrectly identified as that of BELLONA. It was an imposing OCTASTYLE temple, and was rebuilt in the late republic or in Augustan times. It was heavily repaired by Domitian after the fire of Titus in 80.
Reading: Patterson 1992, 196; Richardson 1992, 233.

lares praestites The guardian spirits of the Roman state known only from OVID. In Rome, they had an altar, possibly in the Colline district of the Quirinal and Viminal Hills. There was a festival of the *lares praestites* on May 1. They were also known as *lares publici*.
Reading: Richardson 1992, 233.

lares viales Roman guardian spirits of roads. There were altars dedicated to these deities along the roads outside Rome.
Reading: Scullard 1981, 156.

lar familiaris (pl. *lares familiares*) The guardian spirit of the household. (See *LAR*.)

Lariberus Breus An Iberian god who is known from inscriptions on a series of altar fragments from Hio, Cangas, near Pontevedra, northwestern Spain. At this site, variants of the god's name include Laribreus Brus, Lariberus Breoronis and Lariberus Breoro. The collection of altar fragments and other sculptural fragments from the site implies that it was a cult center of this god.
Reading: Tranoy 1981, 293.

Larocus An Iberian deity who is known from an inscription found near Chaves, northwestern Spain. Larocus is probably the same deity as LARAUCUS.
Reading: Tranoy 1981, 281.

Larunda An obscure Roman goddess, probably a deity of the UNDERWORLD. She was equated with LARA by some ancient authors. There was an annual sacrifice to Larunda at an altar in the Velabrum in Rome on December 23.
Reading: Hammond and Scullard (eds.) 1970, 579.

larvae An alternative name for the Roman evil spirits known as the *LEMURES*.

Latis A Celtic goddess who is known from Cumbria, England. She was a local goddess of watery places, bogs and pools. Inscriptions mentioning this

goddess are known from Fallsteads and from Birdoswald, on Hadrian's Wall.
Reading: Green, M. J. 1992a, 130.

Latobius A Celtic god of mountains and sky who was worshipped in Austria. He was equated with the Roman gods MARS and JUPITER. A dedication to Mars Latobius has been found 6,561 ft. (2,000 m) above sea level on the highest peak of Mount Koralpe, Austria.
Reading: Green, M. J. 1992a, 130.

Latona The Latin name for the Greek goddess LETO, mother of APOLLO and ARTEMIS.

Laverna The Roman goddess who was patron and protector of thieves and impostors. She had an altar in Rome near the gate known as the Porta Laverna.

lead tanks (Fig. 59) Circular lead vessels or tanks found only in Britain. The known examples (about 17 in number) range from 1.48 ft. to 3.15 ft. (0.45 m to 0.96 m) in diameter, and 6 in. to 1.5 ft. (0.16 m to 0.48 m) in height. They range in capacity from just under seven to almost 90 U.S. gallons (27 to 360 liters). They may have had a Christian liturgical function, such as ritual ablution, with a person standing in the tank while water was poured over his or her head, although some are too small for this function. It is also suggested that they were used for *pedilavium*, footwashing undertaken as part of the baptismal rite, which would explain their small size. The tanks were made of sheet lead and usually had two handles. The exterior of the tanks was decorated. Six tanks bore a CHI-RHO monogram, one an alpha and omega, and there were also other symbols of a Christian nature. The tanks may be of fourth-century date.
Reading: Guy 1981; Guy 1989; Watts 1988.

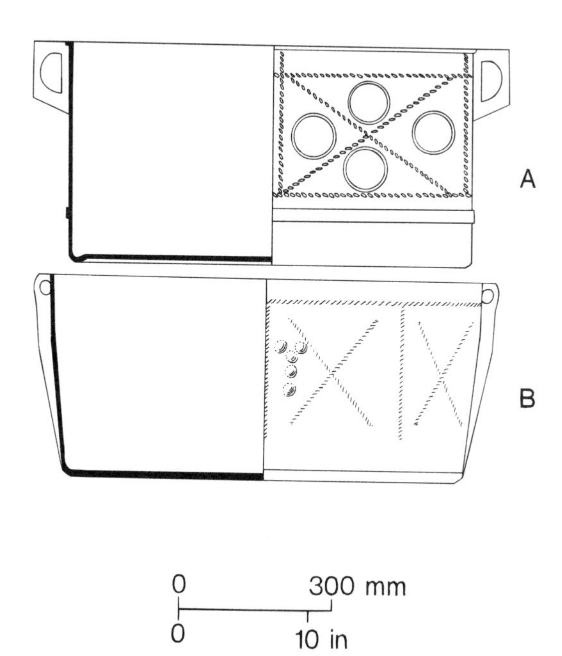

Fig. 59 Two lead tanks from England. A *is from an unknown provenance;* B *is from a villa at Bourton-on-the-Water and weighs 135 kg (297½ lbs).*

lectisternium (pl. *lectisternia*) Banquet for one or more gods. A *lectisternium* was part of a special religious festival, usually expiatory or of supplication, in which a banquet was offered to the gods. Dining couches were laid out for the gods on which they could recline and on which images or symbols representing the gods were publicly displayed. The feast could last several days. A *sellisternium* was a similar festival for goddesses, in which chairs *(sellae)* with cushions and symbols of the deities were prepared. They were for sitting, not reclining.
Reading: Hammond and Scullard (eds.) 1970, 590.

lemures Also known as *larvae*, they were regarded by the Romans as evil spirits or ghosts. They were spirits of the dead who were believed to haunt households on May 9, 11 and 13, the festival days of the LEMURIA. The most terrifying were those who had died young, since they were thought to bear a grudge. They were regarded as ghosts or hostile spirits in contrast to the spirits of dead members of the immediate family who were worshipped in the PARENTALIA.
Reading: Hammond and Scullard (eds.) 1970, 594; Toynbee 1971, 64; Warde Fowler 1899, 107–109.

Lemuria A festival held on May 9, 11 and 13 (successive uneven days, as even-numbered days were considered unlucky) to appease the spirits of the dead *(LEMURES)* at a time when they were supposed to haunt the house. Little is known of the

public rites, although there is information derived from OVID about domestic and private rites. Each head of the household *(paterfamilias)* rose at midnight and made the *MANO FICO* sign, and walked barefoot through the house. As he went, he spat out nine black beans, or else having first washed his hands, cast some black beans over his shoulder. These beans were possibly for the ghosts to eat as ransom for the living members of the household, who would otherwise be carried off by the ghosts. This action was accompanied and followed by other rites designed to drive away the ghosts.
Reading: Toynbee 1971, 64; Warde Fowler 1899, 106–111.

Leno A Celtic god who was the eponymous protective deity of Lérins, Provence, France. Other than dedicatory inscriptions which mention his name, little is known about this god.
Reading: Green, M. J. 1992a, 131.

Lenumius A Celtic god who was linked with the Roman god MARS as MARS LENUMIUS.

Lenus An important Celtic healing god of the Treveri tribe who had sanctuaries at medicinal springs at Trier and Pommern in Germany. Dedications to this god are also known from Britain. Lenus was sometimes equated with the Celtic god IOVANTUCARUS, apparently a protector of youth. Lenus was also equated with MARS at Trier and is more usually referred to in inscriptions as Lenus Mars, rather than Mars Lenus; the fact that the name of the Celtic deity Lenus usually has precedence suggests that Lenus was an established god in the locality before the impact of Roman influence. An inscription from Caerwent, Wales, refers to MARS LENUS equated with OCELOS VELLAUNUS. The sanctuary at Trier was enlarged in the mid-second century, and a large Romano-Celtic temple, baths and a huge altar were built. There may also have been a theater as part of the temple complex. At this Trier sanctuary, Mars Lenus's partner was the Celtic goddess ANCAMNA.
Reading: Green, M. J. 1992a, 142–143 (under *Mars Lenus*); Ross 1974, 226–227.

Lesser Quinquatrus A festival of the guild of flute players *(tibicines)*, who played an important part in religious ceremonies. It took place June 13–15, when they apparently roamed the streets of Rome wearing masks, long robes and making music.

Leto A Greek goddess who was mother of the Greek god APOLLO and the Greek goddess ARTEMIS. She was known to the Romans as Latona and was sometimes equated with the Roman goddess DIANA.

Leucothea (probably meaning "white goddess") A Greek sea goddess who was identified with the Greek goddess INO and sometimes with the Roman deity ALBUNEA.
Reading: Grimal 1986, 259.

libation A sacrifice of liquids offered to the gods by pouring them on the ground or over altars (Fig. 89). The most common liquid was undiluted wine, but other liquids such as milk, honey and even water were used. Libations were also offered to the dead during burial ceremonies and at subsequent ceremonies at the tomb, often by pouring them into the grave.

Liber (or Liber Pater, "Liber the Father") A Roman fertility god who had an important cult on the Aventine Hill in Rome. He shared a temple with the Roman goddess CERES and his female equivalent LIBERA, although he does not appear to have had his own temple in Rome. During a famine in 496 B.C., the SIBYLLINE BOOKS recommended that the worship of DEMETER, IACCHUS and KORE (Greek deities associated with the ELEUSINIAN MYSTERIES) be identified with the Roman gods Ceres, Liber and Libera. There was a temple on the Aventine Hill in Rome where these three deities were worshipped together. Liber was sometimes identified with the North African god Shadrapa (a healing god worshipped by the Carthaginians). As Liber Pater, he was often identified with the Greek god DIONYSUS, even though the god Liber does not appear to have been associated with wine. Liber had a festival (LIBERALIA) on March 17, apparently shared with Libera.
Reading: Hammond and Scullard (eds.) 1970, 607.

Libera A Roman goddess who was the female equivalent and partner of the Roman god LIBER. She was identified with the Greek goddess PERSEPHONE and apparently shared the LIBERALIA festival of Liber on March 17. With the Roman gods CERES and Liber, she was part of an important cult centered on the temple shared by these three deities on the Aventine Hill in Rome.

Liberalia The festival of LIBER PATER and his consort LIBERA on March 17. It was celebrated with sacrifices, crude songs and masks hung on trees. There may have been games but they were no longer held by the time of OVID.
Reading: Scullard 1981, 91–92.

Liberalitas A Roman deity who was the personification of generosity. This deity was invented and used for propaganda purposes to encourage support of the emperor. By the second century, it had become the spirit of the emperor's donative to the soldiers.
Reading: Ferguson 1970, 72.

Libertas A Roman goddess who was the personification of liberty, the condition of a free man (not a slave but not necessarily possessing other rights, including political ones). Under the empire, Libertas came to mean the personification of political liberty. This goddess had a temple on the Aventine Hill in Rome which was founded around 238 B.C. and which was restored by the emperor Augustus. She was sometimes associated with FERONIA and with JUPITER, and there was also a temple of JUPITER LIBERTAS on the Aventine Hill.
Reading: Hammond and Scullard (eds.) 1970, 607.

Libitina A Roman goddess of funerals who supervised burials and rites in honor of the dead. Erroneous etymology connected the words *Libitina* (goddess of funerals) with *Lubentina* (a title probably meaning passionate or pleasurable), and Libitina became equated with VENUS as VENUS LIBITINA or VENUS LUBENTINA. There was a temple dedicated to Venus Libitina in Rome, probably near the Esquiline cemetery. It was here that all the funeral undertakers *(libitinarii)* assembled and where all burials in Rome were registered. By custom a coin was deposited in this temple for each of the dead.
Reading: Richardson 1992, 235; Scullard 1981, 177.

Limentius Also known as Limentinus, this Roman god presided over thresholds of doorways.
Reading: Ogilvie 1969, 11.

lituus A special emblem used by the augurs when taking auspices to mark out a *TEMPLUM*. It was a curved staff with its top shaped like a question mark, similar to a crosier. It was Etruscan in origin. It was not the same shape as the war trumpet, used for giving military signals and also known as a *lituus*.

loculus (pl. *loculi*) A term used for small chambers at the base of temples in which valuables were deposited. These chambers were entered from outside (not inside) the temples, and were sealed by doors. The word *loculus* also meant a pigeonhole or niche in a tomb for the deposition of a cinerary urn.

Loucetius (or Leucetius) A name meaning "lightning" or "brilliant," linked with the Roman god MARS as MARS LOUCETIUS or Loucetius Mars. Loucetius was either a Celtic god or a title.

Lua Mater A Roman goddess of the earth who was a cult partner of SATURN. Her name may mean something like "baneful," and it is possible that she was a goddess of pestilence, by which her suppliants hoped that their enemies would be struck down. She was one of the deities to whom captured arms could be dedicated and burned.
Reading: Hammond and Scullard (eds.) 1970, 620; York 1986, 71–72.

Lucaria A festival held on July 19 and 21. It was celebrated in a large grove *(lucus)* between the Via Salaria and the Tiber River in Rome. Its meaning has been lost, and the festival meant little by the late republic. It may have been held because the Romans hid in this grove after fleeing the Gauls (the battle of Allia in 390 or 387 B.C. being on July 18). It more likely originated in early Rome when the forests were cleared for agriculture and settlement and their spirits had to be propitiated.
Reading: Warde Fowler 1899, 182–185.

Lucina The Roman goddess of bringing things to light, and therefore also of birth. She was often identified with the Roman goddesses DIANA and JUNO and also with the Greek goddess EILEITHYIA.

Lucoubus Arquienis An Iberian god who was probably the same deity as the Iberian god LUGUBUS ARQUIENOBUS.

lucus A sacred grove, sometimes adjoining a temple and part of its precinct, or else a grove with no temple building, dedicated to a particular deity. More usually, a *lucus* was a grove, often near Rome, such as that of the ARVAL PRIESTS. It is thought that the word *lucus* may have the same meaning as a *templum* and did not necessarily contain trees—it was simply the place where a deity lived. (See also GROVES, SACRED; *NEMUS*.)
Reading: Beard 1993; Richardson 1992, 2; Scheid 1993.

ludi Public games (Latin, *ludi*) originally held at some religious festivals, but gradually the entertainment factor of the games became more important than their religious significance. They originated as votive games in honor of JUPITER OPTIMUS MAXIMUS (the LUDI ROMANI), which before about 220 B.C. were the only annual games. Other annual games were established later. New *ludi* were repeatedly decreed and added to the calendar, such as the LUDI APOLLINARES and LUDI VICTORIAE SULLANAE. While regarded as festivals, the games were not strictly festivals known as *FERIAE,* but were regarded as *dies festi* (feast days or holidays in honor of a god). The type of entertainment varied and included chariot races in the circus, gladiatorial fights and theatrical entertainment. In the late republic, games that had formed part of the cult of Hellenistic kings in the east subsequently became part of the cult of Roman generals and administrators. Many games were held in eastern provinces in honor of deities and the IMPERIAL CULT, such as the ROMAIA.
Reading: Friesen 1993, 114–141; Scullard 1981; Warde Fowler 1899; York 1986, 4–5.

Ludi Apollinares (Apolline Games) Games *(LUDI)* in honor of APOLLO which were established in Rome in 212 B.C. during the Second Punic War. They were held every four years, and from 208 B.C. annually on July 13. Apollo was expected to help the Romans in war and as a healing god. The games became very popular and extended back to July 6–13, two days being for circus games and two for theatrical plays. There were also sacrifices to Apollo and everyone present wore garlands. After the games there were six days of markets or fairs *(mercatus)*.
Reading: Scullard 1981, 159–160, 164, 188.

Ludi Capitolini The Latin name for the CAPITOLINE GAMES.

Ludi Florales Annual games *(LUDI)* that took place in the FLORALIA festival.

Ludi Plebeii (Plebeian Games) Games *(LUDI)* that were held November 4–17 in honor of JUPITER. Entertainment such as chariot racing was held in the CIRCUS MAXIMUS. The games were probably established in 220 B.C. by Gaius Flaminius when he was censor. Only the LUDI ROMANI were more important than these games. They were the responsibility of the plebeian aediles.
Reading: Scullard 1981, 196–197.

Ludi Romani (or *ludi magni*) Games *(LUDI)* originally celebrated on the occasion of a triumph. They came to be held September 4–19 in honor of JUPITER OPTIMUS MAXIMUS. Originally they took place only on September 13. They gradually expanded to 10 days by the late republic, and 15 days by the time of Julius Caesar, with an extra day to honor Caesar, so covering half the month. By at least 366 B.C. they had become annual games. On September 13 the *EPULUM IOVIS* ("feast of Jupiter") took place. The games were the responsibility of the curule aediles. They started with a solemn procession from the Capitol to the CIRCUS MAXIMUS, where a sacrifice took place, followed by *ludi circenses* and *ludi scaenici*, including chariot races.
Reading: Hammond and Scullard (eds.) 1970, 569; Scullard 1981, 182–185.

Ludi Saeculares (Secular Games or Tarentine Games) According to legend, these games *(LUDI)* were founded by the first consul in 509 B.C., Publius Valerius Poplicola, at the altar of DIS and PROSERPINA to commemorate its discovery 20 ft. (6.09 m) underground by an ancestor, at a place in the CAMPUS MARTIUS called Tarentum (or Terentum). The games were held every century to ensure the avoidance of pestilence. The appropriate dates in the cycle of the Secular Games were disputed in antiquity. The games included three days and three nights of continuous stage plays. The Secular Games of 17 B.C. culminated in a ceremony at the temple of APOLLO. Detailed records of the games under Augustus (17 B.C.) and Septimius Severus (A.D. 204) were found in inscriptions in 1890 and

1930, 328.08 yds. (300 m) to the northwest of the altar of Dis and Proserpina.
Reading: Palmer 1974, 94–108.

Ludi Taurei quinquennales (Ludi Taurii or Taurian Games) Games *(LUDI)* held on June 25–26 every five years in order to honor the gods of the UNDERWORLD *(DI INFERI)*. Games, including horse racing, were held in the CIRCUS FLAMINIUS. Their last recorded celebration was in 186 B.C. It has been suggested that bullfighting and sacrifice took place, but the derivation of the name is also attributed to the sale of beef to pregnant women in the time of Tarquinius Superbus (the word for bull being *taurus*) which led to an outbreak of plague. The games were therefore instituted to appease the gods of the UNDERWORLD who were responsible for outbreaks of plague.
Reading: Scullard 1981, 156.

Ludi Victoriae Caesaris Games *(LUDI)* in honor of Julius Caesar and of VICTORIA, a goddess closely connected with Caesar. They took place July 20–30. After the battle of Pharsalus in 48 B.C., Julius Caesar vowed these games, which consisted of scenic events and circus games. They were first instituted in honor of his alleged ancestor and patron deity VENUS GENETRIX, and were held on September 26, 46 B.C., the day when the temple to Venus Genetrix in Rome was dedicated. At that time the games were called Ludi Veneris Genetricis. In 45 B.C. the games were transferred from September 26 to July 20–30, and the name of the games was changed to Ludi Victoriae Caesaris.
Reading: Fishwick 1987, 115; Scullard 1981, 167.

Ludi Victoriae Sullanae (Sulla's Victory Games) Games *(LUDI)* held October 26 to November 1 in honor of the goddess VICTORIA. They were established in 81 B.C. to celebrate Sulla's victory on November 1, 82 B.C. over a large army of Samnites at the Porta Collina in Rome. On November 1 (the day of the battle) there were circus games. The games were originally called Ludi Victoriae, but their name was changed, possibly to distinguish them from the Ludi Victoriae Caesaris.
Reading: Scullard 1981, 196.

Lug Possibly a Celtic god, the equivalent of the Irish god Lugh. The worship of a Celtic god called Lug may account for various place names, such as Lugdunum (modern Lyon), France. The Latin name Lugdunum is thought to mean something like "town of Lug" and so reflects the worship of this god by the people of the area. However, there is no evidence from the writings of ancient authors for the existence of this god within the Roman empire, and few inscriptions have been found that might be connected with this god. (See also LUGUBUS ARQUIENOBUS.)
Reading: Fishwick 1987, 99–100; Green, M. J. 1992a, 135–136.

Lugdunum altar An ALTAR of the Three Gauls *(Tres Galliae)* at the confluence of the Rhône and Saône Rivers at Lyon (Lugdunum), in France. It was dedicated to Roma and Augustus in 12 B.C. by Drusus (or possibly constituted in 12 B.C. and dedicated in 10 B.C.). The altar was large and adorned with reliefs. There were statues of VICTORIA on either side. According to Strabo, the altar was engraved with the names of 60 tribes (apparently not on the front face), and nearby were 60 statues, one representing each tribe.

The altar was the first and one of the most important monuments of the IMPERIAL CULT in the western Roman empire, but it was not a temple, as normally seen in the east for the imperial cult. Nevertheless, it was a huge structure set on a large terrace and approached on the east and west by a monumental ramp. Strabo also refers to a second altar, for which there is no supporting evidence. Apart from literary references, the altar was depicted on a series of coins minted at Lugdunum. The altar would have been the focus of sacrifices and other rites at festivals. The cult of ROMA and Augustus at Lugdunum was served by *sacerdotes* (priests). The priesthood of the Three Gauls was a prestigious appointment. In 1958 an inscription was found naming the priest (Gaius Iulius Rufus) who undertook the construction of the amphitheater c. A.D. 19, which would have been the scene of festival games, especially at the August 1 festival. Once a year, the assembly of the Three Gauls met under its chairman (who was a priest); the main purpose of this assembly was to pay cult to the emperor with lavish ceremonies, including games. It probably began on August 1 and lasted for a few weeks.

Later on, the *DIVI* were added to the cult of Roma and Augustus, followed by the construction

of a temple in the vicinity of the altar, probably by Hadrian. Very little is known about the provincial temple at Lugdunum (also known as the temple of the Three Gauls), except that inscriptions of priests were now described as serving *ad templum* (at the temple) rather than *ad aram* (at the altar).
Reading: Fishwick 1987, 97–107, 118–137, 308–316.

Lugubus Arquienobus An Iberian god who is known from an inscription found in an area to the east of Orense, northwestern Spain. This is probably the same deity as Lucoubus Arquienis, an Iberian god known from an inscription found north of Lugo, northwest Spain. It is likely that these deities are linked with the Celtic god LUG and that the names *Arquienis* and *Arquienibus* may relate the deities to a particular tribe or place in northwest Spain.
Reading: Tranoy 1981, 289–290.

Luna The Roman goddess of the moon who was identified with SELENE, the Greek goddess of the moon. She had a temple on the Aventine Hill in Rome, and there was a temple of Luna Noctiluca ("Luna that shines by night") on the Palatine Hill. There were festivals of Luna on March 31 and August 24 and 28.
Reading: Grimal 1986, 262; Hammond and Scullard (eds.) 1970, 625.

Luna, temple of A temple situated on the Aventine Hill in Rome. Its building was attributed to King Servius Tullius. It is known that it was damaged by a storm in 182 B.C. Consular elections were postponed when the temple was struck by lightning in 84 B.C., at the time of Lucius Cornelius Cinna's death. It may have been destroyed in the fire of Nero. Its dedication day was March 31.
Reading: Richardson 1992, 238.

Luperca A Roman goddess who was the wife of the Roman god LUPERCUS. She was identified with the deified she-wolf who suckled Romulus and Remus.

Lupercalia A festival celebrated on February 15, involving purification and fertility rites. It was originally a shepherd festival in honor of LUPERCUS, a pastoral god, to ensure fertility of fields and flocks. The festival was very ancient, and the Romans themselves were uncertain which god was being worshipped. Lupercus seems to have been invented in the Augustan period to account for the rituals. Ancient authors cited INUUS or FAUNUS (both identified with PAN) as the god of Lupercalia.

Worshippers gathered at a sacred cave called the Lupercal at the foot of the Palatine Hill, where Romulus and Remus were supposed to have been suckled by a wolf. Here, the priests called *luperci* sacrificed goats and a dog, and there was an offering of sacred cakes. Two youths of noble family were smeared with sacrificial blood, and the *luperci* clothed themselves with parts of the skin of the sacrificed goats. They ran with some of the magistrates through Rome's streets, striking everyone they met with strips of skin from the goats (called *februa*) to make them fertile. The festival involved much revelry and was very popular. Consequently the early Christian church could not abolish it, and so in 494 Pope Gelasius I made February 15 the Festival of the Purification of the Virgin Mary.
Reading: Warde Fowler 1899, 310–321.

luperci ("wolfmen") A group of male priests who officiated at the festival of LUPERCALIA in Rome. They were divided into two groups or colleges, the Luperci Quinctiales or Quintilii, and the Luperci Fabiani or Fabii, believed to have been founded by Romulus and Remus respectively. Their cult center was the Lupercal. Their total number is unknown; by the late republic they included ex-slaves. The priests may have held temporary posts, possibly coopted. Their main duties were at the ritual of Lupercalia.
Reading: Porte 1989, 117–121.

Lupercus A Roman god who appears to have been invented in the Augustan period to account for the festival of LUPERCALIA. His partner was the Roman goddess LUPERCA.

lustratio ("lustration") The performance of a purification ceremony (a *lustrum*) to provide protection from evil influences and to bring good luck. The objects to be purified were various and could be a town, body of people or piece of land. Every five years the censors held a *lustrum populi* (purification ceremony of the people) in Rome. The ceremony consisted of a solemn and slow procession of a beneficial object, such as an appropriate animal for

sacrifice *(felix hostia)*, around whatever was to be purified (such as the boundaries of a settlement), with prayers and sacrifices being offered at various points on the route. It was designed to loose *(luere)* or free an area from hostile spirits. Specific examples were carried out at the AMBARVALIA and AMBURBIUM.
Reading: Hammond and Scullard (eds.) 1970, 626; Scullard 1981, 26.

lustrum A ceremony of purification (lustration), especially that carried out by the censors every five years at Rome during the republic to mark the end of a census. It also came to mean the five-year period of office of the censor, or any five-year period or long period of time.
Reading: Hammond and Scullard (eds.) 1970, 626.

Luxovius A Celtic god who was the eponymous deity of Luxeuil, France. He is known only from this site, where he was worshipped as the partner of the goddess BRICTA. This divine couple were deities of the thermal spring, where other deities were also worshipped.
Reading: Green, M. J. 1992a, 136.

M

Ma A Cappadocian mother goddess who was the personification of fruitfulness. The cult of this goddess was introduced into Rome by the dictator Lucius Cornelius Sulla around 85 B.C. She was equated with the Roman goddess BELLONA as Ma-Bellona.
Reading: Garcia Y Bellido 1967, 64–70 (Ma-Bellona).

Maband A possible reading of a fragmentary inscription found at Godmanchester, England. (See ABANDINUS.)

Maenads Followers of the god DIONYSUS (or BACCHUS) who were also known as BACCHANTS.

Magaia A native goddess who is known from an inscription on an altar found at Aquae (Baden-Baden), Germany. The altar has a relief sculpture of a seated goddess with a round object (possibly an orb or a fruit) in her right hand.
Reading: Espérandieu 1931, no. 447.

magic The attempt to control events by direct actions and rituals. It springs from the same origin as Roman religion, in a belief in supernatural forces which control the lives of people. The dividing line between a religious ritual (asking for something to happen) and a magic ritual (attempting to directly make that thing happen) is often very fine, and Roman religion contained a strong element of magic. Magic was officially disapproved of, but it appears to have been widely used by private individuals, and there are descriptions of witches in Roman literature. Harmful magic was practiced privately, and came to be repressed by Roman law, whereas non-harmful magic was often absorbed into or became indistinguishable from religious ritual. Magic occurred in practices such as *defixiones* (curse tablets), in *LUSTRATIO* (purification ceremonies) and in offerings to the dead. Harmful magic was illegal and was suppressed not because of disbelief, but rather through fear of its possible consequences. Similarly, early leaders of the Christian church condemned magic as impious rather than as a delusion.
Reading: Gordon 1990c, 252–255; Hammond and Scullard (eds.) 1970, 637–638; Liebescheutz 1979, 126–139; Luck 1985, 30–131; Merrifield 1987.

Magna Mater ("Great Mother") An ancient Anatolian goddess who was also known as AGDISTIS, Cybele, KYBELE or KYBEBE. In Roman times she was generally described as Magna Mater. Originating in Asia Minor, her cult came to be centered on Mount Dindymus at Pessinus in Phrygia, where she was known as Agdistis. Her consort was ATTIS, and there was a great deal of mythology surrounding them both. She was considered to be the mother of all living things—an earth mother goddess and a goddess of fertility and of wild nature, the latter being symbolized by her attendant lions. A characteristic of her cult consisted of states of ecstasy, inducing prophecy and insensibility to pain. She was also said to cause and to cure disease.

Her cult was deliberately brought to Rome in 204 B.C. (during the war with Carthage) after a prophecy in the SIBYLLINE BOOKS and advice from the ORACLE at Delphi. The prophecy stated that the invaders would be driven from Italy if Magna Mater was brought to Rome. The sacred black stone of the goddess was brought to Rome from Pessinus in Phrygia, was temporarily housed in the temple of VICTORIA, and was later placed in a temple on the Palatine Hill which was dedicated to Magna Mater in 191 B.C. There was another temple dedicated to Magna Mater on the Almo River near the Via Appia in Rome and a small temple at the head of the Sacra Via. Shrines for the worship of Cybele were called *metroons.*

The Romans regarded some of the rites of Cybele as excessive, so that the cult was restricted and Roman citizens were forbidden to serve as priests. Restrictions were lifted by Claudius, and worship of Cybele and her consort Attis became part of the state religion and an important mystery religion. The cult spread with the expansion of the empire, and there is evidence for it from many of the provinces. It was remarkably persistent, and the festival and rituals of Cybele were revived in the west under the emperor Eugenius (392–394). It is likely that the cult was suppressed, along with other pagan cults, soon afterwards, but some authorities have argued that the Christian cult of GNOSTICISM was a transformation of the cult of Cybele and point out the similarities between the veneration of Cybele as a mother goddess and that of Mary the Mother of Christ.

The rites of Cybele and Attis included the *TAUROBOLIUM,* self-flagellation and castration of the priests *(GALLI),* and ecstatic dances. The CORYBANTES were priests associated mainly with the cult of Cybele. The main festival of Cybele was the MEGALENSIA. As part of the Cybele cult, a festival of mourning was followed by a joyous ceremony (HILARIA) to celebrate the rebirth of Attis and the start of the new year. Cybele may have been identified with the Celtic goddess ANDARTE.
Reading: Gasparro 1985; Grimal 1986, 26–27 (under *Agdistis*); Hammond and Scullard (eds.) 1970, 303–304; Ferguson 1970, 26–31; Turcan 1989, 35–75; Vermaseren 1977.

Magna Mater, temple of A temple vowed in 204 B.C. and built on the Palatine Hill in Rome at a place called the Germalus, in response to an instruction from the SIBYLLINE BOOKS during a crisis in the Second Punic War. It was built to house the sacred black stone of the goddess which had been brought to Rome in 204 B.C. The temple was dedicated on April 11, 191 B.C. by the praetor Marcus Iunius Brutus, on which day the MEGALENSIA festival was established. In 111 B.C. the temple suffered a fire, but it was restored in 110 B.C. After another fire, it was restored by Augustus in A.D. 3. Elagabalus intended to move the cult image to the temple of Sol Invictus Elagabalus, but this only occurred for a short time, if at all. The temple was still standing in the fourth century. It has been discovered near the west corner of the Palatine Hill. It faced southwest, had a huge concrete podium and was HEXASTYLE with Corinthian columns. It was 36.28 yds. long and 18.70 yds. wide (33.18 m × 17.10 m). It fronted a precinct where the Megalensia festival was held.
Reading: Nash 1962b, 27; Richardson 1992, 242–243.

Maia A Roman goddess who was associated with VULCAN. She appears to have been connected with the growth of living things, and the month of May is probably named after her. She became confused with a much better known Greek goddess of the same name, who was the mother of Hermes. Consequently, she also became associated with MERCURY (the Roman equivalent of HERMES). As a fertility goddess, Maia was also associated with FAUNA. She had a festival on May 15, and because she was sometimes regarded as the consort of Vulcan, celebrations in her honor also took place during the VOLCANALIA on August 23.
Reading: Hammond and Scullard (eds.) 1970, 640.

Maison Carrée One of the best-preserved Roman temples, it is situated at Nîmes (Nemausus) in southern France (Gallia Narbonensis). It was thought to have been built by Marcus Agrippa in 16 B.C., but recent work has shown that the original inscription was in honor of Agrippa's sons Gaius and Lucius and should date to A.D. 1 or 2. The temple measures 13.44 yds. × 27.48 yds. (12.29 m × 25.13 m) and is much smaller than contemporary ones at Rome. It faced the forum and was approached by a broad flight of steps. The facade has six Corinthian columns, with an entrance porch, and additional columns continue down the sides and round the back of the cella as half-engaged columns in the walls (that is, they form part of the wall itself but each column protrudes beyond the line of the wall).
Reading: Amy and Gros 1979; Balty 1960; Barton 1989, 81.

Malakbel A Syrian sun god who was also known as Malachbelus. He was associated at Palmyra with

BAAL SHAMIN and frequently with AGLIBOL. There was a temple to Aglibol and Malakbel at Palmyra which lasted to the end of the second century. There was a shrine dedicated to Sol Malachbelus established by the Palmyrene community at Rome before the cult of SOL (sun) was introduced by the emperor Aurelian.
Reading: Drijvers 1976; Richardson 1992, 365; Teixidor 1969, 34–52.

Mamers An early (Oscan) name for the Roman god MARS.

Mamuralia This festival is recorded for March 14, but it is unclear if it was a separate festival for the bronzesmith Mamurius Veturius, legendary maker of the sacred shields *(ancilia)*, or another name for the EQUIRRIA held on March 14.
Reading: Warde Fowler 1899, 45–50; York 1986, 97.

Mandica An Iberian goddess who is known from an inscription on an altar found at Ponferrada, northwest Spain.
Reading: Tranoy 1981, 298.

Manes The spirits or souls of the dead. Being immortal, they were regarded as gods and were therefore worshipped. Their name is usually accompanied by the words *di* or *dii.* They were worshipped collectively as *DI MANES* (the divine dead) at the festivals of FERALIA, PARENTALIA and LEMURIA. They were later identified with the *DI PARENTES* (the dead of the family), and the concept grew that each dead person had an individual spirit called a *manes* (a plural noun used as a singular noun). Similarly, graves were originally dedicated to the dead collectively (*dis manibus sacrum,* "sacred to the divine dead"). Later in the empire, it became customary to name individuals in such dedications, meaning "sacred to the divine spirit of [the named individual]." The *manes* were regarded as powerful spirits who required cult and propitiation. (See also AFTERLIFE.)
Reading: Hammond and Scullard (eds.) 1970, 643; Lattimore 1962, 90–96 (evidence from epitaphs).

Mania This Roman deity was regarded as mother of the *lares* and also as a goddess of death. She was equated with LARA, also considered to be the mother of the *lares.* Sacrifices were made to her on May 11, possibly as part of the LEMURIA, a festival of the dead. Small images of ugly faces that were hung up as charms or offerings were called *maniae* (sing. *mania*), and it appears that the name of the goddess Mania was used as a "bogeyman" to frighten naughty children.
Reading: Hammond and Scullard (eds.) 1970, 643.

Fig. 60 The mano fico *sign.*

mano fico (Fig. 60) A sign made with hand and fingers curled and the thumb thrust between the middle and index fingers. It was a fertility and good luck charm and was also designed to ward off evil. The gesture has survived to modern times, regarded in some areas a good-luck sign and in others as an insulting gesture. In modern Italian it is now called *mano fica,* taken to mean "fig hand." However, the Italian for "fig" is *fico* (in Latin, *ficus*). In Italian, *fica* is a slang term for the vulva, and the gesture is often thought to represent sexual intercourse. Some Roman amulets combine a *phallus* and a *mano fico* gesture.
Reading: Johns 1982, 73–74, figs. 56, 57.

Manturna A Roman goddess who presided over the preservation of marriage. She was invoked to make a marriage long-lasting.

Maponus A Celtic god who was worshipped in northern Britain and at Bourbonne-les-Bains and Chamalières in France. At Chamalières, he was invoked on a lead curse tablet. *Maponus* means "divine youth" or "divine son." He was sometimes identified with the Greek god APOLLO. The Ravenna Cosmography (a collection of topographical documents dating back to the fifth century) mentions a *locus Maponi* ("place of Maponus"). This was possibly a cult center and may have been at Clochmabenstane, Dumfries and Galloway, Scotland. Dedications to Maponus suggest that he was associated with music and poetry, but on a sculptured stone from Ribchester, England, he is portrayed alongside an unnamed goddess of hunting.
Reading: Green, M. J. 1992a, 140; Ross 1974, 463–466.

Marduk A Syrian god who was originally a Babylonian god. He was the personification of the fertilizing effect of water and was responsible for the growth and ripening of crops. His cult was widespread in Syria and Mesopotamia in the Roman period.

Marica A Roman NYMPH who was the deity of the Liris River (the modern Liri River) in Latium in Italy. She was described by Virgil as wife of the god FAUNUS and mother of King Latinus. She was also equated with the Greek goddess Circe. A wood in Minturnae (modern Minturno) in Latium was dedicated to her.
Reading: Grimal 1986, 272.

Maris An early (Etruscan) name for the Roman god MARS.

Marmar An early name for the Roman god MARS.

Marpiter An alternative name for the Roman god MARS PATER.

marriage Roman marriage was not a religious ceremony but a private act with no prescribed formula of words or written contract. The oldest form of marriage was *CONFARREATIO*. The day of the wedding had to be carefully chosen. It was ill-omened to marry in March, May and in the first half of June (but acceptable after June 15, when the annual refuse had been swept into the Tiber River from the temple of VESTA). It was also ill-omened to marry on all KALENDS, NONES and IDES and succeeding days of each month, on *dies religiosi* and on *dies festi*. Widows could remarry on *dies festi* because they would have fewer guests.

Omens had to be sought and recorded; originally augurs had attended the wedding ceremonies, but by Cicero's time a friend of the family attended with the title *auspex*. This signified approval of the couple's friends. At the marriage, there was a sacrifice and examination of the entrails, but it is uncertain to what deities the sacrifice was offered—sometimes to TELLUS and CERES. After the wedding rites, which probably began in the home of the bride, the festivities moved to the home of the groom. The bridegroom carried the bride into his house to avoid an ill-omened stumble over the threshold. The couple then joined in a religious rite to mark her entry into the new house.

There was no religious ban on divorce. Despite a theological decision that marriage was a sacrament, divorce remained straightforward under CHRISTIANITY.
Reading: Dixon 1992, 61–97; Treggiari 1991.

Mars (Fig. 61) A Roman god of war. He was originally a god of agriculture and guardian of fields and boundaries, at times variously known as Mamers, Maris, Marmor, Marmar or Mavors. He was identified with the Greek god ARES and so assumed the major role of a war god. He was regarded as the son of the Roman goddess JUNO. The month of March was named after him. Mars had an altar (Ara Martis) in the CAMPUS MARTIUS at Rome and was served by the *flamen Martialis*. There was a temple of Mars on the Via Appia outside Rome and another in the CIRCUS FLAMINIUS. The wolf and the woodpecker were his sacred animals. Mars was one of only three gods (with NEPTUNE and APOLLO) to whom a bull might be sacrificed. A combined sacrifice of a bull, boar and ram *(SUOVETAURILIA)* was often made to Mars (Fig. 99).

Mars had a succession of festivals in February, March and October, and there was a festival on June 1. The ARMILUSTRIUM on October 19 was also a festival in honor of Mars. Mars was worshipped

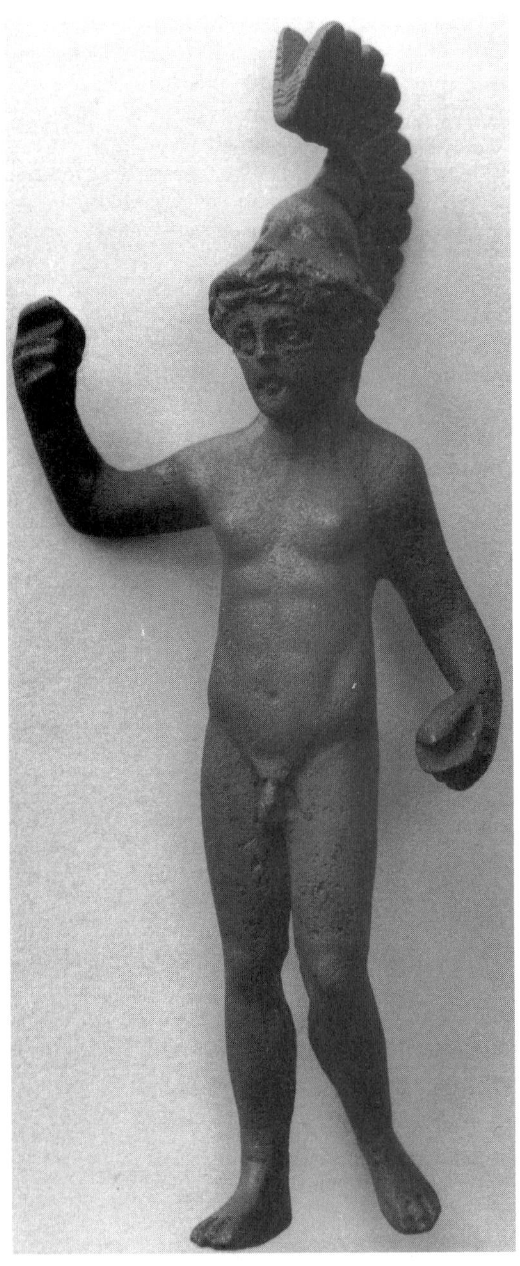

Fig. 61 A votive bronze figurine of Mars found at Lamyatt Beacon, England. He is naked, apart from a plumed helmet. In his right hand he originally held a spear. Height 3.66 in. (93 mm). Courtesy of Somerset County Museums Service.

under a number of epithets and linked with many other deities. Among the Celts, Mars was regarded not only as a war god, but took on roles of peaceful protector, healer and tribal god. He was equated with many Celtic gods, such as COCIDIUS, BELATUCADRUS and BRACIACA.

Reading: Green, M. J. 1992a, 140–144 (discusses many of the Celtic gods equated with Mars); Hammond and Scullard (eds.) 1970, 651; Simon 1990, 135–145; York 1986, 73–76.

Mars, temples of The main temple of MARS in Rome was on the northeast side of the Via Appia outside the Porta Capena *(extra portam Capenam)*, between the first and second milestones. The district came to be known as *ad Martis*. The temple contained a statue of Mars and probably images of wolves. It was vowed during the invasions of the Gauls, and was dedicated on June 1, probably in 388 B.C. The Roman army assembled at this temple before setting off for campaigns.

Another temple to Mars was built in the CIRCUS FLAMINIUS by Decimus Junius Brutus Callaicus, probably after his triumph around 133 B.C. It was designed by a Greek architect, contained a colossal statue of Mars and a naked VENUS, both by Sopas, and the approach to the temple was decorated with verses of the poet Accius. Julius Caesar planned to build an enormous temple to Mars on the site of his lake used for mock sea battles *(naumachiae)*, but the plan was abandoned and the site was used partly for the PANTHEON instead.

Reading: Richardson 1992, 244–245; Scullard 1981, 127; Steinby (ed.) 1993, 222–223.

Mars Alator A Celtic god who was equated with the Roman god MARS. He is known from an inscription on an altar found at South Shields, England, and also from a dedication on a silver-gilt votive plaque or leaf found at Barkway, Hertfordshire, England (Fig. 119). The Celtic name ALATOR has been interpreted as meaning "huntsman" or "he who cherishes," although his identification with Mars might imply that he was a god of war.

Reading: Phillips 1977, 66; Ross 1974, 227–228.

Mars Albiorix A Celtic god who was identified with the Roman god MARS. He was worshipped as

protector of the Albici tribe in southern France, and was also regarded as a mountain god.
Reading: Green, M. J. 1992a, 141.

Mars Barrex A Celtic god who was equated with the Roman god MARS. This god is known only from a dedicatory inscription found at Carlisle, England. An alternative reading of the name on the inscription is Barrecis. The name *Barrex* or *Barrecis* probably means "supreme."
Reading: Ross 1974, 236.

Mars Belatucadrus The Celtic god BELATUCADRUS who was equated with the Roman god MARS. He is known in this form from five inscriptions found in the area of Hadrian's Wall, England.

Mars Braciaca A Celtic god who was equated with the Roman god MARS. This god is known from a single inscription found at Bakewell, England.
Reading: Ross 1974, 234–235.

Mars Camulos The Celtic war god CAMULOS who was linked with the Roman god MARS.

Mars Capriociegus An Iberian god who was linked with the Roman god MARS. This god is invoked in two inscriptions found in the Pontevedra region of northwest Spain.
Reading: Tranoy 1981, 304.

Mars Caturix A Celtic god who was equated with the Roman god MARS as Mars Caturix ("Mars king of combat"). He was worshipped in Gaul, possibly as the tribal god of the Caturiges.
Reading: Green, M. J. 1992a, 141.

Mars Cocidius A Celtic god who was sometimes equated with the Roman god MARS. He is known in the area of north and west Cumbria and around Hadrian's Wall, England. Usually a god of woodland and hunting, COCIDIUS seems to have been regarded as a war god in the instances when he was equated with Mars.

Mars Condatis A Celtic god, CONDATIS, who was sometimes linked with the Roman god MARS. Condatis was god of the confluence ("condate") of rivers and a god of water and healing; Mars Condatis presumably fulfilled a similar function. He is known from inscriptions found at Piercebridge, Bowes and Chester-le-Street, near Hadrian's Wall, England.
Reading: Jones and Mattingly 1990, 275; Ross 1974, 236–237.

Mars Corotiacus The Celtic god COROTIACUS who was identified with the Roman god MARS. He is known only from Martlesham, Suffolk, England, in an inscription on a fragmentary bronze sculpture. The sculpture portrays a warrior (probably the god) riding a horse over a prostrate enemy.
Reading: Green, M. J. 1992a, 142; Ross 1974, 227.

Mars Gravidus The name of the Roman god MARS to which the Palatini, one of the two groups of *SALII* (priests of Mars), were especially devoted. The origin of the name *Gravidus* is disputed, but some etymologists derive it from *gradus*, meaning "step," so that Mars Gravidus could be "Mars the marching god."
Reading: Scullard 1981, 85.

Mars Invictus ("Unconquered Mars") There was a temple dedicated to Mars Invictus at Rome, and a festival of Mars Invictus on May 14.

Mars Latobius A Celtic god who was equated with the Roman god MARS.

Mars Lenumius A Celtic god who was identified with the Roman god MARS. He is known from a dedication to him found at the fort of Benwell on Hadrian's Wall, England. Little else is known about him.
Reading: Ross 1974, 227.

Mars Lenus An important Celtic god of healing who was equated with the Roman god Mars. (See LENUS.)

Mars Loucetius (also Mars Leucetius and Loucetius Mars) The Roman god MARS possibly linked with a Celtic deity. The name *Loucetius* means "lightning" or "brilliant." It is not certain whether Loucetius was a Celtic god, or a Celtic use of the name *Lucetius* for Mars. Loucetius Mars is known from a dedication found at Bath, England, where a divine couple of Loucetius Mars and the Celtic

goddess NEMETONA was worshipped; Mars Loucetius/Loucetius Mars may have been a god of healing since this particular dedication (by a citizen of Trier, Germany) was also on an altar in the temple of SULIS MINERVA at the medicinal springs at Bath. Mars Loucetius is also known from several other places in Europe, such as Mainz, Germany.
Reading: Green, M. J. 1992a, 143; Ross 1974, 228–229.

Mars Medocius A Celtic god who was equated with the Roman god MARS. He is known from an inscription on a bronze panel found at Colchester, England.
Reading: Ross 1974, 236.

Mars Mullo A Celtic god who was equated with the Roman god MARS. The cult of Mars Mullo was popular in northern and northwestern Gaul, in particular in Normandy and Brittany. There is evidence that there was a center of this cult at Rennes, Brittany, which was the tribal capital of the Redones. At Allones, in the Sarthe area of France, Mars Mullo was worshipped as a healer of eye afflictions. The importance of this cult is shown by an inscription that links Mars Mullo with the emperor Augustus. *Mullo* means "mule," and so this god may have been connected with horses or mules, but it appears that his primary function was that of a healer, particularly of eye ailments.
Reading: Green, M. J. 1992a, 143–144.

Mars Nabelcus A local Celtic mountain god who was equated with the Roman god MARS. He was worshipped in the Vaucluse mountains of Provence, on Mount Ventoux and at Moncieux, as well as in other mountain areas of southern France.
Reading: Green, M. J. 1992a, 144.

Mars Nodens A Celtic god of healing, NODENS, who was linked with the Roman god MARS.

Mars Ocelus (Fig. 62) (or Mars Ocelos) A Celtic god referred to in dedications from Caerwent, Wales, and Carlisle, England. He is probably the same as MARS LENUS, who is linked with OCELOS in another dedication from Caerwent, Wales, which refers to Mars Lenus and to Ocelos Vellaunus.
Reading: Ross 1974, 471–472.

Fig. 62 An altar dedicated to Mars Ocelus found at Caerwent, Wales. The inscription reads DEO MARTI OCELO AEL AGVS TINVS OP VSLM ("to the god Mars Ocelus, Aelius Augustinus, optio [a junior officer in a legion] willingly and deservedly fulfilled his vow").

Mars Olloudius A Celtic god who was linked with MARS. Mars Olloudius appears to have been a god of peaceful protection (in contrast to Mars's warlike aspect) and probably also of fertility, prosperity and healing. An image of Mars Olloudius

is known from Custom Scrubs, Gloucestershire, England, where he is accompanied by a *patera* and a double cornucopia, symbolizing abundance.
Reading: Green, M. J. 1992a, 166 (under *Olloudius*).

Mars Pater ("Mars the father") A version of the Roman god MARS who was also known as Marspiter or Marpiter. Roman troops celebrated the birthday of Mars Pater on March 1 with the sacrifice of a bull. As well as being a god of war, Mars Pater had connections with agriculture.

Marspiter An alternative name for the Roman god MARS PATER.

Mars Rigas A Celtic god who was linked to the Roman god MARS. He is known from a single inscription found at Malton, North Yorkshire, England.
Reading: Jones and Mattingly 1990, 275.

Mars Rigisamus A Celtic god who was equated with the Roman god MARS. He is known from dedications found at Bourges, Gaul, and West Coker, Somerset, England, where evidence suggests that there may have been a shrine dedicated to this god. The name *Rigisamus* means "King of Kings" or "Most Kingly" and implies a very high status for this god, beyond the usual roles of Mars.
Reading: Green, M. J. 1992a, 144; Ross 1974, 229.

Mars Rigonemetis ("Mars King of the Sacred Grove"; *nemeton* means "sacred grove") A Celtic god who was linked with the Roman god MARS. This deity is known from an inscription found at Nettleham, Lincolnshire, England, where he was linked to the *NUMEN* of the emperor in the dedication. This association with the emperor implies a high status for the god, but no other dedications to him are known. It is possible that the stone on which the inscription was found was once part of the arch of a temple.
Reading: Green, M. J. 1992a, 144; Ross 1974, 229.

Mars Rudianus A Celtic war god who was equated with the Roman god MARS. He was worshipped in southern Gaul. *Rudianus* means "red," probably (through blood symbolism) reflecting the warlike nature of the deity.
Reading: Green, M. J. 1992a, 181 (under *Rudianus*).

Mars Segomo Possibly a Celtic god equated with the Roman god MARS, meaning "Mars Victorious." Mars Segomo was worshipped by the Sequani tribe in Gaul. *Segomo* is more of a title than a name, and may be an epithet of Mars rather than a separate Celtic deity.
Reading: Green, M. J. 1992a, 188 (under *Segomo*).

Mars Silvanus The Roman god MARS linked with the Roman god SILVANUS. A lead *DEFIXIO* from the shrine at Uley, Gloucestershire, England, is addressed to *deo Marti Silvano*, although *deo Mercurio* ("to the god Mercury") was later written over this inscription, and *deo Silvano* was written in the same text. The god worshipped at Uley was MERCURY, and from the evidence of the lead *defixiones* from the site, it seems that Mercury was identified with Mars and Silvanus at this shrine.
Reading: Tomlin 1993.

Mars Smertrius A Celtic god of abundance who was linked with the Roman god MARS. He is known from a dedication found at Möhn, near Trier, Germany, where a shrine was dedicated to this god and to the Celtic goddess ANCAMNA.
Reading: Green, M. J. 1992a, 193 (under *Smertrius*).

Mars Tarbucelis An Iberian god who was linked with the Roman god MARS. This deity is known from a dedicatory inscription from the Braga region of northern Portugal.
Reading: Tranoy 1981, 304.

Mars Teutates A Celtic war god who was equated with the Roman war god MARS. (See TEUTATES.)

Mars Thincsus (Fig. 63) A Germanic or possibly a Celtic god, known from a dedication found at Housesteads, Hadrian's Wall, England, where he is linked with two goddesses called the ALAISIAGAE; these goddesses are also linked with MARS on another dedication from Housesteads (Fig. 2).
Reading: Green, M. J. 1992a, 144.

Mars Tilenus An Iberian mountain god who was equated with the Roman god MARS. This deity is known from an inscription on a silver plaque found at Quintana del Marco, near La Bañeza,

northern Spain. He is probably the god of the nearby Teleno mountain and therefore probably the same deity as TILLENUS.
Reading: Tranoy 1981, 306.

Mars Ultor ("Mars the Avenger") Ultor was a new title given to MARS under the emperor Augustus in recognition of his victory over the assassins of Julius Caesar at the battle of Philippi in 42 B.C. Augustus ordered a temple of Mars Ultor to be built in Rome.

Mars Ultor, temple of (Fig. 64) ("Mars the Avenger") A temple built by Augustus in the new Forum of Augustus (often called the Forum Martis, Forum of Mars), which formed the temple's huge precinct (120.29 yds. × 57.41 yds.; 110 m × 52.5 m). It was vowed at the battle of Philippi by Octavian (later Augustus) in 42 B.C. to commemorate his defeating Brutus and Cassius and thus avenging the murder of Julius Caesar. It was completed and dedicated on May 12, 2 B.C. The standards recovered by Augustus from the Parthians in 20 B.C. were also kept in this temple. Before this temple was built, the standards may have been kept in another possible temple of Mars Ultor on the CAPITOLINE HILL or in the temple of JUPITER OPTIMUS MAXIMUS.

The OCTASTYLE temple stands at the northwest end of the forum on a high podium approached at the front by a broad flight of steps. It dominated the forum and had an imposing facade of eight Corinthian columns more than 16.40 yds. (15 m) high. The colonnade continued along the sides but not the rear, which was the precinct wall. The cella contained colossal cult statues of Mars, VENUS and Divus Julius and the sword of Julius Caesar. After Augustus was deified, a gold statue of him was

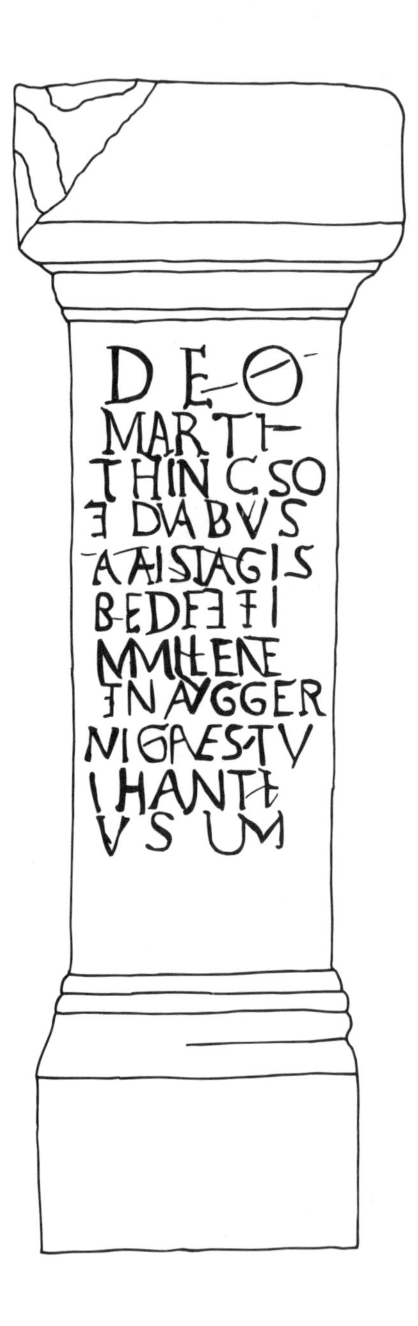

Fig. 63 An altar dedicated to Mars Thincsus and the two Alaisiagae. The inscription reads DEO MARTI THINGSO ET DVABVS ALAESIAGIS BEDE ET FIMMILENE ET N[VMINI] AVG[VSTI] GERM[ANI] CIVES TVIHANTI V[OTUM] S[OLVERUNT] L[IBENTES] M[ERITO] ("To the god Mars Thincsus, to the two Alaisiagae called Beda and Fimmilena and to the spirit of the emperor, German tribesmen of Twenthe willingly and deservedly fulfilled their vow"). The altar was found at Housesteads, Hadrian's Wall, England.

Fig. 64 The remains of the Forum of Augustus at Rome and (left) the temple of Mars Ultor as depicted in a 19th-century illustration.

temporarily placed in the cella, where it lay on a golden bed. The temple and temple precinct were used for enrollment for military training, and as the place from where governors departed for their provinces and where triumphal insignia were kept. The Senate also met in the temple when considering awards of triumphs or receiving reports of military successes.
Reading: Barton 1989, 76–79; Richardson 1992, 160–162, 245–246.

Mars Visucius A Celtic god who was occasionally linked with the Roman god MARS. (See VISUCIUS.)

Mars Vorocius A Celtic god of healing who was equated with the Roman god MARS at the medicinal springs at Vichy, Allier, France. Mars Vorocius was worshipped as a healer of eye afflictions and was depicted as a Celtic warrior.
Reading: Green, M. J. 1992a, 144.

martyrium (Fig. 65) (or *memoria;* pl. *martyria*) Burial place of early Christian martyrs. Originally the term was used for the spot where the martyr

Fig. 65 The martyrium *of St. Philip situated outside the city walls at Hierapolis (Pammukale), Turkey. He was believed to have been martyred here, and the* martyrium *became a place of pilgrimage. It was built at the end of the 4th or beginning of the 5th century. It measures 65½ ft. × 65½ ft. (20 m × 20 m) and was an octagonal building containing eight chapels set within a square structure.*

was killed and buried. These places were venerated by Christians, and chapels and churches came to be built over them. They also acted as a focus for other burials, so that cemeteries grew up around them. As relics of martyrs began to play a prominent part in Christian religion, the name *martyrium* came to be used for any church or chapel containing relics of martyrs. These sites were thought to be especially holy and attracted pilgrims.
Reading: Lane Fox 1988, 419–492 (for martyrs).

Mater Matuta The Roman goddess of growth who also developed into a goddess of childbirth. She may also have been a goddess of dawn, but this is disputed. She was also known as Matuta or Matuta Mater and was later identified with the Greek goddess INO. She had a temple in the FORUM BOARIUM at Rome and also a famous temple at Satricum, Italy, which the Romans spared when they destroyed the city in 346 B.C. Mater Matuta was worshipped at the festival of MATRALIA in June.
Reading: Hammond and Scullard (eds.) 1970, 656; Scullard 1981, 150–151; Simon 1990, 152–157.

Mater Matuta, temple of A temple situated in the Area Sacra di Sant' Omobono at Rome between the FORUM BOARIUM and FORUM ROMANUM, just inside the Porta Carmentalis (Fig. 15). It formed a pair with the adjacent temple of FORTUNA. Both were apparently built in the sixth century B.C. by King Servius Tullius, dedicated on June 11, destroyed by fire in 213 B.C. and rebuilt in 212 B.C. This temple had bright terracotta decoration. Much decorative and votive material belonging to the two temples has been found, including some connected with childbirth and the care of children. The temple was discovered in 1937 under the church of Sant' Omobono. In front of the temple was an archaic U-shaped altar. The cella of the temple was built into the church of Sant' Omobono.
Reading: Richardson 1992, 35–37, 246; Scullard 1981, 150–151.

Matidia (Matidia the Elder, c. 68–119) The only child of Marciana (sister of Trajan), Matidia was a niece of the emperor Trajan. She had two daughters, Sabina, who married the emperor Hadrian, and Matidia the Younger. On the death of her mother, Matidia the Elder received the title *Augusta.* In 117, together with Plotina (wife of Trajan) and Attianus (adviser of Hadrian), she brought Trajan's remains back from Cilicia to Rome. Matidia died in 119, and Hadrian gave his mother-in-law a funeral oration and deified her. Hadrian erected a commemorative temple, with attached halls named for Matidia and her mother Marciana. It appears that Matidia was the first deified female member of the imperial family *(diva)* to have her own temple at Rome.
Reading: Hammond and Scullard (eds.) 1970, 656; Richardson 1992, 246–247.

Matralia Festival of mothers held at Rome on June 11 in honor of Mater Matuta. It was concerned with the birth and care of children and involved rites not fully understood. These rites included the wife of a first marriage decorating the statue of Matuta, a slave girl being beaten in the temple (possibly as a warning to others or as a fertility rite), and sacred cakes *(testuacia)* being cooked in old-fashioned ceramic pots *(testu)* and offered to the goddess. Women prayed to Mater Matuta for their nephews and nieces.
Reading: Scullard 1981, 150–151.

Matres (Fig. 66) Also called Deae Matres or Matronae, these were Celtic mother goddesses, normally worshipped in a triad. The Latin word *matres* means "mothers" (sing. *mater*). They were often portrayed in art, particularly sculpture, usually as three seated women, wearing long robes and accompanied by various symbolic objects. The symbols included cereal crops, bread, fruit and other symbols of plenty, babies and children. The Matres were largely worshipped in northwest Europe under a variety of names and with differing attributes, such as the MATRES DOMESTICAE. Goddesses that have been called Deae Nutrices are apparently connected with the Matres. (See DEA NUTRIX.)
Reading: Green, M. J. 1992a, 155–156 (under Mother-goddess).

Matres Comedovae A triad of Celtic mother goddesses also known as Comedovae. They were worshipped at Aix-les-Bains, France, where they were associated with healing and the medicinal properties of the hot springs.
Reading: Green, M. J. 1992a, 146.

Matres Domesticae A triad of Celtic mother goddesses who are known from inscriptions found

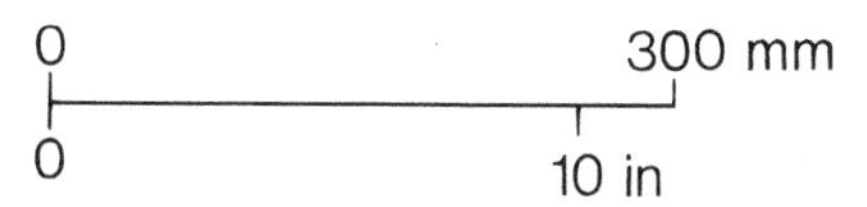

Fig. 66 Relief sculpture from Lyon, France, depicting three goddesses called Matres Augustae. They are sitting with baskets of fruit, and the goddess in the center holds a cornucopia in her left hand and a patera *in her right hand.*

in Britain. Dedications to these deities are known from Chichester, York, Stanwix and Burgh-by-Sands. The name *Domesticae* probably means "goddesses of the homeland."
Reading: Green, M. J. 1992a, 146.

Matres Griselicae Celtic mother goddesses who were worshipped at medicinal springs at Gréoulx, southern France.
Reading: Green, M. J. 1992a, 146.

Matres Nemausicae Celtic mother goddesses also known as the NEMAUSICAE.

Matres Suleviae Celtic mother goddesses also known as the SULEVIAE.

Matronae An alternative name for MATRES or DEAE MATRES (Celtic mother goddesses). The Latin word *matrona* (pl. *matronae*) means "wife," "married woman" or "matron."

Matronae Alhiahenae Celto-Germanic mother goddesses who are known only from an inscription on an altar found at Neidenheim, Germany.
Reading: Elbe 1975, 172.

Matronae Andrustehiae Celto-Germanic mother goddesses who were invoked in an inscription on an altar from the Rhineland, Germany.
Reading: Elbe 1975, 214.

Matronae Audrinehae Celto-Germanic mother goddesses who were invoked in an inscription on an altar from the Rhineland, Germany.
Reading: Elbe 1975, 214.

Matronae Aufaniae Celto-Germanic mother goddesses who were worshipped in the Rhineland, Germany; also known as Aufaniae. They were portrayed as one young woman with long flowing hair, flanked by two older women with large circular bonnets. They wear long robes and carry baskets of fruit. They were also often associated with faunal and floral symbols such as birds, snakes, trees and flowers. A temple at Nettersheim, near Bonn, Germany, was dedicated to these goddesses.
Reading: Green, M. J. 1992a, 146.

Matronae Axsinginehae Celto-Germanic mother goddesses who were invoked in an inscription on an altar from the Rhineland, Germany.
Reading: Elbe 1975, 214.

Matronae Fernovinehae Celto-Germanic mother goddesses who were invoked in an inscription on an altar from the Rhineland, Germany.
Reading: Elbe 1975, 214.

Matronae Udravarinehae Celto-Germanic mother goddesses who were invoked in an inscription on an altar from the Rhineland, Germany.
Reading: Elbe 1975, 214.

Matronae Vacallinehae Celto-Germanic mother goddesses who were worshipped in the Rhineland, Germany. There was an important cult center of these deities at Pesch, near Zülpich, Germany. More than 160 altars dedicated to the Matronae Vacallinehae have been found here, many set up by soldiers of Legion XXX Ulpia. Portrayals of the goddesses show them with large linen head-

dresses, and they are usually accompanied by loaves of bread.
Reading: Green, M. J. 1992a, 146–147.

Matronae Vallabneihae Celto-Germanic mother goddesses who were invoked in an inscription on an altar from the Rhineland in Germany.
Reading: Elbe 1975, 214.

Matronalia Festival of JUNO LUCINA held on the KALENDS (1st) March (the old New Year's Day) and celebrated by women at the temple of Juno Lucina in Rome. Prayers were offered to JUNO and her son MARS, husbands gave their wives presents, and female slaves were feasted by their mistresses.
Reading: Scullard 1981, 87.

Matunus A Celtic god who is known from a dedication found at Risingham, England. *Matunus* means "Divine Bear."
Reading: Ross 1974, 471.

Matuta A Roman goddess also known as MATER MATUTA or Matuta Mater (Matuta the Mother).

mausoleum (pl. *mausolea*) To the Romans, a mausoleum was the same as a TOMB, but it has come to specify a monumental tomb. It was a word apparently first used for Augustus's tomb and was later used for very large and ornate tombs, particularly those of emperors. It derived from the tomb built for Mausolus (satrap of Caria, 377/376–353 B.C.) at Halicarnassus (Bodrum, Turkey).
Reading: Richardson 1992, 351–352.

Mavors An early name for the Roman god MARS.

medicine Roman medicine absorbed much from Greek medicine, so that it was part scientific (mainly from the Greeks), and part magical and religious (mainly from the Romans), resulting in a sometimes bizarre collection of treatments and practices. Most (if not all) Roman deities were attributed some healing powers, but some deities were thought to be particularly beneficial. Their healing powers were sought by PRAYER, VOTIVE OFFERINGS and INCUBATION. Illness was often regarded as a punishment for sin requiring the intervention of the gods. Amulets and magical incantations were widely used to ward off or attempt to cure disease. (See also ANATOMICAL EX-VOTO.)
Reading: Bourgeois 1991; Jackson 1988; Jackson 1990 (contains detailed bibliography).

Meditrina A goddess who seems to have been a late Roman invention to account for the festival of MEDITRINALIA.

Meditrinalia A festival held on October 11. The goddess MEDITRINA appears to have been a late Roman invention to explain the festival, whose origins remain obscure. It was concerned in some way with the new wine vintage, and had some connection with JUPITER. It was an important ceremony in early agricultural Rome.
Reading: Scullard 1981, 192.

Medocius A Celtic god who was linked with the Roman god MARS as MARS MEDOCIUS.

Meduna A Celtic goddess who was associated with springs at Bad Bertrich, Germany. The springs later became a spa, so Meduna may have been a healing goddess.
Reading: Wightman 1970, 138, 226.

Mefitis A Roman goddess of the sulphurous fumes that rise up from the ground. She was sometimes identified with ALBUNEA. It was thought that the sulphurous fumes were responsible for epidemics and plagues, so that Mefitis was sometimes regarded as a goddess of plagues. Her cult was concentrated in the volcanic regions of central and southern Italy, where her main shrine was on the volcano Ampsanctus in Samnium, but it appears that she was worshipped throughout Italy as well. Presumably because of her association with fumes and diseases, her temple at Cremona was outside the city walls. In Rome she had a temple on the Esquiline Hill.
Reading: Grimal 1986, 276; Hammond and Scullard (eds.) 1970, 664.

Megalensia (or Megalesia or, later, Megalesiaca) A festival with games at Rome in honor of Cybele or MAGNA MATER (Greek *meter megale*). It lasted from April 4 to 10. The festival was established in 191 B.C. Festivals in honor of Magna Mater were fixed national holidays, unlike those of ATTIS (see HILARIA). The festival originally consisted of games (Ludi Megale[n]ses or Ludi Megalesiaci) in the CIR-

CUS MAXIMUS; theatrical performances were later added, as were sacrifices and banquets. Magna Mater's priests *(galli)* were allowed to carry her image in procession through Rome to the sound of tamborines and cymbals. They themselves were bloodstained through self-inflicted wounds. On April 10, the day of Cybele's birthday, great games were held in the Circus Maximus. (See also CLODIUS.)
Reading: Scullard 1981, 97–100; Vermaseren 1977, 124–125.

Megara One of the Roman deities known as the FURIES.

Mellonia Also known as Mellona, a Roman goddess who presided over bees and honey.
Reading: Ferguson 1988a, 853.

Melqart ("God of the City") A Phoenician god who was originally a sun god or BAAL of the city of Tyre. He was sometimes identified with the Greek god HERACLES (the Roman HERCULES).

Men A Phrygian or Persian god whose cult spread throughout Asia Minor. He was a god of healing and protection of tombs, as well as a giver of oracles. He was also associated with the moon. Men became linked with the Anatolian god ATTIS and was worshipped in Italy as ATTIS MENOTYRANNUS; a series of inscriptions have been found in Rome and Ostia to this deity.
Reading: Hammond and Scullard (eds.) 1970, 669; Lane 1971, 1975, 1976 and 1978.

Menerva An archaic form of the name of the Roman goddess MINERVA.

Mens Also known as Mens Bona and Bona Mens, a Roman goddess who was the personification of "mind" or "right-thinking". She had a festival on June 8. A temple on the Capitoline Hill in Rome was vowed to Mens in 217 B.C. on advice from the SIBYLLINE BOOKS and was dedicated in 215 B.C.
Reading: Richardson 1992, 251; Scullard 1981, 148.

Mentoviacus An Iberian god who is known from inscriptions on two altars found in the Zamora region of northern Spain. The function of this god is unknown, although it has been suggested that the "via" element of his name means that he was a protector of tracks and roads.
Reading: Tranoy 1981, 298.

Mercury (Figs. 31, 67) Known in Latin as Mercurius and occasionally as Merqurius, Mirqurios or Mircurios, with Mercury as the modern English form. This Roman god was regarded as the son of the Roman goddess MAIA and the Roman god JUPITER. He was identified with the Greek god HERMES. Mercury was a messenger of the gods and a god of trade, particularly the grain trade, and also a god of

Fig. 67 A bronze votive figurine of Mercury found at Lamyatt Beacon, England. He wears a winged hat, shoes and cloak, and holds a money bag in his right hand and a caduceus *in his left hand. Height 2½ in. (64 mm). Courtesy of Somerset County Museums Service.*

abundance and commercial success, especially in Gaul. In Rome he had a temple on the Aventine Hill (Fig. 68). He was often depicted bearing a *caduceus* (a herald's staff with two entwined snakes) and wearing a winged hat and winged shoes. He was also often accompanied by a cockerel (herald of each new day), a ram or goat (a fertility symbol) and a tortoise (a reference to Mercury's invention of the lyre from a tortoise shell). At Rome, Mercury was not assigned a *FLAMEN*, indicating that he was not worshipped at Rome from earliest times, but there was a festival of Mercury on May 15.

Julius Caesar stated that Mercury was the most popular god in Britain and Gaul and was regarded as the inventor of all the arts. In Celtic areas, he was sometimes portrayed with three heads or faces. At Tongeren, Belgium, a statuette of Mercury with three *phalli* (an extra one on his head and one replacing his nose) is probably a good luck and fertility charm, enhanced by using the magical number three. In Celtic areas, Mercury was very often equated with native deities (only the main ones are listed below) and he was frequently accompanied by the Celtic goddess ROSMERTA.
Reading: Combet-Farnoux 1980; Hammond and Scullard (eds.) 1970, 673; Simon 1990, 158–167.

Mercury, temple of (Fig. 68) Situated outside the *pomerium* in Rome on the slope of the Aventine Hill overlooking the CIRCUS MAXIMUS. It was traditionally believed to have been dedicated on Ides of May, 495 B.C. by the centurion *primi pili* Marcus Laetorius. The temple was apparently shared with MAIA, Mercury's mother. It became the center of the guild *(collegium)* of traders and merchants *(mercatores)*. Little is known of its building history and no trace has ever been found. From the evidence of coins, Marcus Aurelius rebuilt the temple, possibly as a circular structure or with a barrel-vaulted roof. It is the only known temple to Mercury in Rome.
Reading: Richardson 1992, 252; Vermeule 1987, 60–61.

Mercury Artaios The Celtic god ARTAIOS who was equated with the Roman god MERCURY. He was worshipped at Beaucroissant, France. He was probably connected with bears and hunting, both as protector of bears and as a protector of bear hunters.
Reading: Green, M. J. 1992a, 148–149.

Fig. 68 The restored temple of Mercury shown on a sestertius *of Marcus Aurelius dated to 172–173, with the legend IMP VI COS III RELIG AVG SC (*"imperator *for the sixth time, consul for the third time, the religion of the emperor [is commemorated], by order of the Senate"). It is shown as a circular temple (or with a barrel-vaulted roof) with attributes of Mercury (cockerel, ram,* caduceus*) on the facade. The coin refers to Mercury apparently coming to the assistance of Marcus Aurelius during a military campaign.*

Mercury Arvernus The Celtic god ARVERNUS who was equated with the Roman god MERCURY. He was worshipped in the Rhineland and was probably a god of that locality. The name *Arvernus* suggests that he was a particular deity of the Arverni tribe, but dedications to Mercury Arvernus do not occur in their territory which was within the Auvergne region of central France.
Reading: Green, M. J. 1992a, 148.

Mercury Cissonius The Celtic god CISSONIUS who was linked with the Roman god MERCURY. This deity is known within a region from Cologne, Germany, to Saintes, France.
Reading: Green, M. J. 1992a, 149.

Mercury Esibraeus An Iberian deity ESIBRAEUS who was linked with the Roman god MERCURY. This deity is known from an inscription found at Medelim, Portugal. It is possible that this is the

same deity as Banda Isibraiegus (see BANDA), who is invoked in an inscription from the nearby village of Bemposta.
Reading: Alarcão 1988, 93.

Mercury Gebrinius The Celtic god GEBRINIUS who was equated with the Roman god MERCURY. He is known from an inscription on an altar found at Bonn, Germany.
Reading: Green, M. J. 1992a, 149.

Mercury Moccus A Celtic god who was equated with the Roman god MERCURY. He is known from evidence at Langres, France. The name *Moccus* ("pig") suggests that he was connected with boar hunting.
Reading: Green, M. J. 1992a, 149.

Mercury Visucius A Celtic god, VISUCIUS, who was equated with the Roman god MERCURY.

Merqurius An early name for the Roman god Mercurius (MERCURY).

Messor A Roman god who presided over reaping and harvesting. He was said by Fabius Pictor in the late third century B.C. to have been invoked by a priest of CERES.
Reading: Ferguson 1988a, 853; York 1986, 60.

metroon Sanctuary containing shrines or temples for the worship of MAGNA MATER (Cybele). The word *metroon* is derived from *meter*, the Greek word for "mother."
Reading: Vermaseren 1977.

Minerva (Fig. 69) A Roman goddess of crafts and trade guilds. She was originally the Etruscan goddess Menrva, and the archaic form of her name was Menerva. She was identified with the Greek goddess ATHENA and sometimes with the Roman goddess NERIO. She appears to have assumed the martial aspect of Athena Promachos ("champion") and was regarded as a goddess of handicrafts and of war. Along with JUPITER and JUNO REGINA, she was one of the three deities of the CAPITOLINE TRIAD. In Noricum and Dalmatia, she was identified with a local goddess FLANONA and was known as MINERVA FLANATICA. In Rome, Minerva had a temple on the Aventine Hill and another in the Forum of Nerva.

Fig. 69 A bronze votive figurine of Minerva found at Lamyatt Beacon, England. She wears a tunic and aegis; *her left hand originally held the rim of a shield and her raised right hand held a spear. Height 2.9 in. (76 mm). Courtesy of Somerset County Museums Service.*

She had festivals on June 19 and September 13, and her main festival (QUINQUATRUS) was on March 19.
Reading: Hammond and Scullard (eds.) 1970, 689; Simon 1990, 168–181.

Minerva, temples of One of Minerva's temples was outside the *pomerium* of Rome on the Aventine Hill, and was probably dedicated on March 19 (year unknown). It was next to, but not aligned with, the temple of DIANA. It was on a podium with a deep pronaos, and was about 24.05 yds. × 49.21 yds. (22m × 45 m). It was older than the Second Punic War, when it is first mentioned. It became a center for a guild of writers and actors and possibly skilled craftsmen.

At the east end of Nerva's Forum (Forum Nervae or Transitorium) was another temple of Minerva, built by Domitian and dedicated by Nerva in 97. Minerva was Domitian's patron deity. The temple had Corinthian columns and was HEXASTYLE on a high podium. The precinct wall had relief sculptures on the frieze and attic which depicted her cult and legends, and Severus Alexander placed colossal statues of the deified emperors here. Much of the temple was still standing until the ruins were demolished under Pope Paul IV in 1606 to be used for building materials. The ruins were often depicted by sixteenth-century artists.
Reading: Fishwick 1987, 210 (note 76); Nash 1962a, 433; Richardson 1992, 167–169; Scullard 1981, 93–94.

Minerva Capta ("Minerva in Captivity") This aspect of the Roman goddess MINERVA had a small temple at the foot of the Caelian Hill in Rome, which seems to have been built when a statue of the goddess was captured at the town of Falerii (Civita Castellana) in Italy in 241 B.C. and was then brought to Rome.
Reading: Palmer 1974, 43; Richardson 1992, 255; Scullard 1981, 94.

Minerva Flanatica FLANONA was the native patron goddess of the city of Flanona (modern Plomin) in the Roman province of Dalmatia. She was identified with the Roman goddess MINERVA, and was worshipped in the area of Istria within Dalmatia.
Reading: Wilkes 1969, 195.

Minerva Medica The Roman goddess MINERVA in her aspect of patron of doctors. She had a temple on the Esquiline Hill in Rome. In 1887 *favissae* (see FAVISSA) containing hundreds of votive objects were discovered, probably belonging to this temple.
Reading: Richardson 1992, 256; Scullard 1981, 93.

miracle A wonderful event demonstrating the power of a deity. The Christian church needed to be able to demonstrate its spiritual authority. This was nowhere better demonstrated than in the performance of miracles. Miracles were proof of sanctity, and the saints who performed them had the role of intercessors between god and the people. This role was more effective if the saint was physically present, so that relics of saints became an important focus for Christians.

Miracles performed by saints, both alive and after their deaths, were a powerful force for recruiting adherents to early CHRISTIANITY, leading to the setting up of *martyria* and the practice of pilgrimage. However, miracles were not the exclusive preserve of Christianity; many pagan deities were believed to perform miracles, the commonest of which were healing deities such as AESCULAPIUS. Roman deities, such as VESTA, were thought to have performed numerous miracles, but in general miracles were more likely to be performed by Oriental deities such as ISIS or SERAPIS.
Reading: Hammond and Scullard (eds.) 1970, 694; Lane Fox 1988, 570–571.

Mircurios An early name for the Roman god MERCURY.

Mirqurios An early name for the Roman god MERCURY.

mithraeum (Fig. 70) (pl. *mithraea*) A temple for the worship of MITHRAS. *Mithraea* were constructed to simulate the cave in which Mithras was supposed to have captured and killed the divine bull, the symbol of life through death. The temples were small and tunnel-like, and some were built partially or wholly underground. They were dimly lit, with a variable amount of rustication. There were benches along the sides for the worshippers. The temples were also known by the name *spelaea* (caves).

Fig. 70 The remains of the mithraeum *situated just outside the fort at Carrawburgh on Hadrian's Wall, England. The building measures 19 ft. × 42 ft. (5.79 m × 12.8 m). The concrete posts represent upright wooden timbers, and there were low wooden benches. At one end were three altars. This* mithraeum *was founded in the early 3rd century, underwent several building phases, and was destroyed in the early 4th century.*

Mithraea were different from most other temples in that the worshippers of Mithras conducted their worship mainly inside rather than outside the temple. The focus of the temple interior was a marble relief or sometimes a painting at one end, portraying Mithras slaying the bull (Fig. 101). This might be flanked by other sculptured scenes or statues and by altars (Fig. 71). There is evidence that at least some of these sculptures were pierced so that illumination from behind could shine through. In the main body of the temple, the central aisle was flanked by raised benches on which the initiates reclined at ritual meals (as seen in Rome in the preserved *mithraea* at Santa Prisca and at San Clemente). At the end opposite the reliefs and altars was a narthex or porch, and there was sometimes a pit used for initiation ceremonies. Various other deities have also been found depicted in *mithraea.* Two common ones are the torch bearers CAUTES (Fig. 19) and CAUTOPATES, and others include the deities that protected each grade of initiate (such as VENUS), and a lion-headed god, encircled by the coils of a snake, who is thought by some to represent Ahriman (power of evil—see MITHRAS). Altars to SOL INVICTUS and to other gods have been found in *mithraea.* Thirteen *mithraea* are known in Rome, arranged in natural caves or adapted in the cellars of preexisting buildings. *Mithraea* are also known across the Roman world. The size of these temples is small, implying that the number of worshippers in any one place was also small.

Reading: Bianchi (ed.) 1979; Hammond and Scullard (eds.) 1970, 694–695; Toynbee 1986.

Mithraeum Domus Barberinorum Three rooms of a first-century house found in Rome in 1936 during building construction work behind the Palazzo Barberini. The westernmost room (measuring 12.96 yds. × 6.83 yds.; 11.85 m × 6.25 m) had been converted into a *MITHRAEUM.* There was a central aisle and raised side benches, and the cult image on the south wall is a large painting of Mithras Tauroctonos, one of the few paintings of MITHRAS, showing him killing a bull.

Reading: Nash 1962b, 72–73; Richardson 1992, 257.

Mithraeum Domus Clementis An early third-century MITHRAEUM found in Rome and built into a first-century house. It was discovered in 1869 under the church of San Clemente, but could not be excavated until after 1914 because of flooding. It consisted of a rectangular room with a low vaulted ceiling and side benches. There were niches and an altar with Mithraic reliefs. The *mithraeum* was deliberately filled with earth when the cult was suppressed.
Reading: Nash 1962b, 75; Richardson 1992, 257.

Mithraeum Domus Sanctae Priscae A MITHRAEUM discovered by the monks of Santa Prisca under the Aventine Hill beneath their church. Excavations were completed in 1958. The *mithraeum* had been built into a room of a private house in the late second century and consisted of a central aisle with side benches. There were niches for the statues of CAUTES and CAUTOPATES and a cult niche with a stucco group of Mithras Tauroctonos. The interior was also painted. It was rebuilt and enlarged around 220, with additional rooms for initiation rites.
Reading: Nash 1962b, 79; Richardson 1992, 257–258.

Mithraeum prope Carceres Circi Maximi A MITHRAEUM in Rome northwest of the *carceres* (starting gates) of the CIRCUS MAXIMUS, but separated from the *carceres* by a narrow street. Four vaulted chambers and a monumental stair discovered during tidying up of the cellars of the Museums of Rome in 1931 may have originally been a public building. In the second half of the third century, three of the four chambers were converted into a *mithraeum*, with benches and niches for statues.
Reading: Nash 1962b, 69; Richardson 1992, 256–257.

Mithraeum Thermarum Antoninianarum A MITHRAEUM discovered in 1912 during excavations of the subterranean vaulted service corridors beneath the Baths of Caracalla in Rome. The largest discovered in Rome, it measures 25.15 yds. × 10.60 yds. (23 m × 9.70 m) and consists of a nave with a black-and-white mosaic floor and low side benches.
Reading: Nash 1962b, 85; Richardson 1992, 258.

Mithraism A mystery religion, the cult of MITHRAS, which spread from Persia and reached Rome in the second half of the first century B.C. It had secret rites and stages of initiation. In the first century A.D., it began to spread through the Roman empire, reaching a peak in the third century, before being suppressed along with other pagan religions at the end of the fourth century. Mithraism was confined exclusively to men and appealed particularly to merchants, soldiers and treasury officials, so that the cult barely touched the civilian population.

Mithraism was an offshoot of Zoroastrianism, which recognized Ahura Mazda as god and sole creator of the universe. Mithraism became virtually a new religion, with its own unique aspects, such as TAUROCTONY. The mythology of Mithraism is very complex. The bull slaying (tauroctony) by Mithras was a central part of Mithraism in the Roman period and was depicted on stone sculptured reliefs in *mithraea.* Because it was a mystery religion, much of the ritual was kept secret, and what little is known of the religion comes from archaeological and epigraphical evidence and from Christian writers who denounced some of the rites as a blasphemous mockery of Christian rituals.

Mithraism had seven grades by which worshippers progressed through successive stages of initiation, when more of the mysteries of the cult were revealed to them. The grades of initiation began with Corax (Raven) and progressed to Nymphus (Bridegroom), Miles (Soldier), Leo (Lion), Perses (Persian), Heliodromus (Courier of the Sun) and Pater (Father). The progress from one grade to the next appears to have been achieved by a ritual during which some kind of ordeal was suffered by the worshipper. Each grade of worshipper had a protective deity and associated emblems: Corax was protected by MERCURY and had a *caduceus* and a cup as emblems; Nymphus was protected by VENUS and had a lamp and veil as emblems; Miles was protected by MARS and had a kit bag and a quiver of arrows as emblems; Leo was protected by JUPITER and had a thunderbolt, fire shovel and *sistrum* as emblems; Perses was protected by the Moon and had a sickle and ears of cereal crops as emblems; Heliodromus was protected by the Sun and had a radiant crown, torch and orb as emblems; and Pater was protected by SATURN and had a staff, Phrygian cap, sickle-like sword and *patera* as emblems. Wall paintings depict the various grades dressed in ritual clothes, according to their grades of initiation, and Corax is shown wearing a raven-head mask. The rites of the cult included a form of baptism, a sealing on the forehead and ceremonial meals.

Astrological elements such as the signs of the zodiac and references to gods identified with planets are prominent in Mithraic art and presumably had some significance in the cult. Various other deities have also been found depicted in *mithraea.* The size of the *mithraeum* is small, implying that the number of worshippers was also small. However, the evidence from dedicatory inscriptions suggests that a large proportion of worshippers were well-to-do and included army officers, wealthy merchants and business men, provincial governors, and in one case, emperors.

Reading: Bianchi (ed.) 1979; Ferguson 1970, 47–49; Hammond and Scullard (eds.) 1970, 694–695; Toynbee 1986; Ulansey 1989 (examines connection with astrology and proposes new interpretation).

Mithras (Fig. 71) The god who was worshipped in the mystery religion of MITHRAISM. He was an ancient Persian (Indo-Iranian) god of truth and light who, in Zoroastrianism, was the agent and supporter of the power of good known as Ahura Mazda, against Ahriman, the power of evil. This struggle of good and light against evil and darkness was central to Zoroastrianism, in which Mithras had various titles, including "Warrior," "Victorious," "Lord of Light," "God of Truth," "Savior from Death" and "Giver of Bliss." In Iranian myth, Mithras was sent to earth by Ahura Mazda to hunt and kill a divine bull that had been Ahura Mazda's first creation; from the bull's blood all living things sprang. In one myth, Mithras was born from a rock and was aided by the Sun who sent his messenger, the raven, to help find the sacred bull. After the bull had been killed, its blood spread over the earth, from which all life sprang. Through this act, the Sun yielded supremacy to Mithras and made a covenant with him. Mithras finally parted from his ally, the Sun, after a ceremonial banquet, which was commemorated by cult followers in a ritual meal.

This broad outline is consistent with the iconography of the cult worshipped by the Romans and with the few Roman Mithraic inscriptions that have survived. More detailed interpretation, drawing heavily on Iranian myths, has been disputed in recent studies, and much of the cult remains unknown. Mithras had close connections with the Sun. Although in myth Mithras came to be acknowledged as superior to the Sun, he later came to be identified with the Sun, and dedications to Sol Invictus Mithras (see SOL INVICTUS) are known. Mithras is usually portrayed wearing a Phrygian cap and trousers.

Fig. 71 An altar dedicated to Mithras. It was found in the mithraeum *at Housesteads, Hadrian's Wall, England. The legend reads DEO SOLI INVICTO MYTRAE SAECVLARI LITORIVS PACATIANVS BF COS PRO SE ET SVIS VSLM ("To the God, Sol Invictus Mithras the Eternal, Litorius Pacatianus, consular* beneficiarius, *pays his vow willingly and deservedly for himself and his").*

Reading: Cumont 1896 (numerous illustrations); Hammond and Scullard (eds.) 1970, 694–695; Vermaseren 1963.

Moccus A Celtic god who was linked with the Roman god MERCURY as MERCURY MOCCUS.

model objects Objects made in a variety of materials, smaller than their normal size, often used as votive offerings. They included baked clay pottery vessels (Fig. 118) and models of tools and weapons. The weapons comprise shields, spears and swords, and even a model ballista (artillery machine) was found at the temple of SULIS MINERVA at Bath, England. Model axes are commonly found on temple sites, and may represent implements of sacrifice. Also common are model wheels, and small bronze enamelled stands designed to stack one on top of another, the purpose of which is unclear. Model *caducei* were offered to MERCURY. The model objects were made in a wide range of materials, including terracotta, bronze, iron, silver, gold, lead, bone and stone. Bronze was most common.
Reading: Bourgeois 1991, 113–204; Green, M. J. 1981; Green, M. J. 1984; Henig 1993b.

Moelius Mordoniecus An Iberian god who is known from an inscription on an altar found at Cornoces, near Orense, northwest Spain. The altar was dedicated in 79 by Lucius Caecilius Fuscus, a soldier of Legion VII Gemina. This is one of the few altars that can be closely dated, because the date of the dedication was included in the inscription.
Reading: Tranoy 1981, 276.

Mogons ("great one") A Celtic god who was worshipped mainly in northern England, particularly in the area around Hadrian's Wall. He is also known from evidence in Germany and eastern France. There appear to be various spellings of this god's name, and dedications to Mogtus, Mogunus, Mogounus and Mountus are all thought to refer to this god. The Celtic goddess MOGONTIA may be connected with this deity.
Reading: Green, M. J. 1992a, 152–153.

Mogons Vitiris The Celtic god MOGONS equated with the Celtic god VITIRIS, known from a single inscription found at Netherby, Cumbria, England.
Reading: Ross 1974, 468–469.

Mogontia A Celtic goddess who is known from an inscription found at Sablon, France. Mogontia may be linked to the Celtic god MOGONS.
Reading: Cüppers *et al.* 1983, 142.

Mogounus Probably an alternative name for the Celtic god MOGONS.

Mogtus Probably an alternative name for the Celtic god MOGONS.

Mogunus Probably an alternative name for the Celtic god MOGONS.

mola salsa A cake of ground barley and salt used in sacrifical meals and rituals. It was prepared by the VESTAL VIRGINS for use at the VESTALIA, at the *EPULUM IOVIS*, and at the LUPERCALIA. To make the sacred cake, the Vestal Virgins had to fetch water from a sacred spring without setting it down on the way back. *Salsa* means "salted" and *mola* can mean "mill" or "millstone" as well as the cake itself.

monasticism Retreat from normal life by single persons or by a community (usually, but not invariably, a single-sex community) to concentrate on the contemplation and worship of God. By the late fourth century, the organized Christian church was very rich, and leading thinkers like JEROME and Martin of Tours began to question its values. This gave impetus to the monastic movement which had been set in motion earlier in the fourth century by single ascetics seeking solitude in the desert in Egypt. Men began withdrawing into the desert in Egypt, Syria and Palestine, away from cities, often setting up small settlements that allowed for both solitude and communal life. Initially, many monks lived off charity or survived by gathering wild herbs and roots, but some organized communities lived by producing and selling goods of all kinds, depending on the skills of the monks. Bishops were not slow to draw on the energies and talent within the monastic movement, and some monastic communities came to be set up within cities. In time, the great monastic houses became the training ground for future bishops and eventually for the offspring of the aristocracy as well. Through the fourth and fifth centuries, monasticism spread westward into Europe, and in the sixth century there is evidence of monks in Ireland.
Reading: Johnson 1980, 139–144.

monumentum Any TOMB for the BURIAL OF THE DEAD, both above and below ground.

Moritasgus A Celtic god who was linked to the Greek god APOLLO as APOLLO MORITASGUS, a healing god sometimes associated with the Celtic goddess DAMONA.

Mors A Roman goddess who was the personification of death.
Reading: Grimal 1986, 296.

Morta A Roman goddess who presided over stillbirths. She was sometimes identified as one of the PARCAE.

mother goddess (Fig. 72) A deity who personified maternal attributes, such as care, nurturing and protection, as well as fertility, increase and abundance. Cybele was known to the Romans as MAGNA MATER ("Great Mother"), and JUNO was often regarded as a form of mother goddess in her various guises. The Celts in particular worshipped many forms of mother goddess, often as a triad, and in Roman inscriptions their names were often prefixed by the word *Matronae* or *Matres.*
Reading: Bourgeois 1991, 21–25; Deyts 1992, 58–68; Green, M. J. 1984, 200–202.

Fig. 72 A small altar found at Carrawburgh, Hadrian's Wall, England. It was dedicated simply to MATRIBVS ("mother goddesses"). Height 9.5 in. (0.24 m).

Mountus Probably an alternative name for the Celtic god MOGONS.

Mullo A Celtic god who was linked with the Roman god MARS as MARS MULLO.

mundus A subterranean ritual pit which was believed to lead to the UNDERWORLD. The one in Rome seems to have been called the *mundus Cereris,* linking the pit with the goddess CERES. The association with Ceres may have been because she was the mother of PROSERPINA. Its location is unknown, possibly on the Palatine Hill. It was closed by a cover except on August 24, October 5 and November 8, which were considered days of ill omen. They were not *dies nefasti,* but no public business was conducted. The cover was regarded as the Gate of Hell, and when lifted, the spirits *(MANES)* of the underworld roamed the streets of Rome.
Reading: Richardson 1992, 259–260; Scullard 1981, 180–181, 197; York 1986, 163–164, 173–174.

Munidia An Iberian god who is known from inscriptions found in the area between the Douro and Tagus Rivers, Portugal, and around Cáceres, western Spain. It is thought that he is the same deity as MUNIS.
Reading: Alarcão 1988, 93; Tranoy 1981, 276–277.

Munis An Iberian god who is known from inscriptions in the area between the Douro and Tagus rivers, Portugal, and around Cáceres, western Spain. It is thought that he is the same deity as MUNIDIA.
Reading: Alarcão 1988, 93.

Murcia An obscure Roman goddess who was also known as Murtea, Murtia and Myrtea. She had a shrine in Rome in the valley between the Aventine Hill (Murcus was an old name for the Aventine Hill) and the Palatine Hill. She appears to have

been regarded as a goddess of sloth. *Murcia* was sometimes used as a title of the Roman goddess VENUS. Little else is known about this deity.
Reading: Richardson 1992, 260.

Muses (Latin, Musae) Greek deities who came to preside over various aspects of art. Originally the number of muses varied from region to region, but during the classical period in Greece, the number of muses was standardized to nine. Gradually, each one came to have a specific function: Calliope was the Muse of epic poetry, Clio the Muse of history, Polyhymnia the Muse of mime, Euterpe the Muse of the flute, Terpsichore the Muse of light verse, Erato the Muse of lyric choral poetry, Melpomene the Muse of tragedy, Thalia the Muse of comedy and Urania the Muse of astronomy. The muses were sometimes linked to HERCULES, and in Rome there was a temple dedicated to Hercules of the Muses in the CIRCUS FLAMINIUS.
Reading: Grimal 1986, 298; Scullard 1981, 157.

music Music played a part in most religious ceremonies (such as at a sacrifice—Fig. 99), often to drown out sounds of ill omen. Double pipes *(tibiae)* were used at most sacrifices, as well as the flute and the lyre. Tamborines and cymbals seem to have been used mainly in orgiastic cults, such as those of MAGNA MATER and BACCHUS, where music played a large part. Rattles were probably widely used, but a special kind of rattle *(SISTRUM)* was used in the cult of ISIS (Fig. 96). Singing of hymns may also have been widely practiced, and a few are known, such as the *CARMEN ARVALE.*
Reading: Hammond and Scullard (eds.) 1970, 713.

Myrtea An alternative name for the Roman goddess MURCIA.

mystery religions (or mysteries) Secret cults which required initiation for admission. Their teachings were supposed to illuminate the mystery of achieving immortality; the teachings themselves were kept as a mystery, to which the faithful were initiated. Mystery religions were brought to Rome from Greece and the east and included the ELEUSINIAN MYSTERIES, MITHRAISM, ORPHISM and the cults of BACCHUS and MAGNA MATER. Mystery religions involved the participation of the individual, unlike the worship of the traditional Roman pagan gods. They involved initiation rites, purification, sacred symbols and rites, and a promise of a happy afterlife. CHRISTIANITY was regarded as a mystery religion.
Reading: Ferguson 1970, 99–131; Hammond and Scullard (eds.) 1970, 716–717.

myths Traditional stories which were often based on historical or supposedly historical events and people. Many myths and legends about the Roman gods had their origins in Greek myths whose gods had a complex mythology. Myths provided the Greeks with their entire early history (which involved their gods). Many Greek myths were a mixture of fact and fiction, and most featured stories about the Greek gods, their activities, relationships and ritual. The myths used by Roman poets were largely borrowed from Greek sources. Most early Roman gods were not anthropomorphic in nature until they became identified with Greek gods, so there is unlikely to have been much scope to invent myths around Roman gods. There is very little surviving evidence for Roman and Italian myths before the Romans adopted many of the Greek myths. Very few Roman gods had any mythology; this was usually a later invention by poets and other writers.
Reading: Bremmer and Horsfall 1987; Grant 1971; Hammond and Scullard (eds.) 1970, 718.

N

Nabelcus A Celtic god who was linked with the Roman god MARS as MARS NABELCUS.

Nabia An Iberian goddess who is known from a number of inscriptions found in Portugal, where her worship was widespread in Lusitania and Callaecia. She is thought to be a goddess of valleys, hills, woods and flowing water. She may be the same deity as NABIA CORONA and NAVIA.
Reading: Alarcão 1988, 93; Tranoy 1981, 281–283.

Nabia Corona An Iberian deity who is known from an inscription found near Penafiel, Portugal, where she was invoked in conjunction with the Roman god JUPITER, a native deity (Lida) and another deity whose name cannot be retrieved. The inscription suggests that she was worshipped as a NYMPH and as a guardian of the Danigi tribe. The epithet *Corona* may mean that she was regarded as the consort of the god CORONUS. It is possible that Nabia Corona is the same deity as Nabia.
Reading: Alarcão 1988, 93; Tranoy 1981, 282.

Nabu An alternative name for the Syrian god NEBU.

Nanai A Syrian goddess who was originally a Babylonian goddess, sometimes equated with ARTEMIS. Her cult was still widespread in Syria and Mesopotamia in the Roman period.

Nantosuelta A Celtic goddess whose name means "winding river" or "meandering brook." She was invoked with the Celtic god SUCELLUS as a divine couple.

naos (pl. *naoi*) A Greek word used in the eastern provinces for a temple, shrine or cult room within a larger structure.
Reading: Price 1984, 134.

Natalis Urbis *(natalis urbis Romae aeternae)* A new festival which Hadrian substituted in 121 for the old PARILIA to mark the "anniversary of the foundation of the eternal city of Rome." It was celebrated across the empire; an altar commemorating the event is known from High Rochester, England, and the festival is recorded on the calendar from Dura-Europus in Syria (the *FERIALE DURANUM*).
Reading: Haynes 1993, 142.

Navia An Iberian goddess who is known from inscriptions found in the area of Guntín, northwest Spain. Here dedications to Navia, Navia Arconunieca and Navia Sesmaca are known. It is possible that the names *Arconunieca* and *Sesmaca* refer to local places or tribes. Navia is probably the same deity as the Iberian goddess NABIA.
Reading: Tranoy 1981, 293–294.

Nebu Also known as Nabu or Nebo, a Syrian god who was originally a Babylonian god. He was the son of MARDUK and was possibly at times equated with APOLLO (although this is disputed). He was particularly associated with BEL. His cult was widespread in Syria and Mesopotamia in the Roman period.
Reading: Teixidor 1969, 106–111.

Necessitas The Roman goddess of necessity who was seen as the personification of the constraining force of destiny. She was identified with the Greek goddess ANANKE, who was also a personification of necessity.

necromancy The summoning of the spirits of the dead to do the bidding of the living, usually for purposes of DIVINATION. Necromancy was considered to be MAGIC or witchcraft and was generally viewed with disapproval or hostility by the Romans. Consequently, practitioners were secretive, and little evidence of their methods has survived. Since spirits of the dead could apparently give oracles and foretell the future, this was probably the main motive for necromancy. The process was probably carried out by people believed to possess magical powers. In a poem, Horace describes two witches performing various rituals in order to raise spirits of the dead to provide oracular answers to their questions.
Reading: Ferguson 1970, 159.

nefastus (or *dies nefastus*, pl. *dies nefasti*) Days when no political assembly was permitted and when it was not permitted to initiate legal business of a civil nature (although such business could be undertaken if a sacrifice was made). Such days were determined by the pontiffs. They were indicated by the letter *N* in calendars. There were 58 such days in the pre-Julian CALENDAR. Days marked *NP* in the calendars were possibly *nefasti publici*, days in which assembly and legal business were not permitted, possibly because of major public festivals. There were 52 such days in the calendars. However, the term *NP* seems to have been used loosely for *N* in some calendars. (See also *ENDOTERCISUS*.)
Reading: Hammond and Scullard (eds.) 1970, 341; York 1986.

Nehalennia A Celtic goddess of seafarers, fertility and abundance. The name *Nehalennia* may mean "steerswoman" or "leader." She is known at two coastal shrines at Domburg and Colijnsplaat, the Netherlands, in the territory of the Morini tribe. Many altars have been found at these sites, and on them Nehalennia is frequently portrayed with symbols of sea travel, such as a steering oar, as well as with symbols of abundance, such as a heap of fruit or a cornucopia. Another frequent accompanying symbol is a dog, usually portrayed in a benign protective pose. The variety of symbolism suggests that the goddess presided over wider activities such as healing, death and rebirth and not just travel at sea. Nehalennia is also known from a dedication at the river port of Cologne, Germany.
Reading: Elbe 1975, 215; Green, M. J. 1992a, 159–160.

Nemausicae (Also known as Matres Nemausicae) Celtic mother goddesses of fertility and healing who were associated with the shrine and spa at the town of Nîmes (Nemausus), France. They were also associated with NEMAUSUS, the eponymous god of that town who presided over the healing spring.
Reading: Green, M. J. 1992a, 160.

Nemausus An ancient local Celto-Ligurian god of Nîmes (Nemausus), France. The Ligurians were pre-Celtic people living in the extreme south of Gaul. Nemausus was probably originally the spirit of the healing springs at Nîmes, where local goddesses of healing and fertility (called NEMAUSICAE or Matres Nemausicae) were also worshipped.
Reading: Green, M. J. 1992a, 160.

Nemesis The Greek goddess of vengeance who came to be worshipped by the Romans. She was also known as ADRASTEA and Adrastia. An UNDERWORLD goddess, Nemesis was always ready to punish impiety and reward virtue. She was sometimes regarded as one of the FURIES.
Reading: Garcia Y Bellido 1967, 82–95.

Nemetona A Celtic goddess of the sacred grove (*nemeton* means "sacred grove"). She was mainly worshipped in the territory of the Nemetes in Germany. She was usually paired with a Celtic version of MARS, such as MARS RIGONEMETIS, MARS LOUCETIUS or Loucetius Mars. A dedication to her and Loucetius Mars, by a citizen of Trier, Germany, has been found at Bath, England.
Reading: Green, M. J. 1992a, 160.

nemus A Latin word denoting a sacred grove dedicated to a deity. One example is the sanctuary of DIANA NEMORENSIS. (See also GROVES, SACRED; *LUCUS*.)
Reading: Scheid 1993.

Nenia The Roman goddess of the dying, of mourning and of the lamentations sung at funerals.

She had a temple outside the Porta Viminalis at Rome.
Reading: Grimal 1986, 231 (under *Indigetes*).

Neoplatonism (sometimes called Platonism) A philosophy sporadically developed over several centuries by various philosophers and given its final form by Plotinus and his pupils in the third century. Plotinus and his pupils combined the philosophy of Plato with elements from the philosophies of Pythagoras, Aristotle and the Stoics. It was an attempt at a comprehensive pagan philosophy which also showed how the individual soul might reach god. Plotinus recognized a single pagan god, with all material things, both good and bad, derived from that god. He did not believe in a battle between good and evil and thought that the ultimate aim was the ascent of the soul to god. This was to be achieved through love, with love of physical and material beauty leading to higher and pure forms of love. As such, Neoplatonism offered pagans a path to "salvation" comparable with CHRISTIANITY and the MYSTERY RELIGIONS, and came to have a great influence on Christian thinking. It was the dominant pagan philosophy from around the mid-third century (in reaction to Christianity) until philosophy schools were closed by Justinian in 529.
Reading: Ferguson 1970, 206–210 (under *Plotinus*); Jackson Knight 1970, 159–172.

Neopythagoreanism Revival of the Pythagorean school of thought in Rome and Alexandria in the first century B.C. It concentrated mainly on theological speculation and symbolism of mystical numbers. It influenced Christian and Jewish thought and merged into NEOPLATONISM. (See also CHRISTIANITY; JUDAISM.)
Reading: Hammond and Scullard (eds.) 1970, 728.

Neptunalia Very little is known of the festival of NEPTUNE, which was held on July 23. It was one of the oldest festivals.
Reading: Hammond and Scullard (eds.) 1970, 729.

Neptune (Fig. 73) (in Latin, Neptunus) An ancient Roman god of water. He was later identified with the Greek god POSEIDON and was therefore later regarded as a sea god. Because of Poseidon's association with horses, Neptune also became identified with the Roman god CONSUS, who was associated with horses. At Rome, there was a temple dedicated to Neptune in the CIRCUS FLAMINIUS within the CAMPUS MARTIUS. Neptune was one of only three gods (with MARS and APOLLO) to whom a bull might be sacrificed. According to legend, Neptune had a companion deity, who is named by some as SALACIA and by others as VENILIA. Neptune had a festival, the NEPTUNALIA, on July 23, and there was another festival in his honor on December 1.
Reading: Grimal 1986, 307–308; Hammond and Scullard (eds.) 1970, 728–729; Richardson 1992, 267 (temple); Vermeule 1987, 62–63; York 1986, 85–86.

Fig. 73 Neptune holding a trident on a denarius *of Septimius Severus of* A.D. *210.*

Nergal A Syrian god of the UNDERWORLD who became equated with the Greek god HERACLES (HERCULES) in the Roman period. He was accompanied by a dog.
Reading: Colledge 1986, 225–226; Teixidor 1969, 112–114.

Nerio A Roman goddess of war who was the personification of valor. She was the ancient cult-partner of the Roman god MARS and was sometimes identified with the Roman goddess BELLONA and occasionally with the Roman goddess MINERVA. Sometimes spoils taken from the enemy were dedicated to Nerio.
Reading: Grimal 1986, 308.

Nerthus A Germanic earth and fertility goddess who was mentioned as riding in procession on a wagon by the Roman historian Tacitus in the *Germania*.
Reading: Green, M. J. 1992a, 161.

Nicaea, Council of the Church in The first Christian ecumenical council, held in 325 in Nicaea (now Iznik in Turkey). ARIANISM was repudiated and orthodox Christian principles were upheld; a declaration to that effect (known as the Nicene Creed) was asserted. The Nicene Creed was named after Nicaea, and it was upheld at the Second Ecumenical Council held in Haghia Eirene at Constantinople in 381 (Fig. 22).

Nicomachus Virius Nicomachus Flavianus, 334–394, a prominent senator, pagan, and friend of Symmachus whose daughter he married. He used violent means to oppose CHRISTIANITY and further the cause of PAGANISM. He supported the pagan rule of the emperor Eugenius, and committed suicide after the victory of Theodosius I.
Reading: Hammond and Scullard (eds.) 1970, 734.

Nike The Greek goddess of victory who was equated with the Roman goddess VICTORIA. Nike was often portrayed with wings. As a symbol of victory over death, Nike was a popular motif in Roman art.
Reading: Hammond and Scullard (eds.) 1970, 735.

Nimmedus Seddiagus An Iberian god who is known from two inscriptions found at d'Ujo, near Mieres, northern Spain.
Reading: Tranoy 1981, 298.

Nixi Also known as Di Nixi, these Roman goddesses were a triad of deities who protected women in childbirth.

Nodens Also known as Nodons or Nudens, a Celtic god of healing found only in Britain. There is no known portrayal of Nodens in human form, but representations of a dog occur which may portray the god or an associated attribute. Dedications to MARS NODENS have been found at Lydney, Gloucestershire, and near Lancaster, Lancashire. There was an important temple complex and healing sanctuary dedicated to Nodens at Lydney.
Reading: Green, M. J. 1992a, 162.

Nodutus A Roman god of stalks of grain plants who presided over their development as far as the joints or nodes.
Reading: Ferguson 1988a, 853.

Nona A Roman goddess who presided over the eighth month of pregnancy (the ninth month, according to the Roman method of inclusive counting). She was sometimes identified as one of the PARCAE.
Reading: Ferguson 1988a, 853.

Nonae Caprotinae (Caprotinae or Nonae Capratinae) The feast of the serving women or maidservants *(ancillarum feriae)*, held on July 7. The name *Nonae Caprotinae* means "Nones of the Wild Fig," *caprificus* being Latin for "wild fig." JUNO CAPROTINA was worshipped at this festival, which may have commemorated an incident when serving women were instrumental in the removal of a threat to Rome by a Latin army after the capture of Rome by the Gauls. An alternative explanation was that the day was called Caprotinae because women in Latium would sacrifice to Juno Caprotina under a wild fig tree on that day. The festival may have been associated with an agricultural festival for the fertility of fig trees. Plutarch suggested that the celebration was in honor of Romulus on the day he disappeared (which was actually on July 5, the POPLIFUGIA).
Reading: Bremmer and Horsfall 1987, 76–88; Scullard 1981, 161–162.

Nones (Latin, Nonae) Nine days before the IDES (the 7th in long months and the 5th in other months). No festivals were held in any month before the Nones (except for the POPLIFUGIA in July). The wife of the *REX SACRORUM* sacrificed a pig or lamb to JUNO in the REGIA, and the holidays *(FERIAE)* of the month were announced on the Nones.
Reading: York 1986, 2.

Noreia The patron goddess of Noricum who had a shrine at Hohenstein, Austria. She was sometimes identified with the Egyptian goddess ISIS.

Nortia An Etruscan goddess of fortune, also called Nurtia. She was sometimes identified with the Roman goddesses FORTUNA and NECESSITAS. She was worshipped at Volsinii (Bolsena) in Italy, where a nail was ritually driven into the wall of her temple during her annual festival. The origin and purpose of this rite are unclear.
Reading: Hammond and Scullard (eds.) 1970, 738.

Novensiles (or Novensides or *di novensiles*) A group of Roman deities who are mentioned before (and were therefore more important than) the INDIGETES in the formula for *DEVOTIO*. Some authorities have suggested that *Novensiles* means "newly settled gods" and thus refers to deities assimilated or imported from other cultures, such as CASTOR and AESCULAPIUS. However, this interpretation is disputed and nothing is known of the Novensiles' function.
Reading: Hammond and Scullard (eds.) 1970, 740.

Nudens An alternative name for the Celtic god NODENS.

number, sacred A number or numeral that had a religious, mystical or magical significance. Several numbers seem to have had special importance for the Romans. The number three was particularly significant, with groups of three deities or three images of a single deity being common (a process known as triplism). The number four was also important, and some prayers were repeated four times. Other sacred numbers appear to have been adopted from the Greeks, such as seven (the traditional number of the planets) and 12 (the number of signs of the zodiac). Odd numbers were considered lucky; odd-numbered days were considered lucky, and even-numbered days less lucky or even unlucky. Most festivals *(FERIAE)* were held on odd-numbered days.
Reading: Hammond and Scullard (eds.) 1970, 742.

numen (pl. *numina*) A divine spirit or power. Originally the Romans thought of places such as woods, springs and caves as supernatural or divine places. They gradually developed the idea, probably under Greek influence, that the places were inhabited by spirits *(numina)*. In time, the spirits accumulated personalities and even names. These early deities were asexual, giving rise to anomalies as they acquired names and personalities. The goddess VENUS was probably originally one of these spirits; in Latin, her name is neuter in form, rather then feminine. *Numina* were expected to be found in material things, such as growing crops, and also in actions such as traveling. In the later Roman period, *numina* were also considered to be abstractions such as "virtue" and "loyalty," and the *numen* of the emperor was often worshipped, especially in Gaul and Britain. Because many deities appear to have developed from *numina*, it is often difficult to define a meaningful distinction between a *numen* and a god.
Reading: Ferguson 1970, 71–73; Ferguson 1988a, 853–854; York 1986.

Numiternus A Roman deity who was worshipped at Atina (modern Atena), to the southeast of Rome. Numiternus may have been the patron god of the Roman *gens* (tribe) called Numitorius.

Nurtia An alternative name for the Etruscan goddess NORTIA.

nymphaeum An ornamental fountain, originally in the shape of a grotto. Some were associated with the nymphs. By the second century they consisted of a decorative wall or facade with columns, statues and falling water, some very ornate and large. *Nymphaea* are found across the empire, but it is difficult to be certain if any particular example was associated with a cult or if it was just an ornamental architectural structure.
Reading: Bourgeois 1992, 107–130.

nymph A female personification of a natural object such as a spring, river, tree or mountain. These spirits were derived from Greek myth, where they were regarded as vague beings who were young and beautiful, fond of music and dancing and long-lived rather than immortal. The cult of nymphs was widespread through the Hellenistic world and under the Roman empire extended to all the provinces. The distinction between a nymph and a goddess is often indistinct. The Celtic deity COVENTINA, for example, was sometimes portrayed as a nymph, as were other goddesses associated with water. There was a temple dedicated to the Nymphs in the CAMPUS MARTIUS in Rome, and several *nymphaea* (shrines dedicated to the nymphs, see *NYMPHAEUM*) were located in various parts of the city. The nymphs were worshipped during the festival of the VOLCANALIA on August 23. They were often worshipped in conjunction with SILVANUS.

Reading: Bourgeois 1991, 26–27; Hammond and Scullard (eds.) 1970, 743–744.

Nyx A Greek goddess who was the personification of night. She was usually regarded as more of a mythological figure than a cult deity, but a dedication to her is known from the temple of the Greek goddess DEMETER at Pergamum, Turkey.
Reading: Hammond and Scullard (eds.) 1970, 744.

O

oath Both solemn oaths and what might today be regarded as profane oaths were used by the Romans to give extra force to their statements. The names of various gods were often used, in the same way that the Christian God was subsequently used. Oaths used in everyday speech are known to have included *medius fidius* or *me dius fidius* ("I call heaven to witness"), which had to be said in the open air (possibly so that the person was not hidden from the god of the sky). Another oath used by men was *me hercule* ("By Hercules"). Women also swore "by Castor" (*mecastor*), and men "by Pollux" (*edepol*).
Reading: Scullard 1981, 147.

Obarator A Roman god who presided over the plowing of fields. He was said by Fabius Pictor in the late third century B.C. to have been invoked by a priest of CERES.
Reading: Ferguson 1988a, 853; York 1986, 60.

Obsequens Julius Obsequens, probably fourth century, an important source of information for prodigies. He compiled tables of prodigies *(Liber Prodigiorum)* which had occurred in the period from 249 B.C. to 12 B.C. The tables for 190 B.C. to 12 B.C. are extant. His work possibly represents a late Roman justification for pagan rites in an increasingly Christian age.
Reading: Hammond and Scullard (eds.) 1970, 744; MacBain 1982, 7–24.

Ocaera An Iberian deity who is known from an inscription on an altar found at San Joao do Campo, northeast of Braga, northern Portugal.
Reading: Tranoy 1981, 277.

Occator A Roman god of harrowing the fields, said by Fabius Pictor in the late third century B.C. to have been invoked by a priest of CERES.
Reading: Ferguson 1988a, 853; York 1986, 60.

Occupo A Roman god of opportunism.

Oceanus (Fig. 74) The Greek god of the ocean (which was regarded as "the great river which surrounded the earth") who was also worshipped by the Romans. His sister and consort was TETHYS, a

Fig. 74 A marble disc 5 ft. (1.52 m) in diameter which originally formed the mouth of a drain at Rome, and on which Oceanus is depicted in relief. It was built into the wall of a medieval church and is now known as Bocca della Verità—Mouth of Truth.

Greek sea goddess who was also worshipped by the Romans.
Reading: Hammond and Scullard (eds.) 1970, 744–745.

Ocelos A Celtic god also known as Ocelus. He is recorded on three inscriptions found in Britain, two of which are from Caerwent, Wales: in one, he was identified with the Celtic god VELLAUNUS in a dedication to "the god Mars Lenus or Ocelos Vellaunus." There is a third dedication to this god from Carlisle, England, where he is invoked as MARS OCELOS.
Reading: Green, M. J. 1992a, 164; Ross 1974, 471–472.

octastyle A temple with eight columns on the main facade.

October horse, sacrifice of *(equus October)* On October 15 (Ides) a chariot race took place in the CAMPUS MARTIUS in Rome, and the right-hand horse of the victorious team was sacrificed by the *FLAMEN MARTIALIS* to MARS at the altar of Mars to ensure good crops. The head was cut off and adorned with a string of loaves. The Sacravienses and the Suburanenses (inhabitants of the Sacra Via and the Subura district) fought for possession of the head of the horse after the sacrifice. If the Sacravienses won, it was nailed to a wall of the Regia. The Suburans (if they won) fastened it to the Mamilian Tower. The blood of the horse was caught and kept until April 21, when VESTAL VIRGINS mixed it with the blood of unborn calves sacrificed six days earlier at the FORDICIDIA.
Reading: Frazer 1913, part V vol. II, 42–44; Richardson 1992, 340; York 1986, 178–179.

Ogmios A Celtic god mentioned by the Greek author Lucian, who traveled in Gaul in the second century. He encountered the cult of Ogmios in Gallia Narbonensis. Ogmios was apparently portrayed as an old bald man, burnt by the sun. He was shown linked to a band of men by a thin gold chain running from his tongue to their ears, apparently to symbolize the fact that he was regarded as the god of eloquent speech. Despite his physical appearance, Ogmios was equated with HERCULES, and Lucian was informed that this was because the Celts associated eloquence with Hercules

Fig. 75 The image of Ops is known only on coins of Antoninus Pius and Pertinax. On this coin of Pertinax, she is shown sitting on a throne and holding ears of wheat. The legend reads OPI DIVIN TR P COS II SC ("To Divine Ops, with tribunician power, in his [Pertinax's] second consulship, by decree of the senate").

because of his strength. Ogmios is also known from two curse tablets from Bregenz, Austria.
Reading: Green, M. J. 1992a, 165.

Olloudius A Celtic god who was worshipped in Britain and Gaul. He was a god of fertility, abundance, healing and peaceful protection and was sometimes equated with the warlike MARS. (See also MARS OLLOUDIUS.)
Reading: Green, M. J. 1992a, 166.

Olympians The major Roman gods were often thought of in groups, the best known being the Olympians. The Olympian gods were JUPITER, JUNO, MARS, VENUS, APOLLO, DIANA, CERES, BACCHUS, MERCURY, NEPTUNE, MINERVA and VULCAN. They paralleled the Greek Olympian gods.

omphalos At Delphi in Greece there was a half-egg-shaped stone regarded as the tomb or egg of the Pytho (in Greek myth, a monster or dragon who was an enemy of APOLLO) and as the navel of the world. Later confusion within the myths appears to make the Pytho an ally or servant (not enemy)

of Apollo, and probably accounts for the name of Apollo's priestess (the Pythia) at the Delphic ORACLE. The omphalos was often copied as a cult object, particularly in stone, and was used for boundary stones and markers.
Reading: Hammond and Scullard (eds.) 1970, 752; Kerény 1951, 135–37.

Opalia The second major festival of OPS, held on December 19, and associated in some way with SATURN.
Reading: Hammond and Scullard (eds.) 1970, 753.

Opiconsivia A festival of OPS, held on August 25. It may also have had some connection with the god CONSUS.
Reading: Hammond and Scullard (eds.) 1970, 753.

Ops (Fig. 75) A Roman goddess of abundance who had the titles CONSIVA ("sower" or "planter") and *Opifera* ("bringer of help"). She was usually associated with the Roman god SATURN. Because Saturn was identified with the Greek god CRONUS, Ops was identified with Cronus's consort, the Greek goddess RHEA. The goddess JUNO was associated with Ops as JUNO OPIGENA. In Rome, there was a small shrine dedicated to Ops Consiva in the Regia, and later a temple on the CAPITOLINE HILL (Fig. 15). She was thought to have originally been a Sabine goddess. Ops had festivals on August 25 (OPICONSIVIA) and December 19 (OPALIA) and was worshipped during the VOLCANALIA on August 23.
Reading: Grimal 1986, 328; Hammond and Scullard (eds.) 1970, 753; Richardson 1992, 277.

oracle (Fig. 76) A form of DIVINATION whereby a deity responds to a question asked by a worshipper. The word *oracle* is used for the place or oracular shrine where prophecies were given, for the agency of the deity giving responses (such as the SIBYLLINE BOOKS) and also for the prophecies. The prophecies were usually given from the deity by a priest or priestess, as obscure or ambiguous responses. In the Greek world, the most famous oracle was the

Fig. 76 The famous oracular shrine of Apollo at Delphi in Greece was located below the theater.

oracular shrine of APOLLO at Delphi, where a priestess (the Pythia) prophesied in a similar manner to the Sibyls (see OMPHALOS for the origin of the Pythia's name). This Delphic oracle continued to be consulted during the Roman period; the first recorded consultation by the Romans was in 216 B.C., but it declined in the first century B.C. Despite a brief revival during Hadrian's reign, it was virtually abandoned by the mid-fourth century.

Several other gods were regarded as providing prophecies, as well as Apollo, including FAUNUS and CARMENTIS. INCUBATION was practiced at the temple of Faunus at Tivoli, Italy, where a sheep was killed and the person consulting the oracle slept in its skin. There were no oracular shrines in Italy to compare with those of Greece, and during the republic the Sibylline books appear to have been the only oracle consulted by the state. At Praeneste in Italy, oracles were given at the temple of Fortuna Primigenia and this became a famous oracle. The prophecies or responses were inscribed on oak tablets called *sortes* ("lots") which were shuffled by a boy who chose one at random and gave it to whoever was consulting the oracle.

Under the empire, with increased worship of Greek and Oriental gods, there was increased interest in oracles. Many books of oracles circulated, and during a time of panic, Augustus seized and burned 2,000 books of prophecies in an attempt to calm the situation.

Reading: Ferguson 1988c; Hammond and Scullard (eds.) 1970, 322–323 (for Delphi in the Greek period); Lane Fox 1988, 168–261; Parke 1988.

Orbona A Roman goddess invoked by parents whose child had died or was in danger of dying. The goddess had a sinister character and was associated with the goddesses FEBRIS and FORTUNA MALA. There appears to have been a shrine or altar dedicated to Orbona at the head of the Sacra Via in Rome.

Reading: Richardson 1992, 277–278.

Orcus A Roman god of death and the UNDERWORLD who came to be identified with the Roman god DIS. Orcus is portrayed in paintings in Etruscan tombs as a hairy, bearded giant. A possible temple existed on the Palatine Hill in Rome.

Reading: Grimal 1986, 328; Richardson 1992, 278.

orgia Secret rites or mysteries, particularly of the god BACCHUS.

Oriental religions Religious cults originating from the eastern provinces. They gained a reasonable following in Rome and Italy by the late republic, mainly because they made a direct appeal to the individual. This was in contrast to other cults, which did not demand particular beliefs and codes of behavior from the individual nor promise the individual enlightenment, happiness or life after death. Most Roman cults offered their followers the favor of the gods, whereas the Oriental religions offered much more. Many were considered as MYSTERY RELIGIONS, and many began as purely private cults. There is evidence, espcially in the west, that the Oriental cults were followed initially by freedmen (ex-slaves), but many cults became wealthy and were absorbed into municipal religious life. Oriental cults that were absorbed include those of ATTIS, MAGNA MATER (Cybele), ISIS, SERAPIS and MITHRAS.

As the empire expanded, Oriental cults grew in strength. However, most Romans did not renounce state religion when initiated into such cults, seeing no conflict between them. The situation was different for only two of the Oriental religions—CHRISTIANITY and JUDAISM, which were never absorbed into pagan Roman religion, although Christianity was later forced into a dominant position by successive emperors. It was the insistence by Christians and Jews that converts must renounce all other religions that was mainly responsible for conflict with the state in the later Roman period. Jews and Christians would not sacrifice to the cult of the emperor and were therefore accused of disloyalty.

Reading: Garcia Y Bellido 1967 (cults in Spain); Tacheva-Hitova 1983 (cults in Moesia Inferior and Thrace).

Orosius Paulus Orosius, c. 380–c. 420, a Christian historian. He was probably from Bracara Augusta in Spain. He took refuge in 414 with St. AUGUSTINE in North Africa following the barbarian Vandal invasion of his homeland. In 417 he composed *Historiae adversum Paganos (History Against the Pagans)*, which was a history of the world to his own day in seven books from a Christian viewpoint. It became a standard history of the ancient world in the Middle Ages.

Reading: Hammond and Scullard (eds.) 1970, 758.

Orpheus A mythical Greek poet and hero from Thrace who was the founder of ORPHISM, a mystery religion connected with the mysteries of the Greek god DIONYSUS. According to legend, Orpheus was a pre-Homeric Greek poet and marvellous lyre player. He descended into the UNDERWORLD to recover his wife Eurydice. On leaving the underworld, with her following, he disobeyed the condition imposed by PERSEPHONE (Greek goddess of the underworld) that he should not look back, and so Eurydice was lost forever. A different myth relates how he was torn to pieces, either by the women of Thrace or by MAENADS (female worshippers of Dionysus). His mythology is complex and varied, but the common theme in all the myths is his return after death. Orpheus became a popular subject for artists and was often portrayed charming animals with music.
Reading: Hammond and Scullard (eds.) 1970, 758.

Orphism A Greek mystery religion associated with ORPHEUS. From about the sixth century B.C. or possibly earlier, there are indications of a mystery cult associated with Orpheus, but it is doubtful whether there was ever a unified cult that could be called Orphism. It was the first Greek religion to have a founder, and it spread to southern Italy. The Derveni papyrus, an ancient book of the late fourth century B.C. found in Greece, gives a commentary on an Orphic religious poem. It indicates that good and evil in human nature were explained by the myth of DIONYSUS ZAGREUS (which involved death and resurrection, and punishment of the wicked). Men were regarded as bearing the guilt of the death of Dionysus Zagreus and had to pay a penalty to PERSEPHONE after death before rising to a higher existence. This Greek myth had as its central doctrine the punishment of individuals after death in the UNDERWORLD. The Orphic cult also recognized reincarnation after death. After three virtuous lives as defined by Orphic doctrine, individuals were supposed to reside in the Isles of the Blessed forever. The body was regarded as evil and the soul as the divine part of the person. Abstinence from killing animals and from eating meat was a feature of Orphism. The high ethical tone and ascetic practices of some adherents of Orpheus in Greece became debased and ridiculed. The cult appears to have waned, but there was a revival of belief during the empire.

Part of Orphism appears to have been a belief in life after death, and the portrayal of Orpheus taming animals with music in some Roman mosaics from Britain has been interpreted as symbolizing a hope of salvation. There are several versions and variations of the legend, which was often used as a theme by poets and Roman mosaicists.
Reading: Black 1986, 150–157 (hope of salvation symbolized in Romano-British mosaics); Hammond and Scullard (eds.) 1970, 759–760.

Osiris In pre-Roman Egyptian religion, Osiris represented the dead Pharaoh, who was brought to a new life and reigned in the UNDERWORLD. He was a god of the underworld and was also associated with fertility. Herodotus identified Osiris with the Greek god DIONYSUS. The Egyptians believed that men and sacred animals became "Osirified" (identified with Osiris) in a new life; SERAPIS was a conflation of Osiris and the sacred bull APIS, and this deity became more common in Hellenistic and Roman times. From Hellenistic times, Osiris was worshipped alongside other Egyptian deities such as Serapis, ISIS, ANUBIS and HARPOCRATES. Elaborate mysteries seem to have been constructed around these deities, with Isis being the central figure: Osiris was thought to have been killed and dismembered by the evil god Seth but was restored to life by Isis. However, in Roman Egypt, Osiris remained primarily a god of the underworld.
Reading: Hammond and Scullard (eds.) 1970, 760.

Osirisantinous The patron god of the new city of Antinoopolis in Egypt which was founded by Hadrian to commemorate ANTINOUS. Osirisantinous was Antinous equated with OSIRIS.

Ovid Publius Ovidius Naso, 43 B.C.–A.D. 17. A Roman poet who wrote the *Fasti*, a poetical calendar of the Roman year, a commentary on the CALENDAR of religious festivals. Only the first six books (January–June) survive. It is an important source of information for Roman religion. It was probably based on an earlier prose commentary by Verrius Flaccus. Ovid is better known for his love poems.
Reading: Frazer 1929; Hammond and Scullard (eds.) 1970, 764.

P

Paganalia A festival of the *pagi* or village communities, possibly a *FERIAE CONCEPTIVAE*. OVID equated this festival with the SEMENTIVAE.
Reading: Hammond and Scullard (eds.) 1970, 767; Warde Fowler 1899, 294–296.

paganism Until Christianity, the concept of paganism did not exist because local traditions of worship were maintained. *Paganus* ("a villager") seems to have become a slang word by the late empire for someone who was not a follower of CHRISTIANITY or for a non-Jew, but who instead had many gods, worshipped statues, and undertook sacrifices.
Reading: Dowden 1992, 46; Hammond and Scullard (eds.) 1970, 767 (under *paganus*).

Palatua The Roman goddess who was the guardian of the Palatine Hill at Rome. This was one of the minor deities who had her own *FLAMEN* (the *flamen Palatualis*).
Reading: York 1986, 70.

Pales A Roman deity of shepherds and sheep. An obscure deity, he was regarded as male by some authorities and female by others. There was also doubt as to whether Pales was singular or plural, and thus whether there was one deity or two. There were festivals of Pales on April 21 (the PARILIA) and on July 7. The second appears to have been a festival of "the two Pales" *(Palibus duobus)*. Pales had a temple at Rome; this is generally thought to have been located on the Palatine Hill, but it may have been situated elsewhere in the city.
Reading: Richardson 1992, 282; Scullard 1981, 104–105.

Pales, temple of A temple was built by Marcus Atilius Regulus after his victory over the Salentini in 267 B.C. Its location is unknown; it was possibly on the Palatine Hill, but being a victory monument, it is more likely to have been on the route of the triumphal procession (CAMPUS MARTIUS or on the Aventine Hill).
Reading: Richardson 1992, 282.

Palici Indigenous deities of Sicily regarded as twin brothers. They were apparently gods of the UNDERWORLD, and their cult centered on three small lakes in the Palagonia plain of Sicily that emitted sulphurous vapours. According to one legend, the Palici were the sons of the Greek god ZEUS, but another makes them the sons of ADRANOS, who was another indigenous god of Sicily.
Reading: Hammond and Scullard (eds.) 1970, 771; Wilson 1990, 278.

Palladium An image of the Greek goddess Pallas Athena (who was identified with MINERVA). According to legend, the image had been sent from heaven by ZEUS to Dardanus, the founder of Troy. The Romans believed that it was a powerful talisman which protected Rome and had been rescued by Aeneas from the fires at Troy and brought to Rome by him. It was kept in the temple of VESTA and was looked after by the VESTAL VIRGINS.
Reading: Hammond and Scullard (eds.) 1970, 771–772.

Pan A Greek god of nature who was equated with the Roman god FAUNUS and also with SILVANUS. Although Faunus and Silvanus do not have the characteristics of a goat, Pan was usually portrayed as half-human and half-goat, with goats' legs, ears

and horns like a SATYR. He was sometimes referred to or depicted in the plural *(Pans)* in much the same way as *Fauns* derived from *Faunus*, and Pan was sometimes even regarded as female. SILENUS was at times equated with Pan. Pan was often depicted in Roman art, including scenes of Bacchic rites.
Reading: Borgeaud 1988; Hammond and Scullard (eds.) 1970, 773; Johns 1982, 42–48.

Panda (or Panda Cela) A Roman goddess who is mentioned by some ancient authors. Little else is known about her.
Reading: York 1986, 164.

Pantheon (Figs. 77a, b) A temple in Rome originally built by Marcus Vipsanius Agrippa, possibly begun in 27 B.C. and completed by 25 B.C. It was built on part of the site of the *naumachia* lake which had been earmarked by Julius Caesar for a huge temple to MARS but never built. It probably had a wooden roof, and was struck by lightning in 22 B.C. and destroyed by the great fire of Titus in A.D. 80. It was rebuilt by Domitian, again probably with a wooden roof. It was struck by lightning and destroyed by fire under Trajan in 110. Although the present-day building has an inscription saying that Agrippa's building was restored, it was actually completely rebuilt by Hadrian (from the evidence of stamps on the building bricks which date to after 126), probably on an entirely new plan. This building was possibly restored under Antoninus Pius, and also in 202 by Septimius Severus. In 609 it was dedicated as a Christian church to St. Mary and All the Martyrs, having apparently been imperial property until then.

Agrippa's building seems to have been rectangular, and is known from Pliny and Cassius Dio to have been called the Pantheon or Pantheum. It was in a large area of the CAMPUS MARTIUS developed by Agrippa. There was no architectural similarity between Hadrian's and Agrippa's buildings. Hadrian's building was a rotunda with a temple-like col-

Fig. 77a The Pantheon in Rome as rebuilt by Hadrian. On the left, part of the rotunda is visible, with the colonnaded pronaos at the front.

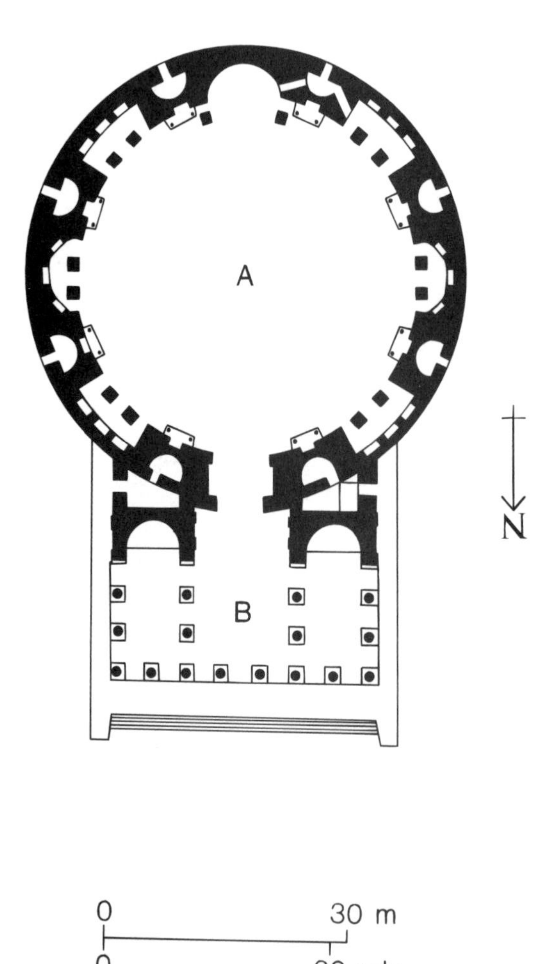

Fig. 77b Plan of the Pantheon as built by Hadrian. A *is the rotunda and* B *indicates the colonnaded pronaos.*

onnaded pronaos in the Corinthian style with a triangular pediment. It resembled a classical temple, with the pediment being very high to hide the dome behind it. The rotunda was 46 yds. (43.2 m; 144 Roman feet) in diameter, far larger than any other ancient domed structure, and was lit by a circular opening *(oculus)* 29.5 ft. (9 m) in diameter at the top of the dome. The dome was of brick-faced concrete 20.34 ft. (6.2 m) thick. The interior was richly decorated in marble, with seven niches for statues. It had a coffered ceiling and huge bronze doors which still survive. It faced north.

Agrippa's building seems originally to have been intended to be named after Augustus (as the Augusteum), which Augustus refused. Statues of many gods may well have been present in the building, but it may not have been a temple or even dedicated to the Pantheon of the Gods—it may have been simply named the Pantheon because of the presence of so many statues of gods. In Rome and Italy there does not seem to have been a cult of all the gods, although this cult is found in the Greek world. Instead, it may have been intended to commemorate the imperial family. Hadrian's building had a temple-like facade, but its interior is quite unlike traditional Roman temples, which tended to be rectangular or stand within a rectangular *templum* (unlike the Pantheon). Again it possibly served no religious function, but was rather an imperial audience chamber used for judicial business and to commemorate Hadrian's family.
Reading: Godfrey and Hemsoll 1986; Richardson 1992, 283–286.

Parcae (sing. Parca) A triad of Roman deities or Fates who were originally assimilated from Greek myths and who represented rather abstract powers of destiny. In Latin, *fate* is *fatum* ("what has been said"), and the Parcae were also sometimes referred to as Fatae (or Fata, if a male was present among the Parcae). The three Parcae were called NONA, DECIMA and MORTA, meaning respectively "nine-month birth" (which was actually the eighth month by the Roman method of calculation), "ten-month birth" (normal by the Roman method of calculation), and "still-birth" (from *mors*, death). The Parcae may originally have been birth-goddesses who became equated with the attributes of the Greek Fates, who were called Clotho, Lachesis and Atropos.

The triplism of the Roman Fates sometimes appears to have encouraged their fusion with the triads of Celtic mother goddesses, who are sometimes portrayed with spindle, distaff and scroll, which were symbols usually associated with the Fates. In an inscription found at Carlisle, England, a triad of mother goddesses is actually called *Parcae.*
Reading: Green, M. J. 1992a, 95 (on the Celtic associations of these deities); Hammond and Scullard (eds.) 1970, 432.

Parentalia (or *dies parentales*) The festival of the dead *(DI MANES)* at Rome, held February 13–21. The last day was for public ceremony, but the

preceding days were for private commemoration of the dead, particularly parents and other ancestors (*DI PARENTES*). During this festival, temples were closed, marriages forbidden, and magistrates did not wear their insignia of office (including *toga praetexta*). Offerings were made to the dead, often by groups of mourners going outside towns and cities to visit their family tombs and have a feast. The Parentalia culminated in the FERALIA on February 21, and on February 22 the CARISTIA was held.
Reading: Hopkins 1983, 233–234; Scullard 1981, 74–75.

Parilia (or Palilia) The festival of PALES on April 21. This seems to have been an ancient agricultural festival for the purification of sheep and shepherds. It fell on what was regarded as the anniversary of Rome's foundation day and so was prominent in the CALENDAR. Sheep pens were cleaned and decorated with greenery, and the sheep were purified in smoke from a bonfire on which sulphur was burnt. Milk and cakes were offered to Pales, and shepherds apparently washed themselves in dew, drank milk and leaped through the bonfire. At the celebration of this festival in Rome, ashes from calves burnt at the FORDICIDIA were sprinkled on the bonfire, although other celebrations at Rome are uncertain. The blood from the October horse sacrifice and that from the calves burnt at the Fordicidia was distributed to shepherds for fumigating their flocks. In 121 Hadrian substituted a new festival of NATALIS URBIS for the old Parilia.
Reading: Richardson 1992, 282–283; Scullard 1981, 104–105.

Partula A Roman goddess who presided over childbirth.
Reading: Ferguson 1988a, 853.

Patelana A Roman goddess who presided over the husks of cereal crops when they are open to allow the ears to emerge.

patera (pl. *paterae*) A broad shallow dish or bowl of a type often used as a sacred libation vessel. It was frequently used as a decorative religious motif and was used especially by the pontiffs in Rome. *Paterae* could be highly decorated and some had a central boss so they could be held in one hand (umbilical *paterae*), and some had a handle. They were made mainly of bronze, silver and pewter. (See also RITUAL VESSELS.)
Reading: Henig 1984, 131–132.

Paulinus of Nola Meropius Pontius Anicius Paulinus, an early Christian poet and letter writer. He was born at Bordeaux, France, in 353 of a wealthy Christian family. He held public office, and then became a priest and, c. 409, bishop of Nola, where he remained until his death in 431. Thirty-three poems on Christian themes have survived. Fifty-one letters written from 393 have also survived and include correspondence with AUGUSTINE and JEROME.
Reading: Hammond and Scullard (eds.) 1970, 791.

Pax (Fig. 78) A Roman goddess who was the personification of political peace. She was identified with the Greek goddess IRENE but was rarely known before the time of Augustus. She is represented on coins as a young woman with a cornucopia in her left hand and an olive branch or staff of MERCURY in her right hand. As well as other shrines, an altar was dedicated in Rome to Pax by the emperor

Fig. 78 The goddess Pax depicted on a silver tetradrachm of 28 B.C. The coin was struck in Asia Minor (probably Ephesus) and celebrates the sole rule of Octavian (later the emperor Augustus). The reverse (shown here) depicts Pax holding a caduceus *and standing on a sword, with a snake rising from a mystical box in the background. The whole is surrounded by a laurel wreath.*

Augustus (ARA PACIS, Fig. 8) to sanctify the reestablishment of peace after the civil war. Later, the temple of Pax was built by Vespasian at Rome.
Reading: Grimal 1986, 349; Hammond and Scullard (eds.) 1970, 793; Richardson 1992, 286–289.

Pax, temple of (Fig. 79) (temple of Peace) A temple built in Rome by Vespasian to commemorate his victory in the civil war and his conquest of Judaea. It was begun in the summer of 71 and was dedicated in 75. It was built by converting the site of the former meat market *(macellum)*. The *TEMPLUM* or precinct was a rectangular colonnaded enclosure about 120.29 yds. × 158.57 yds. (110 m × 145 m) laid out as a formal garden and surrounded by porticoes. It was known as the Templum Pacis, Forum Pacis (Forum of Peace) or Forum Vespasiani. In the center of the portico on the southeast side was the *aedes* or temple flanked by other buildings (including the library of Peace), with six columns also on its facade and an almost square cella behind. In the temple were displayed spoils of war from Jerusalem and works of famous Greek artists, including many of the treasures from Nero's Domus Aurea. The forum was restored by Septimius Severus after the fire of Commodus in 191. It was regarded as one of the most beautiful buildings of Rome.
Reading: Barton 1989, 88–89; Nash 1962a, 439; Richardson 1992, 287.

Pax Augusta ("the peace of Augustus") A version of the Roman goddess of peace, promoted by the emperor Augustus to signify the maintenance of peace at home and abroad. (See also PAX.)
Reading: Hammond and Scullard (eds.) 1970, 793.

pax deorum The concept of "peace with the gods" *(pax deorum)* was maintained by the correct observance of public and private rituals at particular times of the year. Prodigies occurred if the *pax deorum* was broken, which then required expiation. (See PRODIGY.)
Reading: Ogilvie 1969, 23.

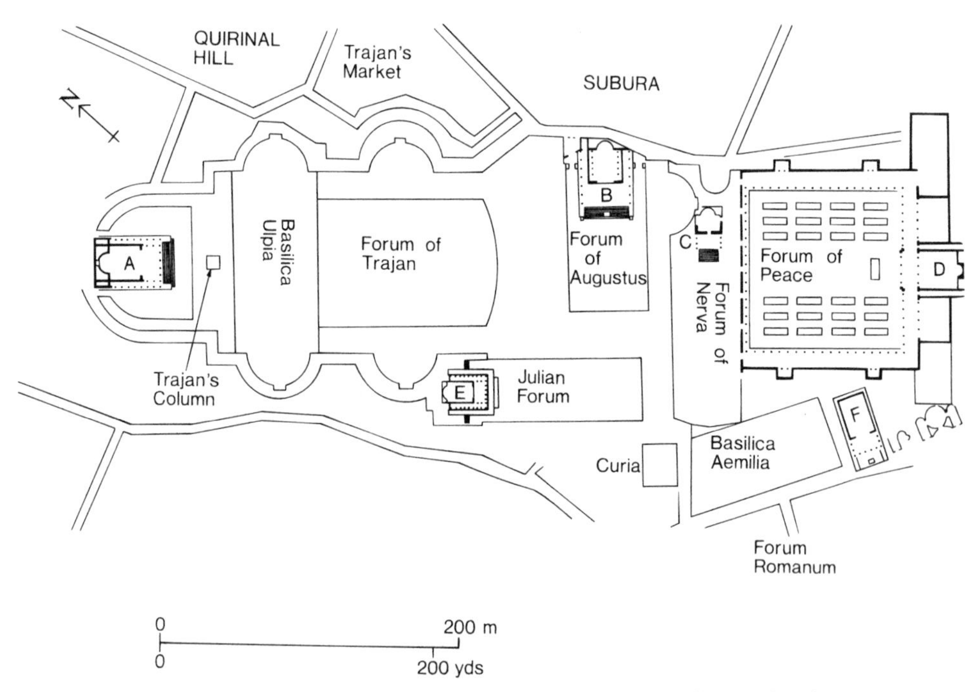

Fig. 79 The temple of Pax (peace) was situated at one end of the Forum of Peace. To the west were several other fora. The major religious sites in this area are: A = temple of Vespasian; B = temple of Mars Ultor; C = temple of Minerva; D = temple of Pax; E = temple of Venus Genetrix; F = temple of Antoninus Pius and Faustina.

Penates (Di Penates or Dei Penates, "gods of the storecupboard") Roman deities regarded as protectors of the household, along with the *lares* (see LAR). They were the spirits of the pantry or larder *(penus)*, and images of these deities were placed in the *atrium* of houses. They were worshipped in close association with the Roman goddess VESTA and with the *lares*. A portion of every family meal was set aside and thrown on the flames of the hearth fire for the Penates and *lares*, and there was always a salt cellar and a small offering of first fruits for them on the table. On the KALENDS, NONES and IDES of every month, they were especially honored with offerings, and the household hearth was decorated with garlands. Any notable event of family life also usually involved a prayer to the Penates and *lares*. There was a festival of the Penates on October 14. The state counterparts of the family Penates were the PENATES PUBLICI.

Reading: Dubourdieu 1989; Hammond and Scullard (eds.) 1970, 797–798.

Penates, temple of A temple situated on the Velia in Rome, although its precise position is uncertain; it probably lay under the platform of Hadrian's temple of VENUS and ROMA. Its date of construction is unknown, but the temple was struck by lightning in 167 B.C., and Augustus is known to have restored it. October 14 was either its dedication or restoration date. It was apparently destroyed in the fire of Nero in 64.

Reading: Richardson 1992, 39, 289; Scullard 1981, 193.

Penates Publici Roman state counterparts of the family PENATES (Di Penates). Their cult was attached to the temple of VESTA at Rome, and there was also a temple to the Penates Publici on the Velia.

Reading: Hammond and Scullard (eds.) 1970, 797–798 (under *Penates*); Richardson 1992, 289 (under *Penates Dei*).

Pergamum, Asclepieium of (Figs. 10, 80) A healing center of AESCULAPIUS at Pergamum, Turkey. It was in a valley outside the city, and was founded in the fourth century B.C. and continued through the Roman period. It was most popular in

Fig. 80 Asclepieium at Pergamum, Turkey, looking northeast across the courtyard, with the theater on the left and the source of the sacred spring in the center.

the second century. The complex included a sacred theater and various temples. The main temple was dedicated to Zeus-Aesculapius and was modeled on the PANTHEON at Rome: Aesculapius was sometimes equated with the Greek god ZEUS. The ASCLEPIEIUM was destroyed in an earthquake sometime between 253 and 260 and was never rebuilt. In the Roman period, the healing sanctuary at Pergamum was ranked the most important, and much information about it is known from the writings of ARISTIDES.
Reading: Jackson 1988, 153–157.

peripteral A temple that was peripteral had columns on all four sides. One that was *peripteral sine postico* had columns down the two long sides and the main facade but the back wall was solid. This was particularly common in Roman temples.

persecution Suppression and punishment (often by execution) of people for their religious beliefs. The Romans were generally very tolerant towards other religions, unless these were considered subversive. In 186 B.C. the Senate banned the BACCHANALIA, and in the provinces DRUIDISM was suppressed under the emperors Tiberius and Claudius. In the first century Rome came into increasing conflict with the Jews; the first of the JEWISH REVOLTS was suppressed by Vespasian and Titus in 70. The Romans also regarded CHRISTIANITY as a troublesome Jewish sect, and Nero had already begun the first persecutions following the fire of Rome in 64. Intermittent persecutions of Christians took place in the next two centuries, and under Septimius Severus there were martyrs in Alexandria, Corinth, Rome and Carthage. More serious persecutions were begun by Decius in 250. The persecutions were officially ended by the Edict of Milan in 313.
Reading: Hammond and Scullard (eds.) 1970, 231–234; Lane Fox 1988, 419–492; Sordi 1983.

Persephone A Greek goddess who was the daughter of ZEUS and DEMETER. She was also known as KORE. She was identified with the Roman goddesses LIBERA and PROSERPINA, but is also invoked in Latin inscriptions under her own name.
Reading: Hammond and Scullard (eds.) 1970, 812 (under *Phersephone*).

personification A virtue or abstract quality represented as a deity. A number of deities were personifications of Roman virtues, either related to the state or to the emperor. Rather than worship the emperor in his own lifetime, it was commonplace to worship his deified virtues. Many of these personifications were regarded as deities and had a recognizable cult. The personified virtues included Abundantia (Abundance), Aequitas (Equity), Aeternitas (Eternity), Annona (Produce), Beatitudo (Beatitude), Bonus Eventus (Successful Outcome), Caritas (Affection), Claritas (Clarity), Clementia (Clemency), Concordia (Concord), Disciplina (Discipline), Fecunditas (Fecundity), Felicitas (Good Fortune), Fides (Honesty), Fortuna (Fortune), Genius (Spirit), Hilaritas (Gaiety), Honos (Honor), Humanitas (Humanity), Indulgentia (Indulgence), Iustitia (Justice), Iuventus (Youth), Laetitia (Joy), Liberalitas (Generosity), Libertas (Freedom), Moneta (Mint), Munificentia (Munificence), Nobilitas (Nobility), Ops (Abundance), Patientia (Patience), Pax (Peace), Perpetuitas (Continuity), Pietas (Dutiful Respect), Providentia (Providence), Pudicitia (Chastity), Quies-Requies (Peace), Religio (Reverence), Salus (Well-Being), Securitas (Security), Spes (Hope), Tranquillitas (Tranquillity), Tutela (Protection), Ubertas (Abundance), Utilitas (Usefulness), Victoria (Victory) and Virtus (Virtue).
Reading: Henig 1984, 76–79; Vermeule 1987.

phallus (Fig. 81) (pl. *phalli*) Fertility was a major preoccupation of Roman life, and the *phallus* (the male organ) was regarded as a good luck symbol and capable of overcoming and averting evil influences. The *phallus* is portrayed in numerous contexts, such as on pottery vessels, buildings and bridges, and as charms and in mosaics. Scenes which today could be regarded as obscene were probably rarely judged as such by the Romans. Some *phalli* apparently bear an eye or pair of eyes, presumably to help combat the Evil Eye. *Phalli* were sometimes combined with the *MANO FICO* sign (Fig. 60). Some gods, such as MERCURY and PRIAPUS, were at times attributed with an oversized *phallus*. Many *phalli* were shown as having an independent nature, with legs, wings and tails. (See also *FASCINUM*.)
Reading: Johns 1982, 61–75.

Philo Philo Judaeus ("Philo the Jew") A prominent member of Alexandria's Jewish community. He was born at Alexandria c. 30 B.C. and lived to c. A.D. 45. He traveled to Rome in 39–40 to persuade the emperor Caligula (Gaius) to exempt the Jews

Fig. 81 A phallus *depicted on the wall of a house situated just inside the Herculaneum Gate at Pompeii. It gave protection and good luck to the home.*

from worshipping the emperor. He was a writer whose extant works (in Greek) include *Legatio ad Gaium* (Embassy to Gaius).

philosophy In the ancient (Greek and Roman) world, philosophy was defined in its widest sense as the pursuit of wisdom, of the knowledge of things and their causes, using both theoretical and practical methods. Philosophy encompassed most aspects of the fields nowadays defined separately as philosophy, science and religion. The Romans were initially suspicious of Greek philosophers, banning them from Rome in 173 B.C. and 161 B.C. By the end of the second century B.C., philosophy was beginning to gain favor at Rome, particularly EPICUREANISM and STOICISM, which became the leading schools of philosophy there. In general, the Romans were more interested in the ethical and religious aspects of philosophy than in theory and speculation. Philosophy remained unknown in non-urban provinces and in the countryside, and tended to be followed by the aristocracy; the majority of the population was content to follow and observe the rites of traditional religion.

The importance of the various schools of philosophy in Roman religion stems from the attempts by philosophers to tackle such questions as what constituted morality, whether gods existed, whether there was life after death (and if so, the form of this AFTERLIFE), and what was the purpose of life. These questions, or parts of them, had previously been the province of various religious cults, often with simplistic and shallow answers. It was the desire for more satisfactory answers to these questions that led to the popularity of the various MYSTERY RELIGIONS, including CHRISTIANITY, and also to an increasing interest in philosophy. (See also NEOPLATONISM; PLATO.)
Reading: Ferguson 1970, 190–210; Meredith 1988.

Phoebus ("bright") A name given to the Greek god APOLLO. As Phoebus Apollo, this deity was regarded as a sun god.

piaculum An offering, typically of a pig, to restore good relations with a god, similar to expiation or atonement.

Picius An Iberian deity who is known from an inscription found at San Pedro de Lourosa, Portugal. It is possible that Picius may be the same deity as Banda Picius (see BANDA).
Reading: Alarcão 1988, 93.

Picumnus A Roman god, the brother of the Roman god PILUMNUS. Both may have originally been ancient agricultural gods. They appear to have been regarded by some as beneficent gods of matrimony and childbirth.
Reading: Grimal 1986, 374; Hammond and Scullard (eds.) 1970, 833.

Picus A Roman god of agriculture who possessed prophetic powers. He usually took the form of Mars' sacred bird, the woodpecker (MARS originally being a god of agriculture). According to legend he was either a son of SATURN or an early king of Latium who was changed into a woodpecker by Circe (a Greek goddess powerful in magic). The Latin word for "woodpecker" was *picus*. (See also CANENS.)
Reading: York 1986, 76, 80.

pietas A sense of duty concerned with moral issues and the maintenance of good relations with family, friends, ancestors, institutions and fellow citizens, as well as with the gods. This is a much wider meaning than in the modern derivative word "piety." The concept of *pietas*, like other abstract concepts, was personalized and deified (see PIETAS). The concept of *CULTUS* was far more important in Roman religion than *pietas*.
Reading: Hammond and Scullard (eds.) 1970, 833.

Pietas A Roman goddess who was the personification of an attitude of respectful duty to the gods, the state, parents and family. She was often portrayed in human form, sometimes accompanied by a stork symbolizing filial duty. During the empire, Pietas was often portrayed on coins to symbolize the moral virtues of the reigning emperor. At Rome, Pietas had a temple in the CIRCUS FLAMINIUS within the CAMPUS MARTIUS and later another in the FORUM HOLITORIUM (Fig. 15). There was a festival of Pietas on December 1.
Reading: Grimal 1986, 373–374; Hammond and Scullard (eds.) 1970, 833; Richardson 1992, 290; Scullard 1981, 198–199.

Pietas Augusta (Fig. 82) ("Pietas of Augustus") A version of the Roman deity PIETAS promoted by the emperor Augustus.

Fig. 82 A coin depicting Pietas Augusta holding a box and turned toward a lighted altar.

Pii Fratelli ("Pious Brothers") Two deities who were worshipped in the plain of Catania in Sicily. According to legend, the two brothers risked their lives to save their parents from an eruption of Mount Etna, and a path in the flames opened up to let them pass unharmed. These deities were portrayed on coins during the republic, and continued to be venerated until the late empire.
Reading: Wilson 1990, 282.

pilgrim From the late Roman period, Christians were moved to visit holy places, and such visitors to holy sites were called pilgrims. Initially the main places of pilgrimage were in the Holy Land, especially Jerusalem, but the number of holy places increased, until by the end of the medieval period there were places of pilgrimage in most parts of Europe. The usual motive for pilgrimage was to pray in a specific holy place or in the presence of a particular holy object, often for a specific benefit such as healing or forgiveness of sins. Other motives included receiving baptism in a specific place (such as in the Jordan River), and as penance or fulfillment of a vow. There were itineraries giving routes for pilgrims.

Pilumnus One of three Roman deities whose function was the protection of newborn babies against the evil tricks of SILVANUS and other evil spirits (see DEVERRA). Pilumnus may have originally been an ancient Roman agricultural god. He was thought by some to have a brother, PICUMNUS, and together they appear to have been regarded as beneficent gods of matrimony and childbirth.
Reading: Grimal 1986, 374; Hammond and Scullard (eds.) 1970, 833.

Pinarii Priests who along with the Potitii were associated with the cult of HERCULES at the ARA MAXIMA before 312 B.C. They were pre-republican in origin and were from the Pinarius *gens*.
Reading: Jones 1990, 246; Warde Fowler 1899, 193.

pipe burial A grave (INHUMATION and CREMATION) provided with a pipe so that wine or other liquids could be poured into the burial as an offering from the living to the dead. Some graves also had holes so that food offerings could be made as well. This was to ensure the wellbeing of the soul in the AFTERLIFE.
Reading: Toynbee 1971, 51–52.

Pisintos A Celtic god who was worshipped at Trier, Germany, where he was equated with the Roman god VERTUMNUS.
Reading: Wightman 1970, 218.

Plato A Greek (Athenian) philosopher who lived c. 427 to c. 347 B.C. He became a follower of the philosopher Socrates. Although Socrates appears in many of Plato's writings, Plato developed his own distinctive philosophy that was based on two main ideas: that human beings could be improved and that the intellect was supreme. In the Greek world, the philosophy of Plato remained a powerful influence. However, Roman adherents disregarded many of the metaphysical and mystical aspects of Plato's philosophy, adopting an intellectual skepticism that replaced certainty of truth with probabilities. The ideas of Plato were modified and developed over several centuries, culminating in the philosophy of Plotinus and his pupils. (See NEOPLATONISM.)

Plouton (or Pluton; Latin, Pluto) An epithet meaning "the rich one" which was applied to the Greek god HADES, who was equated with the Roman god DIS.

Pluto The Latin form of Pluton or Plouton, which was an epithet given to the Greek god HADES who was equated with the Roman god DIS.

Poeninus A Celtic god who was linked with JUPITER as JUPITER POENINUS. It is possible that Poeninus is the same deity as POININUS.
Reading: Dorcey 1992, 75; Green, M. J. 1992a, 127.

Poininus A local Celtic or possibly Thracian god who was equated with the Roman god SILVANUS. This deity is known from an inscription found at Turnovo, Bulgaria. It is possible that Poininus is the same deity as the Celtic god POENINUS.
Reading: Dorcey 1992, 75.

Pollux The brother of CASTOR and one of the two DIOSCURI.

pomerium A strip of land immediately outside a town wall. It was the formal and religious boundary of the town, and was not allowed to be inhabited, plowed or used for burials. When cities such as Rome continued to expand, the *pomerium* was reestablished from time to time by the augurs.
Reading: Richardson 1992, 293–296.

Pomona The Roman goddess of fruit *(poma)*, and particularly of fruit grown on trees. She had a sacred wood called the Pomonal which was 12 miles (19.31 km) outside Rome on the road to Ostia. At Rome, she had her own *FLAMEN* (the *flamen Pomonalis*), but he was the lowest ranking of all the *flamines*, and she does not appear to have had a festival. Poets wrote many stories about Pomona; one identifies her as the wife of PICUS, for whom Picus was said to have rejected the love of Circe, while OVID identifies her as the wife of VERTUMNUS. All these stories are thought to be late inventions.
Reading: Grimal 1986, 387; Hammond and Scullard (eds.) 1970, 856.

pompa A ceremonial sacred procession held during a funeral or as part of a festival. A *pompa circensis* preceded circus games; there would be a parade of contestants, dancers, musicians, precious objects from temple treasuries and people carrying incense and perfume. Statues and other symbols of the gods were carried on special wagons called *tensae.* (See also FUNERALS.)
Reading: Hanson 1959, 81–92.

Ponte di Nona A healing sanctuary or shrine on a small ridge along the Via Praenestina, 24.13 miles (15 km) east of Rome. It seems to have been established in the late fourth or early third century B.C. There were mineral springs on the site, and buildings included a temple, *mansio* (overnight stop for travelers) with baths, a cave-like *NYMPHAEUM* and probably a circular pool. Over 8,000 terracotta ex-votos (votive offerings) have been found, many of hands, feet, eyes and heads (the latter possibly for headaches relating to malaria). It is not certain if these offerings were given in supplication (before healing, in an attempt to get the deity to effect a cure) or as thanks to the (unknown) deity (after the healing). (See also ANATOMICAL EX-VOTO.)
Reading: Jackson 1988, 160–161.

pontifex (pl. *pontifices*) A pontiff, or priest, responsible for state religion. The *collegium pontificum* ("college of pontiffs") was the most important college of priests at Rome, headed by the *pontifex* *maximus* ("greatest pontiff"), the highest-ranking priest in Rome. The *pontifices* had overall control of the state religion. In the monarchy, they formed the religious council of the king, assisting him in the duties of the state cult. The name *pontifex* means literally "bridge builder," which implies that their original function may have been the skilled or magic art of bridge building (a disputed notion). During the republic, they were responsible for the organization of the state religion. It is thought that there were originally three pontiffs, but their number gradually increased to nine by 300 B.C., to 15 under Sulla and 16 under Julius Caesar. Originally, all the pontiffs were male patricians, but after 300 B.C. half of them were plebeians. They were originally coopted, but from 104 B.C. some were selected by popular election. They held the post normally for life.

Pontiffs did not mediate directly between people and the gods. They undertook the ritual duties at the CARMENTALIA, FORDICIDIA, *ARGEI* and celebrations of CONSUS. They had wide-ranging administrative duties, and determined the dates of festivals, of *dies fasti* and of *dies nefasti.* They kept a record of the main events that occurred each year. They also undertook administrative jobs such as the supervision of funerary and tomb law, advised the Senate on religious matters and controlled the behavior of individuals—such as what they could and could not do on days of religious festivals. In theory, pontifical law did not extend beyond Italy. Duties of pontiffs were onerous, although the priesthood remained part-time.
Reading: Beard and North 1990; Hammond and Scullard (eds.) 1970, 860; Porte 1989, 122–127, 131–144.

pontifex maximus (Fig. 83) ("greatest pontiff") Head of the pontiffs. He exercised control over the entire state religion, and so was particularly powerful. From the third century B.C. he was chosen by a form of popular election. The post was held by Julius Caesar, and then by Augustus and all other emperors (until Gratian dropped the title some time between 379 and 383). It became part of the imperial office and denoted the emperor as head of state religion, who could influence religious policy. The official headquarters of the *pontifex maximus* at Rome was the REGIA.
Reading: Hammond and Scullard (eds.) 1970, 860.

Fig. 83 A denarius *of Tiberius (emperor 14–37) struck at Lugdunum. It portrays a seated figure of Livia, wife of the emperor Augustus, holding a branch, and the legend reads PONTIF MAXIM* ("pontifex maximus"). *Courtesy of Somerset County Museums Service.*

Poplifugia An ancient festival held in the CAMPUS MARTIUS in Rome on July 5 (and possibly on July 7, the Nonae Caprotinae), and whose meaning seems to have been lost at an early date. It was held before the NONES, which was highly unusual. It may have been linked with the REGIFUGIUM. *Poplifugia* means, literally, "flights" or "routs of the people." The Romans thought that what was meant was either the flight of the people when Romulus disappeared from view during a storm, or else the flight of the Romans when attacked by the people of Fidenae after the Gauls had sacked Rome. The original meaning of the word *Poplifugia* may not have referred to the Roman people, but to ritual routs of Latin armies *(populi).*
Reading: Palmer 1974, 7–15; Scullard 1981, 159.

Populona Also known as Populonia, she was possibly an early Roman goddess in her own right, although the name *Populona* was more usually linked with JUNO as JUNO POPULONA.

Porrima A Roman goddess of childbirth (possibly the same as PRORSA) who was invoked if the unborn baby was presented head first. (See also CARMENTIS.)
Reading: Richardson 1992, 72.

Portunalia The festival of Portunus which was held on August 17. Some ritual connected with keys was probably performed.
Reading: Scullard 1981, 176.

Portunus Originally a Roman god who protected doors. He also became the protector of harbors, as the word for door *(portus)* gradually changed its meaning to harbor. Portunus was identified with Palaemon, who, in Greek legend, was a son of HERACLES. Portunus was usually depicted holding a key, and his festival was the Portunalia. He was served by his own *FLAMEN*, the *flamen Portunalis*, and it is possible that a surviving temple in the FORUM BOARIUM at Rome was dedicated to him (Fig. 84).
Reading: Hammond and Scullard (eds.) 1970, 866; Scullard 1981, 176.

Portunus, temple of (Figs. 84a, b) One of two surviving well-preserved temples in the FORUM BOARIUM in Rome (the so-called temples of FORTUNA VIRILIS and VESTA). This one was once thought to be the temple of Fortuna Virilis (the other now identified as that of HERCULES VICTOR) but is most likely that of PORTUNUS. It dates to the late republic. The temple stands on a high podium and is approached by steps at the front. It has a TETRASTYLE (four-column) porch. The cella occupied the full

Fig. 84a The temple of Portunus in Rome, looking towards the tetrastyle porch.

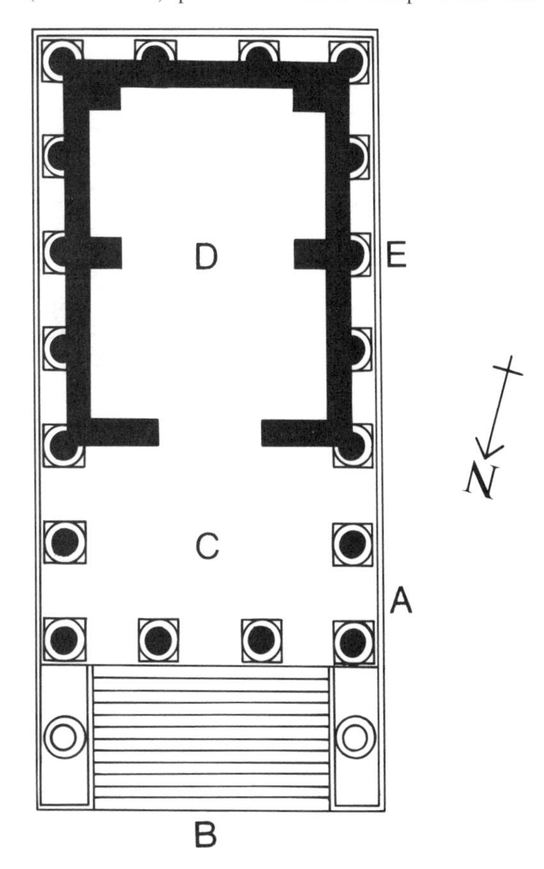

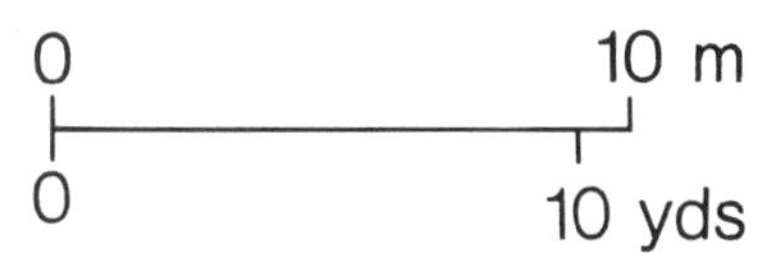

Fig. 84b Plan of the temple of Portunus in Rome. A = podium; B = steps; C = tetrastyle pronaos; D = cella.

width of the podium, and the flanking Ionic columns were built into the side and rear walls of the cella (half-engaged columns). The area around the temple was known as the Portunium and became the center of the flower industry in Rome. It was converted to the church of Santa Maria Egiziaca in 872.
Reading: Barton 1989, 70–73; Richardson 1992, 320; Scullard 1981, 176.

Poseidon Originally the Greek god of earthquakes and water, he came to be regarded as a god of the sea. He was equated with the Roman god NEPTUNE and sometimes with the Roman god CONSUS.
Reading: Hammond and Scullard (eds.) 1970, 866–867.

Postverta Also known as Postvorta, a Roman goddess of childbirth who was invoked in the case of a breech birth. (See also CARMENTIS.)
Reading: Richardson 1992, 72.

Potina Also known as Potica, a Roman goddess who presided over a weaned child's first drink.
Reading: Grimal 1986, 231 (under *Indigetes*).

Potitii Priests (along with the PINARII) in charge of the cult of HERCULES at the ARA MAXIMA before 312 B.C. They were pre-republican in origin and were members of the Potitius *gens.*
Reading: Jones 1990, 246; Warde Fowler 1899, 193.

Praestana A Roman goddess who was probably the same deity as PRAESTITIA. Little else is known about her.

Praestitia A Roman goddess who was apparently associated in some way with excellence. She is probably the same deity as PRAESTANA. Little else is known about her.

prayer Informal and formal prayers were fairly common in Roman religion and were often associated with other rites such as SACRIFICE. They were the only sacred writings of the Romans. Roman prayers took the form of a legalistic bargain with a god: "I am doing this for you (or I am giving this to you), please do this for me." An example of such a prayer is recorded by Cato in *De Agricultura*, 139: "Whether you are god or goddess to whom this grove is dedicated, as it is your right to receive a sacrifice of a pig for the thinning of this sacred grove, and to this intent, I or one at my bidding do it, may it be rightly done. To this end, in offering this pig to you I humbly beg that you will be gracious and merciful to me, to my house and household, and to my children. Will you deign to receive this pig which I offer you to this end." The basis of this prayer is the propitiation of the deity of the wood before the farmer cuts down some of the trees. The legal tone, which exemplifies the Roman attitude to the gods, can be summarized as: "with the sacrifice of this pig I am buying the god's permission to cut down some trees." As with other elements of ritual, the wording of prayers tried to cover all eventualities.

The Roman attitude of prayer was orant, with the face turned towards heaven and their arms and hands outstretched, with palms upwards to display their purity. This appears to have been used by both pagans and Christians, although sometimes Christians only extended their arms horizontally rather than raising their arms and hands to the sky, in order to distinguish themselves from pagans.
Reading: Hammond and Scullard (eds.) 1970, 875; Ogilvie 1969, 24–40.

Priapus A Greek god of the fertility of crops and protection against harm, whose cult spread to Italy. Statues of him seem to have been a common feature of the countryside, but in later times he appears to have been regarded with amusement rather than awe (although still treated as a deity), and he became primarily a god of gardens. His symbol was a *phallus*, and his secondary role is probably linked to the more general use of phallic symbols as protective charms, particularly against the evil eye. Priapus was usually portrayed as a small, sometimes misshapen, man with enormous genitals. According to some myths, Priapus was a son of DIONYSUS and was sometimes worshipped as part of the rites of Dionysus.
Reading: Hammond and Scullard (eds.) 1970, 876; Johns 1982, 50–52.

priest A person who operated in parallel with the *paterfamilias:* the latter performed rites to maintain good relations with the gods on behalf of his family, while priests were officers of religious cults and mediated between the state and gods, performing rites to maintain good relations with the gods on behalf of the state and its people. They were not representatives of the gods on earth, but provided advice on religion, with the Senate making all major decisions about religious matters. They were not moral leaders and were not concerned with the spiritual welfare of the people. Priests originally interpreted civil law, but this function came to be taken over by jurists. Under the empire, the role of priests became less important, but acquiring priesthoods nevertheless remained important. In some cases, the duties of priests were light (such as for the *luperci*, who participated in one annual festival), while others were onerous, especially those of the *pontifices*.

Qualifications varied from priesthood to priesthood and over time. Most priests in the republic were elected from the ranks of patricians; as well as being priests, they usually pursued other occupations (including political ones). Priests—even pontiffs—remained part-time; only the VESTAL VIRGINS were full-time professionals. Priests were not magistrates (although they could hold magistracies), but when performing ritual duties they wore the same *toga praetexta* as the magistrates. Senators could hold only one priestly office, but this rule was broken by Julius Caesar, who was *PONTIFEX MAXIMUS* (from 63 B.C.) and was elected AUGUR and *quindecemvir* in 47 B.C., a trend later followed by Octavian (Augustus) and his successors, who acquired several priesthoods. Eventually plebeians were admitted to most priesthoods, the qualification being freebirth, except for the major *flamines*, SALII and *REX SACRORUM*, where patrician status remained a requirement.

Priests were recruited in different ways, according to the particular priesthood. They could be chosen by the *pontifex maximus*, by cooption by other priests, and by popular election. Normally they were recruited for life, with some exceptions (such as Salian Virgins—*SALIAE VIRGINES*). In the republic, it was customary for a priest on election to provide expensive public entertainment and a feast for his colleagues, and in the empire it seems likely that there was compulsory payment *(summum honorarium)*. There was a hierarchy of priesthoods at Rome, many organized in colleges or groups. The two major colleges were the *augures* and the *pontifices (collegium pontificum)*, the latter also including the *flamines*, the Vestal Virgins and the *rex sacrorum*. Two lesser colleges were the priests who looked after the SIBYLLINE BOOKS *(quindecimviri sacris faciundis)* and the *EPULONES*. Minor priesthoods were arranged in groups *(sodales)* and included the *fetiales*, the ARVAL PRIESTS, the *salii* and the *luperci*. Many priests had precise titles, such as *pontifices*, while others were imprecise, such as *QUINDECIMVIRI SACRIS FACIUNDIS* (the priesthood of fifteen).

Most priests were male, but priestesses served in some cults, usually those of goddesses, the most well known being the Vestal Virgins. There were some women priests outside Rome. For example, a *collegium* of priests *(sacerdotes)* of Jupiter Amon and Barbarus Silvanus at Carthage included two women. There were also priests and priestesses related to such cults as those of ISIS, MITHRAS and MAGNA MATER, whose role, along with that of Christian priests, involved a care for the congregation.

Priests and priestesses are known outside Rome's state religion, and the Roman type of priesthoods spread beyond Rome. For example, there is epigraphic evidence for priests and priestesses who served the cult of ROMA in the eastern provinces. In many of the provinces, priesthoods were confined to the affluent few, often being the culmination of a local provincial career, equivalent to a senior magistracy at Rome. It is likely that temples in areas such as the Celtic provinces of Britain, Gaul and Germany also had priests, but little is known of them except for finds of priestly regalia. However, more is known about official worship in the three Gauls (centered at the Lugdunum altar and temple) than in any other western province because about 40 provincial priests *(sacerdotes)* are attested in numerous inscriptions.

There were also other religious functionaries, such as cleaners of the temples, who did not fulfill the role of priests.

Reading: Beard 1988; Beard and North (eds.) 1990; Fishwick 1987, 317–350 (priests of the three Gauls); Friesen 1993, 76–113 (priests of imperial cult in Asia); Mellor 1975 (includes priesthood of Roma in eastern provinces); Porte 1989; Scullard 1981, 27–31.

Pritona An alternative reading of the name of the Celtic goddess RITONA.

processional objects Various items, such as standards and scepters, carried in religious processions *(pompae)*. Elaborate standards portraying gods accompanied by animals and other attributes are known, but simpler maces or scepters were more common. These were often surmounted with the bust or head of a god, or in some cases that of an emperor, and were made of wood, iron and bronze. Other sacred objects, such as the sacrificial implements, ceremonial vessels used for lustrations, and incense burners were also carried. Garlands and bouquets of flowers and burning incense were used to present the god with sweet smells and pleasing sights. In religious ceremonies carried out by the army, legionary standards and banners were carried in processions.

prodigy *(prodigium*; pl. *prodigia)* An event contrary to the normal course of nature, representing a sign that the *PAX DEORUM* had been broken. Prodigies included the birth of monsters, streams running with blood, rain of milk, earthquakes, and buildings and statues being struck by lightning. They could be interpreted by DIVINATION and were warnings of a disaster, which could only be averted by performing appropriate rituals, such as by an expiatory SACRIFICE *(procuratio)*. Examples of prodigies were mentioned by many writers, but especially by Livy and Julius Obsequens.
Reading: MacBain 1982 (includes an index of prodigies); North 1990.

Promitor A Roman deity who presided over the bringing out of cereal crops from where they had been stored. He was therefore probably a deity of the distribution of the harvest. He was said by Fabius Pictor in the late third century B.C. to have been invoked by a priest of CERES.
Reading: Ferguson 1988a, 853.

pronaos The porch of a temple in front of a cella. In Roman temples, the pronaos was open, usually just with columns (not walls) and could be as long as the cella.

propylaeum A gateway to a sacred precinct, usually marked by elaborate columns and doors. It projected beyond the precinct wall and sometimes projected inside the precinct wall as well.

Prorsa A Roman goddess of childbirth (possibly the same as PORRIMA) who was invoked when the unborn baby was presented head first. (See also CARMENTIS.)
Reading: Richardson 1992, 72.

Proserpina A Roman goddess of germinating seeds and of the UNDERWORLD who was identified with the Greek goddess PERSEPHONE; her name was a mispronunciation of "Persephone." She was the wife of DIS and the daughter of CERES. In 249 and 207 B.C., the Senate ordered special festivals to appease Dis and Proserpina as deities of the underworld. (See also DIS AND PROSERPINA, ALTAR OF.)
Reading: Hammond and Scullard (eds.) 1970, 812.

prostyle A temple with columns on the main facade only, not on the sides of the building.

Providentia A Roman goddess of forethought. She was the personification of providence in the sense of a prescient power capable of creating or altering future events. There was an altar to Providentia Augusta at Rome.
Reading: Richardson 1992, 322.

Prudentius Clemens Aurelius Prudentius Clemens, 348 to after 405, a poet on Christian themes. He was from Saragossa in Spain. He studied rhetoric, became a lawyer and held public office, but c. 392 he turned to writing poetry on Christian themes. His poetry included the *Cathemerinon (Hymns for the Day)*, substantial lyric poems, extracts from which are still sung today. The *Peristephanon* was a collection of poetry to celebrate the Christian martyrs of Spain, Africa and Rome. The *Apotheosis* was concerned with the divinity of Christ and the nature of the Trinity and was over 1,000 lines long. His *Psychomachia (Battle for the Soul)* was an epic allegorical poem on the struggle between virtue and vice, and became very popular in the Middle Ages. Another of his works was *Contra Symmachum (Against Symmachus)*, an argument in two books against paganism and the pagan senator Quintus Aurelius Symmachus.
Reading: Hammond and Scullard (eds.) 1970, 893.

Pudicitia (Fig. 85) A Roman goddess who was the personification of the chastity or modesty of women. In Rome, according to Livy, this goddess was originally worshipped as Pudicitia Patricia ("Pudicitia of the Patricians") at a shrine in the FORUM

Fig. 85 Pudicitia shown as a seated draped figure on a coin. The legend spells her name as PVDICITEA.

Fig. 86 The Puteal Libonis was a large wellhead which was set up in the Forum Romanum at a spot where lightning had struck. It is shown here on a coin of c. 55 B.C. minted by Lucius Scribonius Libo.

BOARIUM, but a rival cult of Pudicitia Plebeia ("Pudicitia of the Plebeians") was established in the Vicus Longus in 296 B.C. The cult was initially restricted to women who had only married once.
Reading: Hammond and Scullard (eds.) 1970, 899–900; Richardson 1992, 322.

pulvinar (pl. *pulvinaria*) A banquet couch with cushions or mattresses on which images of the deities or their symbols were placed after processions *(pompae)* during a *lectisternium* and at other games and ceremonies in honor of the gods. The deities appeared to be participating in the celebrations. The practice reflects the Greek custom of reclining at meals, which was adopted after the Second Punic War by the Romans. Sometimes a space or box was permanently set aside for couches in theaters, amphitheaters and temples. Permanent *pulvinaria* were rare at Rome (one built by Augustus is known at the CIRCUS MAXIMUS), but they were to be found in temples.
Reading: Richardson 1992, 85, 322.

Puta A Roman goddess who presided over the pruning of trees and bushes.
Reading: Ferguson 1988a, 853.

puteal (pl. *putealia*) A wellhead, the structure round the top of the well and its lid. It was also used as a protective ledge or wall built around places where lightning had struck *(BIDENTAL)*. The most famous was the PUTEAL LIBONIS (Fig. 86).
Reading: Hammond and Scullard (eds.) 1970, 901.

Puteal Libonis (Fig. 86) (or Puteal Scribonianum) A large altar-like wellhead *(PUTEAL)* which was set up in the FORUM ROMANUM in Rome on a spot where lightning had struck. It may have been the circular structure which existed in front of the temple of Divus Julius.
Reading: Grant 1970, 220; Hammond and Scullard (eds.) 1970, 901.

Q

Quadruviae Celtic goddesses of crossroads who were also known as Quadriviae, Deae Quadruviae or Deae Quadriviae. There are several dedications to these deities from Germany, such as the altar found at Stuttgart which was dedicated by Serenius Atticus on December 29, 230. An inscription found near Cologne records a dedication *quadriviis, trivis, viis, semitis* ("to the goddesses of the crossroads, road forks, roads and paths").
Reading: Elbe 1975, 208; Espérandieu 1931, no. 557.

quindecimviri sacris faciundis (alternative Latin forms are *quindecimviri, XVviri sacris faciundis, XVviri s.f.*) A college of 15 priests who were in charge of the SIBYLLINE BOOKS. Originally, the Sibylline books were supervised by two priests *(duoviri)*. In 367 B.C. they were increased to 10 priests, known as *decemviri sacris faciundis*. In Sulla's time they were increased to 15, and to 16 under Caesar (although they retained the name of "fifteen"). They were originally male patricians, but included plebeians from 367 B.C. They were originally selected by cooption, but from 104 B.C. some were selected by popular election. Apart from supervising the Sibylline books, they also supervised foreign cults (mainly Greek and Oriental), such as that of MAGNA MATER. They were not priests of these cults, but represented them at official state ceremonies. Recommendations for the nomination of new priests and priestesses for these cults had to be made to this college.
Reading: Beard and North (eds.) 1990; Porte 1989, 144–149.

Quinquatrus March 19, the fifth day after the IDES of March (by the Roman inclusive reckoning). Quinquatrus came to be regarded as the start of a five-day festival and holiday at Rome, the Greater Quinquatrus, due to a misunderstanding of the name (believing it to mean five days, not the fifth day). It was the chief festival of the goddess MINERVA—the first day was considered her birthday and the other four days were circus games. It may have been celebrated at the temple of Minerva on the Aventine Hill and at the temple of Minerva Capta on the Caelian Hill.
Reading: Scullard 1981, 92–94.

Quirinalia Little is known of the festival of QUIRINUS, held on February 17 during the PARENTALIA and on the last day of the FORNACALIA. It was also known as the Feast of the Fools *(stultorum feriae)*.
Reading: Scullard 1981, 78–79.

Quirinus A Roman god who was a member of the original CAPITOLINE TRIAD. He was originally a Sabine god (perhaps a war god) worshipped on the Quirinal Hill before Rome was founded. He was subsequently absorbed into the state religion. He had a wife called HORA. His festival was on February 17. He was served by the *FLAMEN QUIRINALIS*. At Rome, he had an early shrine on the Quirinal Hill and a later temple, which was dedicated in 293 B.C.
Reading: Dumézil 1970, 246–272; Hammond and Scullard (eds.) 1970, 908.

Quirinus, temple of One of the oldest temples in Rome, it was traditionally believed to be founded when Romulus appeared to Julius Proculus in the mid-sixth century B.C. and ordered such a shrine to be built on the site. The earliest record of the temple building was its dedication by Lucius Papirius Cursor in 293 B.C., probably replacing an earlier

one. It was struck by lightning in 206 B.C. and burned in 49 B.C. It was rebuilt by Augustus, who dedicated it on June 29, 16 B.C., the original dedication day being February 17 (QUIRINALIA). This was one of Rome's biggest temples, OCTASTYLE with Doric columns. A statue of Julius Caesar was erected in the temple in 45 B.C. by the Senate. The temple stood on the northwest side of Alta Semita in the gardens of the later Palazzo del Quirinale. It stood until at least the fourth century. A shrine to QUIRINUS may have stood at the Porta Quirinalis.
Reading: Richardson 1992, 326–327.

R

Ratis (also known as Rata) A Celtic goddess who is known from inscriptions found at Birdoswald and Chesters on Hadrian's Wall, England. *Ratis* means "goddess of the fortress."
Reading: Ross 1974, 276.

Rea An Iberian goddess who is known from an inscription on an altar found at Lugo, northwest Spain. It is likely that this goddess formed a divine couple with the god REUS PARAMAECUS, who was also worshipped at Lugo.
Reading: Tranoy 1981, 290.

Redarator An alternative name for the Roman deity REPARATOR.

Rediculus A Roman god worshipped at Rome as the deity who caused Hannibal to retreat from the city gates in 211 B.C. A shrine was erected to him outside the Porta Capena. The deity may also have been known as Rediculus Tutanus—Tutanus was a Roman deity who gave protection in time of trouble.
Reading: Hammond and Scullard (eds.) 1970, 910.

Regia A consecrated *TEMPLUM* in Rome (Fig. 37) containing *sacraria* (shrines). It was believed to have been built by Numa and for a while to have been his house or headquarters and the house of the *PONTIFEX MAXIMUS*. During the republic, it was the official headquarters of the *pontifex maximus*. There was a *sacrarium Martis* ("shrine of Mars") with an image of the god MARS in the Regia; here were kept the *ancilia* and *hasta Martis* (sacred shields and sword of Mars), and the head of the October horse was nailed to the wall if it had been won by the Sacravienses (inhabitants of the Sacra Via area). There was also a *sacrarium Opis Consivae* (shrine of Ops Consiva) which only priests and VESTAL VIRGINS were allowed to enter. The Regia burned in 148 B.C. and was restored, burned again in 36 B.C. and was again restored. It may have been destroyed in the fire of Nero in 64, but is possibly mentioned in a fourth-century inscription. In the Middle Ages it was converted into a private home.
Reading: Richardson 1992, 328–329.

Regifugium Regarded in the late republic as something of an independence day, celebrated on February 24 as an anniversary of the expulsion of the last king from Rome and the beginning of the republic. The origin of this festival is likely to have been quite different, only becoming confused with the expulsion of the king at a late date. The precise meaning of the name is still disputed. It is marked on calendars as *Q R C F (quando rex comitiavit fas)*. Regifugium was not a lucky festival, as it was held on an even-numbered day.
Reading: Hammond and Scullard (eds.) 1970, 911; Scullard 1981, 81–82.

religio A feeling of bond or constraint, usually of prohibition or taboo; religious awe; supersition; religious practice or custom. The Latin noun *religio* covers a wide range of concepts, although there is no word for "religion" as such that was used by the Romans. The adjective *religiosus* meant "superstitious" in a derogatory sense; it could also mean "possessing a religious significance," "reverent," "devout," "forbidden by divine law" and "taboo." A *dies religiosus* was one which was considered to be unlucky, and there was a religious ban on business or other activities on such days.
Reading: Hammond and Scullard (eds.) 1970, 917.

Reparator (or Redarator) A Roman deity who was associated with the preparing of fallow land. He was said by Fabius Pictor in the late third century B.C. to have been invoked by a priest of CERES.
Reading: Ferguson 1988a, 853; York 1986, 60.

Reus Paramaecus An Iberian god who is known from an inscription on an altar found at Lugo, northwest Spain. It is likely that this god formed a divine couple with the Iberian goddess REA, who was also worshipped at Lugo.
Reading: Tranoy 1981, 290.

Reva An Iberian deity who is known from several inscriptions found in northwest Spain, always bearing an accompanying name. Reva Reumiragus is known from near Verin. Reva Eisutus and Reva Laraucus are known from Ginzo de Limia. Laraucus was an Iberian mountain god; this implies that Eisutus and Reumiragus were also deities, but little else is known about them.
Reading: Tranoy 1981, 285–286.

rex sacrorum After the expulsion of the kings in 510 B.C., the office of *rex sacrorum* ("king of sacred things") was established to carry out some of the king's religious functions. The *rex sacrorum* was a sole male priest appointed for life by the *PONTIFEX MAXIMUS*. He was a patrician whose parents had been married by *CONFARREATIO*. He was forbidden from holding any other office. He and his wife (*regina*, "queen"), who herself had some religious duties, performed various state sacrifices and were present at the AGONALIA and REGIFUGIUM. The *rex sacrorum* was superior in civil rank and precedence to the *pontifex maximus*, but inferior in religious authority.
Reading: Beard and North (eds.) 1990; Porte 1989, 89–91.

Rhea A Greek goddess who was the sister and wife of CRONUS and the mother of ZEUS. She was equated with the Roman goddess OPS and sometimes with the Anatolian goddess Cybele (MAGNA MATER).

Ricagambeda A Germanic goddess who is known from an inscription on an altar found at Birrens, Scotland. This goddess is otherwise unknown, but because the dedication was made by soldiers of the Second Cohort of Tungri, Ricagambeda is thought to be a goddess from the German Rhineland, from where the soldiers originated.
Reading: Keppie and Arnold 1984, 9.

Rider-Gods (or Rider-Hunter Gods) There was a widespread cult from c. 1000 B.C. of gods or heroes who appeared as hunters or riders on horseback. Examples include the DIOSCURI (CASTOR and POLLUX) and the DANUBIAN RIDER-GODS. The main god of Thrace and neighboring countries was a Rider God (or Thracian horseman), who was very popular in the Roman period. He appears not to have had a name, but is referred to in inscriptions as "the hero." He has no connection with the Danubian Rider-Gods.
Reading: Hammond and Scullard (eds.) 1970, 924; Hampartumian 1979.

Rigisamus A Celtic god who was linked with the Roman god MARS as MARS RIGISAMUS.

Rigonemetis A Celtic god who was linked with the Roman god MARS as MARS RIGONEMETIS.

Ritona A Celtic goddess of fords and water crossings who was worshipped at Trier and Pachten, Germany. An alternative reading of the name of this goddess is Pritona.
Reading: Green, M. J. 1992a, 176.

ritual An action, or more usually a precise sequence of actions, performed to achieve a religious result. Rituals range from the straightforward washing in holy water (in order to obtain spiritual purity) to massive processions involving thousands of people performing dances, sacrifices and other acts in honor of the gods. While Roman religion was flexible enough to absorb foreign cults, it was nevertheless also highly ritualized. There was a strong element of MAGIC in rituals, and rituals were rigidly observed. The smallest mistake in performance (such as in sacrifices) would render a ritual invalid. Many rituals had been handed down unchanged, and gradually their meaning became forgotten, so that in later times these rituals were barely understood. Rituals were occasionally performed to honor gods whose character and attributes had been forgotten, with only the name of the god surviving.

The Romans had no sacred writings other than the formulae of prayers, and so they were not bound

by dogma. They were free to think and believe what they wanted about their gods, provided that rituals were performed correctly. The gods, though, were regarded as favoring many of the principles of Roman life, such as patriotism, family devotion and a sense of duty, and they were closely associated with these virtues.
Reading: North 1988a.

ritual vessel Flagons and shallow bowls called *paterae* were commonly used in the ritual of sacrifices, for liquids for ritual washing, and for pouring libations. These vessels were made in a range of materials, including silver, pewter, bronze and pottery. Occasionally they bore inscriptions dedicating them to a particular god.

Silver and bronze strainers were also associated with religious use, mainly for removing impurities from wine, although there is a possibility that some strainers could have been used to infuse wine with herbs or drugs. Knives, spoons and platters would have been used in ceremonial feasting and have been found on temple sites, sometimes with dedicatory inscriptions to particular gods. Religious plate was commonly dedicated in the Christian church, especially of silver, and was probably used in the rituals. A large hoard of silver plate found at Water Newton, England, provides excellent examples of such ritual vessels.
Reading: Henig 1984, 131–135.

Robigalia At this ancient agricultural festival held at Rome on April 25, one or more rust- or red-colored dogs and also sheep were sacrificed to appease ROBIGUS, and prayers were offered. This took place at the fifth milestone on the Via Claudia (originally marking the end of Roman territory) in order to prevent blight or mildew from entering Rome's territory and affecting the vines and cereal crops, and to ensure that they properly ripened. The priest in charge was the *FLAMEN QUIRINALIS*.
Reading: Richardson 1992, 301–302.

Robigo A Roman goddess of mildew or grain rust who was the counterpart of the Roman god ROBIGUS.

Robigus A Roman god of mildew or grain rust. He was the counterpart of the Roman goddess ROBIGO. The Romans were uncertain of the sex of Robigus and so at times worshipped both deities. The festival of Robigus was the ROBIGALIA. There was a grove sacred to this deity at the fifth milestone on the Via Claudia (five Roman miles north of Rome).
Reading: Grimal 1986, 405; Hammond and Scullard (eds.) 1970, 925; Scullard 1981, 108–109; York 1986, 113–115.

Roma (Fig. 87) Originally a Hellenistic goddess, Roma was worshipped as the divine spirit of the city and state of Rome. She was mainly worshipped in the eastern provinces, where her cult was established in the early second century B.C., nearly two centuries before the cult was officially sanctioned by Rome. Roma was not worshipped in Rome itself until the time of Hadrian (emperor 117–138), who brought the cult to Rome and built a temple dedicated to VENUS FELIX and Roma Aeterna on the north side of the SACRA VIA. At this time, the nature of the goddess Roma changed, at least at Rome, and she was regarded as a personification of the city of Rome (and so a more abstract and less divine entity) rather than the protective deity worshipped in the east.

In the east, Roma was frequently worshipped in conjunction with a Greek deity, most commonly

Fig. 87 The goddess Roma on a sestertius *of Nero (emperor 54–68). She holds a figure of winged Victory in one hand. Roma is depicted as a warlike figure sitting on armor.*

ZEUS, and during the republic her name was often coupled with the Roman consul or proconsul, who were worshipped as gods in the same way that previous Hellenistic rulers had been worshipped. At Ephesus, for example, there was a shrine of Roma and Publius Servilius Isauricus (proconsul 46–44 B.C.). During the empire, the IMPERIAL CULT was often linked with the cult of Roma as part of the attempt to prevent the emperor from being worshipped as a god while he was alive. Gradually the cult of Roma became absorbed into the general imperial cult as later emperors became more willing to be worshipped as gods during their lifetimes.
Reading: Ferguson 1970, 89–90; Fishwick 1987, 48–51; Mellor 1975 (the cult of Roma in the Greek world; he collates the evidence for inscriptions mentioning Roma).

Roma, temples of There were numerous temples dedicated to the cult of ROMA which were often linked with other cults, such as the IMPERIAL CULT. Likewise, numerous statues of Roma are known to have been erected. The first temples were dedicated not in Rome but in the Hellenistic east. The very first was founded at Smyrna (Izmir, Turkey) in 195 B.C. when the inhabitants appealed to Rome for help against Antiochus III. After the Julio-Claudian period, the name of Roma was eventually dropped from the temples, as later emperors were willing to be worshipped without linkage to Roma as part of the imperial cult.
Reading: Mellor 1975.

Roma and Augustus, temples of At Ancyra in Galatia (Turkey), which was where the provincial assembly met and where the annual games were held, the temple of Augustus and Roma is most famous for the text of Augustus's *Res Gestae (Acts)*, which was inscribed on the inner walls of the temple. At Pergamum, Turkey, the temple of Augustus and Roma became the center of the IMPERIAL CULT in Asia. The organization of the cities of Asia (Koinon of Asia) met annually at this temple when the games were held (the *Romaia Sebasta*).
Reading: Mellor 1975, 89–90.

Romaia Festivals dedicated to ROMA. In Asia Minor the Romaia Sebasta were held at Pergamum in honor of Roma and Augustus at the annual meeting of the Koinon of Asia (cities of Asia)—Sebasta meaning Augustus. They were ostensibly religious games, but came to play an important political role. Other cities in Asia acquired temples dedicated to the IMPERIAL CULT, and the celebrations of these festivals (Romaia) came to be rotated amongst the major cities, and did not remain at Pergamum. Eventually the name of Roma was dropped from the games. In 189 B.C., Romaia were established at Delphi in Greece; however, later references are lacking, and the games at Delphi were either part of the Pythian games there or were overshadowed by them. By the 150s B.C. Romaia were being celebrated in Athens, and also in the second century B.C. at several other Greek cities, particularly linked to preexisting local festivals (such as the Pytheia-Romaia at Megara). In A.D. 2 an important Greek agonistic festival known as Italika Romaia Sebasta was established in Italy as an Italian counterpart of the Romaia Sebasta of Pergamum. It may normally have been called *Sebasta*, and the games may have been celebrated in honor of the emperor and not actually of Roma.
Reading: Mellor 1975.

Roma Quadrata A shrine on the Palatine Hill at Rome in which were deposited objects used by an AUGUR in founding a city—possibly the *LITUUS*, sacrificial implements and a plow.
Reading: Richardson 1992, 333.

Rosalia (or Rosaria) The commemoration of events by the use of roses. The Rosalia was never a public festival, but the Romans were extremely fond of roses and used them on all kinds of occasions. In particular, they were used to commemorate the dead. The graves or tombs of the dead were presumably garlanded with roses at a time of the year (May to August) when they were abundant locally. This particular festival was also known as *dies rosationis* and is attested in inscriptions in many parts of the empire. (See also STANDARD.)
Reading: Hammond and Scullard (eds.) 1970, 936–937; Lattimore 1962, 137–140; Toynbee 1971, 63.

Rosmerta A Celtic goddess whose name means "the great provider." She was usually associated with the Roman god MERCURY; together they formed a divine couple worshipped over much of Europe, particularly in central and eastern Gaul. She was also worshipped in southwest England. In the divine

couple, Rosmerta was a goddess of prosperity and abundance and was often depicted with a cornucopia and *patera.* In other portrayals, the couple is accompanied by purses of money and *caducei.* On a carving from Mannheim, Germany, Rosmerta holds a purse on which a snake lays its head. In Britain, Rosmerta was sometimes shown accompanied by a bucket, and in one carving she has a scepter and a ladle held over a bucket. She was occasionally worshipped on her own as a goddess of plenty, and at Gissey-la-Vieil, France, she was associated with a sacred spring.
Reading: Green, M. J. 1992a, 180.

Rudianus A Celtic war god who was linked to the Roman god MARS as MARS RUDIANUS.

Rudiobus A Celtic god who is referred to in an inscription on a bronze figurine of a horse found at Neuvy-en-Sullias, France. Horses were presumably sacred to this god.
Reading: Green, M. J. 1992a, 181.

Rumina A Roman goddess also known as Diva Rumina. She protected breastfeeding mothers. She had a shrine and a sacred fig tree at the foot of the Palatine Hill at Rome where milk rather than wine was offered as a sacrifice.
Reading: Hammond and Scullard (eds.) 1970, 940.

Rusina A Roman goddess of fields or farmland who was also called Rurina.

Rusor A Roman deity who was associated with the Roman goddess TELLUS. Rusor may mean something like "ploughman."

S

Sabazius Also known as Sabazios, originally a Phrygian or Thracian god of vegetation, especially of barley and wheat. His worship was widespread in Italy during the empire and seems to have been connected with that of MAGNA MATER. He was sometimes identified with the Roman god JUPITER and with the Greek gods ZEUS and DIONYSUS, and assumed their attributes. He is sometimes portrayed with a thunderbolt and eagle, symbols usually associated with Zeus, and sometimes in Phrygian costume. His chief attribute was the snake, and a characteristic of his cult consisted of votive offerings of representations of hands covered with numerous magical symbols and attributes. The fingers on the hands form a symbol of benediction still seen in some Christian rites.
Reading: Hammond and Scullard (eds.) 1970, 941; Turcan 1989, 313–322.

sacellum (pl. *sacella*) An unroofed open-air shrine with an ALTAR sacred to the gods. Such shrines were not associated with temple buildings. The term was also used for the cellar or partly sunken room in a military building which served a religious function and in which the standards were stored.
Reading: Richardson 1992, 2.

sacer A Latin adjective meaning something consecrated to a deity or made divine, as in SACRA VIA. *Sacra* is its feminine form and *sacrum* its neuter form.
Reading: Warde Fowler 1911.

sacerdos (pl. *sacerdotes*) A PRIEST or religious official. This Latin word was rarely used in the republic, and tended to apply to foreign religious functionaries (in particular those of Greek or eastern cults). It was also used for priests (especially female) of individual deities. Later, the term was applied to Roman priests as well. The provincial priests of the IMPERIAL CULT could be *sacerdotes*. The abstract term was *sacerdotium*.
Reading: Beard and North (eds.) 1990.

sacrarium (pl. *sacraria*) A shrine or sanctuary in which sacred implements and objects *(sacra)* were kept. Sacrifices were held at the ancient *sacrarium* of Ops Consiva in the REGIA, which must have been a *templum*. (See OPS.)
Reading: Richardson 1992, 2.

Sacra Via ("Sacred Street") The oldest and best known street in Rome and one which always had great importance. The adjective *Sacra* almost always precedes *Via* (unlike most other street names in Rome where *Via* comes first, such as Via Aurelia and Via Appia). It was the main route from the Palatine Hill down to the FORUM ROMANUM, but its course and level changed drastically over time. It was flanked by many shops and houses. The Sacravienses (inhabitants of the Sacra Via) and Suburanenses (inhabitants of the Subura district) fought for possession of the head of the October horse on October 15. (See OCTOBER HORSE, SACRIFICE OF.)
Reading: Richardson 1992, 338–340.

sacrifice (Figs. 88, 89) (Literally, the performance of a sacred action, from *sacrificium*) A gift to the gods, heroes, emperors and the dead. Sacrifice did not just concern the ritual killing of animals (blood sacrifice), as the term tends to imply nowadays. Both public and private sacrifice were practiced in order to please and maintain relations with the gods, and sacrifices were offered in different ways. For example, a food offering might be shared between the gods and people in a sacrificial feast,

Fig. 88 A sestertius *of Gaius (Caligula) about to sacrifice an ox in front of the temple of Divus Augustus. Gaius is shown with his head covered* (capite velato), *and by him are an altar, ox, and two assistants. Behind is a hexastyle temple. The legend reads DIVO AVG S C (to the divine Augustus by decree of the Senate), and the coin dates to* A.D. *40/41.*

or the food might be given entirely to the gods by burning it all. It is possible to divide sacrificial offerings into various categories according to the motives for the offering (such as offerings made in the expectation of favors). The evidence for the reason for a sacrifice is largely derived from inscriptions on altars, which were themselves set up as sacrifices. Some sacrifices were made at the instigation of the gods, who may have suggested the sacrifice in a dream or by some other sign. Other sacrifices were as a result of consulting oracles (see ORACLE). Sacrifices were also made on anniversaries, such as the anniversary of the founding of Rome (traditionally April 21) and at festivals.

There were various types of gifts, such as cakes, wine, incense, oil and honey, as well as blood sacrifices which involved the slaughter of various animals. The most common form of sacrifice was a VOTIVE OFFERING made in fulfilment of a vow *(ex voto)*, where a person had promised a sacrifice if a god undertook a particular action. There is very little evidence for human sacrifice, although it was practiced in exceptional circumstances.

The slaughter and consumption of an animal was the most popular form of sacrifice. The animal had to be appropriate to the particular god: male for gods, female for goddesses, without blemish, and often of an appropriate color (such as black for gods of the UNDERWORLD). Some sacrifices were of animals considered by some as unfit for human consumption, such as the dogs sacrificed to HECATE. The person desirous of the sacrifice usually made arrangements with the custodian *(aedituus)* of the relevant temple and hired the services of a *victimarius* to kill the animal, and often of a flute player *(tibicen)* as well. Sacrifices were accompanied by music to prevent any sounds of ill-omen being heard, which would mean starting the sacrifice again. The priest kept his head covered with his toga *(CAPITE VELATO)* at all times to guard against sights and sounds of ill-omen.

The precise way an animal was killed for sacrifice was probably important. The head of the animal was usually sprinkled with wine and sacred cake *(mola salsa)* before it was killed. It was stunned with a pole ax and then stabbed with a sacrificial knife. Its blood was caught in a bowl and poured over the altar, and the animal was skinned and cut up. The entrails could be examined by a *HARUSPEX*. They were then roasted on the altar fire and the important

Fig. 89 Relief sculpture of a person about to offer a libation—a bloodless sacrifice—at a lighted circular altar. The sacrifice was to Tutela, who is shown seated with a cornucopia in her left arm. The inscription reads TVTELE SANCTE ("To sacred Tutela").

participants ate the entrails first. The bones and fat were burnt on the altar fire for the gods with other offerings such as wine and cakes. The rest of the animal was cooked for a feast for those taking part.

Blood sacrifices where all the sacrifice was given to the gods were usually performed at times of crisis (such as before a battle), as well as at purification and expiation ceremonies and at the BURIAL OF THE DEAD. A holocaust was a sacrifice which was completely burnt. The combined sacrifice of a pig, sheep and ox *(SUOVETAURILIA)* was made on some occasions (Fig. 99). Sacrifices tended to become an excuse for a good meal or feast, the focus of a celebration, with the distribution of a meal afterwards.

Jews undertook sacrifices to the emperor, as they had on behalf of earlier rulers, until the JEWISH REVOLT (66–70) when this ceased. Only CHRISTIANITY refused sacrifice. Christians were not willing to sacrifice to the emperor because this ritual treated him like a god. In the fourth century, repeated prohibitions of sacrifices were issued by emperors from Constantine I to Theodosius, but animal sacrifices continued to be carried out, even by Christians.
Reading: Hassall 1980; Price 1984, 207–233.

sacrifice, human There is little evidence for human sacrifice, although it was practiced in exceptional circumstances. Victims were usually paired couples (two men and two women). Following various disasters, a pair of Greeks and a pair of Gauls (two men and two women) were buried alive in the FORUM BOARIUM at Rome, probably in 228 B.C., in accordance with instructions from the SIBYLLINE BOOKS. This was repeated in the Forum Boarium after the battle of Cannae in 216 B.C. after consultation of the Sibylline books; Livy (22:57.6) describes this as a most un-Roman rite *(minime Romano sacro)*. In 97 B.C. a senatorial decree outlawed human sacrifice. Human sacrifice may also have been undertaken by non-Roman religious cults. For example, the first-century poet Lucan describes the three Celtic deities ESUS, TARANIS and TEUTATES as requiring human sacrifice. The suspension of *oscilla* (masks or puppets) in trees at the FERIAE LATINAE and SEMENTIVAE may have been a substitute for human sacrifice. The *ARGEI* may have served the same purpose.
Reading: Hammond and Scullard (eds.) 1970, 944; Liebescheutz 1979, 449–450.

Saegon A Celtic god who was linked with the Roman god HERCULES as HERCULES SAEGON. The name *Saegon* may be linked to Segomo, which means "victorious." (See also SEGOMO.)

saints Holy people revered in the Christian religion. Many of the early saints were martyrs killed during persecutions of Christians. The term *martyr* means "witness," and these early saints were important in the spread of CHRISTIANITY because people were impressed that they accepted death rather than renounce Christianity. Another aspect of saintliness was the performance of miracles. It came to be believed that saints could perform miracles after their deaths, so that relics of saints (any physical remains) became important. The places where these relics were kept became centers of Christian worship and pilgrimage. Relics of saints became so important that many forgeries were made. Likewise in the search for saints, many pagan deities were absorbed into the church and "sanitized" as saints (such as St. Brigit, originally a deity of the Brigantes), in much the same way that pagan sites were often converted to Christian use. (See also *MARTYRIUM*; MIRACLE; PILGRIMS.)

Saitada A Celtic goddess who is known from an inscription found in the Tyne Valley, England. The name *Saitada* may mean "goddess of grief."
Reading: Ross 1974, 474.

Salacia A Roman goddess of the sea who was the personification of salt water. She was associated with the Roman god NEPTUNE. Because Neptune was originally a god of fresh water, Salacia was possibly originally a spirit of water from springs.
Reading: Grimal 1986, 410; Hammond and Scullard (eds.) 1970, 945.

saliae virgines (Salian Virgins) Women (probably not freeborn) who were hired as priestesses to accompany the *PONTIFEX MAXIMUS* at an annual sacrifice, probably in the *sacrarium Martis*. They were hired for a short time only each year, and offered the sacrifice dressed in the costume of the *SALII*.
Reading: Beard and North (eds.) 1990; Dumézil 1970, 173; Porte 1989, 104.

salii Priests of MARS. They were divided into two colleges *(sodales)* each of 12 men, the Palatini and the Collini (or Agonenses). These were the "leaping" or "dancing" priests of Mars (from *salire*, to dance) who danced in procession during his festivals. The Palatini were particularly devoted to MARS GRAVIDUS and the Collini were possibly originally associated with QUIRINUS on the Quirinal Hill. The *salii* formed one of the lesser priesthoods *(sodales)* and were pre-republican in origin. They were chosen from patricians whose parents were living when chosen. They were chosen for life but were allowed to resign if they obtained a major magistracy or priesthood. Their headquarters was the Curia Saliorum on the Palatine Hill, in which there was a *SACRARIUM* where the *LITUUS* of Romulus was kept. There was also a Curia Saliorum on the Quirinal where the Salii Collini kept their sacred implements. The records of the *salii* may have been kept here.

The *salii* were in charge of the *ancilia* (shields) which were kept in the *sacrarium Martis* in the REGIA. Their major duties were ritual song and dance through Rome on several days in March and October (the start and finish of the war season), including the QUINQUATRUS and ARMILUSTRIUM. For these processions, they wore archaic military armor and carried arms, halting at certain places to carry out ritual dances (including the *TRIPUDIUM*) and to sing the *CARMEN SALIARE*. The *salii* are also attested in other Italian towns, and at Tibur (Tivoli) they were attached to Hercules.
Reading: Beard and North (eds.) 1990; Porte 1989, 102–107; Richardson 1992, 2, 104–105; Scullard 1981, 85–86.

Salmoxis An alternative name for the UNDERWORLD deity ZALMOXIS.

Salus An old Roman goddess, possibly originally of agriculture and fertility, but who was chiefly known as a goddess personifying health and preservation in general. She came to be identified with the Greek goddess HYGEIA and was sometimes identified with the Italian goddess SEMONIA. During the empire, she was called Salus Publica Populi Romani ("Public Health of the Roman People"). There was a temple of Salus on the Quirinal Hill at Rome, and part of the hill was called Collis Salutaris, probably indicating that a cult of Salus was established there at an early date. Salus was frequently depicted on coins as feeding a sacred snake from a *patera* and holding a scepter, in the same way that Hygeia was often depicted, but earlier coins show her with ears of cereal crops. There was a festival of Salus on August 5.
Reading: Grimal 1986, 411; Hammond and Scullard (eds.) 1970, 948; Marwood 1988; Scullard 1981, 55, 170.

Salus, temple of Little is known about this temple, despite its importance. It was vowed by the consul Gaius Junius Bubulcus Brutus in the Second Samnite War, probably in 311 B.C. He dedicated it, when dictator, on the NONES of August, 302 B.C. It was struck by lightning in 276 B.C., 206 B.C. and 166 B.C., but little damage was done each time. It was damaged by fire in the time of Claudius (41–54) but must have been restored, as it was still standing in the fourth century. It was situated on a part of the Quirinal Hill known as the Collis Salutaris and was probably preceded by an ancient altar or shrine of Salus, as the name was already in existence when the temple was built. It must have been in a prominent position to have been repeatedly struck by lightning. It may have been a temple that stood until the seventeenth century and was previously identified as the temple of SERAPIS built by Caracalla or the temple of SOL built by Aurelian.
Reading: Richardson 1992, 341–342.

Salus Augusta (Fig. 90) (or Salus Augusti) A personification not just of the "health" of the em-

Fig. 90 A silver denarius *of Maximinus I depicting Salus Augusti holding out a* patera *to a snake.*

peror, but also of his "virtue." It was his power to save and preserve which was deified.
Reading: Hammond and Scullard (eds.) 1970, 948; Marwood 1988.

Salus Publica Populi Romani An aspect of the Roman goddess SALUS; this name means "Public Health of the Roman People," and was used during the empire.

Sancta Sophia, basilica of (Haghia Sophia) An early Christian church built at Constantinople (Istanbul, Turkey) beginning in 343. The first church was completed in 360 and was dedicated to Sancta Sophia (Haghia Sophia), which means "Holy Wisdom," an attribute of Christ. This structure, called "the Great Church," was probably comparable in size with the present building on the site. The first church was burnt down on June 9, 404 in a riot caused by supporters of St. John Chrysostom, the Patriarch, who had been removed from his see by the empress Eudoxia. The church was rebuilt by Theodosius II, but on January 15, 532 this too was destroyed by fire, the first day of the Nika revolt. Justinian had the church rebuilt and it was dedicated in 532. Despite damage from earthquakes and neglect, the building has survived to the present. It was converted to a mosque after Constantinople fell to the Turks in 1453 and it is now a museum.
Reading: Mainstone 1988; Mark and Çakmak 1992.

sanctuary A sacred place, usually rural in nature. Sanctuaries consisted of shrines and/or temples dedicated to one or more deities. They could be situated in sacred groves *(nemus, lucus)*, such as the sanctuary of DIANA NEMORENSIS in Italy, and many were situated by sacred springs. Apart from shrines and temples, other buildings were usually present, and many sanctuaries were probably places of pilgrimage, as votive offerings are a common feature. A number may have been visited by the sick, as ANATOMICAL EX-VOTOS have been found at several sites. (See also ASCLEPIEIUM; GROVE, SACRED; SHRINE.)
Reading: Bourgeois 1991 and 1992 (sanctuaries in Gaul).

Sarana A Celtic goddess who is known from evidence at a temple at Szöny, Hungary. She is probably the same deity as the Celtic goddess SIRONA.
Reading: Green, M. J. 1992a, 192.

Sarapis An Egyptian god who is usually known in Latin as SERAPIS.

Sarritor A Roman god of hoeing and weeding, said by Fabius Pictor in the late third century B.C. to have been invoked by a priest of CERES.
Reading: Ferguson 1988a, 853; York 1986, 60.

Satriana A Roman goddess who is known only from an inscription found at Rome, which was recorded in the sixteenth century but is now lost. The goddess is assumed to be the family deity of the *gens* Satria, but nothing else is known about her.
Reading: Richardson 1992, 107.

Sattada A goddess Sattada (or possibly Saiiada) recorded in an inscription on an altar found at Beltingham, near Hadrian's Wall, England. The inscription is problematic in that it records the dedication of the altar by the assembly of the Textoverdi, which is not recognised as a Celtic name. It is thought most likely that the Textoverdi were a native tribe living in the area, and that Sattada was a local native goddess.
Reading: Burn 1969, 126; Rivet and Smith 1979, 470–471.

Saturn (in Latin, Saturnus) An ancient Roman god, possibly of blight and/or of seed sowing. He is known mainly as a god of sowing and had a festival (SATURNALIA) at the winter solstice. In one legend, Saturn was regarded as the husband of the Roman goddess OPS and father of the Roman deity PICUS. LUA MATER was sometimes thought to be his cult partner. Saturn was also identified with the Greek god CRONUS, whose son ZEUS was identified with JUPITER. According to another legend, Saturn came to Italy from Greece after his son, Jupiter, dethroned him and hurled him from the top of Mount Olympus. He founded a fortified village on the Capitol at Rome, which was called Saturnia. The reign of Saturn (like that of JANUS) was regarded as a golden age of prosperity, and Saturn was thought to have taught the people how to cultivate the ground. He had a temple at the foot of the CAPITOLINE HILL in Rome (Figs. 15, 37).
Reading: Grimal 1986, 412; Hammond and Scullard (eds.) 1970, 955–956; Simon 1990, 193–199.

Saturn, temple of A temple situated in the FORUM ROMANUM at Rome at the foot of the CAPITOLINE HILL (Figs. 15, 37). It was dedicated on December 17 (the SATURNALIA). There were differing opinions among the Romans as to when the temple had been built and by whom: it was built in the early republic, possibly by the consuls in 501, 498 or 497 B.C., or in 493 B.C. It was rebuilt by Lucius Munatius Plancus in 42 B.C. and again in the later fourth century (probably after a fire), entirely from used columns, bases and cornices. From republican times, it served as the main state treasury *(aerarium populi Romani* or *aerarium Saturni)*, where cash (mainly of bronze *[aes]*, hence the name) and archives of the Roman state were deposited. The latter included financial documents, laws, *plebiscita* (decrees of the people) and *senatus consulta* (senatorial decrees), and were moved to the Tabularium after 78 B.C.

The surviving podium is that of the rebuilding of Plancus, 24.60 yds. wide × c. 44 yds. long (22.50 m × c. 40 m). It was a HEXASTYLE temple. The *aerarium* must have been under the steps. There was also a much older altar of SATURN in front of the temple. This was traditionally believed to have been founded in the Trojan War or built by HERCULES. Its antiquity is indicated by the fact that worship was undertaken in the Greek rite with the head uncovered (not *CAPITE VELATO*).

Reading: Hammond and Scullard (eds.) 1970, 16; Nash 1962b, 294; Richardson 1992, 343–344; Scullard 1981, 206.

Saturnalia A festival of SATURN originally celebrated on December 17. By the late republic, the festival fluctuated from three to seven days, from December 17 to 23. It was a winter solstice festival to honor Saturn as the god of seed sowing. The festival began with a great sacrifice at the temple of Saturn in Rome, followed by a public feast open to everyone. All business ceased, there was a general holiday, and on this one occasion in the year people were allowed to play gambling games in public. Everyone wore less-formal clothes and soft caps *(pillei)*, slaves were let off their duties and might even be served by their masters. Each household chose a mock king to preside over the festivities. The final days of the festival were known as the Sigillaria.

The Saturnalia was probably the most popular of Roman festivals. Many of the festivities and customs of the Saturnalia were absorbed into the Christian festival of the Nativity of Christ (Christmas); both were generally a time of enjoyment, and other common elements included cheerfulness and goodwill, lighting of candles, friends and family feasting together, the giving of presents, and possibly the wearing of paper hats as a substitute for *pillei.* Saturnalia was in effect replaced by the festival of Christmas on December 25, on the day in honor of SOL INVICTUS; Christmas is first attested in 336.

Reading: Scullard 1981, 205–207.

Saturnus The Latin name for the god SATURN.

satyrs Originally, satyrs were Greek woodland spirits who took part in the rites of DIONYSUS. They were confused with the Greek god PAN, and the Romans identified them with the Roman woodland deities, the Fauns. Satyrs were thought to be half human and half animal and are most commonly portrayed as half human and half goat. They were sometimes regarded as representing the animal side of human nature. They were thought to be lustful and were often portrayed with overlarge genitals chasing females (goddesses, humans and animals). (See also SILENUS.)

Reading: Johns 1982, 82.

Securitas A Roman goddess who was the personification of public and political security. This goddess was most often invoked when there was some imminent threat to the state. She is usually portrayed leaning on a column.

Reading: Hammond and Scullard (eds.) 1970, 970.

Segetia Also known as Segesta, she was a Roman goddess of grain crops ripening above ground. There was a statue of Segetia in the CIRCUS MAXIMUS at Rome.

Reading: Grimal 1986, 231 (under *Indigetes*).

Segomo This was possibly a Celtic god who was equated with MARS as MARS SEGOMO. *Segomo* means "victorious" and may be linked to the title SAEGON by which HERCULES was sometimes known. *Segomo* is more of a title than a name and may be an epithet of Mars rather than a separate Celtic deity. Mars

Segomo was worshipped by the Sequani tribe in Gaul.
Reading: Green, M. J. 1992a, 188.

Seia A Roman goddess who was the guardian of sown seed when it was underground. She had a statue in the CIRCUS MAXIMUS at Rome. This deity was probably one of the INDIGETES.
Reading: Hammond and Scullard (eds.) 1970, 970.

Selene The Greek goddess of the moon who was equated with the Roman goddess LUNA.

Semele A Greek goddess who was the mother of DIONYSUS. She was sometimes equated with the Roman goddess STIMULA.

Sementivae (or Sementinae) A moveable festival, held around January 24–26. It is not clear whether this was one or two festivals, particularly as it was held on two days with an interval of seven days in between. It appears to have been a festival of spring sowing, or for the protection of seed sown the previous autumn, or both. Offerings were made to TELLUS on the first day, and to CERES on the second day, and included a cake of spelt and a pregnant cow. The oxen which had been used in the plowing were adorned with garlands. *Oscilla* (masks or puppets) may have been hung in the trees. OVID equates the festival with the PAGANALIA.
Reading: Scullard 1981, 68; Warde Fowler 1899, 294–296.

Semonia A Roman goddess who was probably an ancient agricultural goddess. She was sometimes identified with SALUS. Little else is known about this deity.

Semo Sancus A Roman god of oaths and treaties. He was also called Sancus, Sanctus and Semo Sancus Dius Fidius; *Sanctus* may be a misspelling. He was an ancient god whose worship was said to have been introduced by the Sabines. He was sometimes considered to be the father of the Sabus, who was the eponymous hero of the Sabines. There is a suggestion that he may have originally been a god of sowing. Semo Sancus came to be equated with DIUS FIDIUS and thus sometimes also identified with HERCULES. There was a dedication at Rome to Semo on the Quirinal Hill, made by a group of bidental priests; a *BIDENTAL* was a place struck by lightning, which suggests that Semo Sancus was also connected with thunder. He had a temple on the Quirinal Hill at Rome and another on the Tiber Island. Another temple of Semo Sancus is known at Velitrae (modern Velletri), Italy.
Reading: Grimal 1986, 411; Hammond and Scullard (eds.) 1970, 972–973; Richardson 1992, 347–348 (temples); Scullard 1981, 147.

Senaicus An Iberian deity who is known from an inscription from Braga, northern Portugal.
Reading: Tranoy 1981, 269.

Sentinus A Roman god who gave consciousness to a newborn child.

Sentona A native goddess who was worshipped in the area of Tarsatica (modern Trsat, near Rijeka, Croatia) in the Roman province of Dalmatia.
Reading: Wilkes 1969, 196.

Septimontia (or Septimontium) A festival (possibly derived from *septem montes*, "seven hills") held on December 11. It was thought to have been a festival conducted by the Montani, those people living on the seven hills within the Servian Wall of Rome, in honor of those hills. However, the name may be derived from *saepti montes* ("enclosed hills") and may only refer to the oldest part of Rome—the Palatine, Velia, Caelian and Esquiline Hills. Sacrifices were offered on each hill. The festival continued to at least the time of Tertullian (c. 160 or 170–c. 230). There is some confusion in ancient sources about the origin of the festival and the places where it was celebrated.
Reading: Richardson 1992, 349–350; Scullard 1981, 203–204.

sepulcretum A cemetery or graveyard. This term was used once by only one Latin author (Catullus).
Reading: Richardson 1992, 351.

sepulcrum Any type of burial place for the interment of a human body or its ashes, regardless of rites.
Reading: Richardson 1992, 351.

Sequana A Celtic goddess of water and healing and a personification of the Seine River at its source northwest of Dijon, France. The source of the river is in a valley in the Châillon Plateau, and a healing sanctuary was dedicated to the goddess Sequana. The goddess was portrayed wearing a diadem and standing in a boat shaped like a duck. The nature of the votive offerings from the site reflects her role as a healing goddess.
Reading: Green, M. J. 1992a, 188–189.

Sequana, sanctuary of Healing sanctuary or shrine (known as *Fontes Sequanae*) dedicated to SEQUANA at the source of the Seine River, 21.75 miles (35 km) northwest of Dijon, France. The sanctuary was established by the Celts, and the Romans later built two temples and other cult buildings around the spring and pool at this site. It became increasingly elaborate, with several buildings in a temple precinct. Several hundred wooden carvings, which had either been buried or hung on buildings in the precinct, have been found in waterlogged deposits. Many were offered to SEQUANA as a goddess of healing, and many are ANATOMICAL EX-VOTOS, representing models of parts of the body.
Reading: Jackson 1988, 163–164.

Serapeum (Fig. 91) A temple of SERAPIS was often known as a Serapeum. At Rome, a temple of Serapis was adjacent to and south of the temple of ISIS. They were known collectively as ISEUM et SERAPEUM. Both were probably built in 43 B.C. They comprised two separate buildings, with a rectangular open square and probably ornamental entrances. Numerous Egyptian obelisks and other sculpture have been discovered nearby. A temple of Serapis (Serapeum) was in the western quarter of Alexandria, Egypt. It was built on a large artificial hill by Ptolemy III Euergetes, and in Roman times was greatly extended. It was destroyed in 391, and is the only temple in Alexandria whose ruins have been excavated.
Reading: Nash 1962a, 510; Richardson 1992, 211–212; Wild 1981.

Serapis An Egyptian god usually known in Latin as Serapis or sometimes Sarapis. Serapis was a conflation of the god OSIRIS and the sacred bull APIS.

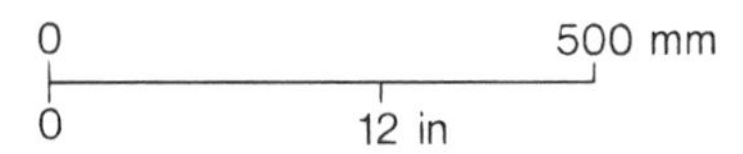

Fig. 91 A late 2nd-century dedicatory inscription for the Serapeum at York, England. It reads DEO SANCTO SERAPI TEMPLVM A SOLO FECIT CL HIERONYMIANVS LEG LEG VI VIC ("Claudius Hieronymianus, commander of the VI Victrix Legion, built this temple from its foundations to the holy god Serapis").

The cult of Serapis seems to have arisen at Memphis in Egypt, in the temple where the sacred bull Apis was kept. According to tradition, the king (Ptolemy I) effectively created the god as a new cult to go with his own power. He established the cult at Alexandria. Serapis was a god of the UNDERWORLD, of the sky and of healing, and was regarded as above fate. He also performed miracles and was equated with many gods such as DIONYSUS, JUPITER, AESCULAPIUS and HELIOS. He was not usually given titles or epithets, although in one inscription he is addressed as Sarapis Polieus ("Serapis of the City").

Although Serapis was the chief god in the cult of Egyptian deities, in the Roman empire he was usually eclipsed by the associated cult of Isis. He was usually portrayed with a benign and bearded face and with a *modius* (a symbol of fertility) on his head. He was sometimes shown seated, with Cerberus (the three-headed dog of HADES) at his right knee and a staff or scepter in his left hand.
Reading: Ferguson 1970, 36–37; Hammond and Scullard (eds.) 1970, 951.

Seth An Egyptian god also known as Set. He was called Typhon by the Greeks. He was a god of upper Egypt who was believed to have killed OSIRIS.
Reading: Hammond and Scullard (eds.) 1970, 982.

Setlocenia A Celtic goddess known from a dedicatory inscription at Maryport, England. *Setlocenia* probably means "she of the long life."
Reading: Ross 1974, 276.

Shadrapa A North African god worshipped by the Carthaginians and sometimes equated with the Roman god LIBER. *Shadrapa* means "Shed heals"; Shed was an ancient Canaanite deity, sometimes equated with the Egyptian god HORUS. Shadrapa was sometimes linked to Horus, but was more usually equated with the Greek god DIONYSUS.
Reading: Picard and Picard 1987, 178.

shrine (Fig. 92) A simple and relatively insubstantial place of worship. The term *shrine* is sometimes used to distinguish those places of worship without a building (such as a *SACELLUM*), although it has also been used as a general term covering a broader range of cult sites. As well as temples, there were probably a great many shrines dedicated to local deities, particularly in rural areas. They probably consisted of little more than an ALTAR or insubstantial building. Relatively few have therefore survived in recognizable form, and it can be difficult to distinguish between shrines and temples from the archaeological evidence. Some shrines were associated with natural places such as groves, springs, sacred pools or rivers. Some of the smaller rectangular, circular or polygonal Romano-Celtic structures which have been interpreted as temples may actually have been shrines. A shrine within a temple was an *aedicula*. There were also portable shrines which were carried in processions and ceremonies. (See also SANCTUARY.)
Reading: Bourgeois 1992; Drury 1980; Woodward and Leach 1993.

Fig. 92 A wall painting at Pompeii, Italy, which shows a portable shrine being carried in a procession. This particular shrine resembles a temple.

Sibyl *(Sibylla)* The name given to various prophetesses, who often had individual names as well. The Sibyl at Cumae in Italy was the most famous. She was believed to have composed the original SIBYLLINE BOOKS, and to have come from the east and settled at Cumae in a cave (unlike any other Sibyls). There were other Sibyls who lived in different places at different times. They prophesied in an ecstatic state, and were thought to be possessed by APOLLO. ALBUNEA was sometimes regarded as a Sibyl. She had a cult at Tivoli, Italy, and her oracular verses were kept with the Sibylline books at Rome. Because of the later Christian interpolations in the Sibylline oracles, the Sibyls were later considered equal to Old Testament prophets, and appear in Christian art and literature. (See also ORACLE.)
Reading: Hammond and Scullard (eds.) 1970, 984; Parke 1988; Potter 1990 (review article of Parke 1988).

Sibylline books (Fig. 93) *(libri Sibyllini)* A collection of verses written in Greek that were consulted as an ORACLE when a crisis threatened Rome. The original collection was believed to have been composed by a prophetess called the SIBYL. She sold some of them to King Tarquin but he refused to buy them all, and so she burned the rest. The books

Fig. 93 A republican coin of Lucius Manlius Torquatus, dating to 54 B.C. On the obverse is the head of the Sibyl, and on the reverse is a tripod and two stars. It was struck at a time when divination by the Sibylline books was especially popular.

were kept in a stone chest beneath the temple of JUPITER OPTIMUS MAXIMUS at Rome, but after the temple and chest were destroyed by fire in 83 B.C., a new collection of oracles was made by 76 B.C. from different copies in many places. These new Sibylline books were transferred by Augustus to the temple of APOLLO on the Palatine Hill in 12 B.C. or earlier. By the mid-first century they were not consulted to the same degree as in the republic. The Sibylline books were supervised by the *QUINDECIMVIRI SACRIS FACIUNDIS*. There were many forgeries of the books as well as interpolations made by Jews and Christians, and fourteen miscellaneous books of oracles still survive.

The books are first known to have been consulted in 496 B.C. during a famine. When consulted, they demanded various courses of action, such as the building of temples, introduction of festivals, and introduction of new cults (such as that of MAGNA MATER in 204 B.C.).

Reading: Dowden 1992, 32–37; Hammond and Scullard (eds.) 1970, 984; Parke 1988; Potter 1990 (review article of Parke 1988).

Silenus A Greek god sometimes identified with the Roman god SILVANUS. Silenus was a deity of wildlife and was represented in art as half man and half animal. In the same way as FAUNS developed from the god FAUNUS, Silenus was often thought of in the plural as *Sileni*. The Sileni were often confused with SATYRS and with the Greek god PAN. It is often difficult to distinguish between portrayals of Sileni and Satyrs in art; Satyrs are usually portrayed as being young, but Sileni are more often regarded as old.

Reading: Howatson (ed.) 1989, 523; Johns 1982, 82, 84.

Silvanae Roman goddesses who were the female counterpart of the Roman god SILVANUS. These deities were mainly worshipped in the Roman province of Pannonia, but are also known from inscriptions found in most of the western empire. They appear to be similar to the nymphs who are normally associated with Silvanus. The number of Silvanae varies, but they are usually portrayed as a triad. Although they are similar to triads of Celtic deities, such as the MATRES, there is no conclusive evidence that the Silvanae were not Roman deities in origin, and they are usually interpreted as a particular type of NYMPH.

Reading: Dorcey 1992, 42–48.

Silvanus (Fig. 94) A Roman god of uncultivated land and woods, agriculture, hunting and boundaries. His cult is known from over 1,100 inscriptions, dating from at least as early as 39 B.C. to A.D. 339. In addition, there are many portrayals in various forms of art, ranging from statues to carved gemstones. His cult was concentrated in Italy, where over half the known dedications to him have been discovered. By contrast, he is hardly mentioned in Latin literature, possibly because he was a popular god of private rather than public religion: he had no state temple, festival or holy day. Silvanus had a great number of titles or epithets, and because his

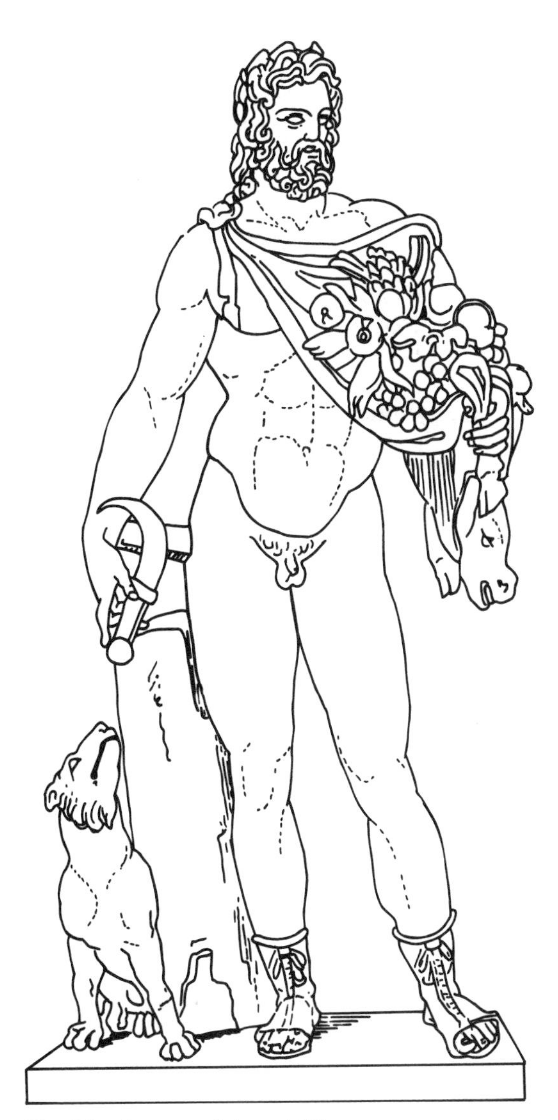

Fig. 94 A statue of the god Silvanus.

sphere of influence overlapped with that of FAUNUS, there was not always a clear distinction between the two gods.

Shrines dedicated to Silvanus were extremely numerous throughout the empire, and were usually very simple. He was often worshipped in conjunction with the nymphs. Particularly in the Roman province of Pannonia, he was worshipped in conjunction with the SILVANAE. Silvanus was sometimes identified with the Greek god SILENUS or with satyrs, but was more often identified with the Greek god PAN. Silvanus was sometimes identified with MARS, and in Gallia Narbonensis he was equated with the Celtic Hammer god. In Britain, he was identified with various local deities such as COCIDIUS in the Hadrian's Wall area, where he was probably a hunting god. He was also linked with NODENS at Lydney, England.

Reading: Dorcey 1992 (full discussion of Silvanus with list of epithets and identifications with other deities); Green, M. J. 1992a, 190–191.

Silvanus Calaedicus A Celtic god linked with the Roman god SILVANUS. This deity is known from a single inscription on an altar found near Logroño, Spain. There is some dispute as to whether the name *Calaedicus* refers to a separate deity or is just another name of Titullus, the person who dedicated the altar. However, *Calaedicus* has been interpreted as meaning "god of the rocky refuge who burns." This would be a suitable deity to be linked with Silvanus, one of whose many functions was the patron of quarrymen (fire was used to break up rock as a standard process in quarrying).

Reading: Dorcey 1992, 62–63.

Silvanus Callirius The Celtic god CALLIRIUS linked with the Roman god SILVANUS. He is known from a dedicatory inscription found at Colchester, England, that occurs on a bronze plaque. It was found buried in a pit near a rectangular shrine. Also in the pit was a small bronze FIGURINE of a stag, which may imply that the god was regarded as a deity who protected stags (as woodland game) and the hunters of stags. Callirius was a local woodland god whose name means "King of the Woodland" or "God of the Hazel Wood."

Reading: Green, M. J. 1992a, 191.

Silvanus Cocidius (Fig. 95) A Celtic god linked with the Roman god SILVANUS. This deity is known from two inscriptions found at Housesteads fort on Hadrian's Wall, England, and at Risingham fort to the north of Hadrian's Wall. At Risingham, the god is portrayed in sculptural relief as a hunter dressed

in a short tunic, carrying a bow and arrow and accompanied by a stag and a dog.
Reading: Dorcey 1992, 54–55.

Silvanus Maglae An inscription to Silvanus Maglae (or possibly Maglaenus) is known from the the Roman province of Pannonia Superior. It is thought that Maglae was a native Celtic god who was equated with the Roman god SILVANUS. However, nothing else is known about this deity, and it is possible that Maglae was merely a local descriptive title of Silvanus.
Reading: Dorcey 1992, 72.

Silvanus Poininus A local Celtic or possibly Thracian god equated with the Roman god SILVANUS. This deity is known from an inscription found at Turnovo, Bulgaria. It is possible that Poininus is the same deity as the Celtic god POENINUS.
Reading: Dorcey 1992, 75.

Silvanus Sinquas A Celtic god equated with the Roman god SILVANUS. This deity is known from an inscription from the Roman province of Belgica.
Reading: Dorcey 1992, 61.

Silvanus Vinotonus The Roman god Silvanus linked with the Celtic god VINOTONUS.

Sinquas A Celtic deity known from two inscriptions from the Roman province of Belgica. In one inscription, Sinquas is equated with the Roman god SILVANUS. Sinquas is also known as *Sinquatis* and *Sinquates* because of differing interpretations of the abbreviated form of the name which appears in the inscriptions.
Reading: Dorcey 1992, 61.

Sirona A Celtic goddess of healing, fertility and regeneration often associated with medicinal springs. She was probably the same deity as SARANA

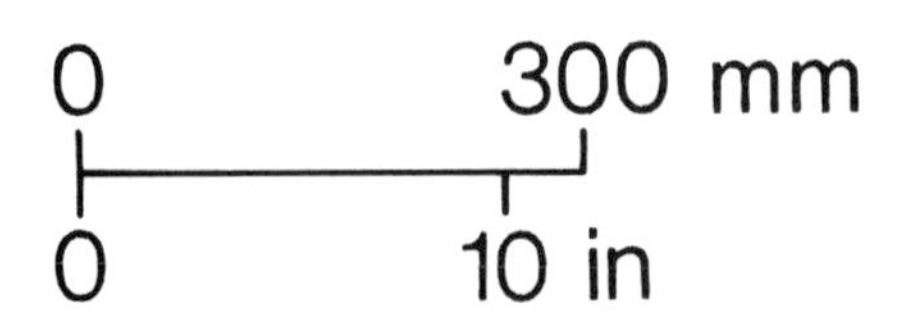

Fig. 95 An altar dedicated to Silvanus Cocidius, found at Housesteads on Hadrian's Wall, England. The inscription reads DEO SILVANO COCIDIO QV FLO RIVS MATERNVS PRAEF COH I TVNG VSLM ("To the god Silvanus Cocidius, Quintus Florius Maternus, prefect of the 1st cohort of Tungrians, willingly and deservedly fulfilled his vow").

and TSIRONA. She was frequently worshipped as the consort of APOLLO (usually APOLLO GRANNUS), and this divine couple was particularly venerated in the territory of the Treveri in Gaul. There was an important SHRINE dedicated to Sirona and Apollo at Hochscheid, between Trier and Mainz, Germany. Here a Romanized temple complex succeeded an unRomanized Celtic shrine. At Hochscheid, Sirona was portrayed wearing a diadem and carrying three eggs, which are symbols of fertility. A snake is shown curling around her arm. Elsewhere, Sirona is sometimes portrayed with cereal crops and fruit. Outside Treveran territory, Sirona was worshipped over a much wider area, from western France to Hungary.
Reading: Green, M. J. 1992a, 191–192; Green, M. J. 1992b, 224–226.

sistrum (Fig. 96) (pl. *sistra*) A rattle commonly used in the worship of ISIS. It was an instrument of Egyptian origin and one of the commonest symbols of the worship of Isis. It consisted of a metal loop with rods across it which made a tinkling sound when shaken. Some *sistra* (particularly their handles) were very ornate. They were normally of bronze, but silver ones are known and even gold was used. They were about 7.5–9.8 in. (190–250 mm) long. *Sistra* were carried and shaken by worshippers as part of the standard rituals of Isis to repel evil or as an expression of joy or mourning,

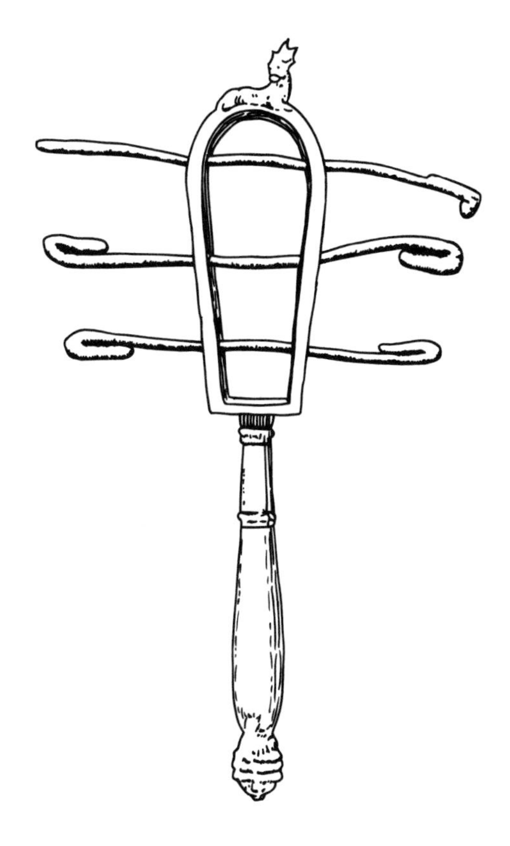

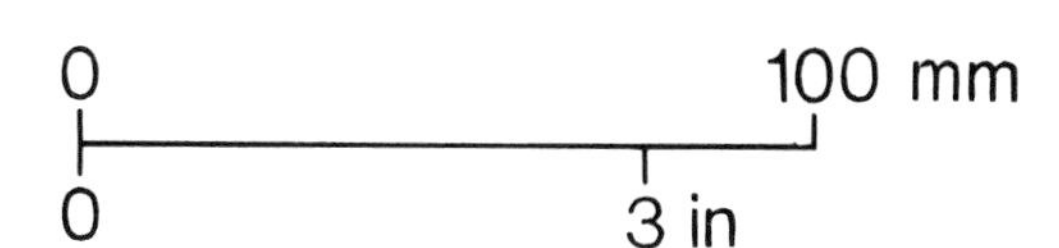

Fig. 96 A bronze sistrum *found at Nîmes, France, in the tomb of a priest of Isis. It has three bronze rods which rattled when shaken.*

situla (pl. *situlae*) A ritual bucket. ISIS is commonly portrayed with a *situla* containing holy Nile River water for sprinkling the worshippers, which was an important element in her cult. *Situlae* were also associated with other cults.

Smertrius A Celtic god of abundance known mainly from inscriptions found in Gaul. The name *Smertrius* appears to mean "the provider." He was sometimes linked with the Roman god MARS and worshipped as MARS SMERTRIUS. At Möhn near Trier, Germany, a shrine was dedicated to the divine couple Mars Smertrius and the Celtic goddess ANCAMNA.
Reading: Green, M. J. 1992a, 193.

snake (Fig. 97) (or serpent) In Greco-Roman thought (as in almost all pagan religions), the snake was beneficent, possessed of healing powers and considered as a *GENIUS* of good (Agathos Daimon). Snakes were valued for apotropaic and prophetic qualities and had a long association with fertility and healing deities and with the spirits of the UNDERWORLD (no doubt due to their ability to disappear into and emerge from crevices). The shedding

Fig. 97 A lararium *in the House of the Vettii, Pompeii, Italy. The wall painting shows the figure of the Genius of the* paterfamilias *between two Lares. Beneath them is the guardian snake of the hearth.*

of their skin each year led to snakes becoming a widespread and powerful symbol of eternal rebirth, and of rejuvenation and renewed health. Snakes were portrayed with various deities. In particular, they were associated with AESCULAPIUS, who often held a snake-entwined staff, as did HYGEIA. At the sanctuary of Epidaurus in Greece, a type of snake *(Elaphe longissima longissima)* was found which was harmless to humans and sacred to Asclepius (Aesculapius). In his cult, snakes were sometimes the intermediary through which the god's cures were performed. When new shrines were established, a snake was fetched from Epidaurus to represent the god. Because of a plague at Rome in 293 B.C., a sacred Aesculapian snake was sent from the Epidaurus sanctuary to Rome as an incarnation of the god (Fig. 1); the snake was apparently instrumental in abating the plague and chose the Tiber Island for its abode, where a temple was built.

Snakes were associated with other healing deities: for example, harmless snakes were allowed to roam freely in the precinct of the temple of Bona Dea Subsaxana (see BONA DEA) at Rome. In art, the snake is also used to represent the *genius*. Snake-headed bracelets with snake-head terminals are common items of Roman jewelry, as were similar spiral finger rings. CHRISTIANITY changed the perception of snakes, making them an enemy of the people and a demon of evil.

Reading: Brouwer 1989, 340–348 (in relation to *Bona Dea*); Green, M. J. 1992b, 182–183, 224–230; Jackson 1988, 142–143; Tudor 1976, 219–224.

sodales Members of minor priesthoods. They included the *fetiales* (see FETIALIS), ARVAL PRIESTS, *SALII* and *luperci.* They ranked below the *collegia* (colleges) of priesthoods. The *sodales Titii* (or *Titienses*) were priests of pre-republican origin about whom little is known. Other *sodales* were instituted at a later date, such as the *sodales Augustales* who were responsible for the cult of Augustus, and the *sodales Hadrianales* who were responsible for the cult of Hadrian.
Reading: Hammond and Scullard (eds.) 1970, 998–999.

Sol The Roman god of the sun. From its earliest days, Rome must have worshipped a solar deity, who later became identified with the Greek god HELIOS. From the first century B.C., this worship of Sol became increasingly important, and SOL INDIGES was probably the same as this deity. There was a temple of Sol and LUNA (usually referred to as the temple of Sol) on the southwestern side of the CIRCUS MAXIMUS in Rome; it was probably built in the first century B.C. There was a festival on August 28. Although the sun had been worshipped as a deity in eastern cults for centuries, at this stage the cult of Sol was not an eastern one. There are many inscriptions to Sol and Luna, but outside Rome and Italy the worship of Sol is less frequent. From the second century the eastern sun worship began to influence Rome, and the ancient Sol cult declined.
Reading: Ferguson 1970, 49–56; Halsberghe 1972, 26–44; Hammond and Scullard (eds.) 1970, 999.

Sol Indiges (possibly meaning "native sun") An early Roman sun god, probably the same as SOL. There was a festival of Sol Indiges on August 9, and this deity may have been worshipped during the AGONALIA on December 11. There was a temple on the Quirinal Hill in Rome which was dedicated on August 9.
Reading: Halsberghe 1972, 33; Hammond and Scullard (eds.) 1970, 999; Scullard 1981, 203.

Sol Invictus (Fig. 98) ("unconquered sun") Also called Sol Invictus El Gabal, Sol Invictus Elagabal, El Gabal and Elagabalus. Sol Invictus was a Syrian sun deity whose cult spread across the empire beginning in the second century, leading to the decline of the traditional cult of SOL in Rome and Italy. The cult was usually known just as Sol Invictus and was associated with MITHRAISM; the epithet *Elagabal* was rarely used until the time of the emperor ELAGABALUS (218–222). In Syria, this sun deity was a BAAL known as El Gabal (or Elagabal). Elagabalus had been a boy-priest of this deity at Emesa in Syria, and may have regarded himself as a reincarnation of the god. After his accession, he actively promoted the worship of this deity, and brought its sacred stone to Rome. Elagabalus attempted to establish Sol Invictus Elagabal as the supreme Roman god and built two temples to Sol Invictus Elagabalus in Rome; one was on the Palatine Hill and the other on the outskirts of the city. However, the excesses of his rule and his assassination checked the growth of sun worship for some time.

Fig. 98 A follis *of Constantine the Great depicting on its reverse the god Sol Invictus. The legend reads SOLI INVICTO COMITI ("To the ally Sol Invictus").*

The sun god (as Deus Sol Invictus) was established as a supreme Roman deity by the emperor Aurelian in the late third century. In 274 Aurelian built a temple to Sol Invictus at Rome and established a college of senators as *pontifices dei Solis* (priests of the sun god). Particularly under Aurelian, the imperial power became closely connected with the cult of the sun, and some coins from this time have the legend SOL DOMINVS IMPERI ROMANI ("Sol Lord of the Roman empire"). Later emperors inherited this connection, and some coins of Constantine bear the legend SOLI INVICTO

COMITI, describing Sol Invictus as "ally" of the emperor.

It has been suggested that the cult of the sun influenced the east-west orientation of burials of the deceased, so that the dead arose to face the rising sun on the day of resurrection. It is more certain that the festival of the birthday of Sol Invictus (on December 25—the midwinter solstice in the Julian calendar) could not be suppressed by CHRISTIANITY. Consequently, in the fourth century (between 354 and 360) the festival was made out to be the celebration of the birthday of Christ instead (which had been previously held on the day of Epiphany on January 6). The festivities of the SATURNALIA, held on December 17–23 and immediately preceding the sun's birthday, also came to be absorbed into the Christian festival of Christmas. Similarly, the proclamation of Sunday as a day of rest in A.D. 321 was originally in honor of the sun god.
Reading: Ferguson 1970, 52–53; Halsberghe 1972; Hammond and Scullard (eds.) 1970, 999 (under *Sol*); Richardson 1992, 142 (the temples).

Sol Invictus, temple of A temple built by the emperor Aurelian after his victories in the east in 273. It was known as Templum Solis Aureliani. The size or form of the temple is not known, but it was renowned for its lavish Oriental decoration. A huge structure recorded by Palladio east of the Via del Corso and west of San Silvestro church in Rome may represent this temple.
Reading: Halsberghe 1972, 142–144; Richardson 1992, 363–364.

Soranus A Sabine sun god who was often identified with APOLLO (as APOLLO SORANUS) and sometimes with DIS PATER. Apollo Soranus was worshipped at the top of Mount Soracte, 26 miles (41.84 km) to the north of Rome, in rites conducted by the Hirpi ("wolves"). These were the priests of the cult, who danced barefoot on burning wood during the rites. According to legend, this priesthood originated when wolves ran off with part of the sacrifice being offered to Dis Pater. The wolves took refuge in a cave which was so full of noxious fumes that it killed their pursuers and spread disease over the countryside. The people then consulted a soothsayer who told them that to appease the gods they must behave like wolves and become predators.
Reading: Grimal 1986, 217; Hammond and Scullard (eds.) 1970, 1,003 (under *Soracte*).

Sortes Vergilianae (Virgilian Lots) The practice of selecting lines of Virgil's poetry at random and interpreting their meaning in order to foretell the future. After the death of the poet Virgil, his fame increased to the point of superstitious reverence. Attempts were made to prophesy the future by opening books of his poetry and reading a line at random. This was widely practiced from Hadrian's time.

Souconna A Celtic deity and personification of the Saône River at Chalon-sur-Saône, France.
Reading: Green, M. J. 1992a, 196.

spelaeum (or *speleum*) A term meaning a cave or grotto and often used for the temples of MITHRAS (which imitated caves) rather than the word *MITHRAEUM.*

Spes A Roman goddess who was the personification of hope. She had a temple in the FORUM HOLITORIUM in Rome (Fig. 15) which had been dedicated in the First Punic War, and another on the Esquiline Hill dedicated to Spes Vetus ("Ancient Hope"). She was sometimes referred to as Spes Populi Romani ("Hope of the Roman People") or as Spes Augusta (meaning "hope of empire through the imperial family"). Spes was sometimes portrayed holding an opening flower and holding up her long skirt as if about to hurriedly run off. She had a festival on August 1.
Reading: Hammond and Scullard (eds.) 1970, 1009; Richardson 1992, 365.

Spiniensis The Roman deity who presided over the digging out of thorn bushes and who guarded the fields against thorns.
Reading: Ferguson 1988a, 853.

spirit A supernatural, incorporeal being. The majority of Roman deities and *numina* were spirits of the local environment. Every place, object and process (even individual trees and rivers) could have its own spirit. Consequently, there were almost limitless numbers of spirits, and most were nameless. In practice, a Roman would not worship all these deities, but only those closely associated with his or her own home and occupation. For example, propitiation of a local river spirit would be necessary to ensure a good water supply and guard against flooding or drowning. (See also *NUMEN*.)

spring, sacred The Romans believed that every spring, pool or river was sacred, and many had shrines associated with them. In Gaul, for example, more than 400 deities are known to have been deities of water or associated with water. There were some particularly popular shrines, such as that of the goddess SEQUANA at the source of the Seine River in France, and the huge healing shrine of SULIS MINERVA at the thermal springs of Bath in England. At Rome, the LACUS IUTURNAE (a shrine associated with the spring of JUTURNA) played an important part in religious rites. (See also FONS, FONTINALIA, NYMPH.)
Reading: Bourgeois 1991 and 1992; Cunliffe (ed.) 1988 (finds from the sacred spring at Bath); Hammond and Scullard (eds.) 1970, 1010.

standard A distinctive emblem on a long pole used as a focal point for each military unit (in the same way as flags were later used). The standards were very important to the army as the embodiment of the luck or power of their military unit. As cult symbols they were worshipped at various times during the year. Tertullian (a Christian writer) stated that the soldiers venerated the standards above all gods. Each permanent military unit (especially legions) had a shrine which was under the care of the First Cohort. In it were kept statues of deities and of the emperor and the standards. In a legionary fortress the standards were kept in a shrine in the *principia* (headquarters building), and if the standards were lost during a campaign, the unit suffering the loss might be disbanded. The standards were tended on feast days, and there was usually an ALTAR dedicated at least to the eagle standard *(aquila)* which each legion possessed. The most important annual festival in which the standards were honored was known as the Rosaliae Signorum (crowning of the standards). This festival is noted in the CALENDAR of Dura-Europus *(FERIALE DURANUM)*, and implies that the standards were garlanded with roses. There are relatively few dedicatory inscriptions that refer to the standards. An altar from High Rochester fort, north of Hadrian's Wall, England, was dedicated to the "Genius and the Standards of the Cohort" by the First Cohort of the Vardulli (a unit of Roman soldiers from Spain). In this case, it is not clear whether the "Genius" is that of the cohort or some other *GENIUS* such as that of the emperor.
Reading: Burn 1969, 148–149; Hammond and Scullard (eds.) 1970, 937 (under *Rosalia*), 1011; Henig 1984, 90–91; Phillips 1977, 62.

Stanna A Celtic goddess who is known from three inscriptions found at Périgueux, France, where she is invoked with the Celtic goddess TELO.
Reading: Green, M. J. 1992a, 208.

Stata Mater Also known as Stata, a Roman goddess who provided protection against fire and was associated with VOLCANUS QUIETUS.
Reading: Hammond and Scullard (eds.) 1970, 1,131 (under *Volcanus*); Richardson 1992, 368.

Statanus An alternative name for the Roman god STATULINUS.

state religion Many different religions existed throughout the Roman world, but there was a collection of beliefs and rituals which was considered by the citizens of Rome to be their particular religion. This was generally known as the "state religion" because it was thought to ensure the preservation and prosperity of the city state. (See Introduction, pp. xvii–xviii.)

Statulinus A Roman god, also known as Statanus or Statilinus, who presided over a child's first attempts to stand up.
Reading: Ferguson 1988a, 853.

Sterculinus A Roman god who presided over the spreading of manure on the fields. Also known as Stercutus or Sterculus, he was thought to have invented the practice of fertilizing by using manure. He was sometimes regarded as the father of the Roman god PICUS and so was identified with SATURN (also regarded as father of Picus).
Reading: Ferguson 1988a, 853.

Stimula A Roman goddess whose function is unknown but who continued to be recognized to the time of Augustine. She had a grove in which the followers of BACCHUS met (until 186 B.C., when the BACCHANALIA was suppressed by the Senate). Stimula was therefore sometimes confused with Semele, the legendary mother of the Greek god DIONYSUS (who was equated with Bacchus).
Reading: Hammond and Scullard (eds.) 1970, 1014; Richardson 1992, 236.

Stoicism A philosophy developed by the Greeks in the late third and early second centuries B.C. after it had been founded by Zeno c. 300 B.C. Zeno's doctrine held that the only real good was virtue and the only real evil was moral weakness. Everything else, such as poverty, pain, and death, were treated with indifference. Happiness was attained by the wise person retaining his or her virtue. Official Roman policy generally favored the Stoics, its most famous proponents being Seneca the Younger and Marcus Aurelius. The Stoics were pantheists and determinists. They believed that people's part in the divine plan was determined, so that they only had freedom in the way that part was played, not a choice of what part to play. Consequently, the Stoics advocated acceptance of whatever life had to offer, good or bad. They also believed that after death the soul left the body and remained in the atmosphere until it was dissolved into the great spirit of the universe. The evidence from inscriptions on tombstones suggests that this philosophy had a significant effect on people's views on religion and the AFTERLIFE.
Reading: Ferguson 1970, 193–194; Hammond and Scullard (eds.) 1970, 1145 (under *Zeno*).

Strenia A Roman goddess of health and vigor. At Rome she had a grove from which twigs were taken and exchanged as presents at New Year. These twigs, called *strenae*, were thought to bring good luck.
Reading: Hammond and Scullard (eds.) 1970, 1019 (under *Strenae*).

Subruncinator A Roman deity who presided over the weeding of the fields. He was said by Fabius Pictor in the late third century B.C. to have been invoked by a priest of CERES.
Reading: Ferguson 1988a, 853; York 1986, 60.

Sucellus ("the good striker") A Celtic Hammer god who is usually portrayed as a mature bearded male with the identifying symbol of a long-handled hammer. He often occurs with a consort, the Celtic goddess NANTOSUELTA ("winding river" or "meandering brook"), who generally carries a model of a house on a long pole. Dedicatory inscriptions to this divine couple are known from Gaul. Some stone carvings depicting similar deities have no dedicatory inscriptions, but are usually taken to be of Sucellus and Nantosuelta. Such images are known from Gaul, Germany and Britain. Sucellus and Nantosuelta are often accompanied by other symbols such as barrels, pots, dogs and ravens, from which it is assumed that they were associated with beneficence, domesticity and prosperity. The hammer may denote a connection with thunder, rain and fertility.
Reading: Green, M. J. 1984, 142–144; Green, M. J. 1992a, 157–158, 200.

Suleviae A triad of Celtic mother goddesses who were worshipped in Gaul, Britain, Germany, Hungary and Rome itself. In Gaul they were sometimes called Matres Suleviae or were identified with the plural form of JUNO as Suleviae Iunones. An altar dedicated to the Suleviae formed part of the religious complex of SULIS MINERVA at Bath, England. The Suleviae were concerned with fertility, healing and regeneration as well as maternity, and their cult was widespread.
Reading: Green, M. J. 1992a, 200.

Sulis Minerva A Celtic healing goddess who was linked with the Roman goddess MINERVA. She was worshipped at the sacred thermal springs at Bath, England, where a pre-Roman shrine was converted to a massive religious complex in the late first century. The springs were enclosed and fed a large ornamental pool, and a temple and bath suite were built nearby. A number of other Celtic and Roman deities were also worshipped in this religious complex, including the SULEVIAE. Dedications to this deity invoke her as Sulis or Sulis Minerva; the Celtic name alway precedes the Roman one, showing that Sulis was the long-established deity of the springs.
Reading: Cunliffe (ed.) 1988; Cunliffe and Davenport 1985a and 1985b; Green, M. J. 1992a, 200–202.

Summanus A Roman god who was closely associated with JUPITER, possibly originally an aspect

of Jupiter rather than a separate deity. Summanus appears to have been the god who wielded thunderbolts (or lightning) by night, as Jupiter wielded them by day. In Rome there was a temple near the CIRCUS MAXIMUS. Sacrifices of black wethers and cakes shaped liked wheels (called *summanalia*) were made to this god. There was a festival of Summanus on June 20.
Reading: Grimal 1986, 428; Scullard 1981, 153–155; York 1986, 134.

Summanus, temple of A temple built during the wars with Pyrrhus (280–275 B.C.), possibly after a statue of SUMMANUS on the pediment of the temple of JUPITER OPTIMUS MAXIMUS had been struck by lightning and the head of the statue was thrown into the Tiber River. This was interpreted as a sign that Summanus wanted his own temple. The temple was probably on the west side of the CIRCUS MAXIMUS, and was itself struck by lightning in 197 B.C. It was dedicated on June 20. It may have been standing in the fourth century but no remains have been found.
Reading: Richardson 1992, 373–374; Scullard 1981, 153–154.

suovetaurilia (Fig. 99) The combined sacrifice of the principal agricultural animals, a boar *(sus)*,

Fig. 99 A boar, ram and a bull being led round a military camp in a ritual procession by the victimarii, *prior to the sacrifice of the animals to Mars (the* suovetaurilia*). They are accompanied by horn and trumpet players. The scene is on Trajan's Column, Rome.*

ram *(ovis)* and bull *(taurus)*. This type of sacrifice was made at certain agricultural festivals and on other occasions such as at the conclusion of a military campaign or a census. These animals were used especially in rites of lustration and they were paraded around the object of lustration before being sacrificed.

superstition The irrational fear of the unknown allied to a false idea of the causes of events. Superstition sprang from the same origin as religion, in a belief in supernatural forces that control the lives of people. Although the entire Roman religion was based on superstition, it was not (in the Roman period) regarded as superstitious in the modern sense. Superstitions and associated charms and rituals are often very ancient and extremely long-lived, since many superstitions current today are attested in Roman literature, such as saying "good health" (nowadays "bless you" is more common) when someone sneezes.

The Latin term *superstitio* may have originally meant prophetic ability or state of religious exaltation; it came to mean superstitious and irrational awe or credulity, most particularly when applied to foreign or non-orthodox religious practices, such as DRUIDISM and JUDAISM, or even the popular religion of the countryside. It could be used in a contemptuous way. In the first and second centuries, the term *superstitio* gradually came to be associated with dangerous foreign religions rather than peasant religions. The retention of pagan beliefs by Christians was later regarded as a form of superstition.
Reading: Gordon 1990c, 237–238, 253; Hammond and Scullard (eds.) 1970, 1,023–1,024; Paoli 1963, 279–291.

Symaethis A Roman water NYMPH who was the daughter of the Roman river god SYMAETHUS and mother of the Roman river god ACIS.
Reading: Grimal 1986, 8 (under *Acis*).

Symaethus The Roman god of the Symaethus River, near Catana, Sicily.

Symmachus Quintus Aurelius Symmachus, c. 340–402. A wealthy Roman noble, a distinguished orator, an ardent supporter of the state pagan religion and the leading opponent of CHRISTIANITY of his time. Extant are 10 books containing more than 900 of his letters which he composed for publication; the first nine books are letters to friends and the tenth is official correspondence comprising 49 dispatches *(relationes)*, including his unsuccessful appeal in 384 to Valentinian II for the restoration of the Altar of Victory (and hence PAGANISM) in the Senate house; Eugenius subsequently restored the altar.
Reading: Hammond and Scullard (eds.) 1970, 1,027–1,028.

synagogue (literally, "a gathering for prayer and reading") Assembly houses for prayer and worship by dispersed Jewish communities far from the temple at Jerusalem. The term *synagogue* primarily denoted the organized group rather than the building itself (which was known as a prayer house). Such houses of prayer date back to at least the third century B.C. in Egypt, and it appears that a deliberate attempt was made to avoid copying the temples of pagan deities. The fundamental difference between pagan temples and early synagogues was that the temples were regarded as the home of gods, with worshippers remaining outside, whereas synagogues were for prayer, worship, study, education, debate, assembly on a Sabbath, and collecting the temple tax and funds for the maintenance of the synagogue. With this difference in function, synagogues were modelled on Greek and Roman assembly halls, with smaller halls for other functions such as legal business. As a result, there is no distinctive architecture or layout that distinguishes early synagogues. Many, if not most, dispersed Jewish communities had a synagogue by the first century A.D., which the Romans classified as *collegia*, and the number of synagogues increased as Jewish communities became more widespread through the empire. Thirteen synagogues are known to have existed in Rome, and even before the destruction of the second temple in Jerusalem in 70, there were many synagogues in Jerusalem itself. There is evidence for many synagogues in the province of Asia, and the one at Alexandria was a huge five-aisled basilica.
Reading: Smallwood 1976.

Syrian Goddess An alternative name for the goddess ATARGATIS.

T

Talassius A Roman god of marriage who was also known as Talassus, Talasius, Talassis or Thalassius. He appears to have been invented to explain the ritual cry of *talassio* when the bride was escorted to the groom's house, the original meaning of which had been lost.

Tameobrigus An Iberian deity who was worshipped at the confluence of the Douro and Támega rivers, Spain.
Reading: Tranoy 1981, 277.

Tanarus A Celtic thunder god who is known from an inscription found at Chester, England, where he was equated with the Roman god JUPITER as Jupiter Optimus Maximus Tanarus. He is also known from an inscription found at Orgon, France and is thought to be the same deity as TARANIS.
Reading: Green, M. J. 1986, 65–67.

Tanit A Carthaginian moon goddess who originated in Phoenicia and was also known as ASTARTE. In the Roman period, she was a mother and fertility goddess, generally known to the Romans as DEA CAELESTIS, JUNO CAELESTIS or VIRGO CAELESTIS. There was a shrine dedicated to Virgo Caelestis on the CAPITOLINE HILL in Rome.
Reading: Ferguson 1970, 215–216.

Taran A Celtic thunder god who is known from an inscription found at Tours, France. He is thought to be the same deity as TARANIS.
Reading: Green, M. J. 1986, 65–67.

Taranis ("thunderer") A Celtic thunder god who was probably the same deity as TANARUS, TARAN, TARANUS, TARANUCUS and TARANUCNUS. Taranis is mentioned by the Roman poet Lucan, who wrote in the first century A.D. about events that took place in the first century B.C. In his poem *Pharsalia* (book I, lines 444–446), he mentions Taranis, whose cult he describes as more cruel than that of Scythian DIANA and which required human sacrifice. Seven altars dedicated to gods whose names are variations of Taranis are known from Britain, Germany, France and the Roman province of Dalmatia. This god was sometimes conflated with the Roman god JUPITER. Jupiter may also be conflated with the Celtic sun-wheel god, and so Taranis has sometimes been identified with the Celtic sun-wheel god. However, there is no direct evidence that Taranis was regarded as a sun god, and it is likely that Jupiter, as omnipotent sky god, combined the functions of both thunder and sun god. Despite being one of the few Celtic gods mentioned in Roman literature, the archaeological evidence does not support Lucan's claim that Taranis was an important and powerful Celtic deity.
Reading: Green, M. J. 1984, 251–57; Green, M. J. 1992a, 205–207.

Taranucnus A Celtic thunder god who is known from inscriptions found at Böckingen and Godramstein, Germany. He is thought to be the same deity as TARANIS.
Reading: Green, M. J. 1986a, 65–67.

Taranucus A Celtic thunder god who is known from an inscription found at Thauron, France, where he is equated with the Roman god JUPITER as Jupiter Taranucus. He is thought to be the same deity as TARANIS.
Reading: Green, M. J. 1986a, 65–67.

Taranus A Celtic thunder god who is known from an inscription found at Scardona (modern Skradin), in the Roman province of Dalmatia, where he was equated with the Roman god JUPITER as Jupiter Taranus. He is thought to be the same deity as TARANIS.
Reading: Green, M. J. 1986a, 66–67.

Tarentum (or Terentum) A place on the edge of the CAMPUS MARTIUS in Rome, near the Tiber River. A small volcanic fissure once emitted vapor here, and it was believed to be a point of communication with the UNDERWORLD. An altar to DIS and PROSERPINA was discovered here; it was uncovered for sacrifices at the LUDI SAECULARES.
Reading: Richardson 1992, 377.

Tarraco, temple at Permission was given by the Senate at Rome in A.D. 15 to build a provincial temple at Tarraco, Spain, which was dedicated to Divus Augustus (specifically Aeternitas, the "eternity" of Augustus). It was the first provincial temple dedicated to the IMPERIAL CULT. From the evidence of coins, it was an OCTASTYLE temple with composite capitals. This temple would have been a focus of worship in the province of Tarraconensis. Building work was started late in Tiberius's reign, and the temple was completed at the start of Vespasian's reign. It was restored by Hadrian at his own expense. It was used as a quarry for the later medieval cathedral at Tarraco, but evidence for it is otherwise slight.

An altar is known to have existed at Tarraco, possibly sited near the temple or else in the lower forum. The date of its erection is uncertain, possibly c. 26 B.C. It was probably a municipal (not a provincial) altar dedicated to ROMA and Augustus.
Reading: Fishwick 1987, 150–154, 171–179.

Tarvostrigaranus ("the bull with three cranes") Probably a Celtic deity. The name is inscribed on a sculptured stone panel found at Paris, France, which depicts a willow tree, a bull and three marsh birds (cranes or egrets). It was part of a monument dedicated to the Roman god JUPITER during Tiberius's reign (14–31) by a guild of sailors. Another relief sculpture on the same monument is inscribed "Esus" (a Celtic god).

A similar sculpture dedicated to Tarvostrigaranus is known from Trier, Germany, dedicated in the first century by Indus, a member of the tribe of Mediomatrici. Representations of MERCURY and ROSMERTA are on another face of this stone, and on another a woodcutter is depicted hacking at a willow tree in which there are the heads of a bull and three marsh birds.

In both the Paris and Trier sculptures, other gods are represented, and the stones form part of a religious dedication. The sculptures contain many elements that occur as symbols in Celtic religion and mythology, such as the bull, the cranes and the number three; the sculptures may represent fertility and the cycle of death and rebirth. It is likely that they are Celtic in origin or have strong Celtic influence, but the exact significance of the Tarvostrigaranus sculpture is unclear.
Reading: Green, M. J. 1992a, 207–208.

taurobolium (Fig. 100) (pl. *taurobolia*) A rite of MAGNA MATER (Cybele) and ATTIS involving the killing of a bull. This ritual originated in Asia Minor, first appearing in the west at Puteoli in Italy in 134 in the cult of VENUS CAELESTIS (which is mentioned in an inscription). It was carried out more frequently from the second quarter of the second century, and spread throughout western provinces, especially Gaul. In about 160 the *taurobolium* became incorporated into the cult of Magna Mater. It was originally a form of SACRIFICE in which the *archigallus* stood in a pit. A similar rite using a ram was known as the *criobolium*.

The ceremonies took place throughout the year, and were not related to the March and April festivals of Magna Mater and Attis. From about the year 225, inscriptions refer to a ceremony with the *vires* (possibly the bull's blood or testicles) being caught in a *cernus* (a sacrifical bowl composed of several attached cups). From about the year 300, the *taurobolium* developed into a baptism rite of blood, and the element of sacrifice was forgotten. The worshipper stood in a pit or ditch, while a bull was sacrificed on a slatted floor above, bathing the person in its blood. Many votive altars commemorating a *taurobolium* or a *criobolium* have been found in nearly every Roman province, particularly in Africa, Italy and Gaul.
Reading: Duthoy 1969; Gasparro 1985, 107–118; Vermaseren 1977, 101–107.

tauroctony (Fig. 101) In MITHRAISM, the ritual slaying of a bull by MITHRAS in a cave. The slaying

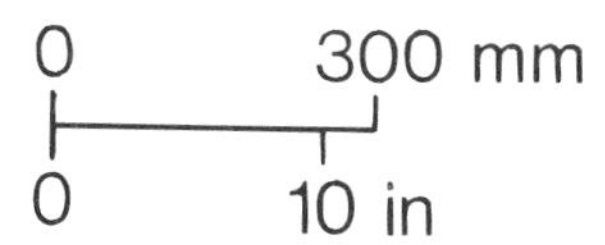

Fig. 100 A taurobolium *altar from Périgueux, France, one of the most ornate altars depicting the* taurobolium. *This side shows the head of a bull and the sacrificial implement and vessels. Another side depicted the bust of Attis in front of a pine tree as well as a bull and a Phrygian cap. The third side showed a ram's head and cymbals, and the fourth bore a dedication.*

Fig. 101 A bull-slaying (tauroctony) relief sculpture of Mithras discovered in about 1877 on the Esquiline Hill in Rome. Height 4 ft., 1 in. (1.25 m).

was often depicted in *mithraea* in sculptured reliefs. The killing of the bull symbolizes Mithras being sent by Ahura Mazda to hunt and kill a divine bull (Ahura Mazda's first creation), from which all living things sprang.
Reading: Cumont 1896 (numerous illustrations).

Tellumo A Roman god who was a male personification of the productive power of the earth and probably the same deity as TELLURUS. He was associated with TELLUS, a Roman goddess who was a female personification of the productive power of the earth.
Reading: York 1986, 69.

Tellura A Roman goddess who was the personification of the productive power of the earth.

Tellurus A Roman god who was probably the same deity as TELLUMO.

Tellus A Roman earth goddess who was a female personification of the productive power of the earth. She was associated with other agricultural deities such as TELLUMO, ALTOR, RUSOR and CERES. She was also known as Tellus Mater ("Tellus Mother"). There was a temple to Tellus at Rome dedicated in 268 B.C. and a festival of Tellus on December 13. She was worshipped, with other deities, in agricultural festivals such as the SEMENTIVAE in January and the FORDICIDIA in April. A sacrifice of a cake made from spelt (a type of wheat producing a fine flour) and a pregnant sow was also made to her on the first day of the festival of Sementivae.
Reading: Hammond and Scullard (eds.) 1970, 1,042; Scullard 1981, 204; Simon 1990, 206–209.

Tellus, temple of Vowed by Publius Sempronius Sophus when an earthquake occurred during a battle with the Picenes. It was dedicated in 268 B.C. The temple was situated in Rome on the Carinae (the western end of the Oppius near the church of San Pietro in Vincoli). It may have been a rebuilding of an earlier temple. The Senate met at the temple once, when it was summoned there by Mark Antony the day after Julius Caesar's assassination.
Reading: Richardson 1992, 378–379.

Telo A Celtic goddess who was the personification of the town of Toulon, France: she was the goddess of the sacred spring around which the town developed. Dedications to Telo are also known from Périgueux, France, where on three occasions she is associated with a Celtic goddess called Stanna.
Reading: Green, M. J. 1992a, 208.

temenos (pl. *temenoi*) The Greek word for a sacred enclosure, often with a temple building or shrine. It was equivalent to a *TEMPLUM*.
Reading: Hammond and Scullard (eds.) 1970, 1,042.

Tempestates Roman goddesses of weather. A temple to the Tempestates was vowed by Lucius Cornelius Scipio, consul in 259 B.C., after he had survived a great storm at sea off Corsica during the First Punic War. It was situated in Rome outside the Porta Capena, possibly near the tomb of the Scipios. The day of dedication was either June 1 or December 23.
Reading: Richardson 1992, 379; Scullard 1981, 127.

temple A building dedicated to a deity. Temples were designed to house a statue of the deity and store votive offerings, and were not intended to provide accommodation for a congregation of worshippers. They accumulated numerous treasures, many of which were ransacked in the early Christian period. Temples were also used as safe deposits; one case of such a purpose was the temple of SATURN.

Many temples may have been preceded by altars or shrines to the deities concerned. The earliest Roman temples were probably built of timber with a skin of decorative plaques and sculptures in terracotta, and later were replaced with more substantial stone buildings. Many of the major temples in Rome were paid for from the spoils of war *(de manubiis)*, built by successful generals to mark their achievements. Others were paid for out of public funds, on authority of the Senate during the republic, or later by order of the emperor. Augustus, probably the most prolific temple-building emperor, is recorded in the *Res Gestae* as having restored 82 temples in 28 B.C. and as having built (or rebuilt) 12 temples. In towns outside Rome, temples appear to have been paid for out of public funds or by leading citizens.

Greek temples usually had their entrance doors at the east end and the cult statue in front of the west wall of the cella, but there appear to have been no fixed rules for the orientation of Roman temples, whose axes often seem to have been determined by the constraints of town planning. The original orientation seems to have been determined by the area of sky in which the AUGUR was taking AUSPICES. There were many styles of temples, and in many areas indigenous styles of architecture were used, such as the Romano-Celtic temples in the Celtic provinces and a mixture of styles in the eastern provinces, suggesting that there was also a continuity of traditional methods of worship.

Apart from priests, temples usually had a staff of servants such as clerks, gatekeepers for security, slaves and menials for general maintenance, acolytes for processions and ceremonies, and in some cases guides and interpreters to look after visitors. Many temples had been destroyed before the Christian period, although a few were converted to churches.
Reading: Barton 1989; Lyttelton 1987 (temples in Asia Minor); Price 1984, 133–169, 249–274 (imperial temples in Asia Minor, including a gazetteer);

Ramage and Ramage 1991 (includes numerous examples with illustrations); Richardson 1992, 1–2.

temple, classical (Figs. 16, 33, 56, 102) A temple that conforms to a particular style, either Greek or Roman. Their common style is a rectangular plan, with columns all or part of the way round. Early Roman classical temples were based on Etruscan traditions. They were raised on a high platform *(podium)* with a broad flight of steps only at the front. There were vaults beneath some podia, which reduced the amount of material used in the construction and could themselves be used for religious rites and storage. At the top of the steps there was a facade of columns (generally HEXASTYLE or OCTASTYLE). On the facade above the columns, there was normally an inscription naming the deity of the temple and perhaps the name of the person who paid for its construction. These inscriptions were frequently made with bronze letters. Behind the facade was a deep entrance porch *(pronaos)*, which could occupy half the length of the temple. Behind this porch was the cella, which contained a statue of the god and possibly a small altar for incense. The cella had solid walls along the side and rear.

Greek classical temples had a small flight of steps all round the building and were designed to be viewed from any angle (Fig. 109); in Roman temples the emphasis was placed on the front of the temple (Fig. 84), with no space to walk round the entire temple. This basic plan gradually evolved from the late republic. This "frontal" type of temple also became more common in the eastern Hellenistic provinces, although Hellenistic architectural styles persisted. Using arches, vaults and domes, the Romans also developed styles of their own, such as the circular temple of VESTA (Fig. 102). There was an altar for sacrifice outside temples, usually placed directly in front of the steps.

Although varying a great deal in plan and details of design, temples recognizable as classical in type are known throughout the empire, although in the Celtic provinces Romano-Celtic temples were far more common, especially outside towns. Even so, it is likely that each main provincial town had at least one classical-style temple.

Reading: Barton 1989; Blagg 1990.

Fig. 102 A medallion of Julia Domna (empress 193–211) showing six Vestal Virgins sacrificing in front of the round temple of Vesta, which had just been rebuilt by the empress.

temple, North African A type of temple style found in North Africa and which has a limited distribution. Its distinguishing feature is a row of three small chambers occupying most, or all, of one side of an enclosure or courtyard. Although often built in classical Roman style, they lack the high podium and impressive facade that are common features of classical temples. They are probably a combination of Roman and Punic traditions of temple architecture; good examples of this type occur at Thugga, Tunisia.

Reading: Charles-Picard 1954.

temple, Romano-Celtic (Figs. 103a, b) Romano-Celtic (or Gallo-Roman) style of temple widespread in the Celtic provinces of Gaul, Germany and Britain, although examples have been found as far east as Budapest (Aquincum) in Pannonia. They are found on villa estates, in major rural sanctuaries (some with theaters and baths) and local cult centers, on hilltops and in towns; some towns (such as Colchester, England, and Trier, Germany) had several Romano-Celtic temples. Many temples were inside or adjacent to Iron Age hill forts and oppida (large settlements or towns), such

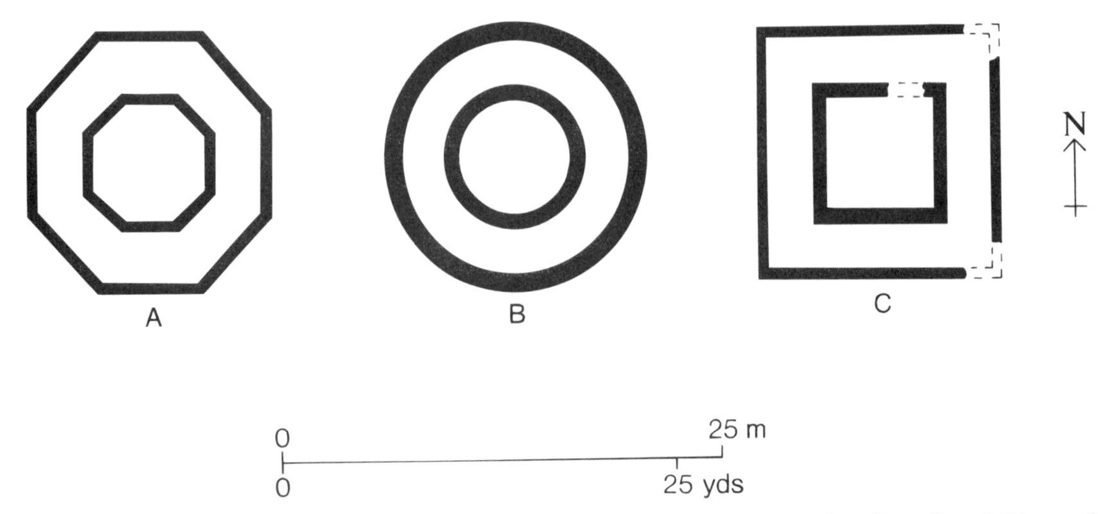

Fig. 103a Plans of Romano-Celtic temples in Gaul. A = Goh-Illis, of octagonal plan; B = Faye-l'Abbesse, of circular plan; C = St. Saëns, of square plan.

Fig. 103b A reconstruction of a Romano-Celtic temple at Schwarzenacker, Germany. It has a square plan and the cella is surrounded by an ambulatory.

as at Maiden Castle, England. Generally, this type of temple is poorly preserved, with only the foundations surviving, and so interpretations regarding their original appearance is open to much dispute. In some cases Romano-Celtic temples were preceded by similar Iron Age timber-built temples or by shrines of usually circular or rectangular plan, and in some instances these buildings continued in use into the Roman period. The implication is that a Celtic type of worship continued from the Iron Age through the Roman period.

Romano-Celtic temples had floor plans of various kinds: square, rectangular, polygonal or circular. The rectangular plan was most common, although the proportions usually approximated to a square. Of polygonal temples, the eight-sided plan was by far the most common, and in some cases a circular cella was surrounded by a polygonal ambulatory. The small central internal chamber (cella) was roofed and many were high-rising towers: at Périgueux, France, the circular cella survives to a height of about 70 ft. (21.33 m). There is some evidence for storage beneath the cella for votive objects. As in other Roman temples, the cella contained a statue and cult objects of the god. There are a few cases where the cella may not have been roofed, such as where it surrounded a sacred pool or spring.

The cella was almost invariably surrounded by a passage or gallery (ambulatory), roofed at a lower level, with some plastered and painted internal and external walls. Some ambulatories were three-sided, and sometimes annexes were attached to one side of the ambulatory. It appears that some ambulatories had solid walls, while others had pillars supported on stub walls, and some had only columns in the form of a portico. Some Romano-Celtic temples seem to have had a classical pronaos at the front of the ambulatory. Access to the cella and ambulatories may have been restricted to the priests. Except where a temple conformed to a town plan by facing on to a street, these temples had their doors facing east or southeast, and many were raised above ground level (often on an earth podium) and approached by a flight of stairs.

Reading: Bourgeois 1992, 201–247; Horne 1986; Horne and King 1980; Rodwell 1980a and 1980b; Wilson 1980; Woodward 1992, 9–50.

templum The word *temple* derives from the Latin word *templum* (pl. *templa*), which originally denoted an area of sky or an area on the ground designated by an AUGUR as that in which he was taking AUSPICES or in which a magistrate could also watch for signs from the gods. It also meant a space on which to erect the shrine of a god or a space in which to conduct business. Roman temple buildings were actually called *aedes*. Because auguries were usually taken at temples, a temple *(aedes)* was usually constructed within an inaugurated area (a *templum*), although an *aedes* could be built upon unaugurated land.

In the first century B.C., the word *templum* came to be used for the temple building, although technically it was not used for temples on unaugurated land: for example, the circular temple of VESTA was an *aedes*, not a *templum*. If a building was only consecrated by the pontiffs, and not by the augurs as well, it was referred to as an *aedes*, not a *templum*, because the consecration was only by the will of men, and not by the will of the gods. (Only the augurs knew the will of the gods.)

Not all *templa* contained an *aedes*. The Senate generally met in the Curia (Senate house) which was itself a *templum*, because by law the Senate had to meet at a place established for augury (that is, a *templum*), since there was always an augural inspection of entrails to determine whether the omens were favorable for discussion of state business. A *templum* as defined by the augurs was usually rectangular or square in plan. Most temples were rectangular, as was the Senate house.

Reading: Richardson 1992, 1–2.

Terminalia An annual ritual on February 23 to worship TERMINUS (god of boundary stones or markers). Rituals (including a sacrifice and feast) were held at boundary stones by the farmers of converging fields, and the boundary stones were garlanded. It was also celebrated at a boundary stone in the temple of JUPITER OPTIMUS MAXIMUS on the CAPITOLINE HILL in Rome.

Reading: Scullard 1981, 79–80.

Terminus The Roman god of boundary stones or markers whose own boundary stone was in the temple of JUPITER OPTIMUS MAXIMUS on the CAPITOLINE HILL in Rome. According to legend, nearly all the resident deities on the Capitol agreed to move by EXAUGURATION to make room for the building of the temple of Jupiter Optimus Maximus;

Terminus alone refused to move. This was regarded as a good omen, signifying the permanence of his cult and Rome. Consequently his shrine was incorporated within the new temple.

When a boundary stone was set up, a religious ceremony took place, a sacrifice was made, and blood and other offerings, along with ashes from the sacrificial fire, were placed in the hole, into which the boundary stone was set. Each boundary stone had its own individual god, and these Termini were worshipped in the Terminalia.

Reading: Grimal 1986, 440; Hammond and Scullard (eds.) 1970, 1,045.

Terminus, shrine of A shrine situated in the cella of JUPITER in the temple of JUPITER OPTIMUS MAXIMUS in Rome. It was marked by a stone which may originally have been an ancient boundary stone. There was an opening *(foramen)* above it in the roof of the temple, because TERMINUS either should not be covered or should be able to see the heavens.

Reading: Richardson 1992, 379–380.

Terra Mater (literally "earth mother") A Roman mother goddess and goddess of the productive power of the earth. She was usually identified with Tellus Mater (see TELLUS).

Reading: Ferguson 1970, 25.

Tertullian Quintus Septimius Florens Tertullianus, the Father of Latin theology and the first major Latin writer in defense of the Church, who greatly influenced the direction and thinking of the Church in the Christian west. He was born c. 160 or 170 in or near Carthage of pagan parents and lived to c. 230. He received a literary and rhetorical education and was converted to CHRISTIANITY before 197, possibly becoming a priest. He composed many works about the history and character of the church. His extant works (31 in all) include *Apologeticus (Apology)*), written c. 197, in which he refutes charges made against Christians of black magic and ATHEISM.

Reading: Hammond and Scullard (eds.) 1970, 1,046–1,047.

Testimonius A Roman deity who presided over the giving of evidence.

Tethys A Greek goddess of the sea who was sister and consort of the Greek god OCEANUS. Both deities were worshipped by the Romans.

Reading: Grimal 1986, 440; Hammond and Scullard (eds.) 1970, 1,047.

tetrastyle A temple with four columns on the main facade.

Teutates A Celtic god who was mentioned by the first-century Roman poet Lucan. Teutates is known from a number of inscriptions found in Britain and Gaul. Inscriptions invoking Toutates, Toutatis and Totatis are usually regarded as variant spellings of this god's name. *Teutates* probably means "protector of the tribe," and he appears to have also been a god of war. He was normally equated with the Roman war god MARS, including a dedication to MARS TEUTATES on a silver plaque found at Barkway, Hertfordshire, England. A dedication to Mars Toutates Cocidius is known from Carlisle, England. Teutates is also sometimes linked with the Roman god MERCURY. A dedication to APOLLO TOUTIORIX is known from Wiesbaden, Germany, and Toutiorix (here linked to the Greek god APOLLO) is thought to be the same god as Teutates. Lucan, who wrote about events that took place in the first century B.C., mentions in his poem *Pharsalia* (book I, lines 444–446) that Teutates was one of three Celtic gods who required human sacrifices.

Reading: Green, M. J. 1992a, 208–209; Ross 1974, 225.

Thalassius An alternative name for the Roman god TALASSIUS.

Thana A native Illyrian deity who is known from an inscription found at Topusko, Croatia. At the same site a dedication to the Illyrian deity VIDASUS and 12 altars dedicated to the Roman god Silvanus have been found. It has been suggested that Thana was equated with DIANA, but there appears to be little evidence to support this suggestion.

Reading: Dorcey 1992, 72.

Theodosius I (the Great) Born c. 346 in Cauca, Spain, eastern emperor from 379, and sole emperor from 392 to 395. He was a devout Christian and dealt severely with heretics, being an adherent of the Nicene Creed (against ARIANISM); he even ordained the death penalty for some extremist sects. In 391 he put an end to all forms of pagan religion in the empire and so founded the Christian state,

for which he acquired his title "the Great." He did not initially ban pagan SACRIFICE, but did cause DIVINATION to cease; nor did he initially close temples, but he allowed fanatical Christians to destroy them or petitioners to take them over. In 390 AMBROSE refused Theodosius I communion for ordering the massacre of 3,000 people at Thessalonica (to avenge the killing of the general Butheric), until he had done penance. In 391 Theodosius closed all temples and banned all forms of pagan worship, probably at the instigation of Ambrose.
Reading: Grant 1985, 270–281; Hammond and Scullard (eds.) 1970, 1,055–1,056; Jones 1964, 170–216.

Thincsus A Germanic or possibly Celtic god who was linked with MARS as MARS THINCSUS.

thyrsus (pl. *thyrsi*) A wand or staff tipped with an ornament resembling a pine cone and sometimes wreathed with ivy or vine leaves (originally to hide a spearhead). *Thyrsi* were carried by worshippers in the rites of BACCHUS.

Tiberinus The Roman god of the Tiber River at Rome (Fig. 1). According to legend, Tiberinus was a tenth-generation descendant of Aeneas and a king of Alba. He was killed by the Albula River, which was renamed Tiber. Another story has Tiberinus as the son of the god JANUS and a water NYMPH from Latium called Camasene. In this version, Tiberinus drowned in the river which came to bear his name. There was an altar and perhaps a shrine dedicated to Tiberinus on the Tiber Island in Rome and a festival of Tiberinus on December 8.
Reading: Grimal 1986, 455; Le Gall 1953; Richardson 1992, 398.

tibicen (pl. *tibicines*) A flute player who played music on a *tibia* (flute) during religious ceremonies, including sacrifices and funerals, to drown out any ill-omened noise. He also played at feasts.
Reading: Warde Fowler 1899, 159; York 1986, 133.

Tillenus An Iberian mountain god who is known from an inscription found at Barco de Valdeorras in the Orense region of northwest Spain. He is the deity of the nearby Teleno mountain and probably the same deity as MARS TILENUS (but with variant spelling).
Reading: Tranoy 1981, 299.

Tisiphone One of the Roman deities known as the FURIES.

tituli sacri Religious dedications on objects (usually altars and votive goods, but sometimes statues and temples) consecrated to the gods. Religious dedications normally begin with the name of the god or gods (in the dative or genitive), followed by the name and status of the dedicator (in the nominative) and a verb or formula, usually abbreviated (such as VSLM, for "he willingly and deservedly fulfilled his vow"). The reason for the dedication is sometimes stated. The verb of dedication is not always expressed but can be understood.

tomb (Figs. 104, 105) A burial place for the dead (CREMATION or INHUMATION) in which it was thought that the dead person continued to live. It was a method of burial reserved for the wealthy, and the tomb was regarded as a sacred place. The term *monumentum* was used by the Romans, but the term

Fig. 104 A tombstone of a man called Ate Aqab from the Yarhai hypogeum *tombs at Palmyra, Syria. Portrait busts, both male and female, closed the burial places* (loculi) *in the* hypogeum.

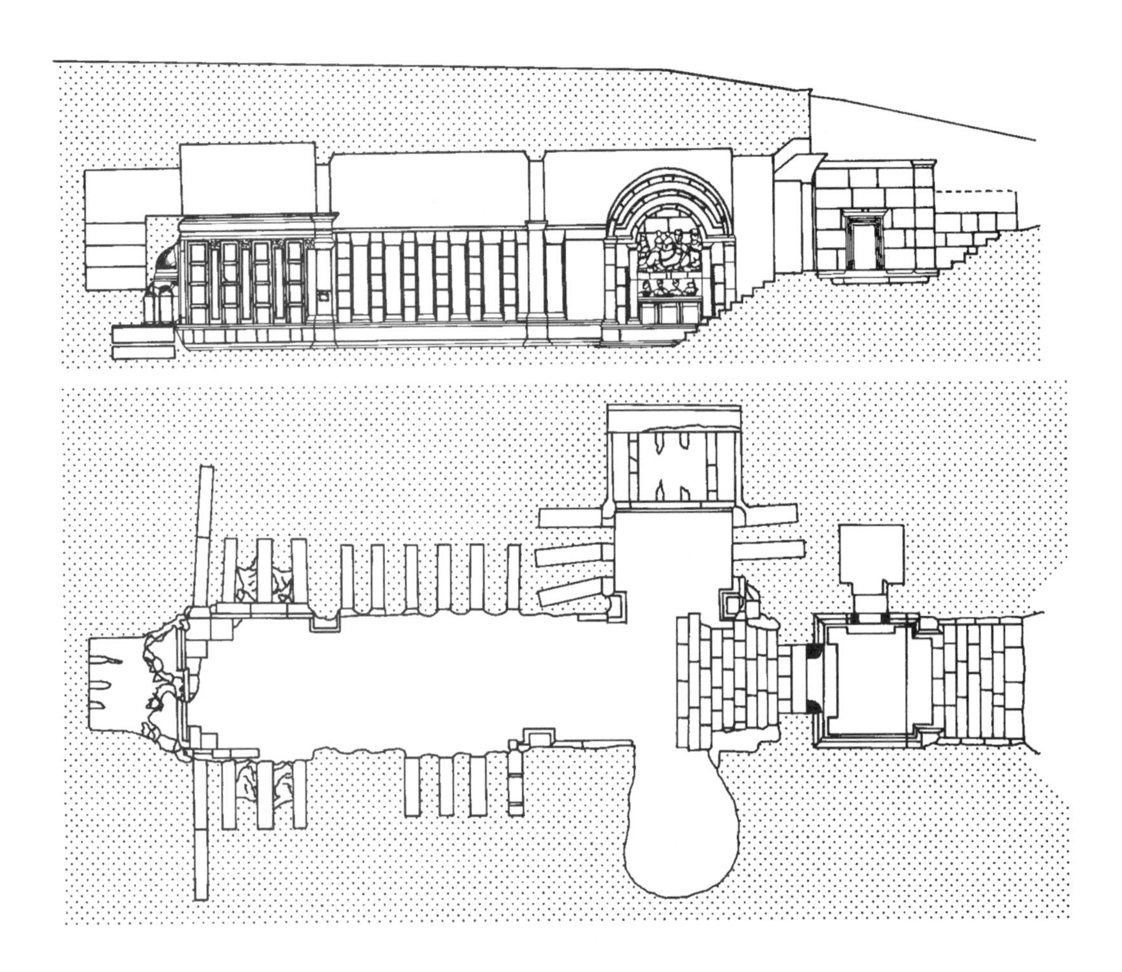

Fig. 105 A section and plan of the Yarhai hypogeum *tombs at Palmyra, Syria. This tomb system comprised a long passage cut into the rock, with* loculi *for burial of the dead. A number of slabs bearing portrait busts of the deceased were found which closed the burials in the* loculi; *some were inscribed with their names. The* hypogeum *was built by Yarhai in* A.D. *108. It could have held a total of 219 inhumations, but its use ceased before it was full.*

MAUSOLEUM came to be applied to many of the imperial tombs. To the Romans, a mausoleum was the same as a tomb, but it has come to mean a monumental tomb, sometimes enclosed within a building. Tombs could range from the very simple to the very ornate; the latter might even have wall paintings in the interior. Tombs of various shapes and sizes were built to accommodate one or more burials in coffins or cremation vessels. Many tombs stood within carefully defined plots of ground, marked at the very least by boundary posts at the corners, or surrounded by a low wall. The most popular forms were the altar tomb, the *aedicula* tomb, the rotunda and the *tumulus*, but numerous shapes and sizes were conceived, including pyramids and tower tombs.The burials of the upper classes were often marked by impressive and sometimes eccentric monuments, like the pyramid-shaped tomb of Gaius Cestius at Rome, either in cemeteries or in prominent positions outside city walls.

It was particularly common in the second and third centuries to treat the dead of one's family as gods, and public funerary monuments became temple-like. Especially in southwest Turkey, there was a tradition of placing sarcophagi on a high column or podium (Fig. 20), and of placing funerary couches (of stone) inside the temple-tombs. There are many tombs in this region modeled upon different types of temple, but inscriptions state that the tomb was *like* a temple rather than actually a temple itself. Large mounds (barrows or *tumuli*) built over the burial were also impressive monuments, examples of which have been found in northern provinces. Rock-cut tombs were used for burial, including catacombs in the late Roman period, the latter mainly by Christians. In Rome, funeral clubs and large households often deposited vessels of cremated remains in a collective tomb called a *COLUMBARIUM*.

Violation of a tomb was a criminal offense, and many tombs have inscriptions or curses warning of the consequences of such violation. The main fear was probably that the soul in the AFTERLIFE would be affected. (See also BURIAL OF THE DEAD.)

Reading: Lattimore 1962 (epitaphs on tombs, including curses); Prieur 1986; Richardson 1992, 351–361 (tombs in Rome); Toynbee 1971.

tombstone A marker of a grave. Many graves (inhumations and cremations) were marked with tombstones and stelae (sing. stele). These varied enormously, but many were sculpted with some representation of the dead, and had a dedicatory inscription. The inscriptions often reflect the religious beliefs of the people (see EPITAPH). Many more graves were probably marked with wooden grave markers which have not survived.

Reading: Abdalla 1992; Lattimore 1962 (epitaphs on tombstones); Toynbee 1971, 245–253.

Totatis Thought to be a variant spelling of TOUTATIS, a Celtic god who is believed to be the same deity as TEUTATES. A silver ring found at York, England, is inscribed with the letters TOT, which have been interpreted as an abbreviation of Totatis.

Reading: Green, M. J. 1992a, 209.

Toutates A Celtic god who is equated with the Celtic god COCIDIUS and the Roman god MARS as Mars Toutates Cocidius. (See TEUTATES.)

Toutatis A Celtic god who is known from an inscription found at Barkway, Hertfordshire, England. Toutatis is thought to be the same god as TEUTATES.

Toutiorix A Celtic deity who is linked with the Greek god APOLLO as APOLLO TOUTIORIX.

tripod An upright bronze ALTAR, resembling a cauldron on three vertical legs with feet. Tripods were used for some sacrifices; their origin lies in the Delphic tripod from which the Pythian priestess at the ORACLE at Delphi gave her responses.

tripudium (pl. *tripudia*) A ritual dance performed in triple time by the *SALII* priests in honor of MARS. It also described the noisy falling to the ground of grain on which the chickens fed, considered to be an omen in AUGURY.

triumph A procession held by victorious kings and generals returning from campaigns. Triumphs had both a military and religious aspect. The original purpose may have been to purify the general and his troops and to offer spoils to JUPITER OPTIMUS MAXIMUS. In Rome the processions started in the CAMPUS MARTIUS, round the Palatine Hill, along the SACRA VIA and ended at the CAPITOLINE HILL.

Reading: Scullard 1981, 213–218; Versnel 1970.

Tsirona A Celtic goddess who is known from an inscription found at Corseul, Brittany. She is probably the same deity as the Celtic goddess SIRONA.
Reading: Green, M. J. 1992a, 192.

Tubilustrium Ceremony of the purification of the trumpets *(tubae)* used in sacred rituals. It was held on the last day of the GREATER QUINQUATRUS (festival of MARS) on March 23 when the *tubae* (sacred trumpets, which were originally war trumpets, but were later used for ceremonial occasions) were purified. It occurred again on May 23. There was a sacrifice of a ewe lamb. The ceremony was held in Rome in a building called the Atrium Sutorium. It was apparently a festival of Mars, and later of MINERVA as well. It is not clear if the army was involved, or if it was merely a ceremony to purify the trumpets used in summoning the assembly on the following day. There was also a festival of VULCAN on May 23 which the Romans came to link with the Tubilustrium, saying that Vulcan was the smith who made the trumpets.
Reading: Richardson 1992, 42; Scullard 1981, 94–95, 123; York 1986, 102.

Tueraeus An Iberian deity who is known from an inscription on an altar found at Feira, Portugal. This deity is possibly the same as Banda Velugus Toiraecus, who is invoked on another altar also found at Feira.
Reading: Alarcão 1988, 93.

tumulus (Fig. 106) (pl. *tumuli*) A type of tomb for the burial of the dead which consists of an artificial circular mound of earth. Some were simple mounds covering a grave, and some covered a chamber. In northwest Europe, *tumulus* is usually described as a barrow or mound. It has a long pre-Roman tradition and is found across much of the Roman world. The Romans themselves adopted its use from the Etruscans. The best-known examples

Fig. 106 A tumulus *with a surrounding wall and an internal chamber for burial of the dead. It is one of several hundred burials of Hellenistic, Roman and Byzantine date in the cemetery at Hierapolis (Pammukale), Turkey.*

in northwest Europe are in Britain, Belgium and the Moselle valley. They occur singly or in groups, and some were surrounded by precinct walls. They covered single and multiple inhumations. They provided a resting place for the souls of the dead, and many of the burials were furnished with grave goods. As with many other types of tomb, it is not known if the style had a particular religious significance.
Reading: Richardson 1992, 352.

Turiacus An Iberian god who is known from an inscription found at Santo Tirso, northwest Portugal. The inscription was a dedication to the god on a votive plaque by Lucius Valerius Silvanus of the Legion VI Victrix. This dates the inscription to the first century.
Reading: Tranoy 1981, 278.

Tutanus A Roman deity who gave protection in time of trouble. (See also REDICULUS.)

Tutela (Figs. 89, 107) (also spelled *Tutula*) Latin word for guardianship or protection and an epithet at times applied to deities. Tutela was also recognized as a divine personification of the abstract concept "protection," as applied to people and things. This type of personification of "protection" is more commonly seen in the form of the goddess TUTILINA whose primary function was that of a guardian or protector.

Tutela Bolgensis An Iberian deity who is known from an inscription found in Cacabelos, near Ponferrada, northern Spain. Tutela means "protector" and implies that the deity was patron of a group of people or a place.
Reading: Tranoy 1981, 306.

Tutela Boudiga A Celtic goddess who is known from an inscription on an altar found in Bordeaux, France, which can be dated to 237. Tutela Boudiga's name means something like "protecting victory," and she appears to have been a goddess of protection and victory. The inscription records fulfillment of a vow by Marcus Aurelius Lunaris after his safe journey from Britain. The name *Boudiga* is linked to Boudicca (also known as Boadicea), the Queen of the British Iceni tribe who led a rebellion against the Romans in A.D. 60.

Fig. 107 An altar from Lyon, France, dedicated to Tutela on June 22, 224, the third year of the reign of Severus Alexander.

Reading: Burn 1969, 50–51.

Tutela Tiriensis An Iberian deity who is known from an inscription on an altar found at Santa Maria de Ribeira, northern Portugal. *Tutela* means "protector" and implies that the deity was protector of a particular place.
Reading: Tranoy 1981, 305.

Tutilina Also known as Tutelina, she was a Roman guardian or tutelary goddess and one who was guardian of the harvest and stored grain. It is possible that she was originally the patron deity of the *gens Tutilia* (the Tutilia clan).

Tyche Originally the Greek goddess of chance or fortune, this deity became attached to various cities during the Roman period. Many cities in the eastern empire adopted her as a guardian deity; among these were Athens, Thera, Selgae, Trapezopolis (in Phrygia), Thasos, Statonicia, Syllium (in Pamphylia), Rhodiapolis, Smyrna and Ephesus. At Mytilene, she was known as Great Tyche of Mytilene. The Roman equivalent of Tyche was FORTUNA, and the adoption of Tyche as a patron in eastern cities is paralleled by the worship of FORTUNA ROMANA at Rome.
Reading: Ferguson 1970, 77–87.

U

Ucuetis A Celtic god who was the partner of the Celtic goddess BERGUSIA.

underworld The resting place of the dead, and the dwelling place of some deities. There were varying beliefs as to the precise nature of the underworld. Souls were thought to go to the underworld (not heaven or hell) after death, although those souls who the underworld gods would not admit were destined to wander homeless forever. The Romans had several gods of the underworld, and there was a belief that the spirits of the dead *(MANES)* lived underground after being buried, probably close to their burial place or in the tomb itself. There was a fear of punishment or torment in the underworld, and some Romans believed in a divine punishment. The poet Virgil described the world of the dead as divided into a limbo, a hell and a heaven (Elysium), but most Romans perceived this as a poetic notion. The idea of Elysium (or Elysian Fields or Isles of the Blessed) was vague and it was thought to be located either in the sky, at the end of the underworld, above the moon, or to be islands in the Ocean. Other views held that the dead lived in the sky or across the ocean. Ideas from Greek myths (such as paying Charon to cross the river Styx to reach the god HADES) were possibly believed by the Romans, as coins are frequently found in Roman burials. The concept of an underworld was profoundly affected by MYSTERY RELIGIONS and by CHRISTIANITY. (See also AFTERLIFE; BURIAL OF THE DEAD; GRAVE GOODS.)
Reading: Lattimore 1962 (evidence from epitaphs).

Uni An ancient Etruscan goddess who was equated with the Roman goddess JUNO.

Unxia A deity of marriage who was concerned with the proper anointing of the bridegroom's door by the bride.

Uranus The Greek god of the heavens who was equated with the Roman god CAELUS.

ustrinum (pl. *ustrina*) A place where a CREMATION of the deceased took place. At Rome, the places of cremation of important people were sometimes commemorated by markers. That of Julius Caesar in the FORUM ROMANUM was marked by an altar.
Reading: Patterson 1992, 198, 199.

Uxellinus A Celtic god who was identified with the Roman god JUPITER as JUPITER UXELLINUS.

V

Vacallinehae Celtic mother goddesses also referred to as MATRONAE VACALLINEHAE.

Vacuna A Roman goddess who was originally an ancient Sabine goddess. Her function had already been forgotten by the time of the poet Horace. At various times, she was identified with BELLONA, DIANA, VENUS, MINERVA and VICTORIA. She had sacred groves at Reate (modern Rieti), Italy, and by the Lacus Velinus (a lake in the same area), and a sanctuary on the banks of the Licenza River, Italy, near Horace's villa.
Reading: Grimal 1986, 464; Hammond and Scullard (eds.) 1970, 1,104; van Buren 1916.

Vaelicus An Iberian god who is known from an inscription found at Postoloboso, central Spain. This is probably the same deity as the Iberian god VELICUS who was worshipped in the same area.
Reading: Knapp 1992, 97.

Vagdavercustis A native goddess who is known from an inscription on an altar found at Cologne, Germany. The altar was decorated with carvings of trees on the side panels; the relief sculpture on the front depicted the dedicator offering a sacrifice in accordance with normal Roman rites. The altar was dedicated by Titus Flavius Constans, the praetorian prefect. This eminent Roman must have been on a mission to Cologne when he made this unusual dedication to a native goddess. Vagdavercustis appears to have been a Celto-Germanic mother goddess, who may have had a link with trees or woods.
Reading: Elbe 1975, 214; Green, M. J. 1992a, 218.

Vagitanus A Roman deity who induced a baby's first cry.
Reading: Ferguson 1988a, 853.

Vagodonnaegus An Iberian god who is known from an inscription on a plaque found at La Milla del Rio, near Astorga, northern Spain. The inscription was an official dedication to the god by the Res Publica Asturica Augusta ("the people of the city of Asturica Augusta"), which was made on their behalf by two magistrates of the city.
Reading: Tranoy 1981, 299.

Vallonia A Roman goddess of valleys who was also known as Vallina.

Varro Marcus Terentius Varro, 116–27 B.C., born in Reate, Italy. One of the most prolific writers in antiquity, author of about 620 books on a wide range of subjects. The *Res Divinae (On Religion)* or *Antiquitates Rerum Humanarum et Divinarum (Human and Divine Antiquities)* was a huge 41-book compilation relating to Roman history and religion; it appeared in 47/46 B.C., and large fragments survive because they were criticized by later Christian writers, including St. AUGUSTINE in his *City of God*, with extensive quotations in his Books 4 to 7. Varro devoted the last 16 books to *res divinae.* There was an introductory book; three books (of which virtually nothing survives) described the three major priestly colleges, three books described shrines, temples and sacred places, three described festivals and games, and three were on public and private rituals. He discussed deities in the last three books.
Reading: Gordon 1990a; Hammond and Scullard (eds.) 1970, 1,107–1,108.

Vasio A Celtic god who personified the native spirit of the Roman town of Vaison-la-Romaine, France. Like other such personifications of places, he presumably was regarded as protector of the

town and its inhabitants. Little else is known about this god.
Reading: Green, M. J. 1992a, 218.

vates Originally a word for a soothsayer or seer; it later came to be used for "poet."

Vediovis Also known as Vedius, Veiovis or Vendius, a Roman god closely connected with the Roman god JUPITER. However, he appears to have been regarded by the Romans as "the opposite of Jupiter" (that is, harmful) and was associated with the UNDERWORLD. Originally a deity of swamps and volcanic movement, he was later identified with APOLLO. There was a temple to this god behind the Tabularium in Rome (Figs. 15, 108), and another on the Tiber Island. An altar to Vediovis was set up at Bovillae to the southeast of Rome. His sacrificial offering is thought to have been a she-goat that was sacrificed by the *ritu humano;* it is not certain whether *ritu humano* means "on behalf of the dead" or "in place of a human sacrifice." He had festivals on January 1, March 7 and May 21. He is little known outside Rome.
Reading: Grimal 1986, 464; Hammond and Scullard (eds.) 1970, 1,110; Scullard 1981, 56–58; Simon 1990, 210–212; York 1986, 86–87.

Vediovis, temples of (Figs. 108a, b) There was a temple of VEDIOVIS on the Tiber Island, vowed in 200 B.C. by the praetor Lucius Furius Purpurio in the battle of Cremona (against the Gauls). It was dedicated on January 1, 194 B.C. (the same day as the dedication of the temple of AESCULAPIUS on the island in 291 B.C.). Another temple was also vowed by Lucius Furius Purpurio, this time as consul in 198 B.C. It was dedicated on March 7, 192 B.C. by Quintus Marcius Ralla. The latter temple was on the CAPITOLINE HILL in Rome (Fig. 15), and was described in Roman times as *inter duos lucos* (between the two groves) or *inter Arcem et Capitolium* (between the two peaks of the Arx and Capitol). It had a rectangular plan with the transverse cella wider than the TETRASTYLE shallow pronaos, and faced south west. It was small and stood on a fairly high podium. It was restored around 78 B.C., perhaps after the Tabularium was built. The temple was discovered in 1939 at the southwest corner of the Tabularium; the original temple foundations were oriented differently from the later rebuilding. The

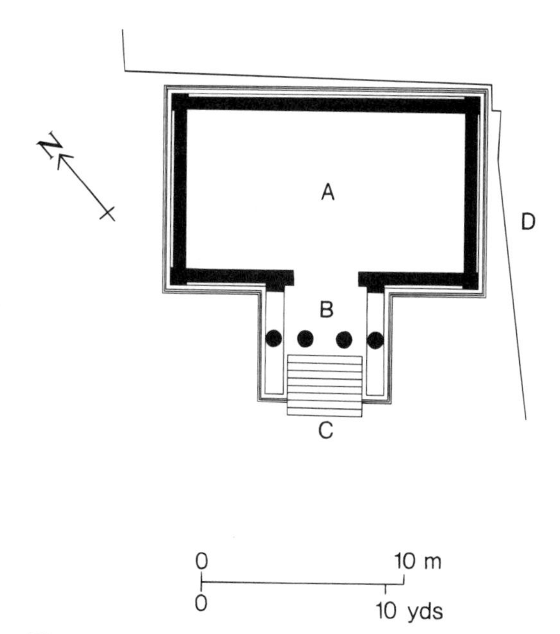

Fig. 108a Plan of the temple of Vediovis on the Capitoline Hill at Rome. A = transverse cella; B = pronaos; C = steps; D = Tabularium.

cult statue of the god was also found, of colossal proportions and similar to statues of APOLLO. It seems to be a first-century B.C. copy of a fifth-century B.C. Greek original.
Reading: Nash 1962b, 490; Richardson 1992, 406; Scullard 1981, 56–58.

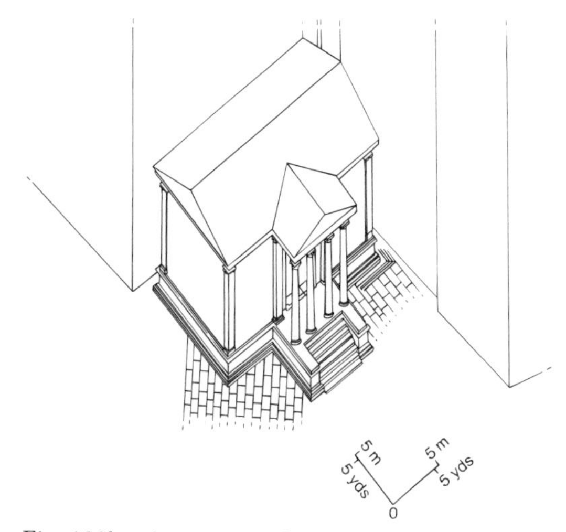

Fig. 108b A reconstructed view of the temple of Vediovis on the Capitoline Hill at Rome.

Vedius An alternative name for the Roman god VEDIOVIS.

Veiovis An alternative name for the Roman god VEDIOVIS.

Velia A high and steep hill in Rome between the Palatine Hill and the Oppian Hill at the head of the SACRA VIA. In the republic its peak was the site of the temple of the PENATES. After the time of Hadrian, it was dominated by the temple of VENUS FELIX AND ROMA AETERNA. It was the scene of various rites, including one of the sacrifices of the SEPTIMONTIA and one of the shrines of the *ARGEI*.
Reading: Richardson 1992, 407–408.

Velicus An Iberian god who was probably the same deity as VAELICUS. He is known from inscriptions found in Spain. There was a shrine dedicated to this god at Postoloboso, central Spain.
Reading: Knapp 1992, 86–93.

Vellaunus A Celtic god who is known from only two inscriptions. One is on a statue base at Caerwent, Wales, where Vellaunus was equated with the Celtic god OCELOS as Ocelos Vellaunus in a dedication addressed to "the god Mars Lenus or Ocelos Vellaunus." The other inscription, from southern Gaul, identifies Vellaunus with the Roman god MERCURY.
Reading: Green, M. J. 1992a, 218–219.

Vendius An alternative name for the Roman god VEDIOVIS.

Veneralia The festival of VENUS VERTICORDIA, held on April 1 (KALENDS). The goddess FORTUNA VIRILIS was also apparently worshipped as part of this festival.
Reading: Scullard 1981, 96–97.

Venilia A Roman goddess whose original nature and function are unclear. Varro implied that Venilia was associated with NEPTUNE, and she came to be regarded by some as a deity of coastal water.
Reading: Hammond and Scullard (eds.) 1970, 1,112.

Venus The Roman goddess of love, beauty and courtesans and the consort of the Roman god MARS. She probably originally presided over the fertility of vegetable gardens, fruit and flowers. Venus was identified with the Greek goddess APHRODITE at an early date and acquired Aphrodite's mythology. In Roman legend, Aeneas (legendary founder of the Roman nation and one of the leaders in the Trojan War) was the son of Anchises (a Trojan prince) and of Venus. A number of other myths and legends also featured Venus.

Venus was closely associated with the Julian family, but it was the Flavian dynasty, beginning with Titus, and subsequent emperors who used Venus extensively as a motif on coins. Venus (as VENUS VICTRIX, VENUS GENETRIX or VENUS FELIX) frequently appeared on coins of the wives, sisters and daughters of the emperors. Venus had a great many titles or epithets including Venus Amica ("Venus the Friend"), Venus Armata ("Armed Venus"), Venus Aurea ("Golden Venus"), Venus Caelestis ("Celestial Venus"), VENUS CLOACINA ("Venus the Purifier"), VENUS ERYCINA ("Venus of Eryx in Sicily"), Venus Felix ("Favorable Venus"), Venus Genetrix ("Venus the Universal Mother"), VENUS LIBITINA (probably meaning "Passionate Venus"), VENUS OBSEQUENS ("Indulgent Venus"), VENUS VERTICORDIA ("Venus the Changer of Hearts") and Venus Victrix ("Venus Victorious").

Venus was also associated with the festival of VINALIA PRIORA in April. Pipeclay FIGURINES resembling the classical Venus (sometimes called "pseudo-Venus" figurines) are probably connected with a Romano-Celtic domestic fertility cult rather than with the worship of Venus.
Reading: Lloyd-Morgan 1986; Room 1983, 319–322 (for titles/epithets of Venus); Schilling 1982 (includes titles of Venus); Simon 1990, 213–228.

Venus Cloacina ("Venus the Purifier") An aspect of the Roman goddess VENUS; also known as Venus Cluacina. She was thought to be derived from the Romans' act of purifying themselves in the vicinity of her statue after the end of the Sabine war, but it appears likely that Cloacina was originally a water deity who became identified with Venus. The statue of Venus Cloacina in Rome was set up on the spot where peace was concluded between the Sabines and the Romans. There was a shrine to this goddess beside the steps of the portico of the Basilica Aemilia in the FORUM ROMANUM in Rome, beside the Cloaca Maxima (great drain). This shrine was portrayed on a coin issued in 39 B.C.

Reading: Nash 1962a, 262–263; Richardson 1992, 92.

Venus Erucina An alternative spelling for VENUS ERYCINA.

Venus Erycina ("Venus from Eryx") Also spelled Venus Erucina. Her cult was introduced to Rome from the sanctuary on Mount Eryx in western Sicily. There were temples of Venus Erycina in Rome on the CAPITOLINE HILL and outside the Porta Collina.
Reading: Hammond and Scullard (eds.) 1970, 1,113; Scullard 1981, 107.

Venus Erycina, temples of There was a temple of VENUS ERYCINA on the CAPITOLINE HILL in Rome, probably in the Area Capitolina, which was vowed by the dictator Quintus Fabius Maximus after he consulted the SIBYLLINE BOOKS following the disaster of the battle of Lake Trasimene in 217 B.C. It was dedicated in 215 B.C. by Quintus Fabius Maximus. It was one of a pair of temples, the other probably dedicated to MENS. The temple was later called Aedes Capitolina Veneris. Another temple at Rome was vowed by Lucius Porcius Licinius in 184 B.C. and was dedicated by him outside the Porta Collina on April 23, 181 B.C., the day of the VINALIA PRIORA. The temple was supposed to be a reproduction of one on Mount Eryx in Sicily, and was apparently frequented by prostitutes. Venus came to receive offerings from the female prostitutes of Rome at this temple during the Vinalia Priora.
Reading: Richardson 1992, 408; Scullard 1981, 107.

Venus Felix ("Favorable Venus") There was a temple of Venus Felix on the Esquiline Hill in Rome, and Hadrian (emperor 117–138) built a temple dedicated to VENUS FELIX AND ROMA AETERNA (Fig. 109) on the north side of the SACRA VIA.
Reading: Richardson 1992, 408.

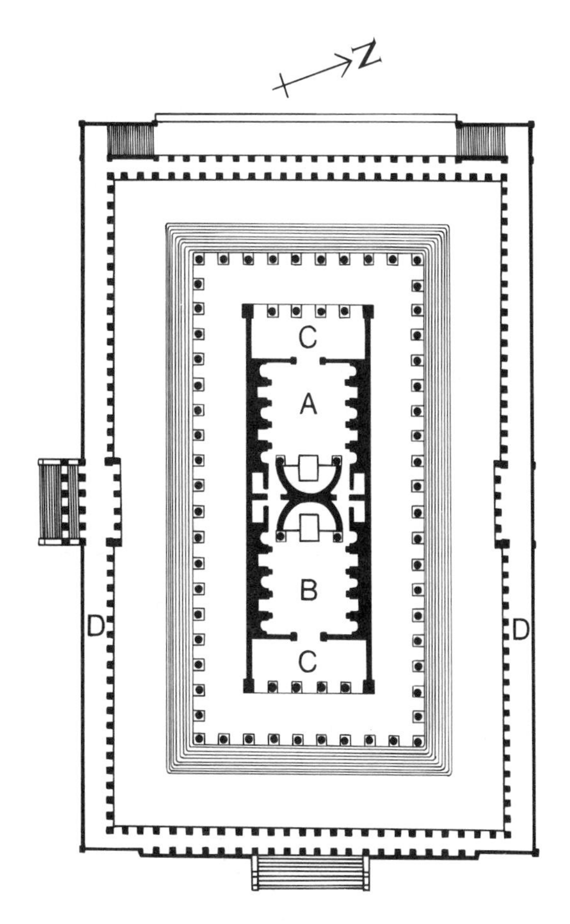

Fig. 109 The double temple of Venus Felix and Roma Aeterna at Rome. A = cella of Roma; B = cella of Venus; C = pronaos; D = colonnade.

Venus Felix and Roma Aeterna, temple of (Fig. 109) A double temple built by Hadrian in Rome, overlooking the Colosseum. It was built on the VELIA on the north side of the SACRA VIA (Fig. 37), on the site of the vestibule of the *domus aurea* which Hadrian demolished, moving the colossal statue (colossus) of SOL (previously Nero). The temple was started on April 21 (PARILIA), A.D. 121 and was probably completed by Antoninus Pius and dedicated in 135. It was dedicated to VENUS FELIX and Roma Aeterna. The temple and colonnades stood on a huge platform 158.57 yds. long and 109.36 yds. wide (145 m × 100 m). The temple stood on a low stepped platform in the Greek style and was of brick-faced concrete with marble. It was DECASTYLE with Corinthian colums. There were two

cellas, back-to-back, one for each goddess—Roma faced west and Venus east. In 307 it was damaged by a fire; it was rebuilt by Maxentius. It may have been destroyed by an earthquake in the ninth century, and the church of Santa Maria Nova was built in its ruins in 847–855. It was rebuilt again as Santa Francesca Romana in 1612.
Reading: Nash 1962b, 496; Richardson 1992, 410.

Venus Genetrix ("Venus the Universal Mother") The Roman goddess VENUS in her role as the ancestress of the Roman people. She had a festival on September 26. She was regarded as the mother of the Julian *gens* to which Julius Caesar belonged. He dedicated a temple to her at Rome.
Reading: Weinstock 1971, 80–90.

Venus Genetrix, temple of In 50 B.C. Julius Caesar vowed a temple on the eve of the battle of Pharsalus to VENUS VICTRIX, but he later chose to build one to VENUS GENETRIX: Julius Caesar was devoted to VENUS, his *gens* being allegedly descended from her. The forum and temple were dedicated by Julius Caesar on the last day of his triumph on September 26, 46 B.C. It was an OCTASTYLE temple built of solid marble on a high podium at the far north end of the colonnaded Julian Forum (Forum Caesaris or Forum Iulium), and the temple and forum were actually completed by Augustus. It may have been one of several buildings in Rome severely damaged in a fire in 80. The temple was rebuilt by Domitian on the original podium and was rededicated by Trajan on May 12, 113. A cult statue of Venus Genetrix was carved by Arcesilas for the temple, and Julius Caesar dedicated numerous works of art in the temple.
Reading: Nash 1962a, 424; Richardson 1992, 165–167.

Venus Libentia An alternative name for VENUS LIBITINA.

Venus Libentina An alternative name for VENUS LIBITINA.

Venus Libertina ("Venus the Freedwoman") It is thought that this aspect of the Roman goddess VENUS was an error, with *Libertina* ("Freedwoman") being mistaken for *Lubentina* (a title probably meaning "pleasurable" or "passionate"). Venus Libertina seems to have been regarded as the same goddess as VENUS LIBITINA.

Venus Libitina Also known as Venus Libentina, Venus Lubentina, Venus Lubentini and Venus Lubentia. The Roman goddess LIBITINA came to be identified with the Roman goddess VENUS: it is thought that this was an error, with Libitina (the goddess of funerals) being mistaken for Lubentina (a title probably meaning "pleasurable" or "passionate"). There was a temple dedicated to Venus Libitina in Rome on the Esquiline Hill.
Reading: Richardson 1992, 409.

Venus Obsequens, temple of (Indulgent or Gracious Venus) A temple dedicated to this aspect of the goddess VENUS was vowed during the Third Samnite War by Quintus Fabius Maximus Gurges. It was begun in 295 B.C. and was dedicated after the war. It was the oldest temple of Venus in Rome, and was situated by the CIRCUS MAXIMUS, probably at the foot of the Aventine Hill. Its dedication day was August 19, the VINALIA RUSTICA. It was built from money levied as fines against women found guilty of adultery.
Reading: Richardson 1992, 409.

Venus Verticordia ("Venus the Changer of Hearts") This aspect of the Roman Goddess VENUS had a festival called VENERALIA on April 1. After consulting the SIBYLLINE BOOKS, a temple to Venus Verticordia was built in Rome in 114 B.C. to atone for the inchastity of three VESTAL VIRGINS. Its dedication day was April 1. Its position is unknown—it was sited in the Vallis Murcia, probably on the slope of the Aventine Hill behind the CIRCUS MAXIMUS.
Reading: Champeaux 1982, 378–395; Richardson 1992, 411; Scullard 1981, 97.

Venus Victrix (Fig. 110) ("Venus Victorious") A temple to this aspect of the Roman goddess VENUS was dedicated by Pompey at the top of his theater in the CAMPUS MARTIUS (Fig. 111) in Rome in 55 B.C., and there was a shrine (probably an altar) of Venus Victrix on the CAPITOLINE HILL. There were festivals of Venus Victrix on August 12 and October 9, and a sacrifice was made to her on the latter date.

Venus Victrix, temple of (Figs. 111a, b) When Pompey built the first permanent stone the-

Fig. 110 The reverse of a silver denarius *showing Venus Victrix standing with a shield. The obverse is of Plautilla (wife of Caracalla). Courtesy of Somerset County Museums Service.*

ater in Rome (in the CAMPUS MARTIUS) in 55 B.C., he built a temple of VENUS VICTRIX at the top of the banks of seats *(cavea)*, so that they resembled temple steps. The whole structure, it was reported, could therefore be dedicated as a temple, not a theater: this may have been Pompey's ploy in order to avoid criticism for having built a permanent place of entertainment. Julius Caesar was assassinated in a hall attached to the portico of this theater when attending a meeting of the Senate. (Senate meetings could take place here, as the structure was a *TEMPLUM*.) The temple was not completed and dedicated until 52 B.C. There was also a series of small shrines to other deities around the top of the *cavea*. Subsequently, numerous theaters associated with temples were built in this way.
Reading: Barton 1989, 79; Hanson 1959, 43–55; Richardson 1992, 411; Scullard 1981, 173.

Veraudinus A Celtic god who was the partner of the Celtic goddess INCIONA. These two deities were worshipped together as a divine couple, but are known only from Widdenberg, Luxembourg. It is likely that they are deities of that specific locality.
Reading: Green, M. J. 1992a, 125–26.

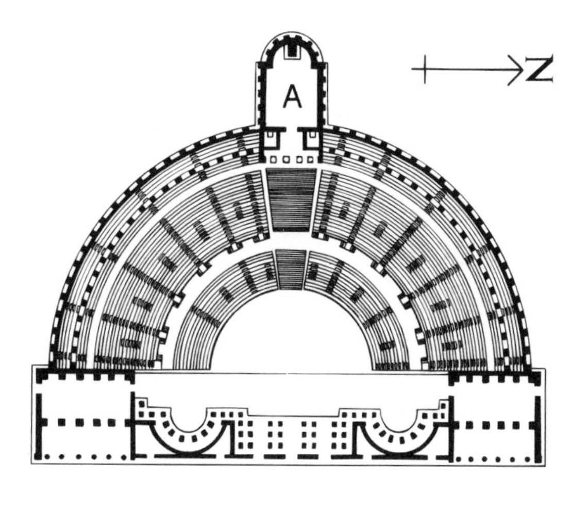

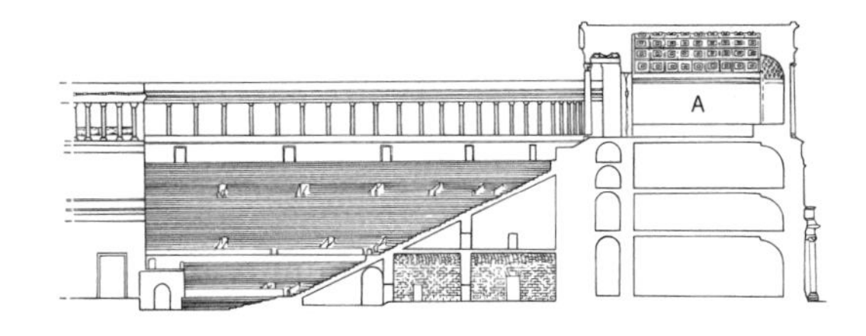

Figs. 111 a and b A plan (a) and section (b) of Pompey's theater, with the temple of Venus Victrix (A) at the top of the banks of seats.

Verbeia A Celtic goddess and personification of the Wharfe River, northern England. An altar dedicated to this goddess is known from Ilkley, North Yorkshire, and an image from the same place may represent the goddess. It depicts a woman with an overlarge head dressed in a pleated robe. In each hand she holds a geometric zigzag, probably representing large snakes.
Reading: Green, M. J. 1992a, 219; Ross 1974, 295.

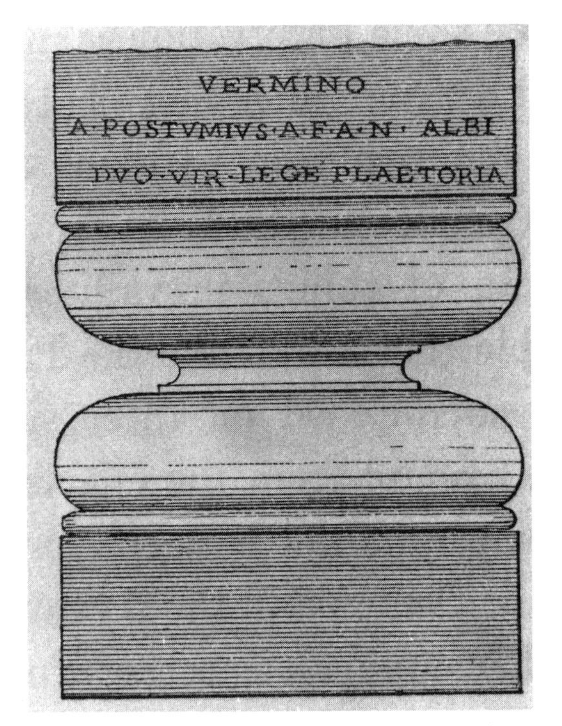

Fig. 112 An hourglass-shaped altar found in Rome dating from c. 175 B.C. It was dedicated to Verminus to avert a disease that was affecting cattle. Height 45.27 in. (1.15 m).

Vercana A Celtic goddess who was associated with springs at Bad Bertrich, Germany. They later became a spa, and so Vercana may have been a healing goddess.
Reading: Wightman 1970, 138, 226.

Verminus (Fig. 112) The Roman god of protection of cattle against disease. This god may have been one of the INDIGETES. An altar to this god was found in 1876, dedicated by the duovir Aulus Postumius Albinus.
Reading: Richardson 1992, 411.

Vernostonus A Celtic god who was the personification of the alder tree (his name means "alder tree"). He is known from an inscription to COCIDIUS Vernostonus found at Ebchester near Hadrian's Wall, England.
Reading: Green, M. J. 1992a, 219.

Veroca An Iberian deity who is known from an inscription found in the Lugo region of northwest Spain. It is possible that this is the same deity referred to as VERORA and VIRRORA VILIAEGUS in inscriptions from the same area.
Reading: Tranoy 1981, 294.

Verora An Iberian deity who is known from inscriptions found in the Lugo region of northwest Spain. It is possible that this is the same deity referred to as VIRRORA VILIAEGUS and VEROCA in inscriptions from the same area.
Reading: Tranoy 1981, 294.

ver sacrum In times of great crisis, the *ver sacrum* ("sacred spring") was performed by dedicating everything born in the spring to a god, usually JUPITER: the animals were sacrificed, and the children were expelled from the country to found a new community when they reached the age of 20. This was a very ancient ceremony which was revived in Rome in 217 B.C., during the Second Punic War, but without the expulsion of children.

Vertumnus A Roman god who was sometimes called Vortumnus. He was originally an Etruscan god, worshipped at Volsinii, Italy, which was captured by the Romans in 264 B.C. Vertumnus appears to have been regarded as a personification of change and so presided over the changes in the seasons. He was also regarded by some as the husband of POMONA, goddess of fruit, and so he came to be seen as a god of orchards and fruit and therefore of fertility. There was a statue of Vertumnus in the Vicus Tuscus at the entrance to the FORUM ROMANUM in Rome, and offerings were made to the god there. He also had a temple on the Aventine Hill in Rome. His festival was on August 13.
Reading: Grimal 1986, 465; Hammond and Scullard (eds.) 1970, 1,114.

Vertumnus, temple of On the Aventine Hill in Rome in the Vicus Loreti Maioris. Marcus Fulvius Flaccus possibly built the temple of VERTUMNUS as a victory offering after a successful siege of Volsinii (Bolsena) in Italy in 264 B.C. Vertumnus was a Volsinian deity, who may have gone over to the Romans by *EVOCATIO*. Flaccus was depicted in tri-

umphal robes on the temple walls. Its dedication day was August 13.
Reading: Richardson 1992, 433.

Vervactor A Roman deity who was associated with the first plowing of the fallow land. He was said by Fabius Pictor in the late third century B.C. to have been invoked by a priest of CERES.
Reading: Ferguson 1988a, 853; York 1986, 60.

Vesta (Fig. 113) The Roman goddess of the hearth fire. She was identified with HESTIA, the Greek goddess of the hearth. In early Rome, the family in each household would gather at the domestic hearth once a day to perform a sacrifice to Vesta. There was a small round temple of Vesta in the FORUM ROMANUM in Rome (Figs. 37, 102), where the fire on her altar was kept constantly burning by the VESTAL VIRGINS. This eternal flame represented the goddess, who was not portrayed by statues in the temple, although the emperor Augustus dedicated an altar and statue to Vesta on the Palatine Hill in part of his house in 12 B.C. The flame in the temple of Vesta was rekindled every year in a ritual on March 1, by rubbing two sticks together. Vesta had a festival on June 9. On May 14, *ARGEI* were thrown into the Tiber River from the Sublician Bridge by the Vestal Virgins.

Fig. 113 The goddess Vesta depicted on a coin issued by Julia Mamaea (mother of Severus Alexander). Courtesy of Somerset County Museums Service.

Reading: Hammond and Scullard (eds.) 1970, 1,116; Simon 1990, 229–239.

Vesta, temple of (Figs. 37, 102) The only known temple of VESTA in Rome was a small round temple in the FORUM ROMANUM within the area known as the ATRIUM VESTAE at the foot of the Palatine Hill. The fire on Vesta's altar was kept constantly burning by the VESTAL VIRGINS in the temple. Men were forbidden to enter the temple. The building was technically a house *(aedes)*, not a temple, and its shape, according to tradition, reflected its original structure, which resembled one of the circular thatched huts of early Rome. According to legend, it was founded by Numa Pompilius, or even earlier by Romulus. The inner sanctum or storehouse *(penus)* possibly contained the PALLADIUM and two small statues of the PENATES (gods of the storehouse, *penus*) which had been brought from Samothrace, as well as other sacred items. However, it is not clear if the Vestal Virgins undertook all their rituals in this temple or elsewhere in the atrium Vestae. The temple was destroyed by fire and rebuilt several times, usually with the sacred objects being rescued. It was closed by THEODOSIUS I in 394. It was excavated mainly in 1899–1900, and part of it has been restored.
Reading: Richardson 1992, 412–413; Scullard 1981, 149; Steinby (ed.) 1993, 141–142.

Vestalia The festival of the goddess VESTA, on June 9. The days before and after this festival were consecrated to Vesta. On June 7 the inner sanctum of the temple in Rome was opened to women; it was closed again on June 15. Vestalia became a holiday for bakers and millers, and the millstones and asses used in milling were garlanded with violets and hung with small loaves. Very little is known about the public celebrations. On June 15 the refuse was swept from the temple of Vesta to an alleyway halfway up the CAPITOLINE HILL, from where it was carried to the Tiber River.
Reading: Scullard 1981, 148–150.

Vestal Virgins (Figs. 102, 114) *(virgines Vestales)* A priesthood of women who guarded the sacred hearth of Rome. There may have originally been two, and then four, Vestals, but their number later increased to six. They were chosen by lot from

Fig. 114 A statue of the Vestal Virgin Flavia Publica which was discovered in the atrium Vestae in 1883. She was a Vestal Virgin in the mid 3rd-century.

candidates selected by the *PONTIFEX MAXIMUS* from virgin girls aged between six and 10 possessing no bodily defect and with living parents. They may have originally been patricians. They were formally required to serve for 30 years, but they usually continued to serve for the rest of their lives. They lived in the Hall of Vesta (atrium Vestae) near the FORUM ROMANUM in Rome. They were maintained at public expense and were controlled by the *pontifex maximus* and had many social and legal privileges. They wore distinctive dress, and had a characteristic hairstyle known as *sex crines* ("six locks") which was otherwise only worn by brides on the day of their marriage. Their purity was all-important and they could be punished (such as by being buried alive) if found unchaste. In 83, for example, Domitian executed three Vestal Virgins for immorality, and in 90 he condemned the chief Vestal, Cornelia, to be buried alive. Vestal Virgins were held in high esteem and could be very influential when intervening on behalf of someone in trouble.

The Vestal Virgins' priesthood was pre-republican in origin, and the first Vestals may have been the successors of the king's daughters who tended the hearth in the palace. They had the duty of watching and tending the sacred hearth of the state in the temple of VESTA in Rome. On March 1 the fire was rekindled ritually by rubbing two sticks together; if the fire went out, it had to be relit in the same way. They undertook other ritual duties such as at the VESTALIA, FORDICIDIA and rites of CONSUS. They made the sacred salt cake (*MOLA SALSA*) used in the Vestalia, *EPULUM IOVIS* and LUPERCALIA, and looked after a number of sacred objects such as the Palladium. In order to make the sacred cake, they had to fetch water from a sacred spring without setting it down on the way back. The salt was specially prepared and mixed with flour.

Reading: Beard and North (eds.) 1990; Porte 1989, 85–88, 121; Scullard 1981, 148–150.

Vestius Aloniecus An Iberian god who is known from two inscriptions and a sculpture found near Pontevedra, on Spain's northwest coast. He is portrayed as a horned god accompanied by sun symbols and may be a version of the Celtic horned god CERNUNNOS. It appears likely that Vestius Aloniecus was a god of regeneration, perhaps linked to the power of the sun.

Reading: Tranoy 1981, 290–291.

Veteres Probably an alternative name of the Celtic deity (or deities) VITIRIS. It is not certain whether this name is singular or plural. Altars dedi-

cated to the Veteres are known from several forts in the area of Hadrian's Wall, England.
Reading: Birley 1973, 111–112.

Vica Pota An ancient Roman goddess of victory who was probably identified with VICTORIA and was later overshadowed by her. Vica Pota had a shrine in Rome at the foot of the slope of the VELIA; the anniversary of the shrine's dedication was celebrated on January 5.
Reading: Richardson 1992, 420; Scullard 1981, 60.

victimarius (pl. *victimarii*) An assistant at sacrifices who undertook the slaughter of the animals (Fig. 99). Under the empire, the *victimarii* were formed into a *collegium* (college). They also dissected the animals so that the *haruspices* could inspect the entrails (see HARUSPEX). A *popa* (pl. *popae*) was a *victimarius* who undertook the actual killing of the animals.
Reading: Hammond and Scullard (eds.) 1970, 1,120.

Victoria (Fig. 115) The Roman goddess of victory, the equivalent of the Greek goddess NIKE, often portrayed with wings. She had a temple on the Palatine Hill in Rome, and a gold statue of Victoria stood in the temple of JUPITER OPTIMUS MAXIMUS on the CAPITOLINE HILL. The statue was sent by Hiero of Syracuse to encourage the Romans after their defeat by Hannibal at the battle of Lake Trasimene in 217 B.C. The emperor Augustus installed an altar to her in the Senate house in 29 B.C. and later established the cult of VICTORIA AUGUSTA ("Victory of the Emperor"). Victoria was an important deity for the Romans and appears regularly on coinage from the late third century B.C. She came to be regarded as the guardian of the empire, and her altar became a symbol of PAGANISM. Victoria had festivals on July 17 and August 1 and was worshipped during the games on July 20 and October 26.
Reading: Hammond and Scullard (eds.) 1970, 1,120; Hölscher 1976 (in German); Simon 1990, 240–247.

Fig. 115 The reverse of an as *of Nero showing winged Victory (Victoria) with a shield inscribed SPQR (the Senate and Roman people), and SC (for* senatus consulto*). Courtesy of Somerset County Museums Service.*

Victoria, Altar of An altar of the goddess VICTORIA, sited in the Curia Iulia (Senate house) in Rome, a building begun by Julius Caesar in 44 B.C. When the altar was dedicated by Octavian (Augustus) in 29 B.C., he installed a statue of Victoria next to it which he also dedicated. The Curia, altar and statue were likely to have been dedicated on the same day (August 28, 29 B.C.). The statue had been brought from Tarentum, Italy, and showed Victoria standing with the tip of her foot on a globe. A golden shield inscribed with Augustus's virtues *(clupeus virtutis)* was also placed in the Curia Iulia near the statue of Victory in 27 B.C. It was dedicated in 26 B.C. Victoria was often depicted holding this shield. The altar came to symbolize the strength of pagan religion in its struggle with CHRISTIANITY. It was removed by Constantius in 357, but was apparently restored (probably by Julian). In 384 SYMMACHUS and other members of the aristocracy pleaded for the altar (and hence paganism) to be restored, but this was resisted by Valentinian II. The altar was restored there by Flavius Eugenius and its use was finally abolished by Gratian.
Reading: Fishwick 1987, 111, 115–116; Rehak 1990; Richardson 1992, 420–421.

Victoria, temple of A temple built by Lucius Postumius Megillus and dedicated by him as consul on August 1, 294 B.C. It was built on the Palatine Hill, traditionally by EVANDER. It is possibly the temple found in the southwestern area of the Pala-

tine Hill just east of the temple of MAGNA MATER. The black stone of Magna Mater was housed temporarily in this temple when it was brought to Rome in 204 B.C. It was one of the first temples to be restored by Augustus.
Reading: Patterson 1992, 204–205; Richardson 1992, 420; Wiseman 1981.

Victoria Augusta ("Victory of the Emperor") Also known as Victoria Augusti, this version of the Roman goddess VICTORIA came into existence during the reign of the emperor Augustus—probably before the first decade A.D., when this goddess is first recorded. She appears to have been a personification of the abstract idea of "victory over enemies of the emperor" (that is, enemies outside the empire rather than rebels within it).
Reading: Fishwick 1987, 116.

Victoria Virgo An aspect of the Roman goddess VICTORIA whose name means "Victory the Virgin." There was a shrine of Victoria Virgo near the temple of Victoria on the Palatine Hill in Rome.
Reading: Scullard 1981, 170.

Vidasus A native Illyrian deity who is known from an inscription found at Topusko, Croatia. At the same site a dedication to the Illyrian deity THANA and 12 altars dedicated to the Roman god SILVANUS have been found. It has been suggested that Vidasus was equated with Silvanus, but there appears to be little evidence to support this suggestion.
Reading: Dorcey 1992, 72.

Vinalia Priora The first of two agricultural festivals held in Rome connected with wine production. It was held on April 23. *Vinalia* is derived from *vinum* ("wine"). Originally in honor of JUPITER, this festival was later connected with VENUS as well. Wine casks filled in the previous autumn were opened, and the first draught of this new wine was offered as a LIBATION to Jupiter. A temple was dedicated to VENUS ERYCINA on April 23, 181 B.C., outside the Porta Collina in Rome, and the Vinalia Priora also became a day when VENUS received offerings from the female prostitutes of Rome at this temple.
Reading: Scullard 1981, 106–108.

Vinalia Rustica An agricultural festival—possibly to celebrate the start of the grape harvest—in which the first grapes were broken off the vine by the *FLAMEN DIALIS*. It was held on August 19, although August is too early for harvesting (which usually takes place at the end of September), and so it may have been a ceremony to protect the vines. The festival was probably associated with JUPITER and later with VENUS. It may have been observed more in the countryside than in the city, as is implied by the word *Rustica*.
Reading: Scullard 1981, 177.

Vindonnus ("clear light") A Celtic god who was linked with the Greek god APOLLO as APOLLO VINDONNUS.

Vinotonus A Celtic god who is known from four inscriptions on altars, all found near the Roman fort of Bowes, North Yorkshire, England. Two of the altars were dedicated to Vinotonus and two to SILVANUS VINOTONUS. The function of this deity is unknown; some authorities have taken the name *Vinotonus* to be connected with viticulture, while others have thought the name a personification of a local stream, but neither interpretation is universally accepted.
Reading: Dorcey 1992, 55; Jones and Mattingly 1990, 275–276.

Viradecthis A Germanic goddess who is known from an inscription on an altar found at Birrens, Scotland. The dedication was made by men of the *pagus Condrustis* serving as soldiers of the garrison at Birrens. The *pagus Condrustis* was an area of the German Rhineland, and other dedications to Viradecthis have been found there.
Reading: Keppie and Arnold 1984, 9.

Virbius A Roman god of the forest who was later identified with the Greek god HIPPOLYTUS. He was worshipped in association with DIANA and EGERIA in a grove at Nemi near Aricia, Italy (the sanctuary of DIANA NEMORENSIS).
Reading: Room 1983, 306–307.

Virgo Caelestis An alternative name for the Carthaginian goddess TANIT. (See also JUNO CAELESTIS.)

Viridios A Celtic god who is known from an inscription found at Ancaster, England. *Viridios* may mean "virile" or "manly."
Reading: Ross 1974, 486.

Viriplaca A Roman goddess who helped wives regain their husband's favor after a quarrel. Viriplaca had a shrine on the Palatine Hill in Rome, to which husbands and wives went to plead their cases; they were then supposed to return home in harmony.
Reading: Richardson 1992, 107.

Virotutis (probably meaning "benefactor of humanity") A Celtic god who was linked with the god APOLLO as APOLLO VIROTUTIS.

Virrora Viliaegus An Iberian deity who is known from an inscription found in the Lugo region of northwest Spain. It is possible that this is the same deity referred to as VERORA and VEROCA in inscriptions from the same area.
Reading: Tranoy 1981, 294.

Virtus (Fig. 116) The Roman deity of "virtue" in the sense of physical and moral excellence, often associated with HONOS. There was a temple of HONOS AND VIRTUS by the Porta Capena in Rome, and a shrine, possibly on the slope of the CAPITOLINE HILL. There was a festival of Virtus on July 17.
Reading: Richardson 1992, 431; Weinstock 1971, 230–233.

Fig. 116 A coin of Galba depicting Honos (right) as a male figure in armor and Virtus (left) as a draped female figure holding a cornucopia.

Visucia A Celtic goddess who was the counterpart of the Celtic god VISUCIUS. She is known from a dedication to a divine couple of MARS VISUCIUS and Visucia from Gaul and to a divine couple of MERCURY VISUCIUS and Visucia from Stuttgart, Germany.
Reading: Espérandieu 1931, no. 595; Green, M. J. 1992a, 220 (under *Visucius*).

Visucius A Celtic god who was worshipped mainly in the frontier area of the empire in Gaul and Germany. His counterpart was the Celtic goddess VISUCIA. He was usually equated with the Roman god MERCURY, as in an inscription from Stuttgart, Germany, but a divine couple of MARS VISUCIUS and a goddess Visucia is known from a dedicatory inscription in Gaul.
Reading: Espérandieu 1931, no. 595; Green, M. J. 1992a, 220.

Visuna A Germanic goddess who is known from an inscription on an altar found at Baden-Baden, Germany.
Reading: Espérandieu 1931, no. 449.

Vitiris (Fig. 117) Probably also called Hvitiris, Vetus, Vitris, Veteris, Hveteris, Hvitris, Vheteris, Vitires and Veteres. A Celtic deity or deities; it is not certain if any of these names is plural. He was worshipped in the Roman period in northern England, in the area of the center and eastern end of Hadrian's Wall. The cult followers appear to have been largely male, and Vitiris was particularly popular among the lower ranks of the army in the third century. However, at least one female cult member is recorded on an inscription found at Great Chesters on Hadrian's Wall. There may have been a center of his cult at Carvoran, also on Hadrian's Wall, where several dedicatory inscriptions have been found, some with the god's name spelled in different ways. Fifty-four inscriptions are known to mention this god. Some of the dedications

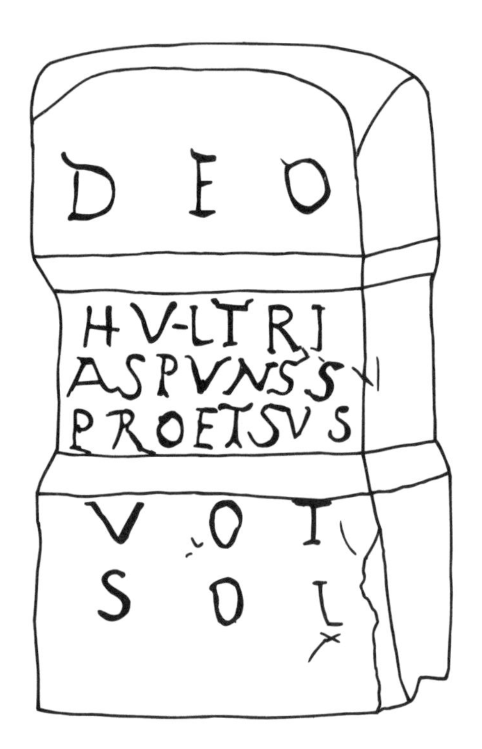

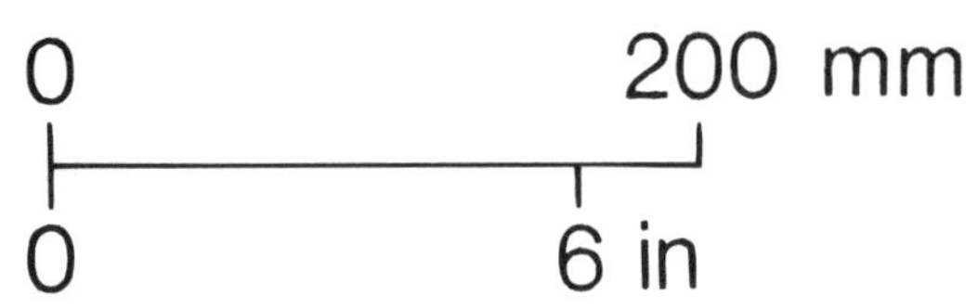

Fig. 117 An altar dedicated to Vitiris (Huitris) found at Housesteads on Hadrian's Wall, England. The legend reads DEO HVITRI ASPVNIS PRO ET SVIS VOT SOL ("To the god Vitiris, Aspuanis pays his vow for [himself] and his").

allude to multiple versions of the god, probably to a trio of deities. One inscription links MOGONS with Vitiris. Some of the altars are decorated with a serpent and a boar. Little is known about the character or function of the deity, who never seems to have been linked with classical Roman deities.
Reading: Green, M. J. 1992a, 220; Jones and Mattingly 1990, 276; Ross 1974, 468–470.

Vitula A Roman goddess of exultation and joy.

Vitumnus The Roman god who was thought to give life to a newborn child.

Volcanalia The festival of VULCAN, held on August 23. Celebrations in honor of MAIA and HORA, both of whom were at times regarded as consorts of Vulcan, also took place on this day. OPS and the nymphs were also worshipped, but their connection with Vulcan is unclear. Little otherwise is known of the festival.
Reading: Scullard 1981, 178–180; York 1986, 160–163.

Volcanus The Latin name for the god VULCAN.

Volcanus Quietus ("Vulcan at Rest") A form of VULCAN, the Roman god of fire. He appears to have been propitiated in order to prevent fires. He was associated with the Roman goddess STATA MATER, whose role was also the prevention of the spread of fire.
Reading: Hammond and Scullard (eds.) 1970, 1,130–1,131.

Volturnalia The festival of VOLTURNUS, held on August 27.

Volturnus The origin of this god is obscure. He seems to have been a river god, perhaps of Etruscan origin, or possibly a wind god. His cult seems to have dwindled by the late republic. He had his own FLAMEN, the *flamen Volturnalis*, and he was variously regarded as the father of the water deity JUTURNA or equated with Eurus, the southeast wind. Volturnus had a festival, the VOLTURNALIA.
Reading: Scullard 1981, 181–182.

Volumna A Roman goddess who presided over childhood. This goddess was probably originally an Etruscan deity. She had a consort called VOLUMNUS.

Volumnus A Roman god who was the consort of VOLUMNA.

Volupia A Roman goddess of pleasure. There was a shrine with an altar dedicated to her near the Porta Romana in Rome (the *sacellum Volupiae*). Here

she was associated with ANGERONA, the Roman goddess of secrecy, who had a statue on the altar. It has been suggested that the two goddesses were different aspects of the same deity.
Reading: Richardson 1992, 433.

Volutina A goddess of the husks of cereal crops when they are folded over the ears.

Vorocius A Celtic healing god who was linked with MARS as MARS VOROCIUS.

Vortumnus An alternative name for the god VERTUMNUS.

Vosegus The Celtic god of the Vosges mountains in eastern Gaul. Vosegus personified the spirit of the mountains and was probably also a god of hunting and protector of the inhabitants of the Vosges forest. Images of a local nature god may represent Vosegus. Some of them portray the god wearing a wolf skin over his shoulders and with his hand on a stag, and he carries a spear, hunting knife, chopper and an open bag containing fruits of the forest such as acorns, nuts and a pine cone. In other portrayals, the god wears a heavy Gallic cloak and carries a piglet under one arm.
Reading: Green, M. J. 1992a, 220–221.

votive offering (ex-voto) (Fig. 118) A form of SACRIFICE made after the fulfillment of a vow (although some of the offerings may have been given in expectation of favors to come). They were permanent gifts to the gods and were also referred to as ex-votos. They could range in size from temples, monumental arches and altars to small coins and FIGURINES, and could also range widely in value. They were often deposited in temples along with the religious plate and cult objects, as well as in sacred springs, fountains and deep pits. In excavations of religious sites, it is often difficult to distinguish casual loss from deliberate votive deposits. Often votive offerings were deliberately broken or damaged, metal objects bent, and coins bent or defaced; it is thought that this was an attempt to "kill" the object as a sacrifice, just as animals sacrificed to the gods were killed. The offerings were probably placed inside the temples or hung on the walls; the temples must have been periodically cleared out when they became full, and the cheaper ex-votos in particular must have been packed into small rooms or buildings or buried in sacred pits: they could not be destroyed as they were the property of the gods.

Fig. 118 Two miniature or model pots from Lamyatt Beacon, England, which were probably deposited as votive offerings. Height approximately 2.36 in. (60 mm). Courtesy of Somerset County Museums Service.

Votive offerings could be made of almost any material, and many of the more perishable items will not have survived. For example, few wooden statuettes or figurines are known, but it is likely that these were common offerings. Objects made specifically as votive offerings were sold in shops at the more important temples and shrines, in some cases imported to the site. For example, pottery figurines were exported from Gaul and the Rhineland to Britain. Items commonly for sale included stone reliefs, bronze figurines, votive plaques, bronze letters, and model (miniature) objects. Stone reliefs depicting gods and goddesses sometimes had a space prepared for the addition of an inscription. Bronze letters (some with gilding) with nail holes are thought to have been used to make up inscriptions, possibly on wooden plaques.

Many votive offerings were made of pottery; these included miniature or model pots, lamps and lamp covers, as well as figurines and incense burners. Rings and brooches of bronze, silver and gold were commonly used as votive offerings, as were gifts of coins and precious metal. For example, more than 12,000 coins have been recovered from the sacred spring at Bath, England. There are also records of valuable antiques being given to shrines and temples. In all these cases, the symbolic act of giving an offering to the gods was enhanced by the fact that the worshipper was giving up a real part of his or her wealth. Offerings of food were probably commonplace, and ANATOMICAL EX-VOTOS are found particularly at healing shrines. (See also MODEL OBJECTS; VOTIVE PLAQUE; VOW.)

Reading: Bourgeois 1991, 113–204; de Cazanove 1993; Hassall 1980; Henig 1993a; Hassall 1993b; Merrifield 1987, 22–57; Woodward 1992, 66–78.

votive plaque (Fig. 119) Many votive offerings took the form of silver (sometimes gilded), gold or bronze plaques (Fig. 53), which could be decorated and bear a dedicatory inscription. Some of these plaques were leaf-shaped (votive leaves) or feather-shaped (votive feathers). Some plaques had triangular handles *(ansae)* on each side. Votive leaves and feathers often had a small hole at the base by which they could be nailed down or suspended by a thread. Some also have representations of gods and/or inscriptions, and a few have been found in Roman Britain with the Christian CHI-RHO symbols flanked by the Greek letters *alpha* and *omega.*

Reading: Bourgeois 1991, 113–204; Henig 1993a; Toynbee 1978.

vow (Latin, *votum,* pl. *vota)* A bargain made with a god, or a promise; if a god granted a favor, the person would do what had been vowed in return. In a PRAYER, the god received a gift whether or not the prayer was answered, but with a vow the god only received a gift if the suppliant's wish was granted. Public vows on behalf of the state promised the gods special sacrifices in return for some favor, often protection from imminent disaster. These vows were recorded in writing, and the records were kept by the pontiffs. Private vows were at times recorded on votive tablets which were deposited in temples. Many have been found, such as at the temple of MERCURY in Uley, England, where they were mostly inscribed on lead sheets, and were largely of the type known as curse tablets. CURSES *(defixiones)* were at times a form of vow.

Annual vows *(vota)* to the gods were undertaken on the emperor's behalf, and were occasions for SACRIFICE. They were attested in Rome and in the provinces.

Once the god performed his part of the transaction, the person was bound by the vow. The initial vow was called the *nuncupatio* (pl. *nuncupationes*) and

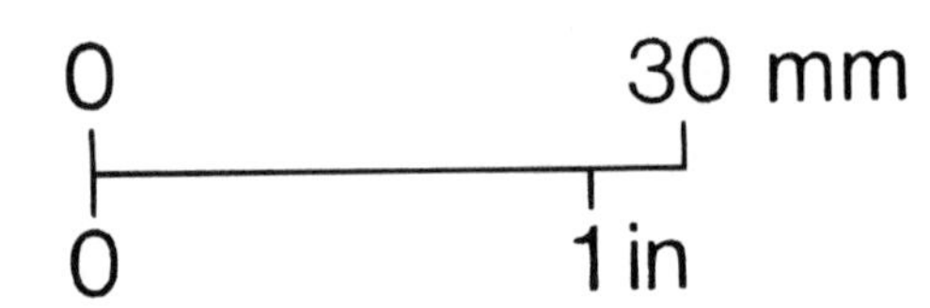

Fig. 119 A silver-gilt votive plaque or leaf dedicated to Mars Alator. It was found at Barkway, Hertfordshire, England.

Fig. 120 An altar from Paris depicting a Gaulish Volcanus (Vulcan), identified by the insciption VOLCANVS. He is shown with a hammer and tongs.

its fulfillment was the *solutio.* Fulfillment of a vow usually took the form of a VOTIVE OFFERING, which might be the deposition of a gift at a shrine or temple. The vow to the god was often the promise of the erection of an ALTAR, and inscriptions are often found on altars fulfilling the vow with the formulae *ex voto* ("in accordance with a vow") or *votum solvit laetus libens merito* ("paid his vow joyfully, freely and deservedly"), usually abbreviated to VSLLM. Inscriptions on many altars show that they were set up in thanks to a god for favors granted freely, rather than in response to a suppliant's vow, while other altars were set up in anticipation of a favor. Many of the latter were *pro salute* ("for the health of") a named person.
Reading: Hammond and Scullard (eds.) 1970, 1,133; Hassall 1980.

Vulcan (Fig. 120) Known in Latin as Volcanus and Vulcanus, an early Roman god of fire and perhaps also of the smithy. He was sometimes given the epithet *Mulciber* ("Smelter of metals"). He had his own *FLAMEN*, the *flamen Volcanalis.* Vulcan was later identified with the Greek god HEPHAESTUS. Vulcan was the father of the fire-breathing monster Cacus. Vulcan had an important cult in Ostia, where he was the patron god. He had festivals on May 23 (TUBILUSTRIUM) and August 23 (VOLCANALIA). In Rome, there was a temple of Vulcan in the CAMPUS MARTIUS which was attributed to Romulus. (See also VOLCANUS QUIETUS.)
Reading: Hammond and Scullard (eds.) 1970, 1,130–1,031; Richardson 1992, 432–433; Simon 1990, 248–255; York 1986, 87–90.

Vulcanus An alternative name for the god VOLCANUS, known in English as VULCAN.

W

wheel motif The spoked wheel symbol was possibly originally a solar symbol related to the Celtic sun god. In the Romano-Celtic world, it is depicted with various gods on nearly 200 stone monuments and in many other representations; in particular, it was associated with the Romano-Celtic sky god (who has no name). The wheel also occurs without the image of a deity, for example, as model (miniature) wheels. The swastika seems to have shared a similar symbolism, and its use seems to have been interchangeable with the wheel.
Reading: Green, M. J. 1984 (includes a gazetteer of examples); Green, M. J. 1986.

wolf *(canis lupus)* A commonplace beast of prey in Roman times, sacred to MARS.

word square (or magic square) A square composed of letters and numbers. Its significance and purpose are uncertain, and very few modern interpretations of word squares are uncontroversial. The most well known is the palindrome ROTAS OPERA TENET AREPO SATOR, several examples of which have been found.

R O T A S
O P E R A
T E N E T
A R E P O
S A T O R

Translated, this means "Arepo the sower holds the wheels with effort." It has often been claimed as Christian in origin. It can be rearranged in a cruciform as PATERNOSTER ("Our Father") twice, sharing the letter *N*, with two letters *A* and *O* (*alpha* and *omega*). Not all examples have been found in Christian contexts, and some are too early in date. It is most likely that it was later adopted by Christians. (See also CHRISTIAN SYMBOLS.)
Reading: Merrifield 1987, 142–147; Thomas 1981, 101–102.

X

Xulsigiae Celtic deities who are known from a shrine in Trier, Germany, which was linked with one of the precincts dedicated to MARS LENUS. They may have been a triad of fertility and mother goddesses, associated with a sacred spring. A clay figure of a *genius cucullatus* was also found at the shrine, and *genii cucullati* were often associated with mother goddesses.
Reading: Green, M. J. 1992a, 228.

Z

Zalmoxis An UNDERWORLD deity who was also known as Salmoxis. He was worshipped in the area of modern-day Romania and Bulgaria. He appears to have originally been a god worshipped by the Getae, a Thracian tribe who had settled in the area around the lower Danube by the fourth century B.C.
Reading: Hammond and Scullard (eds.) 1970, 1,144.

Zeus The chief god in the Greek pantheon who was equated with the Roman god JUPITER.

Zosimus (late 5th century) A Greek pagan historian who attributed the decline of the empire to the rejection of the pagan gods. He was author (in Greek) of *Historia Nova (New History)*, four books on the Roman empire from the time of Augustus to 410 (the sack of Rome). Being a pagan, he was in favor of JULIAN THE APOSTATE, and hostile to Constantine and THEODOSIUS I.
Reading: Hammond and Scullard (eds.) 1970, 1,150.

GLOSSARY

Various technical terms are explained here, but further information can be obtained from Adkins and Adkins 1994.

Aeneas In Roman legend, one of the leaders in the Trojan war, the son of Anchises (a Trojan prince) and of the goddess Venus, and the founder of the Latin city of Lanuvium in Italy.

Africa The province of Africa was formed from conquered territory by the Romans in 146 B.C., roughly equivalent to northeast Tunisia. Further colonies were created along the entire stretch of North Africa.

Alexandria A city in Egypt founded by Alexander the Great and which continued as a center of learning and commerce throughout the Roman period.

amphitheater An elliptical or oval structure, with tiers of seats around an arena, in which gladiatorial and wild beast shows took place.

Anatolia A mountainous area of eastern Turkey bounded by the Pontine Mountains in the north and Zagros mountains in the south. Also used for the entire area of Asia Minor.

Antoninus Pius Roman emperor who succeeded Hadrian in 138; died in 161.

archaic Latin The language of the Roman people from earliest times up to 100 B.C.

Arch of Titus A triumphal arch in Rome commemorating the long siege of Jerusalem and its capture in 70 by Titus.

Asia The Roman province of Asia was territory bequeathed to Rome in 133 B.C., equivalent to part of western Turkey (not modern-day Asia).

Augustus The first Roman emperor, from 27 B.C. to A.D. 14. He was previously known as Octavian.

Aurelian Roman emperor from 270 to 275.

Ausonius Poet who lived c. 310 to 393/395. He taught rhetoric in Bordeaux, retired to Trier after holding official appointments, but returned to Bordeaux. His best-known poem is the *Mosella*, on the beauties of the Moselle River and life around it.

Baths of Caracalla Extensive public baths situated in the southern part of the city of Rome.

Belgica Also known as Gallia Belgica, one of the Roman provinces of northeast Gaul (covering parts of modern-day Belgium, Luxembourg, the Netherlands and Germany).

Brutus Lived c. 85 to 42 B.C., fought with Pompey against Julius Caesar, and was Caesar's prime assassin. He was defeated at Philippi in 42 B.C.

Caligula A nickname ("little boots") for Gaius, Roman emperor 37 to 41.

Cappadocia A Roman province in the eastern part of modern Turkey.

Caracalla Roman emperor from 198 to 217.

Carthage A city founded as a Phoenician colony on the Tunisian coast in the ninth century B.C. (or earlier). It became a wealthy trading power and clashed with Rome in three wars in the third and second centuries B.C. Destroyed by Rome in 146 B.C., it was reestablished as a colony in 29 B.C. and became an important Roman city.

Cassius Gaius Cassius Longinus, a leading conspirator in Julius Caesar's assassination. He was defeated by Antony and Octavian at Philippi in 42 B.C.

Cassius Dio Greek historian and Roman official, lived from 150 to 235. Author of an 80-volume history of Rome.

Cato Cato the Elder or the Censor, lived from 234 to 149 B.C. He had a distinguished military and political career and wrote several treaties, including one on agriculture.

Celts People of the Iron Age who inhabited central and western Europe (north of the Mediterranean region) and who were largely conquered by the Romans.

censor A Roman magistrate. In the republic, this was the highest rank of magistrate, responsible for taking censuses, leasing public land, awarding government contracts and controlling public morals.

Cicero Marcus Tullius Cicero, lived from 106 to 43 B.C. A politician and great orator, as well as a prolific writer, particularly on rhetoric and philosophy.

cinerary urn A container (often of pottery) that held the ashes of the dead.

Claudius Roman emperor (succeeding Caligula) from 41 to 54.

colonies Settlements established by Rome in conquered territories, often for retired legionary veterans.

comitia centuriata Centuriate assembly, originally a military assembly. It was Rome's main legislative body, but rarely legislated after 218 B.C.

Constantine The emperor Constantine I or Constantine the Great, who ruled from 306 to 337.

Constantinople A city founded by Constantine I on the site of Byzantium in 324; it became the empire's new capital. It is now known as Istanbul.

consuls Two annually elected magistrates at Rome, originally in charge of military campaigns. They presided over meetings of the Senate and implemented its decisions.

Corinthian columns The most popular order of Roman architecture was Corinthian. The column capitals were an inverted bell-shape decorated with acanthus leaves.

cursive writing Roman everyday handwriting, used privately and by official scribes; the letters are composed of rounded flowing strokes for ease of writing.

curule magistrates Magistrates (praetors, consuls, censors and curule aediles) who had the right to sit on a special chair *(sella curulis)* as a symbol of their office.

Cyriacus of Ancona A scholar born in 1391 who spent 25 years visiting sites and libraries in Greece and publishing commentaries.

Dalmatia Also known as the province of Illyricum, this was an area of the Dalmatia coast (eastern Adriatic), equivalent to parts of modern Bosnia and Croatia.

dictator A magistrate appointed by the Senate in emergencies and who had supreme military and judicial authority.

Diocletian Roman emperor from 284 to 305 (when he abdicated).

Domitian Roman emperor from 81 to 96.

Domus Aurea Golden House, a huge palace in Rome built by Nero (emperor from 54 to 68), but demolished soon afterward.

Drusus Nero Claudius Drusus, lived from 38 B.C. to 9 B.C., brother of the emperor Tiberius.

duovir Also referred to as duumvir. One of two men who formed a board, usually to perform regular or occasional functions.

Dura-Europus An important Parthian city (now in Syria) on the Euphrates. It was under Roman domination from 165 and was destroyed by the Persians in 256.

east/eastern empire A term to describe the eastern part of the Roman empire, mainly Greek-speaking, and including Greece, Asia Minor, the Levant and Egypt.

emperors Rulers of the Roman world from the end of the republic in 27 B.C.

empire A term sometimes used to describe territory conquered by Rome from the second century B.C. (late republic) onward; more usually it describes the Roman world after the end of the republic in 27 B.C., throughout the five-century period when it was ruled by emperors.

Ephesus Originally a Greek colony, then a Roman city, on the west coast of Asia Minor (now Turkey).

Etruria An area to the north of Rome inhabited by the Etruscans.

Etruscans The people who inhabited Etruria to the north of Rome from the eighth to fifth centuries B.C. They formed a loosely structured but powerful confederation of city-states, with their own language and alphabet.

First Punic War War of Rome against the Carthaginians, 264–241 B.C.

forum A large open space in a town used as a meeting place, marketplace and political center.

Forum of Nerva Forum Nervae or Forum Transitorium. A forum in Rome built by Domitian and dedicated by Nerva in A.D. 97. At its east end was the temple of Minerva.

freedmen Slaves became freedmen or freedwomen by being granted manumission by their owner; they could also buy freedom. Freedmen gained citizenship but were not eligible for public office.

Galatia A Roman province formed in 25 B.C., in the central part of Asia Minor.

Gallia Narbonensis A Roman province in southern France.

Gaul The area bounded by the Alps, the Pyrénées, the Rhine, the Atlantic Ocean and the Mediterranean Sea. It was divided into several Roman provinces whose inhabitants were referred to as Gauls.

gens A Roman family clan or group of families linked by a common name and ancestor.

Germanicus Lived 15 B.C. to A.D. 19. He led military campaigns against Germany and in the east and died in suspicious circumstances in Antioch, Turkey. He was father of the emperor Caligula.

Germans People who lived in an undefined area east of the Rhine River (in Germania) and beyond, and whom the Romans found it difficult to conquer.

Goths A Germanic people originally from southern Scandinavia. They began to invade the Roman empire in the third century.

Greek world The Greek-speaking east (including Greece, Asia Minor, Levant and Egypt), which was conquered by the Romans.

Hadrian Roman emperor from 117 to 138.

Hadrian's Wall A defensive frontier wall with fortlets, turrets and forts built across northern England under the emperor Hadrian.

Hellenistic A term used to describe the Greek world in the eastern Mediterranean and Near East from the death of Alexander the Great (323 B.C.) until its domination by the Romans (approx 30 B.C.).

Horace A lyric poet and satirist. Lived 65 to 8 B.C.

Iberia The Roman name for the Iberian peninsula, comprising modern-day Spain and Portugal.

imperial family The Roman emperor and his family (usually wife and children).

inscriptions Roman writing inscribed in durable materials such as stone or metal, usually of a formal nature.

Janiculum Hill A prominent ridge in Rome on the west bank of the Tiber River, overlooking a large area of the city.

Judaea A Roman province created in 70 after the Jewish Revolt in Jerusalem and the surrounding area; it was later renamed Syria Palaestina.

Julian calendar A reformed calendar introduced by Julius Caesar in 44 B.C.

Julius Caesar Born 100 B.C., he held various military and public offices. In 49 B.C. he started a civil war by crossing the Rubicon River with his army from his province to Italy. He defeated Pompey at Pharsalus in 48 B.C., became a dictator but was assassinated in 44 B.C.

Lanuvium An ancient Latin city in the Alban Hills south of Rome.

Latin The Latin language was originally that of Rome and the territory of Latium but spread to the entire western Roman empire. Latins were pre-Roman inhabitants of Latium.

Latin League An association or confederacy of Latin towns for religious purposes which formed a defensive alliance with Rome in 493 B.C.

Latin towns Towns in Latium, south of Rome, many of which became depopulated from c. 300 B.C. after being incorporated in the Roman state.

Latium An area to the south of Rome between the Apennines and the Tyrrhenian Sea that was populated by Latini (Latins) before the Roman conquest.

legions Units of the army; in the early empire each legion comprised about 5,500 men, including some cavalry.

Ligurian War Campaigns by the Romans against the Ligurians in northern Italy between 238 and 117 B.C.

Linen Books In Latin, *libri lintei*, these were lists of magistrates in Rome which were begun in 509 B.C. They were written on linen around the mid-second century B.C.

Livia Livia Drusilla, lived from 58 B.C. to A.D. 29. Her second husband was the emperor Augustus.

Livy An historian who lived c. 59 B.C. to A.D. 12 or 17. Thirty-five books of his 142-volume history survive.

Lucan A poet, author of the surviving epic poem *On the Civil War* (often called *Pharsalia*). He lived from 39 to 65.

magistrates Elected government officials of Rome, with executive, judicial, legislative, diplomatic, military and religious functions. The term of office was usually one year.

Mark Antony A military leader who lived c. 83 to 30 B.C. After Caesar's assassination he assumed power in Rome with Lepidus. He was challenged by Octavian (Augustus) and civil war ensued. He was defeated at Actium in 31 B.C.

Martial Poet who lived c. 40 to 103/104, and who is particularly known for his epigrams, often satirical and witty.

Mausolus A ruler of an area of southwest Asia Minor 377 to 353 B.C. His tomb, known as the Mausoleum, was one of the Seven Wonders of the World.

Mesopotamia The territory between the Tigris and Euphrates rivers. It was made a Roman province by Trajan but was abandoned by the emperor Hadrian.

mosaics Decorative floors composed of small cubes of stone, tile and other materials.

municipal Relating to a town with the status of *municipium.* It could have Roman citizens or non-citizens and was lower in status than a colony.

naumachia Mock sea battle staged as entertainment in artificial lakes.

Nero Roman emperor from 37 to 68.

Nicaea A town founded in the fourth century B.C. and which remained important under the Roman empire. It is now Iznik in Turkey.

Noricum A Roman province, equivalent to parts of modern-day Slovenia, Italy and Austria.

Numa Pompilius A king of early Rome, who reigned 715–673 B.C.

obelisk An Egyptian monolithic monument. Obelisks were often taken from Egypt for erection in Rome.

Octavian A military leader who defeated Mark Antony at the battle of Actium in 31 B.C. He became the first Roman emperor, and was then known as Augustus.

Palmyra A trading and caravan city between Syria and Babylonia. It became a Roman city, but was always cosmopolitan in nature.

Pannonia A Roman colony equivalent to parts of modern-day Slovenia, Hungary and Croatia.

papyrus A common writing material in the Roman world which was used in rolls. It was made from Egyptian papyrus plants.

Parisi tribe A pre-Roman tribe in the Paris area of France.

paterfamilias The male legal head of the household who had absolute power over his children, married or unmarried.

patricians Privileged citizens from certain Roman families, many of whom were senators and landowners and who controlled the Senate and assemblies, state religion and law.

pediment The triangular or gable end of a ridge roof, particularly in temples.

Persian Relating to Persia (largely modern-day Iran), whose empire expanded to cover much of the eastern Mediterranean. The empire was conquered by Alexander the Great in the fourth century B.C.

Phoenician Relating to Phoenicia, a country along the coast of modern-day Lebanon and Syria. The Phoenicians were a seafaring people who established colonies in Spain and North Africa (including Carthage c. 814 B.C.).

Phrygia Territory in western Asia Minor (including part of the central plateau) which was incorporated into the Roman province of Asia.

plebeians Roman citizens who were not patricians. In the early republic they were excluded from the Senate, public office and important priesthoods.

Pliny the Elder Holder of various public offices, he lived from 23 or 24 to 79. He wrote many works, including his surviving 37-volume *Natural History.*

Porta Collina The Colline Gate (Hill Gate) through the Servian wall on the northeast side of Rome, through which the Via Salaria and Via Nometana passed.

Porta Portuensis The gate to Portus (harbor) through the Aurelian Wall west of the Tiber River in Rome.

Porta Primigenia The first gate through the Servian Wall in Rome near the Tiber River and the Forum Boarium.

porticoes Colonnades, usually forming parts of buildings and surrounding open areas such as gardens.

praetor A senior magistrate in Rome who originally held military command but who later dealt with legal matters and even games and festivals.

Praetorian prefect A commander of the Praetorian Guard (the garrison in Rome). By the late empire, the Praetorian prefect had become deputy to the emperor, with responsibility for finances and supplying the army and civil service.

praetorium The area in which a general's tent was pitched in a military camp, and later a term used for the commander's residence in a fort or fortress.

procurator Title given to governors of some imperial provinces and to collectors of taxes.

province Conquered Roman territory that was governed by magistrates. The Roman empire was divided into numerous provinces.

provincial governors Administrative rulers of Roman provinces, responsible for law and order, justice, security and collection of taxes.

Punic Relating to the territory and people of Carthage (North Africa).

Remus Mythical founder of Rome, along with Romulus, in the eighth century B.C.

republic The period of Rome from 508 B.C. (end of the monarchy) to 27 B.C. (beginning of the empire and rule by emperors).

Res Gestae A work *(Acts)* written by the emperor Augustus on his achievements.

Romanization The assimilation of Roman culture and language by non-Romans.

Romulus Mythical founder of Rome, along with Remus, in the eighth century B.C.

Rubicon A river forming a boundary between Cisalpine Gaul and Italy. Julius Caesar illegally crossed this boundary with troops and thus precipitated a civil war.

Sabine An Italian people living northeast of Rome. They were conquered by the Romans in the Sabine Wars (to 449 B.C.).

Samnites Oscan-speaking people who inhabited the southen Apennines of Italy (an area north of Naples) and who were conquered by Rome.

Scipios, tomb of An enormous tomb built by the Scipio family just after 200 B.C. along the Via Appia outside Rome.

Second Punic War A war of Rome against Carthage (including Hannibal) from 218 to 201 B.C.

Senate A body that advised magistrates in Rome. In the first and second centuries B.C. it was the virtual government in Rome, but its power was greatly curtailed by the emperors.

Senate house The meeting place of the Senate (usually known as a *curia*).

senators A group of unelected men who comprised the Senate (restricted originally to patricians but later extended to plebeians).

Septimius Severus Roman emperor from 193 to 211.

Servius Tullius A king of early Rome who reigned from 579 to 534 B.C.

slaves A large number of slaves made up the population of the Roman world. They had no political rights, but they could be granted or could buy their freedom.

spoils Property looted by soldiers from the conquered (and known as *spolia*).

stele A grave marker, or an upright rectangular slab on which decrees and other documents were inscribed.

stilus Also known as a stylus, an implement with a flat end and a pointed end for writing on waxed tablets.

Strabo A Greek geographer and historian who lived from 64 or 63 B.C. to A.D. 24. His works included a 17-volume *Geography*.

Sublician Bridge The oldest bridge over the Tiber River in Rome, originally built on wood piles *(sublicae)*.

Sulla A politician and military leader who lived c. 138 to 78 B.C. He was involved in a civil war and finally became dictator in 82 B.C.

Syria A Roman province equivalent to parts of modern-day Syria, Lebanon and Turkey.

Tarquinius Superbus Tarquin the Proud, the last king of early Rome from 534 to 509 B.C.

theater Usually a freestanding semi-circular structure with tiered seating and an orchestra and stage. They were used for the performance of plays and increasingly for pantomimes and mimes.

Third Punic War War of Rome against the Carthaginians from 149 to 146 B.C., culminating in the total destruction of Carthage.

Thrace An area equivalent to parts of modern-day Greece, Turkey and Bulgaria that became a Roman province in A.D. 46.

Tiberius Roman emperor who succeeded Augustus in A.D. 14 and died in 37.

Titus Roman emperor from 79 to 81, and who was responsible for the siege and destruction of Jerusalem in 70.

toga Formal outer garment of Roman male citizens which was draped in a complicated way round the body.

Trajan Roman emperor who reigned from 98 to 117.

Treveri Pre-Roman inhabitants of the territory around Trier in Germany.

triumvirs A board of three men. The term *triumvirate* was used for the alliances of Pompey, Crassus and Julius Caesar and of Octavian, Antony and Lepidus.

tunic The basic garment worn by the Romans with short sleeves and tied round the waist with a belt.

Tuscan style An order of architecture with simple plain columns and entablatures.

Ubii tribe A German tribe to the east of the Rhine River who provided the Roman army with recruits.

Vandals A Germanic people who migrated southwards and attacked Roman territory beginning in the third century, invading Gaul, Spain and Africa in the fifth century and capturing Rome in 455.

Veii An Etruscan town 12 miles (20 km) from Rome which the Romans besieged and captured in 396 B.C.

Verres Governor of Sicily who was prosecuted by Cicero in 70 B.C. for extortion.

Vespasian Roman emperor from 69 to 79.

Via Appia Appian Way, a Roman road from Rome to Brindisi.

Via Flaminia A Roman road from Rome to Rimini.

Via Latina A Roman road from Rome to Casilinum (near Capua).

Virgil A Roman poet who lived from 70 to 19 B.C., best known for his epic poem the *Aeneid.*

vulgar Latin The everyday speech of uneducated people.

west/western Europe The territory conquered by Rome in western Europe (including Britain, France, Italy, Austria, Spain, Portugal) and part of North Africa. It became largely Latin-speaking.

BIBLIOGRAPHY

Abdalla, A. 1992. *Graeco-Roman Funerary Stelae from Upper Egypt.* Liverpool: University Press.

Adkins, L., and Adkins, R. 1985. "Neolithic axes from Roman sites in Britain." *Oxford Journal of Archaeology* 4, 69–75.

Adkins, L., and Adkins, R. A. 1994. *Handbook to Life in Ancient Rome.* New York: Facts On File.

Alarcão, J. de. 1988. *Roman Portugal. Volume I: Introduction.* Warminster: Aris and Phillips.

Alcock, J. 1986. "The concept of Genius in Roman Britain." In M. Henig and A. King (eds.), *Pagan Gods and Shrines of the Roman Empire*, pp. 113–133. Oxford: Oxford University Committee for Archaeology Monograph 8.

Allason-Jones, L., and McKay, B. 1985. *Coventina's Well. A Shrine on Hadrian's Wall.* Hexham: Trustees of Clayton Collection, Chesters Museum.

Amy, R., and Gros, P. 1979. *La Maison Carrée de Nîmes.* Paris: Gallia supplement 38.

Austen, P. S., and Breeze, D. J. 1979. "A new inscription from Chesters on Hadrian's Wall." *Archaeologia Aeliana* 77, 5th series, 115–126.

Balty, J. Ch. 1960. *Etudes sur la Maison Carrée de Nîmes.* Brussels: Latomus.

Barton, I. M. 1989. "Religious buildings." In I. M. Barton (ed.), *Roman Public Buildings*, pp. 67–96. Exeter: University of Exeter.

Barton, I. M. (ed.), 1989. *Roman Public Buildings.* Exeter: University of Exeter.

Bauchhenss, G., and Noelke, P. 1981. *Die Iupitersäulen in den Germanischen Provinzen.* Köln: Rheinland-Verlag, and Bonn: Rudolf Habelt Verlag.

Beard, M. 1988. "Roman priesthoods." In M. Grant and R. Kitzinger (eds.), *Civilization of the Ancient Mediterranean. Greece and Rome. Volume II*, pp. 933–939. New York: Charles Scribner's Sons.

Beard, M. 1993. "Frazer et ses bois sacrés." In *Les Bois Sacrés. Actes du Colloque International de Naples 1989*, pp. 171–180. Naples: Collection du centre Jean Bérard, 10.

Beard, M., and North, J. (eds.), 1990. *Pagan Priests. Religion and Power in the Ancient World.* London: Duckworth.

Bianchi, U. (ed.), 1979. *Mysteria Mithrae. Proceedings of the International Seminar on the 'Religio-Historical Character of Roman Mithraism, with Particular Reference to Roman and Ostian Sources' Rome and Ostia 28–31 March 1978.* Leiden: E. J. Brill.

Billows, R. 1993. "The religious procession of the Ara Pacis Augustae: Augustus' *supplicatio* in 13 B.C." *Journal of Roman Archaeology* 6, 80–92.

Bird, J.; Chapman, H.; and Clark, J. (eds.), 1978. Collectanea Londiniensia. *Studies in London archaeology and history presented to Ralph Merrifield.* London: London and Middlesex Archaeological Society.

Birley, R. 1973. "Vindolanda-Chesterholm 1969–

1972." *Archaeologia Aeliana* 1, 5th series, 111–122.

Black, E. W. 1986. "Christian and pagan hopes of salvation in Romano-British mosaics." In M. Henig and A. King (eds.), *Pagan Gods and Shrines of the Roman Empire*, pp. 147–158. Oxford: Oxford University Committee for Archaeology Monograph 8.

Blagg, T. F. C. 1982. "A Roman relief-carving of three female figures, found at Lincoln." *Antiquaries Journal* 62, 125–126.

Blagg, T. F. C. 1986. "The cult and sanctuary of Diana Nemorensis." In M. Henig and A. King (eds.), *Pagan Gods and Shrines of the Roman Empire*, pp. 211–219. Oxford: Oxford University Committee for Archaeology Monograph 8.

Blagg, T. F. C. 1990. "The temple at Bath (Aquae Sulis) in the context of classical temples in the western European provinces." *Journal of Roman Archaeology* 3, 419–430.

Blagg, T. F. C. 1993. "Le mobilier archéologique du sanctuaire de Diane *Nemorensis*." In *Les Bois Sacrés. Actes du Colloque International de Naples 1989*, pp. 103–109. Naples: Collection du centre Jean Bérard.

Boardman, J.; Griffin, J.; and Murray, O. 1988. *The Roman World.* Oxford and New York: Oxford University Press; first published 1986 as two volumes.

Borgeaud, P. 1988. *The Cult of Pan in Ancient Greece.* Chicago, London: University of Chicago Press, translation of 1979 *Recherches sur le dieu Pan.*

Bourgeois, C. 1991. *Divona I Divinités et ex-voto du culte Gallo-Romain de l'eau.* Paris: De Boccard.

Bourgeois, C. 1992. *Divona II Monuments et sanctuaires du culte Gallo-Romain de l'eau.* Paris: De Boccard.

Bowder, D. (ed.), 1980. *Who was who in the Roman world 753 B.C.– A.D. 476.* Oxford: Phaidon.

Braithwaite, G. 1984. "Romano-British face pots and head pots." *Britannia* 15, 99–131.

Bremmer, J. N., and Horsfall, N. M. 1987. *Roman Myth and Mythography.* London: University of London Institute of Classical Studies.

Broise, H., and Scheid, J. 1993. "Etude d'un cas: le *lucus deae Diae* à Rome." In *Les Bois Sacrés. Actes du Colloque International de Naples 1989*, pp. 127–170. Naples: Collection du centre Jean Bérard.

Brouwer, H. H. J. 1989. *Bona Dea. The sources and a description of the cult.* Leiden, New York: E. J. Brill.

Brown, P. 1972. *Religion and Society in the Age of Saint Augustine.* London: Faber and Faber.

Browning, R. 1975. *The Emperor Julian.* London: Weidenfeld and Nicolson.

Bruneaux, J. L. 1988. *The Celtic Gauls: Gods, Rites and Sanctuaries.* London: Seaby.

Burn, A. R. 1969. *The Romans in Britain. An Anthology of Inscriptions.* Oxford: Basil Blackwell.

Champeaux, J. 1982. *Fortuna. Recherches sur le culte de la Fortune à Rome et dans le monde romain des origines à la mort de César. I Fortuna dans la religion archaïque.* Rome: Ecole Française de Rome.

Champeaux, J. 1987. *Fortuna. Recherches sur le culte de la Fortune à Rome et dans le monde romain des origines à la mort de César. II Les Transformations de Fortuna sous le République.* Rome: Ecole Française de Rome.

Charles-Picard, G. 1954. *Les Religions de L'Afrique Antique.* Paris: Librairie Plon.

Clayton, P. A., and Price, M. J. 1988. *The Seven Wonders of the Ancient World.* London and New York: Routledge.

Colledge, M. A. R. 1986. "Interpretatio Romana: the Semitic populations of Syria and Mesopotamia." In M. Henig and A. King (eds.), *Pagan Gods and Shrines of the Roman Empire*, pp. 221–230. Oxford: Oxford University Committee for Archaeology Monograph 8.

Combet-Farnoux, B. 1980. *Mercure Romain. Le culte public de Mercure et la fonction mercantile à Rome de la République archaïque à l'époque augustéenne.* Rome: Ecole Française de Rome.

Conlin, D. A. 1992. "The reconstruction of Antonia Minor on the Ara Pacis." *Journal of Roman Archaeology* 5, 211–215.

Coulston, J. C., and Phillips, E. J. 1988. *Corpus Signorum Imperii Romani (Corpus of Sculpture of the Roman World), Great Britain, Volume I, Fascicule 6. Hadrian's Wall West of the North Tyne, and Carlisle.* New York and Oxford: Oxford University Press.

Crook, J. A. 1967. *Law and Life of Rome.* London: Thames and Hudson.

Cumont, F. 1896. *Textes et Monuments Figurés relatifs aux mystères de Mithra. Vol. 2.* Brussels: H. Lamertin.

Cunliffe, B. (ed.), 1988. *The Temple of Sulis Minerva*

at Bath. Volume 2 The Finds from the Sacred Spring. Oxford: University Committee for Archaeology.

Cunliffe, B., and Davenport, P. 1985a. *The Temple of Sulis Minerva at Bath. Volume 1 (II): The Site.* Oxford: University Committee for Archaeology.

Cüppers, H., *et al.* 1983. *La Civilisation Romaine de la Moselle à la Sarre.* Mayence: Philipp von Zabern.

Cüppers, H. (ed.), 1990. *Die Römer in Rheinland-Pfalz.* Stuttgart: Konrad Theiss.

Curchin, L. A. 1991. *Roman Spain. Conquest and Assimilation.* London: Routledge.

de Cazanove, O. 1993. "Suspension d'ex-voto dans les bois sacrés." In *Les Bois Sacrés. Actes du Colloque International de Naples 1989*, pp. 111–126.

DeLaine, J. 1990. "The *balneum* of the Arval brethren." *Journal of Roman Archaeology* 3, 321–324.

Deyts, S. 1992. *Images des Dieux de la Gaule.* Paris: Editions Errance.

Dixon, S. 1992. *The Roman Family.* Baltimore: The Johns Hopkins University Press.

Dorcey, P. F. 1992. *The Cult of Silvanus. A Study in Roman Folk Religion.* Leiden, New York and Köln: E. J. Brill.

Dowden, K. 1992. *Religion and the Romans.* London: Bristol Classical Press.

Drijvers, H. J. W. 1976. *The Religion of Palmyra.* Leiden: E. J. Brill.

Drury, P. J. 1980. "Non-classical religious buildings in Iron Age and Roman Britain: a review." In W. Rodwell (ed.), *Temples, Churches and Religion: Recent Research in Roman Britain with a Gazetteer of Romano-Celtic Temples in Continental Europe*, pp. 45–78. Oxford: British Archaeological Report 77, part i.

Drury, P. J. 1984. "The temple of Claudius at Colchester reconsidered." *Britannia* 15, 7–50.

Dubordieu, A. 1989. *Les origines et Le Développement du Culte des Pénates à Rome.* Rome: Ecole Française de Rome.

Dumézil, G. 1970. *Archaic Roman Religion with an appendix on the Religion of the Etruscans. Vols 1 & 2.* Chicago and London: The University of Chicago Press.

Dunbabin, K. M. D. 1990. "*Ipsa deae vestigia . . .* Footprints divine and human on Graeco-Roman monuments." *Journal of Roman Archaeology* 3, 85–109.

Duthoy, R. 1969. *The Taurobolium, Its Evolution and Terminology.* Leiden: E. J. Brill.

Elbe, J. von. 1975. *Roman Germany. A Guide to Sites and Museums.* Mainz: Verlag Philipp von Zabern.

Espérandieu, E. 1931. *Recueil Général des Bas-relief, Statues et Bustes de la Germanie Romaine.* Paris and Brussels; republished in 1965 by The Gregg Press Inc., New Jersey.

Etienne, R. 1958. *Le culte impérial dans la péninsule Ibérique d'Auguste à Dioclétien.* Paris: E. De Boccard.

Fairless, K. J. 1984. "Three religious cults from the northern frontier region." In R. Miket and C. Burgess (eds.), *Between and Beyond the Walls. Essays on the Prehistory and History of North Britain in Honour of George Jobey*, pp. 224–242. Edinburgh: John Donald Publishers.

Fears, J. R. 1988. "Ruler worship." In M. Grant and R. Kitzinger (eds.), *Civilization of the Ancient Mediterranean. Greece and Rome. Volume II*, pp. 1,009–1,025. New York: Charles Scribner's Sons.

Ferguson, J. 1970. *The Religions of the Roman Empire.* London: Thames and Hudson.

Ferguson, J. 1988a. "Divinities." In M. Grant and R. Kitzinger (eds.), *Civilization of the Ancient Mediterranean. Greece and Rome. Volume II*, pp. 847–860. New York: Charles Scribner's Sons.

Ferguson, J. 1988b. "Roman cults." In M. Grant and R. Kitzinger (eds.), *Civilization of the Ancient Mediterranean. Greece and Rome. Volume II*, pp. 909–923. New York: Charles Scribner's Sons.

Ferguson, J. 1988c. "Divination and oracles: Rome." In M. Grant and R. Kitzinger (eds.), *Civilization of the Ancient Mediterranean. Greece and Rome. Volume II*, pp. 951–958. New York: Charles Scribner's Sons.

Fishwick, D. 1967. "*Hastiferi.*" *Journal of Roman Studies* 57, 142–160.

Fishwick, D. 1972. "Templum Divo Claudio Constitutum." *Britannia* 3, 164–181.

Fishwick, D. 1987. *The Imperial Cult in the Latin West. Studies in the Ruler Cult of the Western Provinces of the Roman Empire. Volume I 1 & 2.* Leiden, New York, Copenhagen and Cologne: E. J. Brill.

Fishwick, D. 1991. "Seneca and the temple of Divus Claudius." *Britannia* 22, 137–141.

Frazer, J. G. 1913. *The Golden Bough. A Study in*

Magic and Religion. Part V: Spirits of the Corn and of the Wild. Volume II. Reprinted by Macmillan, London, 1990.

Frazer, J. G. 1929. *Publii Ovidii Nasonis Fastorum Libri. The Fasti of Ovid.* London: Macmillan in 5 volumes; reprinted 1973 by Georg Olms Verlag, Hildesheim and New York.

Freyburger, G. 1986. *Fides. Étude sémantique et religieuse depuis les origines jusqu'à l'époque augustéenne.* Paris: Les Belles Lettres.

Friesen, S. J. 1993. *Twice Neokoros. Ephesus, Asia and the Cult of the Flavian Imperial Family.* Leiden, New York and Cologne: E. J. Brill.

García Y Bellido, A. 1967. *Les Religions Orientales dans l'Espagne Romaine.* Leiden: E. J. Brill.

Gascou, J., and Janon, M. 1985. *Inscriptions Latines De Narbonnaise (I.L.N.), Fréjus.* Paris: Éditions du Centre National de la Recherche Scientifique, Gallia, 44th supplement.

Gasparro, G. S. 1985. *Soteriology and mystic aspects in the cult of Cybele and Attis.* Leiden: E. J. Brill.

Gergel, R. A. 1990. "Roman cult images." *Journal of Roman Archaeology* 3, 286–289.

Godfrey, P., and Hemsoll, D. 1986. "The Pantheon: temple or rotunda?" In M. Henig and A. King (eds.), *Pagan Gods and Shrines of the Roman Empire,* pp. 195–209. Oxford: Oxford University Committee for Archaeology Monograph 8.

Gordon, R. 1990a. "From Republic to Principate: priesthood, religion and ideology." In M. Beard and J. North (eds.), *Pagan Priests. Religion and Power in the Ancient World,* pp. 179–198. London: Duckworth.

Gordon, R. 1990b. "The veil of power: emperors, sacrificers and benefactors." In M. Beard and J. North (eds.), *Pagan Priests. Religion and Power in the Ancient World,* pp. 199–231. London: Duckworth.

Gordon, R. 1990c. "Religion in the Roman Empire: the civic compromise and its limits." In M. Beard and J. North (eds.), *Pagan Priests. Religion and Power in the Ancient World,* pp. 233–255. London: Duckworth.

Grant, M. 1970. *The Roman Forum.* London: Weidenfeld and Nicolson.

Grant, M. 1971. *Roman Myths.* London: Weidenfeld and Nicolson.

Grant, M. 1973. *The Jews in the Roman World.* London: Weidenfeld and Nicolson.

Grant, M. 1985. *The Roman Emperors. A Biographical Guide to the Rulers of Imperial Rome 31 B.C.–A.D. 476.* London: Weidenfeld and Nicolson.

Grant, M., and Kitzinger, R. (eds.), 1988. *Civilization of the Ancient Mediterranean. Greece and Rome. Volume II.* New York: Charles Scribner's Sons.

Green, H. J. M. 1986. "Religious cults at Roman Godmanchester." In M. Henig and A. King (eds.), *Pagan Gods and Shrines of the Roman Empire,* pp. 29–55. Oxford: Oxford University Committee for Archaeology Monograph 8.

Green, M. J. 1981. "Model objects from military areas of Roman Britain." *Britannia* 12, 253–269.

Green, M. J. 1984. *The Wheel as a Cult-Symbol in the Romano-Celtic World, with Special Reference to Gaul and Britain.* Brussels: Latomus.

Green, M. J. 1986a. "Jupiter, Taranis and the solar wheel." In M. Henig and A. King (eds.), *Pagan Gods and Shrines of the Roman Empire,* pp. 65–75. Oxford: Oxford University Committee for Archaeology Monograph 8.

Green, M. J. 1986b. *The Gods of the Celts.* Totowa, New Jersey: Barnes and Noble; Gloucester: Alan Sutton.

Green, M. J. 1992a. *Dictionary of Celtic Myth and Legend.* London: Thames and Hudson.

Green, M. J. 1992b. *Animals in Celtic Life and Myth.* New York and London: Routledge.

Grenier, J.-C. 1977. *Anubis Alexandrin et Romain.* Leiden: E. J. Brill.

Grimal, P. 1986. *The Dictionary of Classical Mythology.* Oxford: Basil Blackwell. First published 1951, English translation by A. R. Maxwell-Hyslop.

Guy, C. J. 1981. "Roman circular lead tanks in Britain." *Britannia* 12, 271–276.

Guy, C. J. 1989. "The Oxborough lead tank." *Britannia* 20, 234–237.

Halsberghe, G. H. 1972. *The Cult of Sol Invictus.* Leiden: E. J. Brill.

Hammond, N. G. L., and Scullard, H. H. (eds.) 1970. *The Oxford Classical Dictionary.* Oxford: Oxford University Press.

Hampartumian, N. 1979. *Corpus Equitis Thracii (CCET), IV Moesian Inferior (Romanian Section) and Dacia.* Leiden: E. J. Brill.

Hanson, J. A. 1959. *Roman theater-temples.* Princeton: Princeton University Press.

Hassall, M. W. C. 1980. "Altars, curses and other

epigraphic evidence." In W. Rodwell (ed.), *Temples, Churches and Religion: Recent Research in Roman Britain with a Gazetteer of Romano-Celtic Temples in Continental Europe*, pp. 79–89. Oxford: British Archaeological Report 77, part i.

Haynes, I. P. 1993. "The Romanization of religion in the *auxilia* of the Roman imperial army from Augustus to Septimius Severus." *Britannia* 24, 141–157.

Henig, M. 1980. "Art and cult in the temples of Roman Britain." In W. Rodwell (ed.), *Temples, Churches and Religion: Recent Research in Roman Britain with a Gazetteer of Romano-Celtic Temples in Continental Europe*, pp. 91–113. Oxford: British Archaeological Report 77, part i.

Henig, M. 1984. *Religion in Roman Britain.* London: Batsford.

Henig, M. 1986. " 'Ita intellexit numine inductus tuo': some personal interpretations of deity in Roman religion." In M. Henig and A. King (eds.), *Pagan Gods and Shrines of the Roman Empire,* pp. 159–169. Oxford: Oxford University Committee for Archaeology Monograph 8.

Henig, M. 1993a. "Votive objects: images and inscriptions." In A. Woodward and P. Leach, *The Uley Shrines. Excavation of a ritual complex on West Hill, Uley, Gloucestershire: 1977–9,* pp. 90–112. London: English Heritage.

Henig, M. 1993b. "Votive objects: weapons, miniatures, tokens, and fired clay accessories." In A. Woodward and P. Leach, *The Uley Shrines. Excavation of a ritual complex on West Hill, Uley, Gloucestershire: 1977–9,* pp. 131–147. London: English Heritage.

Henig, M., and King, A. (eds.), 1986. *Pagan Gods and Shrines of the Roman Empire.* Oxford: Oxford University Committee for Archaeology Monograph 8.

Heyob, S. K. 1975. *The cult of Isis among women in the Graeco-Roman world.* Leiden: E. J. Brill.

Hölscher, T. 1967. *Victoria Romana.* Mainz: Philipp von Zabern.

Hopkins, K. 1983. *Death and Renewal. Sociological Studies in Roman History. Volume 2.* Cambridge and New York: Cambridge University Press.

Hörig, M., and Schwertheim, E. 1987. *Corpus Cultus Iovis Dolicheni (CCID).* Leiden and New York: E. J. Brill.

Horne, P. D. 1986. "Roman or Celtic temples? A case study." In M. Henig and A. King (eds.), *Pagan Gods and Shrines of the Roman Empire*, pp. 15–24. Oxford: Oxford University Committee for Archaeology Monograph 8.

Horne, P. D., and King, A. C. 1980. "Romano-Celtic temples in continental Europe: a gazetteer of those with known plans." In W. Rodwell (ed.), *Temples, Churches and Religion: Recent Research in Roman Britain with a Gazetteer of Romano-Celtic Temples in Continental Europe*, pp. 369–555. Oxford: British Archaeological Report 77, part ii.

Howatson, M. C. (ed.), 1989 (2nd ed.). *The Oxford Companion to Classical Literature.* Oxford and New York: Oxford University Press.

Hutchinson, V. J. 1986a. "The cult of Bacchus in Britain." In M. Henig and A. King (eds.), *Pagan Gods and Shrines of the Roman Empire,* pp. 135–145. Oxford: Oxford University Committee for Archaeology Monograph 8.

Hutchinson, V. J. 1986b. *Bacchus in Roman Britain: The Evidence for His Cult.* Oxford: British Archaeological Report 151, 2 volumes.

Hutchinson, V. J. 1991. "The cult of Dionysos/Bacchus in the Graeco-Roman world: new light from archaeological studies." *Journal of Roman Archaeology* 4, 222–230.

Jackson, R. 1988. *Doctors and Diseases in the Roman Empire.* London: British Museum Publications.

Jackson, R. 1990. "Roman doctors and their instruments: recent research into ancient practice." *Journal of Roman Archaeology* 3, 5–27.

Jackson Knight, W. F. 1970. *Elysion. Ancient Greek and Roman beliefs concerning life after death.* London: Rider and Company.

Jenkins, F. 1978. "Some interesting types of clay statuettes of the Roman period found in London." In J. Bird et al. (eds.), Collectanea Londiniensia. *Studies in London archaeology and history presented to Ralph Merrifield,* pp. 148–162. London: London and Middlesex Archaeological Society.

Johns, C. 1982. *Sex or Symbol. Erotic Images of Greece and Rome.* London: British Museum Publications.

Johns, C. 1986. "Faunus at Thetford: an early Latin deity in Late Roman Britain." In M. Henig and A. King (eds.), *Pagan Gods and Shrines of the Roman Empire,* pp. 93–103. Oxford: Oxford University Committe for Archaeology Monograph 8.

Johnson, P. 1980. *A History of Christianity.* Har-

mondsworth: Pelican; originally published 1976 by Weidenfeld and Nicolson, London.
Jones, A. H. M. 1964. *The Later Roman Empire 284–602. A Social, Economic and Administrative Survey. Vol. 1.* Oxford: Basil Blackwell.
Jones, B., and Mattingly, D. 1990. *An Atlas of Roman Britain.* Oxford: Basil Blackwell.
Jones, J. M. 1990. *A Dictionary of Ancient Roman Coins.* London: Seaby.
Kater-Sibbes, G. J. F. 1973. *Preliminary catalogue of Sarapis Monuments.* Leiden: E. J. Brill.
Kater-Sibbes, G. J. F., and Vermaseren, M. J. 1975a. *Apis, I The Monuments of the Hellenistic-Roman Period from Egypt.* Leiden: E. J. Brill.
Kater-Sibbes, G. J. F., and Vermaseren, M. J. 1975b. *Apis, II Monuments from outside Egypt.* Leiden: E. J. Brill.
Kater-Sibbes, G. J. F., and Vermaseren, M. J. 1977. *Apis, III Inscriptions, Coins and Addenda.* Leiden: E. J. Brill.
Keay, S. J. 1988. *Roman Spain.* London: British Museum Publications.
Keppie, L. J. F., and Arnold, B. J. 1984. *Corpus Signorum Imperii Romani (Corpus of Sculpture of the Roman World), Great Britain, Volume I, Fascicule 4. Scotland.* New York and Oxford: Oxford University Press.
Kerényi, C. 1951. *The Gods of the Greeks.* London: Thames and Hudson.
Knapp, R. C. 1992. *Latin Inscriptions from Central Spain.* Berkeley, Los Angeles and Oxford: University of California Press.
Koeppel, G. M. 1992. "The third man: restoration problems on the north frieze of the Ara Pacis Augustae." *Journal of Roman Archaeology* 5, 216–218.
Koester, H., and Limberis, V. 1988. "Christianity." In M. Grant and R. Kitzinger (eds.), *Civilization of the Ancient Mediterranean. Greece and Rome. Volume II*, pp. 1,047–1,073. New York: Charles Scribner's Sons.
Lane, E. N. 1971. *Corpus Monumentorum Religionis Dei Menis, volume I, The Monuments and Inscriptions.* Leiden: E. J. Brill.
Lane, E. N. 1975. *Corpus Monumentorum Religionis Dei Menis (CMRDM), volume II, The Coins and Gems.* Leiden: E. J. Brill.
Lane, E. N. 1976. *Corpus Monumentorum Religionis Dei Menis (CMRDM), volume III, Interpretations and Testimonia.* Leiden: E. J. Brill.
Lane, E. N. 1978. *Corpus Monumentorum Religionis Dei Menis (CMRDM), volume IV, Supplementary Men-inscriptions from Pisidia.* Leiden: E. J. Brill.
Lane Fox, R. 1988. *Pagans and Christians.* Harmondsworth and New York: Viking Penguin; first published 1986 by Alfred A. Knopf, New York.
Lattimore, R. 1962. *Themes in Greek and Latin Epitaphs.* Urbana: University of Illinois Press.
Leclant, J., and Clerc, G. 1972. *Inventaire Bibliographique des Isiaca (IBIS), Répertoire Analytique des Travaux Relatifs à la Diffusion des Cultes Isiaques 1940–1969 (A–D).* Leiden: E. J. Brill.
Leclant, J., and Clerc, G. 1974. *Inventaire Bibliographique des Isiaca (IBIS), Répertoire Analytique des Travaux Relatifs à la Diffusion des Cultes Isiaques 1940–1969 (E–K).* Leiden: E. J. Brill.
Leclant, J., and Clerc, G. 1985. *Inventaire Bibliographique des Isiaca (IBIS), Répertoire Analytique des Travaux Relatifs à la Diffusion des Cultes Isiaques 1940–1969 (L–Q)* Leiden: E. J. Brill.
Leclant, J., and Clerc, G. 1991. *Inventaire Bibliographique des Isiaca (IBIS), Répertoire Analytique des Travaux Relatifs à la Diffusion des Cultes Isiaques 1940–1969 (R–Z).* Leiden: E. J. Brill.
Le Gall, J. 1953. *Recherches Sur Le Culte du Tibre.* Paris: Presses Universitaires de France.
Liebeschuetz, J. H. W. G. 1979. *Continuity and Change in Roman Religion.* Oxford: Clarendon Press.
Lloyd-Morgan, G. 1986. "Roman Venus: public worship and private rites." In M. Henig and A. King (eds.), *Pagan Gods and Shrines of the Roman Empire*, pp. 179–188. Oxford: Oxford Committee for Archaeology Monograph 8.
Luck, G. 1985. *Arcana Mundi: Magic and the Occult in the Greek and Roman Worlds.* Baltimore and London: The Johns Hopkins University Press.
Lyttelton, M. 1987. "The design and planning of temples and sanctuaries in Asia Minor in the Roman imperial period." In S. Macready and F. H. Thompson (eds.), *Roman Architecture in the Greek World*, pp. 38–49. London: Society of Antiquaries.
MacBain, B. 1982. *Prodigy and expiation: a study in religion and politics in Republican Rome.* Brussels: Latomus.
Macready, S., and Thompson, F. H. (eds.), 1987. *Roman Architecture in the Greek World.* London: Society of Antiquaries.

Macdonald, W. 1968. *Early Christian Byzantine Architecture.* London: Studio Vista.

Mainstone, R. J. 1988. *Haghia Sophia. Architecture, Structure and Liturgy of Justinian's Great Church.* London: Thames and Hudson.

Manfrini-Aragno, I. 1987. *Bacchus dans les Bronzes Hellénistiques et Romains. Les Artisans et Leur Répertoire.* Lausanne: Bibliothèque Historique Vaudoise.

Mark, R., and Çakmak 1992. *Haghia Sophia from the Age of Justinian to the Present.* Cambridge and New York: Cambridge University Press.

Marwood, M. A. 1988. *The Roman Cult of Salus.* Oxford: British Archaeological Reports International Series 465.

McManners, J. (ed.), 1990. *The Oxford Illustrated History of Christianity.* Oxford and New York: Oxford University Press.

Mellor, R. 1975. *The Worship of the Goddess Roma in the Greek World.* Göttingen: Vandenhoeck & Ruprecht.

Meredith, A. 1988. "Later philosophy." In J. Boardman *et al.*, *The Roman World*, pp. 288–307. Oxford and New York: Oxford University Press.

Merrifield, R. 1987. *The Archaeology of Ritual and Magic.* London: Batsford.

Miket, R., and Burgess, C. (eds.), 1984. *Between and Beyond the Walls. Essays on the Prehistory and History of North Britain in Honour of George Jobey.* Edinburgh: John Donald Publishers.

Mócsy, A. 1974. *Pannonia and Upper Moesia. A History of the Middle Danube Provinces of the Roman Empire.* London and Boston: Routledge & Kegan Paul.

Nash, E. 1962a. *Pictorial Dictionary of Ancient Rome Volume 1.* London: A. Zwemmer Ltd.

Nash, E. 1962b. *Pictorial Dictionary of Ancient Rome Volume 2.* London: A. Zwemmer Ltd.

Neverov, O. 1986. "Nero-Helios." In M. Henig and A. King (eds.), *Pagan Gods and Shrines of the Roman Empire*, pp. 189–194. Oxford: Oxford Committee for Archaeology, Monograph 8.

North, J. A. 1988a. "Sacrifice and ritual: Rome." In M. Grant and R. Kitzinger (eds.), *Civilization of the Ancient Mediterranean. Greece and Rome. Volume II*, pp. 981–986. New York: Charles Scribner's Sons.

North, J. A. 1988b. "The afterlife: Rome." In M. Grant and R. Kitzinger (eds.), *Civilization of the Ancient Mediterranean. Greece and Rome. Volume II*, pp. 997–1,007. New York: Charles Scribner's Sons.

North, J. 1990. "Diviners and divination at Rome." In M. Beard and J. North (eds.), *Pagan Priests. Religion and Power in the Ancient World*, pp. 51–71. London: Duckworth.

Ogilvie R. M. 1969. *The Romans and Their Gods in the Age of Augustus.* London: Chatto and Windus; reprinted 1986 as *The Romans and Their Gods* by The Hogarth Press, London.

Pailler, J.-M. 1988. *Bacchanalia. La répression de 186 av. J.-C. à Rome et en Italie: vestiges, images, tradition.* Rome: Ecole Française de Rome.

Paladino, I. 1988. *Fratres Arvales. Storia di un collegio sacerdotale romano.* Rome: L'Erma di Bretschneider.

Palmer, R. E. A. 1974. *Roman Religion and Roman Empire. Five Essays.* Philadelphia: University of Pennsylvania Press.

Palmer, R. E. A. 1990. "Cults of Hercules, Apollo Caelispex and Fortuna in and around the Roman Cattle Market." *Journal of Roman Archaeology* 3, 234–244.

Paoli, U. 1963. *Rome. Its People, Life and Customs.* London: Longmans.

Parke, H. W. 1988. *Sibyls and Sibylline Prophecy in Classical Antiquity.* London and New York: Routledge.

Patterson, J. R. 1992. "The City of Rome: from Republic to Empire." *Journal of Roman Studies* 82, 186–215.

Phillips, E. J. 1977. *Corpus Signorum Imperii Romani (Corpus of Sculpture of the Roman World), Great Britain, Volume I, Fascicule 1. Hadrian's Wall East of the North Tyne.* Oxford: Oxford University Press.

Picard, G. C., and Picard, C. 1987. *Carthage. A survey of Punic history and culture from its birth to the final tragedy.* Translated by Dominique Collon, London: Sidgwick and Jackson; first published in 1968.

Piggott, S. 1968. *The Druids.* London: Thames and Hudson.

Popa, A., and Berciu, I. 1978. *Le culte de Jupiter Dolichenus dans la Dacie Romaine.* Leiden: E. J. Brill.

Porte, D. 1989. *Les Donneurs de Sacré. Le prêtre à Rome.* Paris, Les Belles Lettres.

Potter, D. 1988. "Pagans and Christians." *Journal of Roman Archaeology* 1, 207–214.

Potter, D. 1990. "Sibyls in the Greek and Roman world." *Journal of Roman Archaeology* 3, 471–483.

Price, S. R. F. 1984. *Rituals and Power. The Roman imperial cult in Asia Minor.* London and New York: Cambridge University Press.

Prieur, J. 1986. *La Mort dans L'Antiquité Romaine.* Ouest France.

Ramage, N. H., and Ramage, A. 1991. *The Cambridge Illustrated History of Roman Art.* Cambridge and Melbourne: Cambridge University Press.

Reece, R. (ed.), 1977. *Burial in the Roman World.* London: Council for British Archaeology.

Rehak, P. 1990. "The Ionic temple relief in the Capitoline: the temple of Victory on the Palatine?" *Journal of Roman Archaeology* 3, 172–186.

Richardson, L. 1988. *Pompeii. An Architectural History.* Baltimore and London: The Johns Hopkins University Press.

Richardson, L. 1992. *A New Topographical Dictionary of Ancient Rome.* Baltimore and London: The Johns Hopkins University Press.

Rivet, A. L. F., and Smith, C. 1979. *The Place-Names of Roman Britain.* London: Batsford.

Rodwell, W. 1980a. "Temple archaeology: problems of the present and portents for the future." In W. Rodwell (ed.), *Temples, Churches and Religion: Recent Research in Roman Britain with a Gazetteer of Romano-Celtic Temples in Continental Europe*, pp. 211–241. Oxford: British Archaeological Report 77, part ii.

Rodwell, W. 1980b. "Temples in Roman Britain: a revised gazetteer." In W. Rodwell (ed.), *Temples, Churches and Religion: Recent Research in Roman Britain with a Gazetteer of Romano-Celtic Temples in Continental Europe*, pp. 557–585. Oxford: British Archaeological Report 77, part ii.

Rodwell, W. (ed.), 1980c. *Temples, Churches and Religion: Recent Research in Roman Britain with a Gazetteer of Romano-Celtic Temples in Continental Europe.* Oxford: British Archaeological Report 77, part i.

Rodwell, W. (ed.), 1980d. *Temples, Churches and Religion: Recent Research in Roman Britain with a Gazetteer of Romano-Celtic Temples in Continental Europe.* Oxford: British Archaeolgical Report 77, part ii.

Room, A. 1983. *Room's Classical Dictionary.* London and Boston: Routledge & Kegan Paul.

Ross, A. 1974. *Pagan Celtic Britain.* London: Cardinal Edition, Sphere Books; originally published in 1967 by Routledge & Kegan Paul with different pagination.

Ross, A., and Robins, D. 1989. *The Life and Death of a Druid Prince. The Story of an Archaeological Sensation.* London and Sydney: Rider.

Rostovtzeff, M. 1917–18. "Roman Cirencester, Appendix III, Note on the Matres—or Nutrices—relief from Cirencester." *Archaeologia* 69, 204–209.

Scheid, J. 1975. *Les Frères Arvales. Recrutement et origine sociale sous les empereurs julio-claudiens.* Paris: Presses Universitaires de France.

Scheid, J. 1993. "*Lucus, nemus.* Qu'est-ce qu'un bois sacré?" In *Les Bois Sacrés. Actes du Colloque International de Naples 1989*, pp. 13–20. Naples: Collection du centre Jean Bérard, 10.

Schilling, R. 1982 (2nd ed.). *La Religion Romaine de Vénus depuis les origines jusqu'au temps d'Auguste.* Paris: Editions E. de Boccard.

Schwartz, S. 1988. "Judaism." In M. Grant and R. Kitzinger (eds.), *Civilization of the Ancient Mediterranean. Greece and Rome. Volume II*, pp. 1,027–1,045. New York: Charles Scribner's Sons.

Scullard, H. H. 1981. *Festivals and Ceremonies of the Roman Republic.* London: Thames and Hudson.

Simon, E. 1968. *Ara Pacis Augustae.* Tübingen: Verlag Ernst Wasmuth.

Simon, E. 1990. *Die Götter der Römer.* Munich: Hirmer Verlag.

Simpson, C. J. 1993. "Once again Claudius and the temple at Colchester." *Britannia* 8, 1–6.

Small, J. P. 1982. *Cacus and Marsyas in Etrusco-Roman Legend.* Princeton: Princeton University Press.

Smallwood, E. M. 1976. *The Jews under Roman Rule. From Pompey to Diocletian.* Leiden: E. J. Brill.

Soffe, G. 1986. "Christians, Jews and Pagans in the Acts of the Apostles." In M. Henig and A. King (eds.), *Pagan Gods and Shrines of the Roman Empire*, pp. 239–256. Oxford: Oxford Committee for Archaeology Monograph 8.

Sordi, M. 1983. *The Christians and the Roman Empire.* Translated by A. Bedini. London and Sydney: Croom Helm.

Speidel, M. P. 1978. *The Religion of Iuppiter Dolichenus in the Roman Army.* Leiden: E. J. Brill.

Steinby, E. M. (ed.), 1993. *Lexicon Topographicum Urbis Romae Volume I, A–C.* Rome: Quasar.

Stephens, G. R. 1984. "The metrical inscription

from Carvoran, RIB 1791." *Archaeologia Aeliana* 12, 5th series, 149–156.

Stevenson, J. 1978. *The Catacombs. Rediscovered monuments of early Christianity.* London: Thames and Hudson.

Syme, R. 1980. *Some Arval Brethren.* Oxford: Clarendon Press.

Tacheva-Hitova, M. 1983. *Eastern Cults in Moesian Inferior and Thracia (5th century* B.C.*–4th century* A.D.*).* Leiden: E. J. Brill.

Teixidor, J. 1979. *The Pantheon of Palmyra.* Leiden: E. J. Brill.

Thomas, C. 1980. "Churches in late Roman Britain." In W. Rodwell (ed.), *Temples, Churches and Religion: Recent Research in Roman Britain with a Gazetteer of Romano-Celtic Temples in Continental Europe*, pp. 129–164. Oxford: British Archaeological Report 77, part i.

Thomas, C. 1981. *Christianity in Roman Britain to* A.D. *500.* London: Batsford.

Tomlin, R. S. O. 1988. "The curse tablets." In B. Cunliffe (ed.), *The Temple of Sulis Minerva at Bath. Volume 2: The Finds from the Sacred Spring*, pp. 59–277. Oxford: University Committee for Archaeology.

Tomlin, R. S. O. 1993. "The inscribed lead tablets: an interim report." In A. Woodward and P. Leach, 1993. *The Uley Shrines. Excavation of a ritual complex on West Hill, Uley, Gloucestershire: 1977–9*, pp. 113–130. London: English Heritage.

Toynbee, J. M. C. 1961. "The 'Ara Pacis Augustae.' " *Journal of Roman Studies* 51, 153–156.

Toynbee, J. M. C. 1971. *Death and Burial in the Roman World.* London: Thames and Hudson.

Toynbee, J. M. C. 1973. *Animals in Roman Life and Art.* London: Thames and Hudson.

Toynbee, J. M. C. 1978. "A Londinium votive leaf or feather and its fellows." In J. Bird *et al* (eds.), 1978 Collectanea Londiniensia. *Studies in London archaeology and history presented to Ralph Merrifield.* pp. 128–147. London: London and Middlesex. Archaeological Society.

Toynbee, J. M. C. 1986. *The Roman Art Treasures from the Temple of Mithras.* London: London and Middlesex Archaeological Society.

Tranoy A. 1981. *La Galice Romaine. Recherches sur le nord-ouest de la péninsule ibérique dans l'Antiquité.* Paris: Publications du Centre Pierre.

Treggiari, S. 1991. *Roman Marriage.* Iusti Coniuges *from the Time of Cicero to the Time of Ulpian.* Oxford: Clarendon Press.

Trell, B. L. 1988. "The temple of Artemis at Ephesos." In P. A. Clayton and M. J. Price. *The Seven Wonders of the Ancient World*, pp. 78–99. London and New York: Routledge.

Tudor, D. 1976. *Corpus Monumentorum Religionis Equitum Danuvinorum (CMRED). II. The Analysis and Interpretation of the Monuments.* London: E. J. Brill.

Turcan, R. 1989. *Les cultes orientaux dans le monde romain.* Paris: Les Belles Lettres.

Ulansey D. 1989. *The Origins of the Mithraic Mysteries.* New York: Oxford University Press.

van Buren, A. W. 1916. "Vacuna." *Journal of Roman Studies* 6, 202–204.

Vanggaard, J. H. 1988. *The Flamen. A Study in the History and Sociology of Roman Religion.* Copenhagen: Museum Tusculanum Press.

Vermaseren, M. J. 1963. *Mithras, the Secret God.* London: Chatto & Windus.

Vermaseren M. J. 1977. *Cybele and Attis, the Myth and the Cult.* London: Thames and Hudson.

Vermeule, C. 1987. *The Cult Images of Imperial Rome.* Rome: Giorgio Bretschneider.

Versnel, H. S. 1970. *Triumphus. An Inquiry into the origin, development and meaning of the Roman triumph.* Leiden: E. J. Brill.

Warde Fowler, W. 1899. *The Roman Festivals of the Period of the Republic. An Introduction to the Study of the Religion of the Romans.* London: Macmillan and Co.

Warde Fowler, W. 1911. "The original meaning of the word *sacer.*" *Journal of Roman Studies* 1, 57–63.

Watts, D. J. 1988. "Circular lead tanks and their significance for Romano-British Christianity." *Antiquaries Journal* 68, 210–222.

Webster, G. 1986. *The British Celts and Their Gods Under Rome.* London: Batsford.

Weinstock, S. 1971. *Divus Julius.* Oxford: Clarendon Press.

Wightman, E. M. 1970. *Roman Trier and the Treveri.* London: Rupert Hart-Davis Ltd.

Wild, R. A. 1981. *Water in the Cultic Worship of Isis and Sarapis.* Leiden: E. J. Brill.

Wilkes, J. J. 1969. *Dalmatia.* London: Routledge and Kegan Paul.

Wilson, A. N. 1992. *Jesus.* London: Sinclair-Stevenson.

Wilson, D. R. 1980. "Romano-Celtic Temple Architecture: how much do we actually know?" In W. Rodwell (ed.), *Temples, Churches and Religion: Recent Research in Roman Britain with a Gazetteer of Romano-Celtic Temples in Continental Europe*, pp. 5–30. Oxford: British Archaeological Report 77, part i.

Wilson, R. J. A. 1990. *Sicily under the Roman Empire.* Warminster: Aris and Phillips.

Wiseman, T. P. 1981. "The temple of Victory on the Palatine." *Antiquaries Journal* 61, 35–52.

Witt, R. E. 1971. *Isis in the Graeco-Roman World.* London: Thames and Hudson.

Woodward, A. 1992. *English Heritage Book of Shrines and Sacrifices.* London: Batsford/English Heritage.

Woodward, A., and Leach, P. 1993. *The Uley Shrines. Excavation of a ritual complex on West Hill, Uley, Gloucestershire: 1977–9.* London: English Heritage.

York, M. 1986. *The Roman Festival Calendar of Numa Pompilius.* New York, Berne and Frankfurt: Peter Lang.

INDEX

This index is designed to be used in conjunction with the many cross-references within the A-to-Z entries. The main A-to-Z entries are indicated by **boldface** page references. The general subjects are subdivided by both descriptives and A-to-Z entries. Page references followed by "f" indicate figures; page references followed by "g" indicate glossary items.

A

B

D

E

F

G

J

K

L

M

N

Q

R

S

U

V

W

X

Y

Z